ALL·IN·ONE

CIPM®

Certified Information Privacy Manager

EXAM GUIDE

ABOUT THE AUTHOR

Peter H. Gregory, CIPM, CDPSE, CISA, CISM, CRISC, CISSP, DRCE, CCSK, is a 30-year career technologist and a security leader in a telecommunications company. He has been developing and managing information security management programs since 2002 and has been leading the development and testing of secure IT environments since 1990. Peter has also spent many years as a software engineer and architect, systems engineer, network engineer, and security engineer. He has written many articles, whitepapers, user manuals, processes, and procedures throughout his career, and he has conducted numerous lectures, training classes, seminars, and university courses.

Peter is the author of more than 40 books about information security and technology, including *Solaris Security, CISM Certified Information Security Manager All-In-One Exam Guide,* and *CISA Certified Information Systems Auditor All-In-One Exam Guide.* He has spoken at numerous industry conferences, including RSA, Interop, (ISC)² Congress, ISACA CACS, SecureWorld Expo, West Coast Security Forum, IP3, Source, Society for Information Management, the Washington Technology Industry Association, and InfraGard.

Peter serves on advisory boards for cybersecurity education programs at the University of Washington and the University of South Florida. He was the lead instructor for nine years in the University of Washington certificate program in applied cybersecurity, a former board member of the Washington State chapter of InfraGard, and a founding member of the Pacific CISO Forum. Peter is a 2008 graduate of the FBI Citizens Academy and a member of the FBI Citizens Academy Alumni Association. He is also a member of the IAPP, ISACA, and (ISC)².

Peter resides with his family in Washington state and can be found online at www .peterhgregory.com.

About the Technical Editor

John Clark, CIPP/E, CIPT, FIP, CDPSE, CISSP, CISA, CISM, is an information security executive advisor to CISOs, CIOs, boardrooms, and business executives. John has contributed to many articles, blogs, and presentations addressing privacy program management and has spoken on the topic at industry conferences. With more than 20 years of experience in information security and privacy, he has developed a passion for working with clients to develop sustainable, business-aligned information security and privacy management programs that can be applied to emerging regulations with minimal change. In addition to earning multiple industry certifications, John has a bachelor's degree in management information systems and an MBA from the University of Houston.

ALL·IN·ONE

CIPM®

Certified Information Privacy Manager

EXAM GUIDE

Peter H. Gregory

New York   Chicago   San Francisco
Athens   London   Madrid   Mexico City
Milan   New Delhi   Singapore   Sydney   Toronto

CIPM® Certified Information Privacy Manager All-in-One Exam Guide

1 2 3 4 5 6 7 8 9   LCR   25 24 23 22 21

Library of Congress Control Number: 2021935422

ISBN   978-1-260-47409-1
MHID   1-260-47409-7

Sponsoring Editor	Technical Editor	Production Supervisor
Wendy Rinaldi	John Clark	Thomas Somers
Editorial Supervisor	**Copy Editor**	**Composition**
Janet Walden	Lisa Theobald	KnowledgeWorks Global Ltd.
Project Manager	**Proofreader**	**Illustration**
Neelu Sahu,	Rick Camp	KnowledgeWorks Global Ltd.
KnowledgeWorks Global Ltd.	**Indexer**	**Art Director, Cover**
Acquisitions Coordinator	Ted Laux	Jeff Weeks
Emily Walters		

*To my wife Rebekah, my mother, Nathan, Shannon,
and my extended family for their encouragement and
support over the past sixteen years.*

*To current and aspiring privacy professionals everywhere
who own the mission of protecting personal information
about customers, employees, and constituents.*

CONTENTS AT A GLANCE

CONTENTS

ACKNOWLEDGMENTS

I am immensely grateful to Wendy Rinaldi for affirming the need to have this book published on a tight timeline. My readers, including current and future privacy managers, deserve nothing less.

Heartfelt thanks to Emily Walters for proficiently managing this project, facilitating rapid turnaround, and equipping me with the information and guidance I needed to produce the manuscript.

I want to thank my former consulting colleague, John Clark, who took on tech reviewing the manuscript. A Fellow of Information Privacy and a member of the International Association of Privacy Professionals, John carefully and thoughtfully scrutinized the entire draft manuscript and made scores of practical suggestions that have improved the book's quality and value for readers.

Next, I want to thank my former consulting colleague, Greg Tyler, with whom I worked in a consulting role in data protection projects. His insight has been invaluable to our clients and to me. Also, I want to thank Kate Schenker, ITIL, CTPRP, for her records management expertise and insight.

Many thanks to Janet Walden and Neelu Sahu for managing the editorial and production ends of the project and to Lisa Theobald for copy editing the book and further improving readability. I appreciate KnowledgeWorks Global Ltd. for expertly rendering my sketches into beautifully clear line art and laying out the pages. Like stage performers, they make hard work look easy.

Many thanks to my literary agent, Carole Jelen, for her diligent assistance during this and other projects. Sincere thanks to Rebecca Steele, my business manager and publicist, for her long-term vision and for keeping me on track.

Virtually all of the work producing this book was completed during the COVID-19 pandemic. In addition to life's everyday pressures and challenges, everyone involved in this project stayed on task and completed their typical high-quality work on schedule. This effort was likely quite difficult for some of you. I admire your drive and your dedication to serve our readers with nothing but the best. Privacy professionals around the world depend upon it.

Despite having written more than 40 books, I have difficulty putting into words my gratitude for my wife, Rebekah, for tolerating my frequent absences (in the home office) while I developed the manuscript. This project could not have been completed without her loyal and unfailing support and encouragement.

INTRODUCTION

The information revolution has transformed businesses, governments, and people in profound ways. Virtually all business and government operations are now digital, resulting in everyone's personal details stored in information systems.

Two issues have arisen out of this transformation: the challenge to safeguard personal information from criminal organizations, and the challenge to ensure that personal information is used only for clearly stated purposes. Difficulties in meeting these challenges have helped create and emphasize the importance of the cybersecurity and information privacy professions. Numerous security and privacy laws, regulations, and standards have been enacted and created, imposing a patchwork of new requirements on organizations and governments to enact specific practices to protect and control the use of our personal information.

These developments continue to drive demand for information privacy, information security professionals, and leaders in both privacy and security. These highly sought-after professionals play a crucial role in developing better information privacy and security programs that result in reduced risk and improved confidence.

The Certified Information Privacy Manager (CIPM) certification, established by IAPP in 2013, will light the path for tens of thousands of privacy and security professionals who need to demonstrate competence in the privacy field. The International Association of Privacy Professionals (IAPP), the creator of the Certified Information Privacy Manager, the Certified Information Privacy Professional (CIPP), the Certified Information Privacy Technologist (CIPT), and other certifications, is one of the world's leading privacy management and professional development organizations.

Purpose of This Book

Let's get the obvious out of the way: this is a comprehensive study guide for the privacy professional who needs a reliable reference for individual or group-led study for the CIPM certification. The content in this book contains the information that CIPM candidates are required to know. This book is one source of information to help you prepare for the CIPM exam but should not be thought of as the ultimate collection of *all* the knowledge and experience that IAPP expects qualified CIPM candidates to possess. No one publication covers all of this information.

This book also serves as a reference for aspiring and practicing privacy professionals and leaders. The content required to pass the CIPM exam is the same content that practicing privacy professionals need to be familiar with in their day-to-day work. This book is an ideal CIPM exam study guide as well as a desk reference for those who have already earned their CIPM certification.

The pace of change in the privacy and information security industries and professions is high. Rather than contain every detail and nuance of every law, practice, standard, and technique in privacy and security, this book shows the reader how to stay current in the profession. Indeed, this pace of change is one of many reasons that IAPP and other associations require continuous learning to retain one's certifications. It is just as important to understand key facts and practices in privacy and stay current as they continue to change.

This book is also invaluable for privacy professionals who are not in a leadership position today. You will gain considerable insight into today's privacy challenges. This book is also useful for IT, security, and business management professionals who work with privacy professionals and need to improve their understanding of what they are doing and why.

Finally, this book is an excellent guide for anyone exploring a privacy career. The study chapters explain all the relevant technologies, techniques, and processes used to manage a modern privacy program. This is useful if you are wondering what the privacy profession is all about.

How This Book Is Organized

The remainder of this book is logically divided into four major sections:

- **CIPM study material** Chapters 1 through 6 contain everything a studying CIPM candidate is responsible for. This same material is a handy desk reference for aspiring and practicing privacy professionals.

- **Appendix A** Here you'll find a lengthy description of the risk management life cycle, a vital business process in the information security and information privacy professions. Risk management helps business leaders make purposeful business decisions concerning privacy and information security.

- **Practice exams** Appendix B explains how to access the online CIPM practice exam accompanying this book.

- **Glossary** You'll find definitions for more than 350 terms used in the privacy profession.

Information privacy is a big topic, and it depends heavily upon sound information security practices. Many security and audit topics are summarized in this book, and there are numerous references to two other books that offer considerable depth in information security:

- *CISM Certified Information Security Manager All-In-One Exam Guide*
- *CISA Certified Information Systems Auditor All-In-One Exam Guide*

Earning and Maintaining the CIPM Certification

In this section, I'm going to talk about

- What it means to be a CIPM professional
- IAPP and its code of professional conduct
- The certification process
- Preparing for and taking the exam
- How to maintain your certification
- How to get the most from your CIPM journey

Congratulations on choosing to become a Certified Information Privacy Manager! Whether you have worked for several years in the field of privacy or have just recently been introduced to the world of privacy and information security, don't underestimate the hard work and dedication one needs to obtain and maintain CIPM certification. Although ambition and motivation are required, the rewards can far exceed the effort.

You may not have imagined you would find yourself working in the privacy world or looking to obtain a privacy certification. Perhaps the explosion of privacy laws led to your introduction to this field. Or possibly you have noticed that privacy-related career options are increasing exponentially, and you have decided to get ahead of the curve.

By selecting the CIPM certification, you're hitching your wagon to the IAPP star. Founded in 2000, IAPP has more than 50,000 members, many of whom have earned one or more of its certifications: CIPM (established in 2013), CIPP (Certified Information Privacy Professional), CIPT (Certified Information Privacy Technologist), and FIP (Fellow of Information Privacy).

IAPP's certifications are accredited by the American National Standards Institute (ANSI) under the ISO/IEC 17024:2012 standard. This means that IAPP's certification program is certified as having the highest quality, integrity, and reliability available. Not all professional certifications are so certified; before investing your time and energy in a certification, see that it is ANSI certified.

I have put together this information to help you understand the commitment you'll need to prepare for the exam and to maintain your certification. It is my wish to see you pass the exam with flying colors. I've also included information and resources to help you maintain your certification and to represent yourself proudly in the professional world of privacy with your new credentials.

If you're new to IAPP, I recommend you tour the web site and become familiar with the available guides and resources. If you're near one of the local IAPP KnowledgeNet chapters in 50-plus countries, consider taking part in the activities and even reaching out to the chapter board for information on local meetings, training days, conferences, and study sessions. You may meet other privacy professionals who can give you additional insight into the CIPM certification and the privacy profession.

CIPM certification primarily focuses on privacy program operations. It certifies the individual's knowledge of information privacy strategy development, building and managing a privacy program, preparing for and responding to privacy incidents, and information security. Organizations seek out qualified personnel for assistance with developing and maintaining strong and effective privacy programs, and a CIPM-certified individual is a great candidate for this.

Benefits of CIPM Certification

Obtaining the CIPM certification offers several significant benefits:

- **Expands knowledge and skills; builds confidence**   Developing knowledge and skills in privacy and data protection, building and managing a privacy program, and responding to privacy incidents can prepare you for advancement or expand your scope of responsibilities. The personal and professional achievement can boost your confidence and encourage you to move forward and seek new career opportunities.

- **Increases marketability and career options**   Because of various legal and regulatory requirements, such as the Health Insurance Portability and Accountability Act (HIPAA), Gramm–Leach–Bliley Act (GLBA), the European General Data Protection Regulation (GDPR), the California Consumer Privacy Act (CCPA), the Virginia Consumer Data Protection Act (CDPA), and the California Privacy Rights Act (CPRA), demand is growing for individuals with experience in developing and running privacy programs. Besides, obtaining your CIPM certification demonstrates to current and potential employers your willingness and commitment to improving your privacy knowledge and skills. Having a CIPM certification can provide a competitive advantage and open up many opportunities in various industries and countries.

- **Meets employment requirements**   Many government agencies and organizations are requiring certifications for positions involving privacy and information security. While the privacy certifications are relatively new, it's only a matter of time before government agencies and the privacy industry requires a leading privacy certification for its privacy professionals.

- **Builds customer confidence and international credibility**   Prospective customers needing privacy work will have faith that the quality of the strategies proposed and executed by certified professionals are in line with internationally recognized practices and standards.

Regardless of your current position, your ability to demonstrate knowledge and experience in the areas of privacy can expand your career options. The certification does not limit you to privacy or privacy management; it can provide additional value and insight to those currently holding or seeking the following positions:

- Executives such as chief privacy officers (CPOs), data protection officers (DPOs), chief operating officers (COOs), chief financial officers (CFOs), chief compliance officers (CCOs), and chief information officers (CIOs)
- Records management executives and practitioners
- Marketing management executives and practitioners
- IT management executives such as CIOs, chief technology officers (CTOs), directors, managers, and staff
- Chief audit executives, audit partners, and audit directors
- Compliance executives and management
- Security and audit consultants

Finally, because privacy and cybersecurity are so closely related, many cybersecurity leaders and professionals see their span of responsibilities expanding to include privacy. Soon, cybersecurity professionals lacking privacy certifications and experience may find themselves disadvantaged in their organizations and in the employment market.

Becoming a CIPM Professional

To become a CIPM professional, you are required to pay the exam fee, pass the exam, and agree to uphold IAPP ethics and standards. To keep your CIPM certification, you are required to take and document at least 20 continuing education hours every two years and pay maintenance fees. This life cycle is depicted in Figure 1.

IAPP has published several important publications that describe the latest CIPM certification and the certification process. Since no published book can keep up with

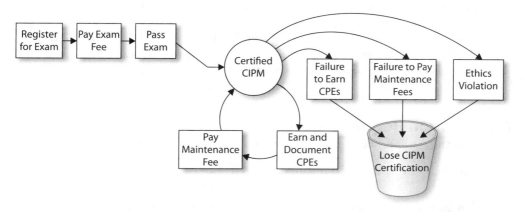

Figure 1 The CIPM certification life cycle

minute changes, I recommend obtaining copies of these publications to ensure that you have the most up-to-date information available:

- **IAPP Privacy Certification Candidate Handbook – Procedures and Policies**   This book describes IAPP certifications and the certification process in general. The latest edition of this publication describes onsite as well as remote certification exams. The entire content of the IAPP Code of Professional Conduct, Application Statement, and Confidentiality Agreement are included in the publication. This is available at https://iapp.org/certify/candidate-handbook.

- **Outline of the Body of Knowledge (BOK) for the Certified Information Privacy Manager (CIPM)**   This publication contains the complete outline of all of the knowledge required of a CIPM candidate. This book closely follows this publication's outline. This document is available at https://iapp.org/certify/get-certified/cipm/.

- **Examination Blueprint for the Certified Information Privacy Manager (CIPM)**   This publication provides a brief look at the CIPM body of knowledge and specifies the number of exam questions that will appear for each section. This is available at https://iapp.org/certify/get-certified/cipm/.

- **Certified Information Privacy Manager (CIPM) Study Guide**   This publication describes the requirements for earning the CIPM certification, the Exam Blueprint, and the Body of Knowledge outline—all in one document. This can be found at https://iapp.org/certify/free-study-guides/; you will need to register to obtain your free copy.

IAPP Membership
While paying the biennial US$250 maintenance fee is the least expensive option for maintaining the CIPM certification, certification holders can instead choose to join IAPP as a member for US$275 per year. IAPP members have access to a trove of members-only content that includes daily news and analysis, discussion groups, resource and research materials, and free training.

Certification Requirements
The following outlines the primary requirements for becoming certified:

- **Purchase the exam**   Candidates are required to pay a one-time exam fee, currently US$550, and must take the exam within one year of purchase.

- **Pay initial certification maintenance fee**   You are required to pay the initial certification maintenance fee, currently US$250 for the first two-year term. Failure to do so will result in your CIPM not being activated upon receiving a passing score. Alternatively, you may become a member of IAPP and pay an annual membership fee of US$275, which includes your certification maintenance.

- **Pass the exam** Candidates must receive a passing score on the CIPM exam.
- **Code of Professional Conduct** All IAPP certified individuals are required to support the IAPP Code of Professional Conduct, which appears in the "IAPP Privacy Certification Candidate Handbook."
- **Education** Those who are certified must adhere to the CIPM Continuing Professional Education Policy, which requires a minimum of 20 continuing professional education (CPE) hours each two-year period.

Privacy Work Experience

Readers familiar with professional certifications in the professions of information technology and information security may notice the lack of a requirement for work experience for the CIPM. Although the CIPM is a knowledge certification, it would be more difficult for someone with no privacy work experience to pass the exam. This is because the exam requires far more than memorization of facts and terms, but also relies on professional judgment gained only from work experience. That said, if you have experience in IT management or operations, IT security management or operations, and data management experience, you will have some of the foundational knowledge already. This book will help to close your knowledge gaps regardless of your starting point.

IAPP Code of Professional Conduct

Becoming a CIPM professional means you agree to adhere to the IAPP Code of Professional Conduct. The code of conduct is a formal document outlining those things you will do to ensure the utmost integrity and to best support and represent the organization and certification.

The IAPP code of ethics requires IAPP certification holders to do the following:

- Conduct yourself professionally at all times.
- Represent your IAPP certifications honestly.
- Maintain professional knowledge.
- Follow all IAPP policies and requirements.

You can find the full text of the IAPP Code of Professional Conduct in the "IAPP Privacy Certification Candidate Handbook."

The Certification Exam

IAPP offers certification throughout the year at numerous testing centers as well as remotely proctored exams you can take at home or at work. I highly recommend you plan ahead and register early, particularly if you plan to take the exam at a test center, as space may be limited.

NOTE As is the case with professional certifications and examinations, the terms, conditions, locations, and rules for certification exams are likely to change from time to time. Readers should thoroughly examine the logistics described in the "IAPP Privacy Certification Candidate Handbook" for the most current information.

Once you have registered for the exam, you will receive one or more e-mail messages that describe the steps you must undergo to take the CIPM exam. You may be directed to select a location to take your exam, or you may be directed to meet the requirements to take the exam remotely. As you decide about test locations, dates, and other conditions, IAPP or a third-party exam service will send you confirmations.

 CAUTION It is essential that you thoroughly understand the rules regarding the exam. Failure to abide by these rules may result in your disqualification for the CIPM certification.

Whether you take the exam remotely or at a test center, you will be supervised by a proctor. Examination candidates should expect to be monitored by video surveillance to ensure that no one can cheat on the exam.

Each registrant has 2-1/2 hours to take the 90-question computerized exam. Each multiple-choice question has four answer choices; test-takers can select only one *best* answer. You can skip questions and return to them later, and you can also flag questions that you want to review later if time permits. While you are taking your exam, the time remaining will appear on the screen.

When you have completed the exam, you are directed to close the exam. At that time, the exam may display your preliminary pass or fail status, with a reminder that your score and passing status are subject to review.

Exam questions are derived from analysis conducted by IAPP. The areas selected represent those tasks performed in a CIPM's day-to-day activities and represent the background knowledge required to develop and manage an information privacy program. You can find more detailed descriptions of the task and knowledge statements in the "CIPM Study Guide."

The CIPM exam is quite broad in its scope. The exam covers six job practice areas, as shown in Table 1.

Domain	CIPM Job Practice Area	% of Exam
1	Developing a Privacy Program	21–22%
2	Privacy Program Framework	14–15%
3	Privacy Operational Lifecycle: Assess	21–22%
4	Privacy Operational Lifecycle: Protect	20%
5	Privacy Operational Lifecycle: Sustain	8–9%
6	Privacy Operational Lifecycle: Respond	14–15%

Table 1 CIPM Exam Practice Areas

Independent committees have been developed to determine the best questions, review exam results, and statistically analyze the results for continuous improvement. Should you come across a horrifically difficult or strange question, do not panic. IAPP may have written this question for another purpose: a few questions may be included for research and analysis purposes and will not count against your score. The exam contains no indications in this regard, so you should consider every question as one that contributes to the final score.

Exam Preparation

The CIPM certification requires a great deal of knowledge and experience from the CIPM candidate. You need to map out a long-term study strategy to pass the exam. The following sections offer some tips and are intended to help guide you through and beyond exam day.

Before the Exam

Consider the following list of tips on tasks and resources for exam preparation. They are listed in sequential order.

- *Read the exam candidate's guide.* For information on the certification exam and requirements for the current year, find the Certified Information Privacy Manager (CIPM) Study Guide. Go to https://iapp.org/certify/free-study-guides/ and click CIPM.

- *Register for the exam.* If you are able, register early for any cost savings and to solidify your commitment to moving forward with this professional achievement.

- *Schedule your exam.* Find a location (where applicable), date, and time—and commit.

- *Become familiar with the CIPM body of knowledge.* The body of knowledge serves as the basis for the exam and requirements. Read this book, and take the online practice exams described in Appendix B.

- *Know your best learning methods.* Everyone has a preferred learning style, whether it's self-study, a study group, an instructor-led course, or a boot camp. Try to use a study program that leverages your strengths.

- *Self-assess by taking practice exams.* Run through the online practice exam questions (see Appendix B for information).

- *Study iteratively.* Depending on how much work experience in privacy you have already, I suggest you plan your study program to take at least two months but as long as six months. During this time, periodically take the online practice exams and note your areas of strength and weakness. Once you have identified your weak areas, focus on those areas weekly by rereading the related sections in this book and retaking practice exams, and note your progress.

- *Avoid cramming.* We've all seen the books on the shelves with titles that involve last-minute cramming. Just one look on the Internet reveals various web sites that cater to teaching individuals how to cram for exams most effectively. Research sites claim that exam cramming can lead to colds and flu, sleep disruptions, overeating, and digestive problems. One thing is certain: many people find that good, steady study habits result in less stress and greater clarity and focus during the exam. Because of the complexity of this exam, I highly recommend the long-term, steady-study option. Study the job practice areas thoroughly. There are many study options. If time permits, investigate the many resources available to you.

- *Find a study group.* Contact your local IAPP KnowledgeNet chapter to see whether these options are available to you; go to https://www.iapp.org/connect/communities/chapters/ for more information. Use your local network to find out whether there are other local study groups and other helpful resources.

- *Check your confirmation letter.* Recheck your confirmation letter. Do not write on it or lose it. Put it in a safe place, and take note of the exam's date, time, and place. Note this on your calendar. If you are taking the exam at a testing center, confirm that the location is the one you selected and located near you. Understand all specific requirements and plan ahead.

- *Check logistics.* If you are taking the exam at a test center, check the candidate's guide and your confirmation letter for the exact time required to report to the test site. Check the site a few days before the exam—become familiar with the location and tricks to getting there. If you are taking public transportation, be sure you are looking at the schedule for the day of the exam. If your CIPM exam is scheduled on a weekend, public transportation schedules may differ from weekday schedules. If you are driving, know the route and where to park your vehicle. If you are taking the exam online, check the "IAPP Privacy Certification Candidate Handbook" and your confirmation letter for your exam's exact time and ensure that you have the required equipment, software, and materials available.

- *Pack what you need.* If you are taking the exam at a test center, place your confirmation letter and a photo ID in a safe place, ready to go. Your ID must be a current, government-issued photo ID that matches the name on the confirmation letter and must not be handwritten. Examples of acceptable forms of ID are passports, driver's licenses, state IDs, green cards, and national IDs. Make sure you leave food, drinks, laptops, cell phones, and other electronic devices behind, as they are not permitted at the test site.

- *Get some sleep.* Make sure you get a good night's sleep before the exam. Research suggests that you should avoid caffeine at least four hours before bedtime, keep a notepad and pen next to the bed to capture late-night thoughts that might keep you awake, eliminate as much noise and light as possible, and keep your room at a comfortable temperature for sleeping. In the morning, rise early so as not to rush and subject yourself to additional stress.

Day of the Exam

On the day of the exam, follow these tips:

- *Dress comfortably.* Certification exams are difficult and require long periods of intense concentration. It is important, therefore, to ensure you will be comfortable as possible physically. Avoid tight-fitting clothes, and dress in layers to stay comfortable throughout the exam.

- *Arrive early.* If you are taking the exam at a test center, check the Bulletin of Information and your confirmation letter for the exact time you are required to report to the test site. The confirmation letter or the candidate's guide explains that you must be at the test site *no later* than approximately 30 minutes *before* testing time. The examiner will begin reading the exam instructions at this time, and any latecomers will be disqualified from taking the test and will *not* receive a refund of fees.

- *Observe test center rules.* There may be rules about taking breaks. The examiner will discuss this along with exam instructions. If you need something at any time during the exam and are unsure as to the rules, be sure to ask first.

- *Answer all exam questions.* Read questions carefully, but do not try to overanalyze. Remember to select the *best* answer. There may be several reasonable answers, but one is *better* than the others. If you aren't sure about an answer, you can mark the question and return to it later. After going through all the questions, you can return to the marked questions (and others) to read them and consider them more carefully. Above all, try not to overanalyze questions, and do trust your instincts. Do not rush through the exam; there is plenty of time to take as much as a few minutes for each question. But at the same time, watch the clock so that you don't find yourself going so slowly that you won't be able to answer every question thoughtfully.

- *Note your exam result.* When you have completed the exam, you should see your preliminary pass/fail result. Your results may not be in large, blinking text; you may need to read the fine print to see your preliminary results. If you passed, congratulations! If you did not pass, do observe any remarks about your status; you will be able to retake the exam—there is information about this on the IAPP web site.

If You Did Not Pass

If you did not pass your exam on the first attempt, don't lose heart. Instead, remember that failure is a stepping stone to success. Thoughtfully take stock and determine your improvement areas. Go back to this book's practice exams and be honest with yourself regarding those areas where you need to learn more. Reread the chapters or sections where you require additional study. If you participated in a study group or training, contact your study group coach or class instructor for advice on studying the topics you need to master. Take at least several weeks to study those topics, refresh yourself on other topics, and then give it another go. Success is granted to those who are persistent and determined.

After the Exam

A few days to a few weeks from the exam date, you will receive your exam results by e-mail or postal mail. Each job practice area score may be noted in addition to the overall final score.

Those unsuccessful in passing will also be notified. These individuals will want to closely examine the job practice area scores to determine areas for further study. They may retake the exam as many times as needed on future exam dates, as long as they have registered and paid the applicable fees. Regardless of pass or fail, exam results will not be disclosed via telephone, fax, or e-mail (except for the consented e-mail notification).

Retaining Your CIPM Certification

There is more to becoming a CIPM professional than merely passing an exam, submitting an application, and receiving a paper certificate. Becoming a CIPM professional is not merely a destination; instead, it should be considered a lifestyle. Those with CIPM certification are required to agree to abide by the code of ethics, meet ongoing education requirements, and pay annual certification maintenance fees. Let's take a closer look at the education requirements and explain the fees involved in retaining certification.

Continuing Education

The goal of continuing professional education requirements is to ensure that individuals maintain CIPM-related knowledge to help them better develop and manage privacy and security management programs. To maintain CIPM certification, individuals must obtain 20 continuing education hours over each two-year period. Each CPE hour is to account for one hour of active participation in educational activities.

IAPP's CPE Policy can be accessed at https://iapp.org/certify/cpe-policy/.

What Counts as a Valid CPE Credit?

For training and activities to be utilized for CPEs, they must involve technical or managerial training directly applicable to information privacy, information security, and information privacy and security management. The following list of activities has been approved by the CIPM certification committee and can count toward your CPE requirements:

- Academic class attendance
- Reading a book, eBook, or audiobook
- Coaching or mentoring a colleague or employee
- Attending industry events (full list at https://iapp.org/about/industry-events/)
- Attending IAPP board presentation
- Attending IAPP certification training
- Attending IAPP conferences
- Attending IAPP KnowledgeNet events
- Attending non-IAPP conferences or events
- Proctoring an IAPP exam

- Publishing a book or article
- Performing research, studying, or training
- Speaking at an industry event
- Teaching a course

For more information on what is accepted as a valid CPE credit, see the CPE Policy (https://iapp.org/certify/cpe-policy/).

IAPP CPE Central

IAPP looks out for its members; a great example is CPE Central (https://iapp.org/certify/cpe-central/), a site where IAPP members can search for many different kinds of educational content, including books, whitepapers, news, tools, training, videos, and web conferences. Much of the available content is free, so there's no argument for not being able to afford continuing education and training.

Tracking and Submitting CPEs

Not only are you required to submit a CPE tracking form for the annual renewal process, but you also should keep detailed records for each activity. Records associated with each activity should include the following:

- Name of attendee
- Name of sponsoring organization
- Activity title
- Activity description
- Activity date
- Number of CPE hours awarded

It is in your best interest to track all CPE information in a single file or worksheet. IAPP has developed a tracking form for your use in the CPE Policy. Consider keeping all related records such as receipts, brochures, and certificates in the same place. You should retain documentation throughout the two-year certification period and for at least two additional years. This is especially important, as you may someday be audited. If this happens, you would be required to submit all paperwork as proof of your continuous learning. So why not be prepared?

For new CIPMs, the annual and two-year certification period begins on the first day of the month following the date the CIPM was earned. You must earn and register your CPEs on IAPP's web site before your CIPM certification expires. Though IAPP will send you reminders, I recommend you make annually recurring calendar entries to remind you to earn and enter your CPEs. It's possible that those CPE and renewal reminders from IAPP will be caught in your spam filter, or you might just not see them if you receive a lot of e-mail.

Notification of compliance from the certification department is sent after all the information has been received and processed. Should IAPP have any questions about the information you have submitted, someone from the organization will contact you directly.

Sample CPE Submission

Table 2 contains an example of a CPE submission. I recommend you also create a worksheet where you document your CPEs. Table 3 contains an example worksheet representing one's CPE records.

Select applicable certification(s):
☐ CIPM
☐ CIPP
☐ CIPT
Activity: (select from the dropdown list)
Activity Date: **Credits Earned:**
Notes: (write down the name of the event here)

Table 2 Sample CPE Submission Form

Activity Title/Sponsor	Activity Description	Date	CPE Hours	Support Docs Included?
IAPP presentation	CCPA compliance	2/12/2021	1	Yes (receipt)
IAPP presentation	Security in SDLC	3/12/2021	1	Yes (receipt)
Regional Conference, RIMS	Compliance, risk	1/15–17/2021	6	Yes (CPE receipt)
Brightfly webinar	Governance, risk, and compliance	2/16/2021	3	Yes (confirmation e-mail)
ISSA board meeting	Chapter board meeting	4/9/2021	2	Yes (meeting minutes)
Presented at ISSA meeting	Privacy management presentation	6/21/2021	1	Yes (meeting notice)
Published an article in XYZ	Journal article on GDPR	4/12/2021	4	Yes (article)
Vendor presentation	Learned about GRC tool capability	5/12/2021	2	Yes
Employer-offered training	Change management course	3/26/2021	7	Yes (certificate of course completion)

Table 3 Sample CPE Recordkeeping

Certification Maintenance Fees

To remain CIPM certified, you must pay maintenance fees every other year or your IAPP membership fees every year.

 TIP Because you may not receive an e-mail reminder, I recommend you create calendar entries or other suitable ways to remind you to record your CPEs and pay your certification maintenance or IAPP membership fees.

Revocation of Certification

A CIPM-certified individual may have his or her certification revoked for the following reasons:

- Failure to complete the minimum number of CPEs during the period
- Failure to document and provide evidence of CPEs in an audit
- Failure to submit payment for maintenance fees
- Failure to comply with the Code of Professional Conduct, which can result in investigation and ultimately lead to revocation of certification

If you have received a revocation notice, you will need to contact the IAPP at appeal@iapp.org or https://iapp.org/about/contact/ for more information.

Summary

Becoming and being a CIPM professional is a lifestyle change, not just a one-time event. It takes motivation, skill, good judgment, persistence, and proficiency to be a strong and effective contributor in the world of privacy. The CIPM was designed to help you navigate the privacy world with greater ease and confidence.

In the following chapters, each CIPM domain is discussed in detail, and additional reference material is presented. Not only is this information useful for studying before the exam, but it is also meant to serve as a resource throughout your career as a privacy professional.

Developing a Privacy Program

In this chapter, you will learn about
- Developing a privacy vision
- Ensuring business alignment
- Developing a privacy and security strategy
- Resources needed to develop and execute a privacy and security strategy
- Obstacles to strategy development and execution
- Privacy program communications

This chapter covers Certified Information Privacy Manager job practice I, "Developing a Privacy Program." The domain represents approximately 22 percent of the CIPM examination.

The genesis of a privacy program is a vision in the mind of a privacy leader. The privacy leader imagines the existence of a privacy program complete with policy, governance, and operations that together ensure the proper collection, use, handling, protection, and disposal of personal information.

The Privacy Vision

Organizations, including private companies, nonprofits, nongovernment organizations (NGOs), and governments, collect and store personal information about customers, citizens, employees, volunteers, and others. Privacy in the context of personal information includes two main components: the proper collection, handling, management, and use of personal information, and the protection of personal information.

The first component, proper collection, handling, management, and use of personal information, is often implemented in the form of data governance. This is a field in itself that includes policies and processes to ensure that all important data, including personal information, is used in accordance with policy and with management oversight and approval. The next component, proper protection of personal information, is generally implemented in the form of cybersecurity. As a practice, cybersecurity has existed for decades and continues to evolve as an art.

Program Approaches

There is more than one way to crack an egg. Similarly, there are several ways to approach the vision and mission of privacy. There is no single, correct approach; in fact, several approaches can be used to attack the matter of privacy. Numerous factors influence the approach, ranging from executive culture to regulatory obligations as well as risk tolerance and risk appetite. Perhaps a good starting point is to consider the typical stakeholders, which include

- Legal
- Human resources (HR)
- Information technology (IT)
- Cybersecurity
- Marketing and sales
- Business units or departments

Some organizations may include additional stakeholders.

Privacy Objectives

Organizations have various reasons for putting resources into a privacy function. Not all organizations and their circumstances are alike, although they share some common threads. Two primary objectives are most often used:

- Avoidance of regulatory problems
- Enhancement of customer experience

You may note the stark contrast between these objectives. In the first, the organization is moving *away* from something (regulatory trouble), while in the second, the organization is moving *toward* something (improved customer experience and market competitiveness). It is said that all human action is driven by two basic emotions: fear and love. The primary objective of a privacy program appears to be so aligned.

Executive Sponsorship

Executive sponsorship is the formal or informal approval to commit resources to a business problem or challenge. Privacy is no exception: without executive sponsorship, privacy will be little more than an unrealized idea.

In its simplest form, the business case for implementing a privacy program comes down to one or two points: the consequences for failing to implement a privacy program and the benefits enjoyed from implementing a program. These can be expressed in financial terms or in terms of image, brand, reputation, and/or market share.

The other dimension related to sponsorship is this: How much privacy is enough? Cybersecurity executives and their corporate counterparts have been arguing a similar point for decades: How much security is enough? Both questions can be answered by understanding the organization's current state, its desired future state, and the costs and consequences involved.

Business Alignment

As vision gives way to strategy, the organization's privacy leader must ensure that the information privacy program fits in with the rest of the organization. This means that the program needs to align with the organization's highest level of guiding principles, including the following:

- **Mission**   Why does the organization exist? Who does it serve and what products and services are provided?

- **Goals and objectives**   What achievements are projected to be accomplished, and when does the organization want to achieve these objectives?

- **Strategy**   What activities need to take place to fulfill the organization's goals and objectives?

To be business aligned, privacy and security professionals should be aware of several characteristics of the organization, including these:

- **Business model and processes**   These include the organization's data flows (particularly flows of personal information), its use of information systems, and its sources of revenue.

- **Sources and uses of personal information**   At the core of a privacy program, it's vital that all sanctioned and unsanctioned uses of personal information are understood, documented, rationalized, and managed.

- **Culture**   This includes how personnel in the organization work, think, and relate to one another. Of utmost importance is the cultural attitude toward the treatment of personal information.

- **Asset value**   This includes information the organization uses to operate, which often consists of intellectual property such as designs, source code, production costs, and pricing, as well as sensitive information related not only to the organization's personnel but to its customers, its information processing infrastructure, and its service functions as well.

- **Risk tolerance**   Risk tolerance for the organization's privacy and information security programs needs to align with the organization's overall tolerance for risk.

- **Legal obligations**   What external laws and regulations govern what the organization does and how it operates? These laws and regulations include Gramm–Leach–Bliley Act (GLBA), General Data Protection Regulation (GDPR), California Consumer Privacy Act (CCPA), and Health Insurance Portability and Accountability Act (HIPAA). Also, contractual obligations with other parties often shape the organization's legal behaviors and practices.

- **Market conditions**   How competitive is the marketplace in which the organization operates? What are the organization's strengths and weaknesses when compared to its competitors? How does the organization want its privacy and security differentiated from its competitors?
- **Privacy law enforcement**   Are regulators and other authorities actively enforcing privacy laws and regulations, or are those laws "paper tigers" that stand unenforced? Organizations are generally reluctant to devote resources to changing business models, business processes, and information systems to comply with laws that may not be enforced.

Goals and Objectives

An organization's goals and objectives specify the activities that are to take place in support of the organization's overall strategy. Goal and objective statements are typically imperatives that describe the development or improvement of business capabilities. For instance, goals and objectives may be related to increases in capacity, improvements of quality, or the development of entirely new capabilities. Goals and objectives further the organization's mission, helping it to continue to attract new customers or constituents, increase market share, and increase revenue and/or profitability.

Risk Appetite

Each organization has a particular "appetite" for risk, although few have documented that appetite. ISACA (www.isaca.org) defines *risk appetite* as "the level of risk that an organization is willing to accept while in pursuit of its mission, strategy, and objectives, and before action is needed to treat the risk."

Risk capacity is related to risk appetite. ISACA defines *risk capacity* as "the objective amount of loss that an organization can tolerate without its continued existence being called into question."

Generally, only highly risk-averse and regulated organizations such as banks, insurance companies, and public utilities will tangibly document and define their risk appetite. Other organizations are more tolerant of risk and make individual risk decisions based on gut feelings or qualitative risk analyses. However, because of increased regulation, as well as influence and mandates by customers, many organizations are finding it necessary to document and articulate their risk postures and appetites. This is an emerging trend in the marketplace but is still relatively new to many organizations.

In a properly functioning corporate risk management program, the chief information security officer (CISO) or chief risk officer (CRO) is rarely the person who makes a risk-treatment decision and is rarely accountable for that decision. Instead, the CISO or CRO is a *facilitator* for risk discussions that eventually lead to risk treatment decisions. The only time the CISO or CRO would be the accountable party would be when risk treatment decisions directly affect the risk management program itself, such as in the selection of a governance, risk, and compliance (GRC) tool for managing and reporting on risk.

The data privacy officer (DPO) plays a similar role in privacy-related risk decisions. Like the CISO and CRO, the DPO is a domain expert and guides the business toward decisions that align with applicable laws, internal policies, and the expectations of its affected constituents. Generally, business leaders will make those decisions.

Establish a Data Governance Model

When properly implemented, *governance* is a process whereby senior management exerts strategic control over business functions through policies, objectives, delegation of authority, and monitoring. Governance is management's continuous oversight of an organization's business processes to ensure that they effectively meet the organization's business vision and objectives.

Organizations often establish governance through a committee or designated position that is responsible for setting long-term business strategy and making changes to ensure that business processes continue to support the business strategy and the organization's overall needs. Effective governance is enabled through the development and enforcement of documented policies, standards, requirements, and various reporting metrics.

Data Governance

Data governance is management's visibility and control over the use of information in an organization. By defining strict and tangible consequences for the failure to protect and use personal information transparently, privacy laws have ushered in the emergence of policies and practices that shine a light on data collection, usage, and protection. Organizations are now accountable for confronting data sprawl and indiscriminate use of personal information.

A typical data governance structure contains the following:

- High-level policy and related standards defining data management practices
- Defined roles and responsibilities for data management
- Key controls
- Assessments of key controls to ensure that they are effective
- Methods of reporting to management the descriptions of incidents, activities, and assessments

A key prerequisite to effective data governance is organizational change management—that is, management must have visibility into and control over changes made to business processes. Organizations lacking organizational change management will find that processes will change—including new and changed uses of personal information that may be contrary to policy—without management's awareness.

Governance Models

As organization leaders develop a vision for data governance, they need to be aware of the structure and scope of the organization. It is the author's belief that existing structures should be leveraged as much as possible when designing new corporate management or governance structures. For example, if information security in a global organization is highly distributed, then data governance and privacy perhaps should also be highly distributed. On the other hand, if information security and privacy are highly centralized, then data governance probably should be as well.

Other factors come in to play for data governance, such as local laws for privacy, information security, cross-border data flow, and data sovereignty. Further, local laws may have differing norms for both minimum and maximum data retention. The geographic reach of an organization's operations adds complexity and begs for at least local involvement if not local control.

There are no easy answers with regard to governance models: privacy, security, and data management leaders need to understand the organization and internal and external influencers and capabilities, and then proceed with a model that is best supported and most likely to succeed. Management will need to continue to monitor the program and should be willing to make adjustments as needed.

Policies and Standards

In the context of data governance, data policies and standards define the required behavior of personnel associated with data architecture, data management, and data usage. Data governance policies and standards will address topics including

- Approvals required for the acquisition of new data sources
- Approvals required for new or changed uses of existing data sources
- Safeguards to protect data from unauthorized access and use

Policies and standards will also define roles and responsibilities and imply the development of controls.

Roles and Responsibilities

A data governance charter or policies and standards should define roles and responsibilities concerning the management of data, including

- Decisions for access to data and databases
- Reviews of access rights to data and databases
- Decisions and reviews for uses of data and databases
- Ownership of individual controls
- Investigations into misuse and unauthorized access to data and databases

Readers versed in information security will recognize these roles and responsibilities as essential parts of a comprehensive information security program.

Control Objectives and Controls

Following the development of policies, standards, roles, and responsibilities, control objectives and controls can be developed. Control objectives and individual controls specify key desired outcomes to ensure that data governance policies will be carried out.

The functional areas where controls will be developed include

- Approvals for the acquisition of new data sources
- Approvals for new uses of data

- Monitoring of data usage
- Approvals for requests to access data
- Reviews of access to data

Organizations will develop processes and procedures that include these controls.

Assessments

The effectiveness of policies and controls cannot be fully known unless they are assessed or audited. The criticality of controls and the applicability of specific regulations will determine the approach and rigor needed to assess controls, whether they are reviewed, assessed, or audited.

Prior to recently enacted privacy laws, many organizations paid little attention to risks associated with the protection and use of personal information. Overall and focused risk assessments concerning the use of personal information are warranted, however.

Assessing controls alone addresses their effectiveness but may overlook aspects of privacy and security where no controls exist. Control assessments and risk assessments should be included in the organization's overall risk management life cycle, as discussed in Appendix A and in more detail in *CISM Certified Information Security Manager All-In-One Exam Guide*.

Reporting

Governance is incomplete if management is uninformed of routine business activities and incidents that occur in a program. Management needs to be periodically informed of how many incidents occur and how effective they have been at circumventing controls, and the effectiveness of incident response, corrective actions, and improvements.

Privacy Governance

Privacy governance is a set of established activities that typically focuses on several fundamental principles and outcomes. These focused activities are designed to enable management to have a clear understanding of the state of the organization's privacy program, its current risks, its direct activities, and its alignment to the organization's business objectives and practices. A goal of the privacy program is enabling the fulfillment of the privacy strategy, which itself will continue to align with the business, business objectives, and developing regulations. The processes supporting these principles and outcomes include privacy policy, data governance, compliance, risk management, and cybersecurity. Whether the organization has a board of directors, council members, commissioners, or some other top-level governing body, governance begins with establishing top-level strategic objectives that are translated into actions and roles and responsibilities through policies, processes, procedures, and other activities downward through each level in the organization.

Privacy is a business issue, and organizations that are not yet properly managing or adequately protecting personal information have a business problem. The reason for this is almost always a lack of understanding and commitment by boards of directors and senior executives. For many, privacy is viewed as a security issue that focuses on data protection problems at the tactical level, and it's not about data usage at all. The challenge is that, because of a lack of awareness or experience in privacy, organizations still struggle with how to organize, manage, and communicate about privacy successfully at the executive leadership and boardroom levels.

To manage privacy successfully, organizations need to understand that privacy is also a people issue. When people at each level in the organization—from board members to individual contributors—understand the importance of privacy and security within their own roles and responsibilities, an organization will be in a position of reduced risk. This reduction in risk or identification of potential privacy or security events results in fewer incidents with less impact on the organization's ongoing reputation and operations.

NOTE Because modern privacy practices are heavily influenced by privacy laws such as the EU GDPR, the CCPA, and the California Privacy Rights Act (CPRA), organizations should rely upon qualified legal counsel as a part of the overall governance process. Including legal counsel helps to ensure that the organization's privacy policies and practices comply with these and other laws.

Think of privacy as having two main components: proper data management and usage, and data protection—commonly referred to as cybersecurity, data security, or information security. A privacy program cannot succeed without effective cybersecurity. Further, cybersecurity cannot succeed without a solid foundation in IT and IT operations. IT is the enabler and force multiplier that facilitates business processes that fulfill organization objectives. Without effective IT governance, privacy and information security governance practices will not reach their full potential. Figure 1-1 shows how the business vision, strategy, and objectives of privacy and information security governance flow downward in an organization through its privacy and IT security strategies, policies, standards, and processes.

NOTE Although CIPM certification is not directly tied to IT governance, this implicit dependence of privacy and security governance on IT governance cannot be understated. IT and security professionals specializing in IT governance itself may be interested in ISACA's Certified Information Security Manager (CISM) and Certified in the Governance of Enterprise IT (CGEIT) certifications, which specialize in these domains.

Although IT governance, information security governance, and privacy governance may be separate activities, in many organizations, these activities will closely resemble or rely upon one another. Many issues will span IT, security, and privacy governance bodies, and many individuals will participate actively in all three areas. Some organizations may integrate IT, information security, and privacy governance into a single set of participants, activities, and business records. The most important thing is that organizations figure out how to establish governance programs that are effective for achieving formally established business outcomes.

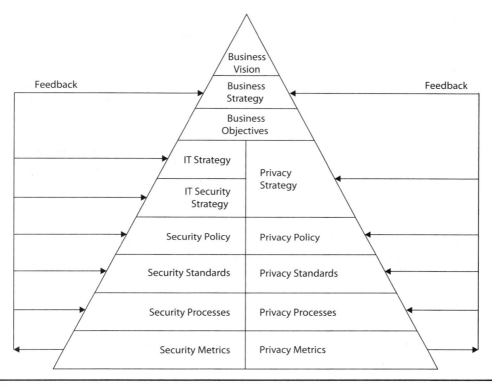

Figure 1-1 Business vision flows downward in an organization.

Privacy governance will enable alignment of the organization's privacy program with customer or constituent expectations, applicable regulations, identified risks, and business needs. An objective of privacy governance is to provide assurance of the proper protection and use of personal information from a strategic perspective to ensure that required privacy practices align with the business practices.

Here are some of the artifacts and activities that flow out of sound privacy governance:

- **Program objectives**   The desired capabilities or end states, ideally expressed in achievable, measurable terms.
- **Established legal basis**   The manner in which the organization may lawfully collect and process personal information about data subjects.
- **Consent**   The mechanisms through which the organization directly or indirectly obtains permission from data subjects to collect and process their personal information.
- **Strategy**   The plan to achieve one or more objectives.
- **Policy**   The mission, objectives, and goals of the overall organization that align with constituent expectations and applicable laws.

- **Priorities**   The main concerns of the privacy program, which should flow directly from the organization's mission, objectives, and goals. Whatever is most important to the organization as a whole should be relevant to privacy and information security.

- **Standards**   The technologies, protocols, and practices used by IT that should reflect the organization's needs. On their own, standards help to drive a consistent approach to solving business challenges; the choice of standards should facilitate solutions that meet the organization's needs in a cost-effective and secure manner.

- **Processes**   The formalized descriptions of repeated business activities that include instructions to applicable personnel. Processes include one or more procedures, as well as definitions of business records and other facts that help workers understand how things are supposed to be done.

- **Controls**   The formal descriptions of critical activities performed to ensure desired outcomes.

- **Program and project management**   The ways in which the organization's privacy, security, and IT programs and projects are organized and performed, which should be in a consistent manner that reflects business priorities and supports the business.

- **Metrics/reporting**   The formal measurement of processes and controls that management can understand and measure.

- **Review/audit**   The formal evaluation of processes and controls to determine their effectiveness.

To the greatest possible extent, privacy governance in an organization should be practiced in the same way that the organization performs cybersecurity, IT, and overall corporate governance. Privacy governance should mimic organizational and/or security and IT governance processes, or it may be integrated into corporate, cybersecurity, or IT governance processes.

Though privacy governance contains the elements just described, strategic planning is also a key component of governance. Strategy development is discussed in the next section.

Privacy and Security: Together or Separate?

Should privacy and security be managed separately or together? Although there's no right or wrong answer, know this: privacy cannot succeed without information security. The objectives of a privacy program are the protection and proper handling of personal information. The protection part is done by information security, and the proper handling part is solely the domain of privacy.

Privacy needs information security to be successful. Security is a prerequisite to privacy, but privacy adds more: the proper *handling* of information and its *protection*.

This is why privacy and security are discussed hand-in-hand throughout this chapter and this book. To discuss privacy alone, without security, tells only half of the entire story that needs to be told.

Factors Influencing Privacy Governance

An organization's privacy program must focus on several internal and external events and activities. Privacy managers realize that some of these factors can be influenced to some degree, while others are entirely out of the managers' sphere of influence. We must be informed and able to react to these influencers.

The Nature of Personal Data and Information   Much of the information contained in information systems is about people. In both government and business organizations, information systems keep track of property owners, taxpayers, voters, citizens, patients, clients, customers, and potential customers. Often, the information retained about people is sensitive in nature, sometimes even secret, and all parties have a vested interest in the adequate protection and proper handling of that information.

In most situations, transactions between individuals and businesses, governments, and healthcare organizations are considered confidential, not to be disclosed, and to be used for official business purposes only. When this information migrated from paper to information systems, and along with advancements in information technology, organizations developed numerous techniques by which additional value could be obtained from the information about their citizens, patients, customers, and constituents. Abuses of these practices have given rise to privacy laws intended to curb such activities.

Privacy laws are discussed in detail in this section. Note that there are many variances among these laws in the following areas:

- **Definitions of personal information**   Privacy laws sometimes provide specific, sometimes vague definitions of which type of data is considered sensitive and which is not. Most laws consider the aggregation of someone's name, together with other items, such as financial account numbers, medical records, political affiliation, and more, as personal information that is to be safeguarded and used within stated guidelines.

- **Data subject rights**   Privacy laws define a number of rights that vary somewhat from one regulation to another. These rights cover transparency and limitations of use, adequate protection, personal data correction, and data removal.

- **Protection of personal information**   Laws require organizations to take measures to ensure the adequate protection of personal information so that it cannot be accessed, altered, stolen, or destroyed by unauthorized parties.

- **Use of personal information**   Laws require transparency regarding the uses of personal information so that persons can be aware of these uses.

- **Notification of breach**   Laws require organizations to disclose to affected individuals any instances in which their personal information was improperly accessed, used, or compromised.

- **Jurisdiction**   Many privacy laws today are *extraterritorial*, meaning that they intend to regulate the activities of organizations located outside of political boundaries.

Data privacy and data protection laws are being enacted at a relatively fast pace, as a reflection of vast expansions of the collection and use of personal information, abuses and breaches by the organizations collecting and using personal data, and still-developing social norms regarding the definitions and expectations of privacy.

The Imperfect Lexicon of Privacy

As in every profession, privacy and information security professions include some special vocabularies. In the privacy profession, there are the terms *personal information* and *data subject request*. Are there really distinctions and valid reasons why "personal information" uses the term "information" while "data subject request" uses the term "data"?

Looking at dictionary definitions, data and information have similar definitions. However, if we go deeper and more specific, we find definitions (in this case, from www.diffen.com) along these lines: "Data are simply facts or figures—bits of information, but not information itself. When data are processed, interpreted, organized, structured, or presented so as to make them meaningful or useful, they are called information. Information provides context for data."

Perhaps this is a clue. The remainder of this exercise is left to the reader.

Privacy Governance Drivers

Whether you attribute the emergence of sweeping data privacy laws to citizen backlash, politicians knee-jerk reacting to that backlash, or merely a coming of age, organizations everywhere are becoming aware of the fact that people's privacy rights matter, and that ignoring these rights can land an organization in hot water. For the most part, organizations are being forced to change their practices, their information systems, and sometimes even their business models to align with the new reality: organizations must be transparent about how they obtain, collect, process, and pass on personal information.

Governance is management's sharpest tool for getting things done. With regard to privacy laws such as the GDPR, CCPA, and CPRA, organizations have put governance structures in place to oversee the transformation in their business processes and information systems from practices of opaqueness to practices of transparency. In many cases, this transformation has meant an about-face on internal practices. Indeed, this has prompted numerous (dare I say the majority of) organizations to "discover" how they are using personal information internally, as though the proverbial foxes have been in charge of the henhouse.

Simply put, privacy governance is all about keeping organizations out of trouble with regulators, outraged citizens, and the courts. Many organizations have had no desire to change their business models, and many complain that it will hurt them financially. Just as the do-not-call lists and laws have curbed the use of unsolicited robo-calls in the United States, privacy laws will forever alter business models that include mining and monetizing personal data behind the dark curtains of organizations' marketing machinery.

While the foregoing portrays the darker side of some organizations, many others were already "doing the right thing" with regard to transparency in managing personal data. For them, the new journey to privacy compliance has been less impactful. All are moving toward new expected norms, which are expected to change still further.

Because privacy governance is generally driven by emerging privacy laws, many organizations have legal counsel in their governance structure as experts on the law and its interpretation. As even more privacy laws are enacted, and as case law begins to emerge, organizations will be watching privacy laws develop and will adjust their systems, processes, and business models accordingly.

The flexibility and capabilities of information systems make it all too easy for organizations to exceed implicitly or explicitly stated purposes for the collection and use of personal information, leading to potential abuses and overreach. As a privacy manager, you must understand the workings of the business with regard to the data it collects about natural persons—how that data is collected, how it is used, and how it is protected. These things should be considered when you're building out a privacy governance structure, but the type of information used by the organization will drive the priority that is given to managing data usage and protection. Privacy governance, then, is needed to ensure that the organization's data management and data protection activities do not lead to incidents that can bring harm to affected persons or the organization itself.

Establish a Privacy Program

Establishing a privacy program requires the development of a strategy. Business, technology, privacy, and security professionals have many different ideas about the meaning of a strategy and the techniques used to develop a strategy, and this can result in general confusion. Although a specific strategy itself may be complex, the concept of a strategy is quite simple. A strategy can be defined as "the plan to achieve an objective." The effort to build a strategy requires more than saying those six words. Again, however, the idea is not complicated. The concept is this: Understand where you are now and where you want to be. The strategy is the path you must follow to get from where you are (current state) to where you want to be (strategic objective).

The remainder of this section explores strategy development in more detail.

Strategy Objectives

As stated, a strategy is a plan to achieve an objective. The objective (or objectives) is the desired future state for the organization's privacy and security posture and level of risk.

There are, in addition, objectives *of* a strategy:

- **Strategic alignment**   The desired future state, and the strategy to get there, must be in alignment with the organization and *its* strategy and objectives.

- **Effective risk management**   Privacy and security programs must include a risk management policy, processes, and procedures. Without risk management, decisions are made blindly and often without regard to their consequences or level of risk.

- **Value delivery**   The desired future state of a privacy or security program should include a focus on continual improvement and increased efficiency. No organization has unlimited funds for privacy and security; instead, organizations need to reduce the right risks for the lowest reasonable cost.

- **Resource optimization**   Similar to value delivery, strategic goals should efficiently utilize available resources. Among other things, this means having only the necessary staff and tools required to meet strategic objectives.

- **Performance measurement**   While strategic objectives need to be SMART (specific, measurable, attainable, relevant, and timely), the ongoing privacy and privacy-related business operations should themselves be measurable, enabling management to drive continual improvement.

- **Assurance process integration**   Organizations typically operate one or more separate assurance processes in silos that are not integrated. An effective strategy would work to break down these silos and consolidate assurance processes to reduce hidden risks.

All of these should be developed in a way that makes them measurable. The metrics for a privacy program should include these objectives.

Risk Objectives

A vital part of strategy development is the determination of desired risk levels. One of the inputs to strategy development is the understanding of the current level of risk, and the desired future state may also have a level of risk associated with it.

It is quite difficult to quantify risk, even for the most mature organizations. Getting risk to a reasonable "high-medium-low" value is simpler, though less straightforward, and difficult to do consistently across an organization. In specific instances, the costs of individual controls can be known and the costs of theoretical losses can be estimated, but doing this across an entire risk-control framework is tedious and uncertain, because the probabilities of occurrence for threat events amount to little more than guesswork.

 NOTE   A key part of a security or privacy strategy may well be the reduction of risk (it could also be cost reduction or compliance improvement). When this is the case, the strategist will need to employ a method for determining before-and-after risk levels that are reasonable and credible. For the sake of consistency, a better approach would be the use of a methodology—however specific or general—that fits with other strategies and discussions involving risk.

Strategy Resources

A strategy describes the process by which goals and objectives are to be met. Before an organization can develop a privacy and security strategy, it must first understand what privacy and security measures are currently in place. Existing resources paint a picture of an organization's current capabilities, including policies, procedures, behaviors, skills, practices, and posture. The gap between the current state and future state can then be filled via tasks and projects involving technologies, skills, policies, and practices.

Two types of inputs must be considered: those that will influence the development of strategic objectives and those that define the current state of privacy and security programs and their protective controls. The following inputs must be considered before objectives are developed:

- Risk assessments
- Threat assessments

When suitable risk and threat assessments have been completed, a privacy or security strategist can then develop strategic objectives; or, if objectives have already been created, the strategist can determine whether these strategic objectives will satisfactorily address risks and threats identified in those assessments.

Privacy and security strategists can examine several other inputs to help them understand the workings of the current privacy and security program. Many of these activities are more security-centric than privacy-centric, because a successful privacy program requires an effective security program as a foundation. These activities include the following:

- **Program charter**   The organization may have a privacy program charter that defines strategy, roles and responsibilities, objectives, and other matters.

- **Risk assessment**   A risk assessment can reveal privacy and security risks present in the organization, and it helps the strategist understand threat scenarios and their estimated impacts and frequency of occurrence. Risk assessment results provide the strategist with valuable information about the types of resources required to bring risks down to acceptable levels. This is vital for developing and validating strategic objectives.

- **Threat assessment**   A threat assessment offers information about the types of threats most likely to have an impact on the organization. It provides an additional perspective on risk, because the assessment focuses on external threats and threat scenarios, regardless of the presence or effectiveness of preventive or detective controls.

 NOTE   A threat assessment is an essential element of strategy development. Without a threat assessment, strategic objectives may fail to address important threats, which would result in a privacy or security strategy that would not adequately protect the organization.

- **Vulnerability assessment**   A vulnerability assessment helps the strategist better understand the current privacy and security postures of the organization's processes and infrastructure. The vulnerability assessment may target personnel, business processes, network devices, appliances, operating systems, subsystems such as web servers and database management systems, and applications—or any suitable combination thereof.

- **Maturity assessment**   A maturity assessment provides valuable information about the maturity of business processes so that the strategist will better understand whether processes are orderly, organized, consistent, measured, examined, and periodically improved.
- **Audits**   Internal and external audits can tell the strategist quite a bit about the state of the organization's privacy and security programs. A careful examination of audit findings can potentially provide significant details on regulatory compliance, control effectiveness, vulnerabilities, disaster preparedness, or other aspects of the program—depending on the objectives of those audits.

NOTE   The topic of audits is discussed in considerable detail in *CISA Certified Information Systems Auditor All-In-One Exam Guide*.

- **Policies**   An organization's privacy and security policies, as well as its practices with regard to these policies, may say a great deal about its desired current state. Privacy and security policies can be thought of as an organization's internal laws and regulations with regard to the protection and proper use of personal information and other assets. Examining current privacy and security policies can reveal a lot about what behaviors are required in the organization. Assessments, discussed earlier in this list, help a strategist understand the organization's compliance with its policies.

NOTE   Many organizations align the structure of their privacy and security policies with the privacy and security control frameworks they have adopted.

- **Standards**   Privacy and security standards describe, in detail, the methods, techniques, technologies, specifications, brands, and configurations to be used throughout the organization. As with privacy and security policies, privacy and security managers must understand the breadth of coverage, strictness, compliance, and last review and update of the organization's standards. These all indicate the extent to which an organization's privacy and security standards are used—if at all.
- **Guidelines**   The very presence of current and actionable guidelines may signal a higher than average maturity level. Most organizations don't get any further than creating policies and standards, so the presence of proper guidelines means that the organization may have (or had, in the past) sufficient resources or prioritization to make documenting guidance on policies important enough to undertake. According to their very nature, guidelines are typically written for personnel who need assistance on compliance with policies and standards.

- **Processes and procedures** An organization's processes and procedures may speak volumes about its level of discipline, consistency, risk tolerance, and the maturity of not only its privacy and security programs but also of IT and the business in general. Like other types of documents discussed in this section, the relevance, accuracy, and thoroughness of process and procedure documents are indicators of maturity and commitment to robust privacy and security programs. Strategists need to confirm whether processes and procedures are actually followed, or if they are merely written artifacts.

- **Architecture** An organization's documentation of systems, networks, data flows, and other aspects of its environment gives privacy and security strategists much useful information about how the organization has implemented its information systems and the business processes supported by the organization. Documentation in the form of architecture diagrams is as important as written policies, standards, guidelines, and other artifacts. The strategist needs to determine whether the organization's architecture supports the organization's goals, objectives, and operations.

- **Controls** The strategist should look for artifacts and interview personnel to determine whether specific controls are in place. The presence of documentation alone may not indicate whether controls are being utilized or whether documentation is just more shelfware. Interviewing personnel and observing controls in action are better ways to determine whether controls are in use. Internal and external audits also help the strategist understand the controls' effectiveness. A strategist will also need to understand whether the controls in place are part of a control framework such as ISO/IEC 27701, ISO/IEC 27001, NIST 800-53, CIS CSC (Center for Internet Security Critical Security Controls), GLBA, HIPAA, or PCI DSS (Payment Card Industry Data Security Standard).

- **Skills and knowledge** An inventory of skills gives the strategist an idea of what staff members are able to accomplish. Understanding skills at all levels helps the strategist understand the types of work that the current staff is able to perform, where minor skills gaps exist, and where the strategist may recommend additional staff through hiring, contracting, or professional services. A key consideration to keep in mind is the potential for a major shift in practices and technologies. A good example is if the organization has been "playing it loose" with personal information and has not yet adopted data governance and data management practices that are required in modern privacy programs. If the staff lacks knowledge about these practices, the organization will struggle to put them in place to comply with applicable privacy regulations.

- **Metrics** Properly established metrics will serve as a guide for the long-term effectiveness of privacy and security controls and processes. Evaluating metrics helps the strategist understand what works well and where improvement opportunities reside. The strategist can then design end states with more certainty and confidence.

- **Assets** The strategist needs to determine whether the organization has sufficient formal asset management practices and records to keep track of its hardware (including virtual machines and other virtual assets), software, and data. Asset management is a key activity for both privacy and security programs—there's a saying often used among information security professionals: "You cannot protect what you do not know about."

- **Risk ledger** The presence of a risk ledger can give the strategist a great deal of insight into risk management and risk analysis activities in the organization. Depending on the detail available in the risk ledger, a strategist may be able to discern the scope, frequency, quality, and maturity of risk assessments; the presence of a risk management and risk treatment process; and whether records of incidents exist.

- **Risk treatment decision records** When available, risk treatment records reveal what issues warranted attention, discussion, and decisions. Coupled with the risk ledger, this information can provide a record of issues tackled by the organization's risk management process.

- **Insurance** The privacy or security strategist may want to know whether the organization has cybersecurity insurance or any general insurance policy that covers some types of cyber events and incidents. As important as having cyber insurance is, equally important is the reason the organization purchased it, such as compliance requirements, customer requirements, prior incidents, or a risk treatment decision. It is vitally important to understand the terms of any cyber-insurance policy. Though the amounts of benefits are important, the most important aspects of a cyber-insurance policy are its terms, conditions, and exclusions.

- **Data management practices** The strategist needs to understand whether the organization implements formal data management practices, including but not limited to a data classification policy, an internal privacy policy, and any tooling that exists (such as data loss prevention [DLP] in its many forms) to provide visibility and control over the movement and use of personal information and other sensitive data.

- **Critical data** Privacy and security strategists need to understand the nature and use of an organization's critical data. It's important to understand the term "critical." There are at least three common uses of the term when associated with data: critical operational data, highly sensitive (including personal information) data, and critical market data (including intellectual property and other competitive data).

- **Critical systems** Aside from critical data, organizations have systems that are critical to the operation of business processes and of other systems. They may not store critical data, but their cessation can still bring the organization to a halt.

- **Business impact analysis**   A business impact analysis (BIA) identifies an organization's business processes, the interdependencies between processes, the resources required for process operation, and the impact on the organization if any business process is incapacitated for a time for any reason. It is also useful for privacy and security professionals aside from business continuity purposes, because it gives the security strategist a better idea of which business processes and systems warrant the greatest protection.

NOTE   The presence of a recent BIA provides a strong indication of the organization's maturity through its intention to protect its most critical processes from disaster scenarios. Correspondingly, the absence of a BIA suggests that the organization does not consider business continuity and disaster recovery (BCDR) strategically important.

- **Privacy and security incident logs**   Privacy and security incident logs provide the strategist with a history of privacy and security incidents that have occurred in the organization. Depending on the information captured in the incident logs, the strategist may be able to discern the maturity of the organization's privacy and security programs, especially its incident response program. The lack of incident logs is a good indicator of the lack of an incident response process.

- **Outsourced services**   The degree to which an organization has outsourced its business applications to the cloud is not the concerning matter. Instead, what's important is the amount of due care exercised in the process of outsourcing— namely, whether a formal third-party risk management (TPRM) program is in place.

- **Culture**   The culture of an organization can tell the strategist a lot about the state of privacy and security. Many people mistakenly believe that privacy and information security are all about the technology. Although technology is part of privacy and security, people are the most important aspect of a privacy and security program. No amount of technology can adequately compensate for an employee's incorrect attitude and understanding about protecting an organization's information assets or about mishandling of personal information. People are absolutely key.

CAUTION   When considering an organization's culture, the strategist needs to rely more upon the organization's actual operations rather than its statements of culture and values. The actual organizational culture may not align with the organization's claims.

- **Maturity**   The characteristics of privacy and security management programs discussed in this list all contribute to the overall maturity of the organization's program. By itself, the maturity level of the program doesn't tell the strategist anything about the program's details. The strategist's observations of the overall program will provide a visceral feeling for its overall maturity.

- **Risk appetite**   Undocumented in most organizations, risk appetite can be discerned through the record of risk treatment decisions and observation of an organization's executive culture. Even then, however, the attitude and culture of risk appetite may differ from an organization's actual practices.

Privacy Program Strategy Development

After performing risk and threat assessments and carefully reviewing the state of privacy and security programs through the examination of artifacts, the strategist can develop strategic objectives. Generally speaking, strategic objectives will fall into one or more of these categories:

- Improvements in data management processes
- Improvements in protective controls
- Improvements in incident visibility and response
- Reductions in risk, including compliance risk
- Reductions in cost
- Increased resiliency of key business systems

These categories all contribute to strategic improvements in an organization's privacy and security programs. Depending on the current and desired future state of privacy and security, objectives may represent large projects or groups of projects implemented over several years to develop broad new capabilities, or they may be smaller projects focused on improving existing capabilities.

Here are some examples of broad, sweeping objectives for developing new privacy and security capabilities:

- Define and implement a data loss prevention (DLP) system to provide visibility and control over the movement of personal information.
- Define and implement a security information and event management (SIEM) system to provide visibility into privacy, security, and operational events.
- Define and implement a privacy incident response program.
- Define and implement a security awareness learning program.

Here are examples of objectives for improving existing capabilities:

- Integrate vulnerability management and GRC systems.
- Link privacy awareness and access management programs so that staff members must successfully complete privacy awareness training to retain access to systems containing personal information.

Once one or more objectives have been identified, the strategist will undertake several activities that are required to meet the objectives. These activities are explained in the remainder of this section.

NOTE   The strategist must consider many inputs before developing objectives and strategies to achieve them. These inputs serve a critical purpose: to help the strategist understand the organization's current state. The journey to developing and achieving a strategy is not possible without understanding the journey's starting point. These are discussed in the previous section, "Strategy Resources."

Gap Analysis

In developing privacy and security strategies and objectives, privacy and security professionals may often spend too much time focusing on the end goals and not enough time on the current state of the organization's privacy and security program. Without having sufficient knowledge of the current state, the strategist will find that accomplishing objectives will be more difficult and achieving success will be less certain.

A gap analysis helps the strategist understand missing capabilities and augment existing capabilities to achieve the desired end state. When performing a gap analysis, the strategist examines the present condition of processes, technologies, and people. The analysis focuses on several aspects of a privacy or security program, including one or more of the items discussed earlier in the "Strategy Resources" section.

When examining all of this and other information about an organization's privacy and security programs, the strategist should bring the appropriate measure of skepticism. There is much to know about what information is found, but the absence of information may speak volumes as well. Here are some considerations:

- **Absence of evidence is not evidence of absence**   This time-honored adage applies to artifacts in any program. For instance, a sparse or nonexistent incident log may be an indication of several things: the organization may not have the required visibility to know when an incident has taken place, the organization's staff may not be trained in the recognition of incidents, or the organization may be watching only for "black swan" events and may be missing commonplace incidents.

- **Freshness, usefulness, and window dressing**   When it comes to policy, process, and procedure documentation, it is important to find out whether documents are created for appearances only (in which case they may be well-kept secrets except by their owners) or whether they are widely known and utilized. A look at these documents' revision histories tells part of the story, while interviewing the right personnel completes the picture by revealing how well the documents' existence is made known and whether they are really used.

- **Scope, turf, and politics**   In larger organizations, privacy and security managers need to understand current and historical practices with regard to roles and responsibilities for privacy, security, and related activities. For example, records for a global security program may reflect only what is occurring in the Americas, even though there may be nothing found in writing to the contrary.

- **Reading between the lines**   Depending upon the organization's culture and the ethics of current or prior privacy and security personnel, records may not accurately reflect goings-on in the program. In other words, there may be overemphasis, underemphasis, distortions, or simply "look-the-other-way" situations that may result in records being incomplete.

- **Off the books**   For various reasons, certain activities and proceedings in a privacy or security program may not be documented. For example, certain incidents may conveniently *not* be present in the incident log—otherwise, external auditors might catch the scent and go on a foxhunt, causing all manner of unpleasantries.

- **Regulatory requirements**   When examining each aspect of a privacy or security program, the program manager needs to ask one important question: Is that activity included because it is required by regulations (with hell and fury from regulators if absent) or because the organization is managing risk and attempting to reduce the probability and/or impact of potential threats?

A common approach to determining the future state in a gap analysis is to determine the current maturity of a process or technology and compare that to the desired maturity level. Continue reading in the next section for a discussion on maturity levels.

Strengths, Weaknesses, Opportunities, and Threats Analysis

Strengths, weaknesses, opportunities, and threats (SWOT) analysis is a tool used in support of strategic planning. SWOT involves introspective analysis, where the strategist asks questions about the four components of the object of study:

- **Strengths**   What characteristics of the business give it an advantage over other businesses?

- **Weaknesses**   What characteristics of the business put it at a disadvantage?

- **Opportunities**   What elements in the environment could the business use to its advantage?

- **Threats**   What elements in the environment threaten to harm the business?

SWOT analysis involves the use of a matrix of the four elements, shown in Figure 1-2.

Capability Maturity Models

The capability maturity model concept has been around for many years. One of the most significant developments for privacy and security practitioners was made by the Software Engineering Institute (SEI) at Carnegie Mellon University with its development of the Capability Maturity Model Integration (CMMI). The CMMI was developed in 2002 as an enhancement to a previous Capability Maturity Model framework and is now maintained by the CMMI Institute, a subsidiary of ISACA. The CMMI continues to be expanded and has multiple areas of focus such as product and service development, service delivery, and data management. Although the CMMI is perhaps the most broadly

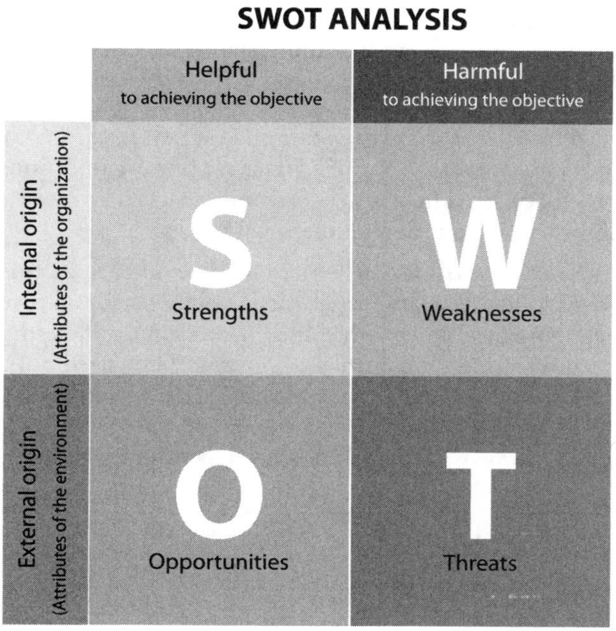

Figure 1-2
A SWOT matrix
with its four
components
(Courtesy of
Xhienne)

SWOT ANALYSIS

referenced maturity model, maturity models in other technology disciplines have also been developed, such as the Systems Security Engineering Capability Maturity Model (SSE-CMM) developed by the International Systems Security Engineering Association (ISSEA) and the ITIL Maturity Model, now maintained by AXELOS.

Maturity models provide a standardized method for defining practices and improving capabilities of a process. The CMMI uses five levels of maturity to describe the formality and performance of a process:

- **Level 0: Incomplete**   This represents a process that does not exist in entirety. Some CMMI illustrations do not show Level 0.

- **Level 1: Initial**   This represents a process that is ad hoc, inconsistent, unmeasured, and unrepeatable.

- **Level 2: Managed**   This represents a process that is performed consistently and with the same outcome. It may or may not be well-documented.

- **Level 3: Defined**   This represents a process that is well-defined and well-documented and the capability is more proactive rather than reactive.

- **Level 4: Quantitatively Managed**   This represents a quantitatively measured process with one or more metrics.

- **Level 5: Optimizing**   This represents a measured process that is under continuous improvement.

Not all strategists are familiar with maturity models. Strategists unaccustomed to capability maturity models need to understand two important characteristics of the models and how they are used:

- *Level 5 is not the ultimate objective.* Most organizations' average maturity level targets range from 2.5 to 3.5. There are few organizations whose mission justifies level 5 maturity. The cost of developing a level 5 process or control is often prohibitive and out of alignment with risks.

- *Each control or process may have its own maturity level.* It is neither common nor prudent to assign a single maturity level target for all controls and processes. Instead, organizations with skilled strategists can determine the appropriate level of maturity for each control and process. They need not all be the same. Instead, it is more appropriate to use a threat-based or risk-based model to determine an appropriate level of maturity for each control and process. Some will be 2, some will be 3, some will be 4, and a few may even be 5.

 TIP The common use of capability maturity models is the determination of the current maturity of a process, together with analysis, to determine the desired maturity level process by process and technology by technology.

Roadmap Development

Once strategic objectives, risk and threat assessments, and gap analyses have been completed, the strategist can begin to develop roadmaps to accomplish each objective. A roadmap is a list of steps required to achieve a strategic objective. The term *roadmap* is an appropriate metaphor because it represents a journey that, in the details, may not always appear to be contributing to the objective. But in a well-designed roadmap, each task and each project gets the organization closer to the objective.

A roadmap is just a plan, but the term is often used to describe the steps required by an organization to undertake and accomplish a long-term, complex, and strategic objective. Often a roadmap is thought of as a series of projects—some running sequentially, others concurrently—that an organization uses to transform its processes and technology to achieve the objective.

Figure 1-3 depicts a roadmap for an 18-month identity and access management project.

A roadmap should be a top-down endeavor, following the usual hierarchy of control of an organization's operations. The roadmap may contain one or more of the following elements:

- **Policy development** Sweeping changes in organization practices around data protection and data management will probably require policy changes to codify expected behaviors and system characteristics. While not generally required in most industries, structuring the organization's security policy with one or more relevant standards or frameworks is nonetheless a common practice. Privacy controls may be adopted from ISO/IEC 27701 or the NIST Privacy Framework.

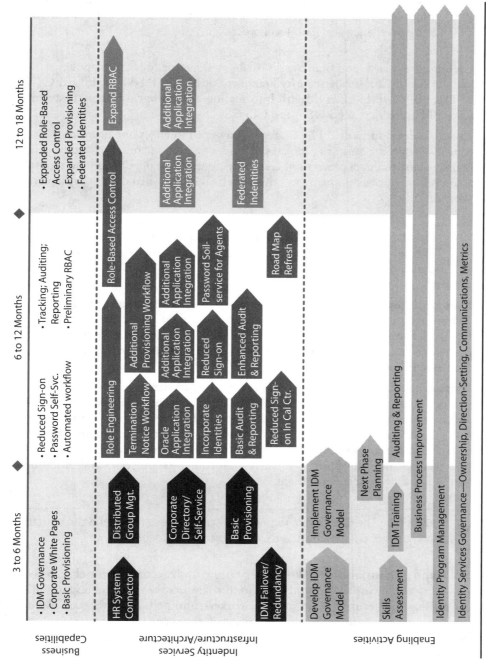

Figure 1-3 Sample roadmap for identity and access management initiative (Courtesy *Hi-Tech Security Solutions* magazine)

NOTE ISO/IEC 27701 is an excellent guide for implementation of a Privacy Information Management System (PIMS) that includes not only controls but also governance and high-level processes.

Common standards and frameworks used as a structure for security policy include NIST CSF (Cybersecurity Framework), NIST SP 800-53, ISO/IEC 27001, HIPAA/HITECH (Health Information Technology for Economic and Clinical Health Act), PCI DSS, and CIS CSC.

- **Controls development**   The strategist may need to enact one or more controls in specific business processes to ensure desired outcomes related to data management and data protection. Generally, controls are developed (and retired) as a result of a risk assessment, and this may be the case when developing a privacy program strategy.

 EXAM TIP   CIPM candidates are not expected to memorize the contents of control frameworks for the exam but are expected to understand their purposes and uses.

- **Standards development**   Changes in policies, controls, or underlying technologies may necessitate that one or more standards be developed or updated. Though standards are often developed with regard to topics such as passwords and encryption, privacy-related standards can be developed on topics such as aggregation and de-identification.
- **Processes and procedures**   Often, the purpose of a new privacy or security strategy is an increase in the maturity of privacy- or security-related technologies and activities in an organization. And because many organizations' privacy and security maturity levels are low, often this means that many important tasks are poorly documented or not documented at all. The desired increase in maturity may compel an organization to identify undocumented processes and procedures and assign staff to document them.

 EXAM TIP   The CIPM exam requires that candidates understand the structure and uses of policies, standards, guidelines, and procedures.

- **Roles and responsibilities**   When the strategy involves changes in technologies or processes (as they usually do), this may, in turn, impact the roles and responsibilities for privacy and security personnel, IT workers, and perhaps other staff. When business processes are added or changed, it often means that changes need to be made to the roles and responsibilities of personnel. There may also be new positions, requiring the development of charter documents and job descriptions.

- **Training and awareness**   Execution of a new privacy or security strategy often has a broad reach, impacting technology as well as policies, standards, processes, and procedures. This results in new information, in many forms and for several audiences, including general privacy and security awareness, updated policies and procedures, and new information systems.

Developing a Business Case

Many organizations require the development of a business case prior to approving significant expenditures on privacy or security initiatives. A *business case* is a written statement that describes the initiative and describes its business benefits. Following are the typical elements included in a business case:

- **Problem statement**   This is a description of the business condition or situation that the initiative is designed to solve. The condition may be a matter of compliance, a finding in a risk assessment, or a capability required by a customer, partner, supplier, or regulator.

- **Current state**   This is a description of the existing conditions related to the initiative.

- **Desired state**   This is a description of the future state of the relevant systems, processes, or staff.

- **Success criteria**   These are the defined items that the program will be measured against.

- **Requirements**   These are required characteristics and components of the solution that will remedy the current state and bring about the desired future state.

- **Approach**   This is a description of the proposed steps that will result in the desired future state. This may include alternative approaches that were considered, with reasons why they were not selected. If the initiative requires the purchase of products or professional services, business cases may include proposals from vendors. Alternatively, the business case may include a request for proposal (RFP) or request for information (RFI) that will be sent to selected vendors for additional information.

- **Plan**   This will include costs, timelines, milestones, vendors, and staff associated with the initiative.

Mature organizations utilize an executive steering committee that evaluates business cases for proposed initiatives and makes go/no-go decisions for initiatives. Business cases are often presented to a steering committee in the form of an interactive discussion, providing business leaders with the opportunity to ask questions and propose alternative approaches.

Business cases should include the following characteristics:

- **Alignment with the organization**   The business case should align with the organization's goals and objectives, risk appetite, and culture.

- **Alignment with regulations**   A business case should cite and align with applicable privacy and data protection regulations.
- **Statements in business terms**   Problem statements, current state, and future state descriptions should all be expressed in business terms.

Establishing Communications and Reporting

Effective communications and reporting are critical elements of successful privacy and security programs. Because success depends mainly on people, in the absence of effective communications, they won't have the required information to make good privacy- and security-related decisions. Without regard for privacy or information security, the results of decisions may include the emergence of unacceptable risks and even harmful incidents.

These are common forms of communications and reporting that are related to privacy and information security:

- **Board of director meetings**   Discussions of strategies, objectives, risks, incidents, and industry developments keep board members informed about privacy and security in the organization and elsewhere.
- **Governance and steering committee meetings**   Discussions of privacy and security strategies, objectives, assessments, risks, incidents, and developments guide decision-makers as they discuss strategies, objectives, projects, and operations.
- **Privacy and security awareness**   Periodic communications to all personnel help keep them informed on changes in privacy and security policies and standards, good privacy and security practices, and risks they may encounter such as phishing and social-engineering attacks.
- **Privacy and security advisories**   Communications on potential threats help keep affected personnel aware of developments that may require them to take steps to protect the organization from harm.
- **Privacy and security incidents**   Communications internally as well as with external parties during an incident keep incident responders and other parties informed. Organizations typically develop privacy and security incident plans and playbooks in advance, which include business rules on internal communications as well as with outside parties, including customers, regulators, and law enforcement.
- **Metrics**   Key metrics are reported upward in an organization, keeping management, executives, and board members informed as to the effectiveness and progress in the organization's privacy and security programs.

As the organization builds or expands a privacy or security program, it's best to utilize existing communications channels and add relevant privacy and security content to those channels, as opposed to building new, parallel channels. Effective privacy and security programs make the best use of existing processes, channels, and methods in an organization.

Obtaining Management Commitment

The execution of a privacy or security strategy requires management commitment. Without that commitment, the strategist will be unable to obtain funding and other resources to implement the strategy.

Getting management commitment is not always a straightforward endeavor. Often, executives and board members are unaware of their fiduciary responsibilities as well as the potency of modern threats and related incidents. Management in many organizations mistakenly believe that they are unlikely targets of hackers and cybercriminal organizations because their companies are small or uninteresting. Further, the common perception of executives and senior managers is that privacy and security tactical problems are solved with "firewalls and antivirus software" and that privacy and information security are in no way related to business issues and business strategy.

If top management lacks a strategic understanding about privacy and security, a privacy or security strategist will need to embark on efforts to inform executives on one or more aspects of modern privacy or information security management. When success is elusive, it may be necessary to bring in outside experts to convince executives that the privacy or security manager is not attempting to build a kingdom, but is instead trying to build a basic program to keep the organization out of trouble. As part of developing an effective communication approach, the strategist should not use fear, uncertainty, or doubt in an attempt to move the leadership team toward adopting the strategy. The better approach, as noted in this section, is to relate it to the leadership team in business terms and opportunities to improve business functions.

Strategy Constraints

Although the development of a new strategy may bring hope and optimism to the privacy or security team, there is no guarantee that changes in an organization can be implemented without friction and even opposition. Instead, the privacy and security manager should anticipate and be prepared to maneuver around, over, or through many constraints and obstacles.

No privacy or security manager plans to fail. However, the failure to anticipate obstacles and constraints may result in the failure to execute even the best strategy. The presence of an excellent strategy, even with executive support, does not mean that obstacles and constraints will simply step out of the way. Instead, these issues represent the realities of human behavior, as well as structural and operational realities that may present challenges to the privacy and security manager and the organization as a whole. There is apt meaning to the phrase "the devil is in the details."

Typical constraints, obstacles, and other issues include the following:

- **Basic resistance to change**   It is basic human nature to be suspicious of change, particularly when we as individuals have no control over it and have no say about it. Change is bad, or so we tend to think. "We've always done it this way" is a common refrain. Strategists need to consider methods of involving management and staff members in anticipated changes, such as town hall meetings, surveys, and cross-functional committees.

- **Culture**   Organizational culture can be thought of as the collective consciousness of all workers, regardless of rank. Privacy and security strategists should not expect to change the culture significantly but instead should work with the culture when developing and executing the privacy or security strategy.

- **Organizational structure**   The strategist must understand the organization's command-and-control structure, which is often reflected by the organizational chart. However, there may be an undocumented aspect of the org chart, which is actually more important: this indicates who is responsible for what activities, functions, and assets.

- **Staff capabilities**   A strategy cannot be expected to succeed if the new or changed capabilities do not align with what staff members are able to do. A gap analysis to understand the present state of the organization's privacy or security program (discussed earlier in this chapter) needs to consider staff knowledge, skills, and capabilities. Where gaps are found, the strategy needs to include training or other activities to impart the necessary skills and language to staff.

NOTE   When an organization lacks staff with specific knowledge about privacy or security techniques or tools, organizations may look to external resources to augment internal staff. The strategist needs to consider the costs and availability of these resources. Consultants and contracts in many skill areas are difficult to find; even larger firms may have backlogs of several months as a result.

- **Budget and cost**   The strategist must determine, with a high degree of precision, all of the hard and soft costs associated with each element of a strategy. Often, executive management will want to see alternative approaches; for example, if additional labor is required, the strategist may decide to determine the costs of hiring additional personnel versus the cost of retaining consultants or contractors.

- **Time**   Realistic project planning is needed so that everyone will know when project and strategy milestones will be completed. Project and strategy timelines must take into account all business circumstances, including peak period and holiday production freezes (where IT systems are maintained in a more stable state), and external events such as regulatory deadlines, audits, and other significant events that may impact schedules.

- **Legal and regulatory obligations**   An organization may include items in its strategy that represent business capabilities that are required for legal or regulatory reasons. The enactment of new privacy laws are specifically the subject of this book and represent considerable changes in practices in many organizations. The extraterritorial nature of some new privacy laws complicates this further.

- **Acceptable risk**   Initiatives in the privacy or security strategy need to align with executive management's risk appetite. However, increased pressure from privacy regulations may also be impacting risk appetite and forcing organizations to build more structures and defenses than they would otherwise choose to do.

The Obstacle of Organizational Inertia

Every organization has a finite capacity to undergo change. This is a fact that is often overlooked by overly ambitious strategists who want to accomplish a great deal in too short a time. I have coined the term "organizational inertia" to represent an analogy to Newton's laws of motion: an object either remains at rest or continues to move at a constant velocity, unless acted upon by a force. In an organization, this means that things will be done in the same way until some force requires the organization to change what is done or how things are done. The greater amount of change that is needed, the greater the outside force is required to implement the change.

The nature of organizational inertia, or its resistance to change, is threefold:

- Operational people changing their processes and procedures
- Learning curve
- Human resistance to change

Structure the Privacy Team

As a privacy leader develops the organization's privacy program strategy, the program will include various routine privacy operations that must be performed. The privacy leader will need to determine what positions will be required and what activities they will perform.

The privacy leader should consider whether any existing staff across the organization can take on some privacy responsibilities. For instance, the security operations team that monitors systems and networks for security events can be leveraged to also monitor data loss prevention (DLP) systems for possible file-handling violations—even though it may be privacy team members who investigate these matters. In another example, in-house legal counsel may be able to take on the responsibility for interpreting privacy regulations and advising personnel regarding compliance obligations. Finally, existing crisis communications capabilities can be used in the event of a privacy incident or breach.

This section discusses not only the roles solely dedicated to privacy, but also the privacy responsibilities of other positions in the organization. Privacy is not a wholly separate function in an organization; instead, many existing personnel, as well as executives, play key roles in an organization's overall privacy program.

Roles

Privacy and information security governance are most effective when every person in the organization knows what is expected of them. More mature organizations develop formal roles and responsibilities that establish clear expectations for personnel with regard to their part in all matters related to the protection and proper use of systems and personal information.

In the context of organizational structure and behavior, a *role* is a description of normal activities that employees are obliged to perform as part of their employment.

Roles are typically associated with a *job title* or *position title*, a label assigned to each person that designates his or her place in the organization. Organizations strive to adhere to more or less standard position titles so that other people in the organization, upon knowing someone's position title, will have at least a general idea of a person's role in the organization.

Typical roles include the following:

- IT auditor
- Systems engineer
- Privacy analyst
- Accounts receivable manager
- Service desk technician

A position title also often consists of a person's *rank,* which denotes a person's seniority, placement within a command-and-control hierarchy, span of control, or any combination of these. Typical ranks include the following, in order of increasing seniority:

- Supervisor
- Manager
- Senior manager
- Director
- Senior director
- Executive director
- Vice president
- Senior vice president
- Executive vice president
- President
- Chief executive officer
- Member, board of directors
- Chairman, board of directors

This should not be considered a complete listing of ranks. Larger organizations also include the modifiers "assistant" (as in assistant director), "general" (general manager), "associate" (a junior position), and "first" (first vice president).

A *responsibility* is a statement of outcomes that a person is expected to support. Like roles, responsibilities are typically documented in position descriptions and job descriptions. Typical responsibilities include the following:

- Perform monthly corporate expense reconciliation.
- Troubleshoot network faults and develop solutions.
- Audit internal privacy controls and prepare exception reports.

In addition to specific responsibilities associated with individual position titles, organizations typically include general responsibilities in all position titles. Examples include the following:

- Understand and conform to information security policy, data protection policy, harassment policy, and other policies.
- Understand and conform to a code of ethics and behavior.

Activity	Responsible	Accountable	Consulted	Informed
Request user account	End user	End user manager	IT service desk, end user manager	Asset owner, security team
Approve user account	Asset owner	Chief operating officer	End user manager, security team	End user, internal audit, IT service desk
Provision user account	IT service desk	IT service manager	Asset owner	End user, end user manager, security team, privacy team
Audit user account	Internal auditor	Internal audit manager	Asset owner, privacy manager	IT service desk, IT service manager, end user manager, privacy team

Table 1-1   Typical RACI Chart Defining Responsible Parties and Their Roles

In the context of privacy and information security, an organization assigns roles and responsibilities to individuals and groups to meet the organization's privacy and security strategies and objectives.

RACI Charts

Many organizations utilize Responsible-Accountable-Consulted-Informed (RACI) charts to denote key responsibilities in business processes, projects, tasks, and other activities. A RACI chart assigns levels of responsibility to individuals and groups. The development of a RACI chart helps personnel determine roles for various business activities. A typical RACI chart is shown in Table 1-1.

The same RACI chart can also be depicted as a second example in Table 1-2. This RACI chart specifies the roles carried out by several parties in the user account access request process:

The meanings of the four roles in a RACI chart are as follows:

- **Responsible (R)**   The person or group that performs the actual work or task.

- **Accountable (A)**   The person who is ultimately answerable for complete, accurate, and timely execution of the work. This person often manages those in the Responsible role.

- **Consulted (C)**   One or more people or groups who are consulted for their opinions, experience, or insight. People in the Consulted role may be subject-matter experts for the work or task, or they may be owners, stewards, or custodians of an asset associated with the work or task. Communication with the Consulted role is two-way.

(continued)

- **Informed (I)**   One or more people or groups who are informed by those in other roles. Depending on the process or task, the Informed role may be told of an activity before, during, or after completion. Communication with Informed is one-way.

Several considerations must be taken into account when assigning roles to individuals and groups in a RACI chart, including the following:

- **Skills**   Some or all individuals in a team assignment, as well as specifically named individuals, need to have the skills, training, and competence to carry out tasks as required.
- **Segregation of duties**   Critical tasks, such as the user account provisioning the RACI chart, must be free of segregation-of-duties conflicts. This means that two or more individuals or groups are required to carry out a critical task. In this example, the requestor, approver, and provisioner roles cannot be assigned to the same person or group.
- **Conflict of interest**   Critical tasks must not be assigned to individuals or groups when such assignments will create conflicts of interest. For example, a user who is an approver cannot approve a request for his or her own access. In this case, a different person must approve the request—while also avoiding a segregation-of-duties conflict.

There are some variations of the RACI model, including PARIS (Participant, Accountable, Review Required, Input Required, Sign-off Required) and PACSI (Perform, Accountable, Control, Suggest, Informed).

Activity	End User	Manager	IT Service Desk	IT Service Manager	Asset Owner	CFO	Internal Audit	Audit Manager	Security Team	Privacy Team
Request user account	R	A	I		I				I	
Approve user account	I	C	I	I	R	A	I		C	
Provision user account	I	I	R	A	C				I	I
Audit user account		I	I	I	C		R	A	I	IC

Table 1-2   Example RACI Chart for an Access Request Process

Board of Directors

The board of directors is a body that oversees organizational activities. Depending on the type of organization, board members may be elected by shareholders or constituents, or they may be appointed. This role can be either paid or voluntary in nature.

Activities performed by the board of directors, as well as directors' authority, are usually defined by a constitution, bylaws, or external regulation. The board of directors is typically accountable to the owners of the organization or, in the case of a government body, to the electorate or to another agency.

In many cases, board members have a *fiduciary duty*. This means they are accountable to shareholders or constituents to act in the best interests of the organization with no appearance of impropriety, conflict of interest, or ill-gotten profit.

In private industry, the board of directors is responsible for appointing a chief executive officer (CEO) and possibly other executives. The CEO, then, is accountable to the board of directors and carries out the board's directives. Board members may also be selected for any of the following reasons:

- **Investor representation** One or more board members may be appointed by significant investors to give them control over the organization's strategy and direction.

- **Business experience** Board members bring outside business management experience, which helps them develop successful business strategies for the organization.

- **Access to resources** Board members bring business connections, including additional investors, business partners, suppliers, or customers.

Often, one or more board members will have business finance experience to bring financial management oversight to the organization. In the case of US public companies, the Sarbanes–Oxley Act requires board members to form an audit committee; one or more audit committee members are required to have financial management experience. External financial audits and internal audit activities are often accountable directly to the audit committee to perform direct oversight of the organization's financial management activities. As the issues of privacy and information security become more prevalent in discussions at the executive level, some organizations have added a board member who is technically savvy or have formed an additional committee often referred to as the technology risk committee.

The board of directors is generally expected to require that the CEO and other executives implement a corporate *governance* function to ensure that executive management has an appropriate level of visibility and control over the operations of the organization. Executives are accountable to the board of directors to demonstrate that they are effectively carrying out the board's strategies.

Many, if not most, organizations are highly dependent upon information technology for their daily operations. Many also process personal information for their workforce and often for their customers or constituents. As a result, privacy and information security are important topics to boards of directors. Today's standard of due care for corporate boards requires that they include privacy and information security considerations in the strategies they develop and the oversight they exert on their organizations. In its publication, *Cyber-Risk Oversight,* the National Association of Corporate Directors (NACD) has developed five principles about the importance of information security:

- Principle 1: Directors need to understand and approach cybersecurity as an enterprise-wide risk management issue, not just an IT issue.
- Principle 2: Directors should understand the legal implications of cyber risks as they relate to their specific circumstances.
- Principle 3: Boards should have adequate access to cybersecurity expertise, and discussions about cyber-risk management should be given regular and adequate time on board meeting agendas.
- Principle 4: Boards should set the expectation that management will establish an enterprise-wide cyber-risk management framework with adequate staffing and budget.
- Principle 5: Board management discussions about cyber risk should include identifying which risks to avoid, which to accept, and which to mitigate or transfer through insurance, as well as specific plans associated with each approach.

The wording of these information security principles makes them entirely relevant to the mission of protecting personal information and to its proper usage.

Executive Management

Executive management is responsible for carrying out directives issued by the board of directors. In the context of privacy and information security management, this includes ensuring that the organization has sufficient resources available to implement privacy and security programs and to develop and maintain controls to protect critical assets and personal information.

Executive management must ensure that priorities are balanced. In the case of IT, privacy, and security, these functions are usually tightly coupled but are sometimes in conflict. IT's primary mission is the development and operation of business-enabling capabilities through the use of information systems. In contrast, the missions of privacy and information security include protection, compliance, and proper usage. Executive management must ensure that these sometimes-conflicting missions successfully coexist.

Following are some typical IT-, privacy-, and security-related executive position titles:

- Chief information officer (CIO)
- Chief technology officer (CTO)
- Chief privacy officer (CPO) or data protection officer (DPO)
- Chief information security officer (CISO)

To ensure the success of the organization's privacy and information security programs, executive management should be involved in three key areas:

- **Ratification and enforcement of corporate privacy and security policies**   This may take different forms, such as formal minuted ratification in a governance meeting, a statement for the need for compliance along with a signature within the body of the privacy or security policy document, a separate memorandum to all personnel, or other visible communication to the organization's rank and file that stresses the importance of and need for compliance to the organization's privacy and information security policies.

- **Leadership by example**   Executive management should lead by example and not exhibit behavior suggesting they are "above" policy; that is, executives should not have the appearance of enjoying special privileges of a nature that suggests that one or more policies do not apply to them. Instead, their behavior should visibly support privacy and security policies that all personnel are expected to comply with.

- **Ultimate responsibility**   Executives are ultimately responsible for all actions carried out by the personnel who report to them. Executives are also ultimately responsible for all outcomes related to organizations to which operations have been outsourced.

Privacy and Security Steering Committees

Many organizations form a security and privacy steering committee—separate or combined—consisting of stakeholders from many (if not all) of the organization's business units, departments, functions, and key locations. Some organizations will separate privacy and security into separate committees, especially if there are differences in membership or focus.

A privacy or security steering committee may have a variety of responsibilities, including the following:

- **Risk treatment deliberation and recommendation**   The steering committee may discuss relevant risks and potential avenues of risk treatment, and may develop recommendations for said risk treatment for ratification by executive management.

- **Prioritization, discussion, and coordination of IT, privacy, and security projects**   The steering committee members may discuss various IT, privacy, and security projects to resolve any resource or scheduling conflicts. They may also address potential conflicts between multiple projects and initiatives and work out solutions.

- **Review of recent risk assessments**   The steering committee may discuss recent risk assessments to develop a shared understanding of their results, as well as discuss remediation of findings.

- **Discussion of new laws, regulations, and requirements**   The committee may discuss new laws, regulations, and requirements that may impose changes in the organization's operations. Committee members can develop high-level strategies that their respective business units or departments can further build out.

- **Review of recent privacy and security incidents**   Steering committee members can discuss recent privacy and security incidents and their root causes. This often can result in changes in processes, procedures, or technologies to reduce the risk and impact of future incidents.

Reading between the lines, the primary mission of a steering committee is to identify and resolve conflicts and to maximize the effectiveness of privacy and security programs, as balanced among other business initiatives and priorities.

Business Process and Business System Owners

Business process and system owners are typically nontechnical personnel in management positions in an organization. While they may not be technology or compliance experts, in many organizations, their business processes are enhanced by IT in business applications and other capabilities. In the context of information privacy, the term "business system" includes databases containing personal information.

Remembering that IT, privacy, and information security functions serve the organization, and not the other way around, business process and business system owners are accountable for making business decisions that sometimes impact the use of IT, the use of personal information, the organization's security posture, or any combination of these. A simple example is a decision on whether an individual employee should have access to specific personal information. While IT or security may have direct control over which personnel have access to what information, the best decision is a policy-backed business decision by the manager responsible for the information.

The responsibilities of business process and business system owners include the following:

- **Access grants**   Process owners decide whether individuals or groups should be given access to the system, as well as the level and type of access.
- **Access revocation**   Process owners should decide when individuals or groups no longer require access to a system, signaling the need to revoke that access.
- **Access reviews**   Process owners should periodically review access lists to determine whether each person and group should continue to have their access.
- **Subject inquiries and requests**   Process owners receive privacy-related inquiries from data subjects in the form of queries about personal data usage, corrections to personal data, opt-in and opt-out requests, requests to be removed, and complaints.
- **Configuration**   Process owners determine the configuration needed for systems and applications, ensuring their proper function and support of applications and business processes.
- **Function definition**   In the case of business applications and services, process owners determine which functions will be available, how they will work, and how they will support business processes. Typically, this definition is constrained by functional limitations within an application, a service, or a product.

- **Process definition**   Process owners determine the sequence, steps, roles, and actions carried out in their business processes.

- **Physical location**   Process owners determine the physical location of their systems. Factors influencing location choices include physical security, proximity to other systems, proximity to relevant personnel, and data protection and privacy laws.

Often, business and system owners are nontechnical personnel, so it may be necessary to translate business needs and applicable laws and regulations into technical specifications.

 EXAM TIP   For the exam, do not confuse the terms *business owner* and *system owner* with persons who possess a majority of shares of the organization. Instead, these terms connote responsibility for business operations.

Custodial Responsibilities

In many organizations, system owners are not involved in the day-to-day activities related to the management of their systems, especially when those systems are applications and the data used by them. Instead, somebody (or several people) in the IT organization acts as a proxy for system owners and makes access grants and other decisions on their behalf. Although this is a common practice, it is often carried too far, resulting in the system owner being virtually unaware, uninvolved, and uninformed. Instead, system owners should be aware of, and periodically review, activities carried out by people, groups, and departments making decisions on their behalf.

The most typical arrangement is that people in IT make access decisions on behalf of system owners based on established policies and practices. Except in cases where there is a close partnership between these IT personnel and system owners, these IT personnel often do not adequately understand the business nature of systems or the implications when certain people are given access to them. Most often, far too many staff members have access to systems, usually with higher privileges than necessary.

Privacy by Design

Privacy by design involves proactively embedding privacy as a default capability into the design and operation of IT systems, networked infrastructure, and business practices. The principle of privacy by design is explicitly stated in GDPR Article 25, "Data protection by design and by default." This principle should be included in every organization's privacy policy, whether the organization is subject to GDPR or other privacy regulations.

This is easier done for new information systems that benefit from a "clean-sheet" design. It is more difficult and costly to retrofit existing information systems developed before modern privacy laws were enacted.

EXAM TIP You should remember that privacy by design and by default are key tenets of the GDPR and are only implied by other privacy regulations.

Chief Privacy Officer

Some organizations, typically those that manage large amounts of personal information related to employees, customers, or constituents, will employ a CPO. Some organizations have a CPO because applicable regulations such as GLBA require it. Other regulations such as HIPAA, the Fair Credit Reporting Act (FCRA), and GLBA place a slate of responsibilities upon an organization that compels them to hire an executive responsible for overseeing compliance. Others have a CPO because they store massive amounts of personal information and have chosen to appoint an executive-level individual to be responsible for managing the privacy program.

The roles of a CPO typically include safeguarding personal information and ensuring that the organization does not misuse the personal information at its disposal. Because many organizations with a CPO also have a CISO, the CPO's duties mainly involve oversight into the organization's proper handling and use of personal information.

The CPO is sometimes seen as a customer advocate, and often this is the actual role of the CPO, particularly when regulations require a privacy officer.

Another similar title with similar responsibilities includes the data protection officer or data privacy officer (DPO). While responsibilities may be similar to those of the CPO, it is important to highlight that DPOs are expected to operate in strictly an oversight of governance role. In some cases, a CPO may not be able to fulfill the role of a DPO, particularly in organizations where the CPO has responsibility for implementing data processing activities or systems that will enable data processing activities.

NOTE Many smaller organizations appoint an existing staff member as the acting privacy officer.

Does GDPR Require a DPO?

Much discussion and debate has ensued over GDPR's requirements for organizations to hire or retain a DPO. The GDPR is somewhat vague on the matter. Section 4, Article 37 reads:

The controller and the processor shall designate a data protection officer in any case where:

(a) the processing is carried out by a public authority or body, except for courts acting in their judicial capacity;

> (b) the core activities of the controller or the processor consist of processing operations which, by virtue of their nature, their scope and/or their purposes, require regular and systematic monitoring of data subjects on a large scale; or
>
> (c) the core activities of the controller or the processor consist of processing on a large scale of special categories of data pursuant to Article 9 or personal data relating to criminal convictions and offences referred to in Article 10.
>
> The key language is included in subsections (a) and (b), which have some subjectivity. When it comes to GDPR, most companies are obliged to assign a DPO.

 NOTE Smaller organizations can consider retaining a consulting CPO, sometimes known as a virtual CPO or fractional CPO. This individual can also act as a strategic advisor to help the organization build its privacy program.

Chief Information Security Officer

The CISO is the highest ranking information security title in an organization. A CISO will develop business-aligned security strategies that support present and future business initiatives and will be responsible for the development and operation of the organization's information risk program, and the development and implementation of security policies, security incident response, and perhaps some operational security functions.

In some organizations, the CISO reports to the chief operating officer (COO) or the CEO. In other organizations, the CISO may report to the CIO, chief legal counsel, or another executive in the organization.

Other titles with similar responsibilities include the following:

- **Chief security officer (CSO)** A CSO often is responsible for physical security and workplace safety in addition to cybersecurity.

- **Chief information risk officer (CIRO)** Generally, this position represents a change of approach to the CISO position, from being protection-based to being risk-based.

- **Chief risk officer (CRO)** This position is responsible for all aspects of risk, including information risk, business risk, compliance risk, and market risk. This role is separate from IT.

Many organizations do not have a CISO but instead have a director or manager of information security who reports farther down in the organization chart. There are several possible reasons for organizations not having a CISO, but generally, it can be said that the organization does not consider information security as a strategic function.

This will hamper the visibility and importance of information security and often results in information security being a tactical function concerned with basic defenses such as firewalls, antivirus software, and other tools. In such situations, responsibility for strategy-level information security implicitly lies with some other executive, such as the CIO. This situation often results in the absence of a security program and the organization's general lack of awareness of relevant risks, threats, and vulnerabilities.

For small to medium-sized organizations, a full-time strategic security leader may not be cost-effective. In these situations, it is advisable to contract with a virtual CISO (vCISO) to assist with strategy and planning. The benefit of this type of approach for organizations that may not require or cannot afford a full-time person is that it enables the organization to benefit from the knowledge of a seasoned security professional to assist in managing the information security program.

Software Development

Positions in software development are involved in the design, development, and testing of software applications and often include the following:

- **Systems architect**   This position is usually responsible for the overall information systems architecture in the organization. This may or may not include overall data architecture as well as interfaces to external organizations.

- **Systems analyst**   A systems analyst is involved with the design of applications, including changes in any application's original design. This position may develop technical requirements, program design, and software test plans. If an organization licenses applications developed by other companies, the systems analyst designs interfaces to other applications.

- **Software engineer/developer**   This position develops application software. Depending upon their level of experience, people in this position may also design programs or applications. In organizations that utilize purchased application software, developers often create custom interfaces, application customizations, and custom reports.

- **Software tester**   This position tests changes in programs made by software engineers/developers.

While the trend toward outsourcing applications has resulted in organizations infrequently developing their own applications from scratch, software development roles persist in organizations. Developers are needed to create customized modules within software platforms, as well as integration tools to connect applications. Still, most organizations have a smaller number of developers than they did decades ago.

 EXAM TIP   You should remember that the regulatory requirements of privacy by design usually rest with the systems architect and others who drive design decisions for organizations that develop software that processes personal information.

Rank Sets Tone and Gives Power

A glance at the highest ranking privacy and information security positions in an organization reveals much about executive management's opinion of privacy and information security in larger organizations. Executive attitudes about privacy and security are reflected in the privacy and security leaders' titles, which may resemble the following:

- **Privacy manager or security manager**   Privacy and information security are tactical only and often viewed as consisting only of basic tactical controls. The privacy and security managers have no visibility into the development of business objectives. Executives consider privacy and security as unimportant and based on simple practices only.

- **Privacy director or security director**   Privacy and information security are essential, and the director has moderate decision-making capability but little influence on the business. A director in a larger organization may have little involvement in overall business strategies and little or no access to executive management or the board of directors.

- **Vice president**   Privacy and information security are strategic objectives but do not influence business strategy and objectives. The vice president will have some access to executive management and possibly the board of directors.

- **CISO/CIRO/CSO/vCISO/CPO/DPO**   Privacy and information security are strategic objectives, and business objectives are developed with full consideration for risk. The C-level security and privacy personnel have free access to executive management and the board of directors.

Data Management

Positions related to data management are responsible for developing and implementing database designs and for maintaining databases. These personnel will be carrying out some of privacy's design principles. These positions are concerned with data within applications, as well as data flows between applications:

- **Data manager**   This position is responsible for data architecture and data management in larger organizations.

- **Database architect**   This position develops logical and physical designs of data models for applications. With sufficient experience, this person may also design an organization's overall data architecture.

- **Big data architect**   This position develops data models and data analytics for large, complex data sets.

- **Database administrator (DBA)**   This position builds and maintains databases designed by the database architect and those databases that are included as part of purchased applications. The DBA monitors databases, tunes them for performance and efficiency, and troubleshoots problems.

- **Database analyst**   This position performs tasks that are junior to the DBA, carrying out routine data maintenance and monitoring tasks.

- **Data scientist**   This position applies scientific methods, builds processes, and implements systems to extract knowledge or insights from data.

 EXAM TIP   CIPM candidates need to understand that the roles of data manager, big data architect, database architect, database administrator, database analyst, and data scientist are distinct from data owners. The data owner role governs the business use of, and access to, data in information systems, while the others are IT department roles for managing data models and data technology.

Network Management

Positions in network management are responsible for designing, building, monitoring, and maintaining voice and data communications networks, including connections to outside entities and the Internet:

- **Network architect**   This position designs data and voice networks and designs changes and upgrades to networks as needed to meet new organization objectives.

- **Network engineer**   This position implements, configures, and maintains network devices such as routers, switches, firewalls, and gateways.

- **Network administrator**   This position performs routine tasks in the network, such as making configuration changes and monitoring event logs.

- **Telecom engineer**   Positions in this role work with telecommunications technologies such as telecom services, data circuits, phone systems, and conferencing systems.

Systems Management

Positions in systems management are responsible for architecture, design, building, and maintenance of servers and operating systems. This may include desktop operating systems as well. Personnel in these positions also design and manage virtualized environments as well as microsegmentation:

- **Systems architect**   This position is responsible for the overall architecture of systems (usually servers), in terms of both the internal architectures and the relationships between systems.

- **Systems engineer**   This position designs, builds, and maintains servers and server operating systems.

- **Storage engineer**   This position designs, builds, and maintains storage subsystems.

- **Systems administrator**   This position performs maintenance and configuration operations on systems.

Operations

In larger organizations, positions in operations are responsible for day-to-day operational tasks that may include networks, servers, databases, and applications:

- **Operations manager**   This position is responsible for overall operations that are carried out by others. Responsibilities include establishing operations shift schedules and assisting staff members.

- **Operations analyst**   This position may be responsible for developing operational procedures; examining the health of networks, systems, and databases; setting and monitoring the operations schedule; and maintaining operations records.

- **Controls analyst**   This position monitors batch jobs and performs data entry work and other tasks to make sure they are operating correctly.

- **Systems operator**   This position monitors systems and networks, performs backup tasks, runs batch jobs, prints reports, and performs other operational tasks.

- **Data entry**   This position is responsible for keying batches of data from hard copy or other sources.

- **Media manager**   This position maintains and tracks the use and whereabouts of backup tapes and other media.

Privacy Operations

Though few organizations have personnel in a privacy operations function, the staff in many business departments have access to personal information of the organization's workforce or to its customers or constituents. These business functions include

- Human resources
- Sales and marketing
- Customer support
- Warranty or assurance services
- Business operations

Workers in these and other business functions need to be aware of the implications of having access to personal information and the organization's privacy policy, so that their day-to-day work does not run afoul of privacy policy or applicable laws.

NOTE For the most part, it's more important that you know that an organization has assigned various privacy responsibilities to designated personnel than to know the structure of the organization (or org chart).

Security Operations

Positions in security operations are responsible for designing, building, and monitoring security systems and security controls to ensure the confidentiality, integrity, and availability of information systems:

- **Security architect** This position designs security controls and systems such as authentication, audit logging, intrusion detection systems (IDSs), intrusion prevention systems (IPSs), and firewalls.
- **Security engineer** This position designs, builds, and maintains security services and systems that are designed by the security architect. Such systems include firewalls, IDSs and IPSs, web application firewalls (WAFs), web content filters, cloud access security brokers (CASBs), and others.
- **Security analyst** This position examines logs from firewalls, IDSs, and audit logs from systems and applications. A security analyst could also have other responsibilities, such as performing security reviews, performing risk analyses, and maintaining security-related business records. This position may also be responsible for issuing security advisories to others in IT.
- **Access administrator** This position is responsible for accepting approved requests for user access management changes and performing the necessary changes at the network, system, database, or application level. Often, this position is carried out by personnel in network and systems management functions; in larger organizations, user account management is performed by information security or in a separate user access department.

Privacy Audit

Positions in privacy audit are responsible for examining process design and for verifying the effectiveness of privacy policies and controls:

- **Privacy audit manager** This position is responsible for audit operations and scheduling and managing audits.
- **Privacy auditor** This position performs internal audits of privacy controls to ensure that they are being operated properly.

The topic of auditing privacy programs and operations is discussed in Chapter 5.

Security Audit

Positions in security audit are responsible for examining process design and for verifying the effectiveness of security controls:

- **Security audit manager**   This position is responsible for audit operations and scheduling and managing audits.
- **Security auditor**   This position performs internal audits of IT controls to ensure that they are being operated properly.

 NOTE   Although a privacy and security audit may not be a formal internal audit function, those performing security audits need to be able to exercise independence from the functions they audit.

Service Desk

Positions at the service desk are responsible for providing frontline support services to IT and IT customers:

- **Service desk manager**   This position serves as a liaison between end users and the IT service desk department.
- **Service desk analyst**   This position provides frontline user support services to personnel in the organization. This is sometimes known as a help-desk analyst.
- **Technical support analyst**   This position provides technical support services to other IT personnel and perhaps also to IT customers.

Quality Assurance

In larger organizations, positions in quality assurance (QA) are responsible for evaluating IT systems and processes to confirm their accuracy and effectiveness:

- **QA manager**   This position facilitates quality improvement activities throughout the IT organization.
- **QC manager**   This position tests IT systems and applications to confirm whether they are free of defects.

Other Roles

Other roles in IT organizations include the following:

- **Third-party risk management manager**   This position assesses third-party service providers to ensure that their practices do not result in unacceptable risks to the protection of sensitive information, particularly personal information of customers, constituents, or employees.

- **Vendor manager**   This position is responsible for maintaining business relationships with external vendors, measuring their performance, and handling business issues.
- **Program manager**   This position manages teams of project managers and oversees larger and more complex projects.
- **Project manager**   This position creates project plans and manages IT projects.

General Staff

The rank and file in an organization may or may not have explicit privacy or information security responsibilities. This is determined in part by executive management's understanding of the broad capabilities of information systems and the personnel who use them. It also determines executives' understanding of the human role in privacy and information security.

Typically, general staff privacy- and security-related responsibilities include the following:

- Understanding and compliance with organization privacy and security policy
- Acceptable use of organization assets, including information systems and personal information
- Proper judgment, including proper responses to people who request access to personal information or request that staff members perform specific functions (the primary impetus for this is the phenomenon of social engineering and its use as an attack vector)
- Reporting of privacy- and security-related matters and incidents to management

Organizations with a more mature privacy and security culture use standard language in job descriptions that specifies general responsibilities for the protection of assets, systems, and personal information.

Competency

Privacy leadership, together with the human resources function, need to establish means for ensuring that all staff have the necessary competencies to perform their roles correctly. In understanding individual staff competencies, an organization can consider prior experience, certifications, and training, and can bolster individual workers' competence as necessary to ensure that processes and tasks are performed correctly and timely.

These activities should be intentional, documented, and applied fairly across relevant parts of the workforce.

Privacy Program Communications

Key categories of communications help an organization's workforce better understand the principles and policies related to information privacy.

Privacy Training and Awareness

Personnel are the primary weak point in an organization's privacy and cybersecurity status. Personnel are generally considered the largest and most vulnerable portion of an organization's attack surface, and for good reason: most breaches start with a social-engineering attack, often via e-mail, or they start with the unintended misuse of personal information.

Many organizations conduct security awareness training so that personnel are aware of these common attacks, as well as several other topics that mainly fall into the category known as *Internet hygiene*, which is the safe use of computers and mobile devices, particularly while accessing the Internet. Organizations also must provide privacy awareness training that enables personnel to be aware of the expectations regarding the proper collection, storage, transmission, and use of customer, constituent, and employee personal information as well as the tools and processes the organization has in place to enable personnel to adhere to these expectations.

Training Objectives

The primary objective of privacy and security awareness programs is the keen awareness, on the part of all personnel, of the proper handling of personal information, the reality of the different types of attacks that they may be subject to, and what they are expected to do in various situations. Further, personnel must understand and comply with an organization's acceptable use policy, privacy policy, security policy, code of ethics or code of conduct, and other applicable policies.

Better privacy and security awareness training programs include opportunities for personnel to practice skills, with testing at the end of training sessions. In computer-based training, users should be required to pass the test successfully with a minimum score—70 percent is a typical minimum score to complete the course.

The best privacy and security awareness training courses, whether in-person or online, are engaging and relevant. Although some organizations conduct privacy and security awareness training for compliance purposes, many organizations have a genuine interest in their personnel getting the most value out of the training. The point of privacy and security awareness training is, after all, the reduction of risk.

Business records should be created, recording when each employee receives training. Many organizations are subject to privacy and security regulations that require personnel to complete awareness training; business records provide ample evidence of users' completion of their training.

Creating or Selecting Content

Privacy and security managers need to develop or acquire awareness training content for personnel in the organization. The content that is selected or developed should be

- **Understandable**   The content should make sense to all personnel. A common mistake that security and privacy managers make is to create or select content that is overly technical and difficult for many nontechnical personnel to understand.

- **Relevant**   The content should be applicable to the organization and its users. For example, training on the topic of cryptography would be irrelevant to the vast majority of personnel in most organizations. Irrelevant content can cause personnel to disengage from further training.

- **Actionable**   The content should ensure that personnel know what to do (and not do) in common scenarios.

- **Memorable**   The best content will give personnel opportunities to practice their skills at some of the basic tasks important to privacy and security, including selecting and using passwords, reading and responding to e-mail, making good decisions about the use of personal information, and interacting with persons inside and outside the organization.

Audiences

When planning an awareness training program, privacy and security managers need to understand the entire worker population and their various roles in the organization. This helps managers understand what training subject matter is relevant to which groups of workers. Managers need to ensure that all workers get all the training they need and not overburden personnel with training that is not relevant to their jobs.

For example, workers in a large retail organization fall into four categories:

- **Corporate workers**   These persons all use computers, and most of them use mobile devices. Most have access to sensitive information, including personal information about customers and/or employees.

- **Retail floor managers**   These persons work in retail store locations and use computers daily in their jobs.

- **Retail floor cashiers**   These persons work in retail store locations. They do not use computers, but they do collect payments by cash, check, and credit card.

- **Retail floor workers**   These persons work in retail store and warehouse locations and may use computers for single tasks only.

Privacy and security managers should package awareness training so that each audience receives relevant training. In this example, retail floor workers probably need little Internet or computer-related security awareness training, but instead would receive training on physical security and workplace safety topics. Cashiers need training on fraud techniques (counterfeit currency, currency counting fraud, and matters related to credit card payments such as skimming). Corporate workers and retail floor managers should probably receive full-spectrum privacy and security training since they all use computers and many have access to personal information and sensitive information. Retail floor managers should also receive all of the training delivered to retail floor workers and cashiers because they also work at retail locations and supervise these personnel.

NOTE Privacy training ensures that all personnel understand the organization's privacy policies, practices, and expectations.

Information Workers Workers in an organization who have contact with the personal information of employees, customers, or constituents should receive privacy awareness training. Information workers need to be aware of the organization's policies on the protection and proper use of personal information, so that the organization is less likely to suffer a privacy breach caused by poor judgment.

Technical Workers Technical workers in an organization, typically IT personnel, should be trained in security techniques relevant to their positions. Technical workers are responsible for system architecture and system and network design, implementation, and administration. Without security training, these workers may unknowingly have lapses in judgment that could result in significant vulnerabilities that could lead to compromises.

Technical workers also need privacy awareness training to be aware of the proper handling of personal information. This is especially important for the organization, to ensure that information systems will be designed and configured to bring about the greatest possible protection and sound handling of personal information.

Software Developers Software developers typically receive little or no education on privacy by design or secure software development in colleges, universities, and tech schools. The art and science of privacy by design and of secure coding, then, is new to many software developers. Training for software developers helps them to be more aware of the common mistakes made by software developers, including these:

- Vulnerabilities that permit injection attacks
- Broken authentication and session management that can lead to attackers accessing other user sessions
- Cross-site scripting
- Broken access control
- Security misconfiguration
- Sensitive data exposure
- Insufficient attack protection
- Cross-site request forgery
- Use of components with known vulnerabilities
- Underprotected APIs

This list, which changes from time to time, is published by the Open Web Application Security Project (OWASP, at www.owasp.org), an organization that helps software developers better understand the techniques needed for secure application development and deployment.

Privacy and security training for software developers should also include protection of the software development process itself. Topics in secure software development generally include the following:

- Protection of source code
- Reviews of source code
- Care when using open-source code
- Testing of source code for vulnerabilities and defects
- Archival of changes to source code
- Protection of systems used to store source code, edit and test source code, build applications, test applications, and deploy applications

Note that some of these aspects are related to the architecture of development and test environments and may not be needed for all software developers.

Third Parties   Privacy and security awareness training needs to be administered to all personnel who have access to personal information through any means. Because this may include personnel who are employees of other organizations, those workers need to participate in the organization's privacy and security awareness training. In larger organizations, the curriculum for third-party personnel may be altered somewhat, since portions of the privacy and security awareness training content may not apply to outsiders.

New Hires   New employees, as well as consultants and contractors, should be required to attend privacy and security training as soon as possible. There is a risk that new employees could make mistakes early in their employment and prior to their training if they are not yet familiar with all of the practices in the organization.

Better organizations link access control with privacy and security training: new employees are not given access to systems until after they have completed their privacy and security training. This gives new workers added incentive to complete their training quickly, since they want to be able to get access to corporate applications and get to work.

Training Schedule

Regular awareness training is required by some regulations, and most privacy and security awareness programs include at least annual refresher training for all workers. Annual training should be considered the minimum. A well-structured program can offer awareness and training in small bits throughout the year to help keep privacy, security, and Internet safety a part of every worker's day-to-day thinking process and to help them avoid common mistakes. Further, because handling procedures, protective techniques, and attack techniques change quickly, regular refresher training helps workers be aware of these developments.

Training takes time, and people tend to put it off for as long as possible. Workers can be offered incentives to complete their training through various types of rewards. For example, workers who complete their training in the first week can be awarded gift cards or other prizes.

Organizations generally choose one of two options for annual training:

- Train the entire organization all at once.
- Train groups of workers on their hire-month anniversaries.

Communication Techniques

Privacy and security awareness training programs often utilize a variety of means for imparting information-handling procedures, Internet hygiene, and safe computing information to its workers. Communication techniques often include

- **E-mail**   Privacy and security managers may occasionally send out advisories to affected personnel to inform them of recent developments, such as a new phishing attack. Occasionally, a senior executive will send a message to all personnel to emphasize that privacy and security are every worker's job and that they are to be taken seriously.
- **Internal web site**   Organizations with internal web sites or web portals may, from time to time, include privacy and security content.
- **Video monitors, posters, and bulletins**   Sometimes, a privacy or security message can be delivered on monitors, posters, or bulletins on various topics that keep people thinking about privacy and security.

Maintaining an Awareness Program

Privacy laws, regulations, and practices are changing and evolving at a fast pace. This can provide particular challenges to personnel who develop and deliver privacy training to an organization's workforce. Just as an organization's legal counsel (or other designee) researches regulatory and legal developments in information privacy informs the CPO and privacy operations about these changes, those maintaining privacy training need to be informed as well, so that they can make required changes to training materials.

Chapter Review

An organization's vision for a privacy program needs to include data protection as well as data usage functions. To be effective, the privacy program vision may also need to include IT governance if this is lacking.

Executive sponsorship is the formal or informal approval to commit resources to a business problem or challenge. Privacy is no exception: without executive sponsorship, privacy would be little more than an idea.

As vision gives way to strategy, the organization's privacy leader must ensure that the information privacy program fits in with the rest of the organization. This means that the program needs to align with the organization's highest level guiding principles.

Governance is a process whereby senior management exerts strategic control over business functions through policies, objectives, delegation of authority, and monitoring. Governance is management's continuous oversight of an organization's business processes to ensure that they effectively meet the organization's business vision and objectives.

Data governance is management's visibility and control over the use of information in an organization. Privacy programs will have difficulty succeeding in its absence.

Privacy governance involves established activities that typically focus on several fundamental principles and outcomes designed to enable management to have a clear understanding of the state of the organization's privacy program, its current risks, its direct activities, and its alignment to the organization's business objectives and practices.

To manage privacy successfully, organizations need to understand that privacy is also a people issue. When people at each level in the organization—from board members to individual contributors—understand the importance of privacy and security within their own roles and responsibilities, an organization will be in a position of reduced risk.

Privacy governance will enable alignment of the organization's privacy program with customer or constituent expectations, applicable regulations, identified risks, and business needs. An objective of privacy governance is to provide assurance of the proper protection and use of personal information from a strategic perspective to ensure that required privacy practices align with business practices.

Establishing a privacy program requires the development of a strategy. Among business, technology, privacy, and security professionals, there are many different ideas about the meaning of a strategy and the techniques used to develop a strategy, and this can result in general confusion. Although a specific strategy itself may be complex, the concept of a strategy is quite simple. A strategy can be defined as "the plan to achieve an objective."

A vital part of strategy development is the determination of desired risk levels. One of the inputs to strategy development is the understanding of the current level of risk, and the desired future state may also have a level of risk associated with it.

Depending on the current and desired future state of privacy and security, objectives may represent large projects or groups of projects implemented over several years to develop broad new capabilities, or they may be smaller projects focused on improving existing capabilities.

Once strategic objectives, risk and threat assessments, and gap analyses have been completed, the strategist can begin to develop roadmaps to accomplish each objective.

Although the development of a new strategy may bring hope and optimism to the privacy or security team, there is no guarantee that changes in an organization can be implemented without friction and even opposition. The privacy and security manager should anticipate and be prepared to maneuver around, over, or through many types of constraints and obstacles.

As a privacy leader develops the organization's privacy program strategy, the program will include various routine privacy operations that must be performed. The privacy leader will need to determine what positions will be required and what activities they will perform. The privacy leader should consider whether any existing staff across the organization can take on some privacy responsibilities.

Privacy and information security governance are most effective when every person in the organization knows what is expected of them. More mature organizations develop formal roles and responsibilities that establish clear expectations for personnel with regard to their part in all matters related to the protection and proper use of systems and personal information.

The role of a CPO typically includes safeguarding personal information and ensuring that the organization does not misuse the personal information at its disposal. Because many organizations with a CPO also have a CISO, the CPO's duties mainly involve oversight into the organization's proper handling and use of personal information.

Privacy leadership, together with the human resources function, must establish means for ensuring that all staff members have the necessary competencies to perform their roles correctly.

Many organizations conduct security awareness training so that personnel are aware of common attacks, as well as several other topics that are considered Internet hygiene, which is the safe use of computers and mobile devices while accessing the Internet. Organizations also must provide privacy awareness training that enables personnel to be aware of the expectations regarding the proper use of customer, constituent, and employee personal information.

Because privacy laws, regulations, and practices are changing and evolving at a fast pace, it is important to ensure that privacy awareness training programs remain current.

Quick Review

- Privacy and security programs should be in alignment with the organization's overall mission, goals, and objectives. This means that the chief privacy officer, chief information security officer, and others should be aware of, and involved in, strategic initiatives and the execution of the organization's strategic goals.

- An organization's definitions of roles and responsibilities may or may not be in sync with its culture of accountability. For instance, an organization may have clear definitions of responsibilities documented in policy and process documents and yet may rarely hold individuals accountable when preventable security events occur.

- Privacy and information security is the responsibility of every person in an organization; however, the means for assigning and monitoring privacy and security responsibilities to individuals and groups vary widely.

- Privacy and security strategists should be mindful of each organization's tolerance for change within a given period of time. While much progress may be warranted, the amount of change that can be reasonably implemented within a short amount of time is limited.

- Although it is important for privacy and security strategists to understand the present state of the organization when developing a strategic roadmap, the strategist must proceed with the knowledge that there can never be a sufficient level of understanding. Even if the most thorough snapshot has been taken, the strategist must understand that the organization is slowly (or perhaps quickly) changing. Execution of a strategic plan is intended to accelerate changes in certain aspects of an organization that is slowly changing anyway.

- Each organization has its own practice for the development of business cases for the presentation, discussion, and approval for strategic initiatives.

- Privacy and security strategists must anticipate obstacles and constraints affecting the achievement of strategic objectives and consider refining those objectives so that they can be realized.

Questions

1. Privacy governance is most concerned with:

   A. Privacy policy

   B. Security policy

   C. Privacy strategy

   D. Security executive compensation

2. A gaming software startup company does not employ penetration testing of its software. This is an example of:

   A. High tolerance of risk

   B. Noncompliance

   C. Irresponsibility

   D. Outsourcing

3. A privacy strategist is developing a privacy awareness program. What is the best method for ensuring that employees have retained important content?

   A. Measure the time it takes for employees to complete training.

   B. Include competency quizzes at the end of training sessions.

   C. Note how quickly employees complete training after being asked.

   D. Include videos in privacy training content.

4. Privacy responsibilities are included in which of these IT positions?

   A. Security engineer

   B. Application developer

   C. Database administrator

   D. All of these

5. The best first step in building privacy operations is:

    A. Perform a risk assessment.

    B. Identify requirements.

    C. Perform data discovery.

    D. Conduct a penetration test.

6. The best definition of a strategy is:

    A. The objective to achieve a plan

    B. The plan to achieve an objective

    C. The plan to achieve business alignment

    D. The plan to reduce risk

7. Which of the following should be considered a prerequisite when building a privacy program?

    A. Executive support

    B. Approved privacy policy

    C. Appointing a CPO

    D. Performing a risk assessment

8. As part of understanding the organization's current state, a privacy strategist is examining the organization's privacy policy. What does the policy tell the strategist?

    A. The level of management commitment to privacy

    B. The maturity level of the organization

    C. The compliance level of the organization

    D. None of these

9. While gathering and examining various privacy-related business records, the privacy officer has determined that the organization has no privacy or security incident log. What conclusion can the privacy officer make from this?

    A. The organization does not have privacy or security incident detection capabilities.

    B. The organization has not yet experienced a privacy or security incident.

    C. The organization is recording privacy or security incidents in its risk register.

    D. The organization has effective privacy policies.

10. The tool that permits senior management to observe and control an organization is known as:

    A. Training

    B. Control

    C. Policy

    D. Governance

11. A privacy strategist has examined a business process and has determined that personnel who perform the process do so consistently, but there is no written process document. The maturity level of this process is:

    A. Initial

    B. Repeatable

    C. Defined

    D. Managed

12. A privacy strategist has examined several business processes and has found that their individual maturity levels range from managed to optimizing. What is the best future state for these business processes?

    A. All processes should be changed to managed.

    B. All processes should be changed to optimizing.

    C. There is insufficient information to determine the desired end states of these processes.

    D. Processes that are managed should be changed to defined.

13. Which of the following roles should include responsibility for monitoring a DLP system for alerts?

    A. Systems engineering

    B. Database management

    C. Security operations

    D. Privacy manager

14. A privacy strategist is seeking to improve the privacy program in an organization with a strong but casual culture. What is the best approach here?

    A. Conduct focus groups to discuss possible avenues of approach.

    B. Enact new detective controls to identify personnel who are violating policy.

    C. Implement security awareness training that emphasizes new required behavior.

    D. Lock users out of their accounts until they agree to be compliant.

15. A privacy strategist recently joined a retail organization that operates with slim profit margins and has discovered that the organization lacks several important privacy capabilities. What is the best strategy here?

    A. Insist that management support an aggressive program quickly to improve the program.

    B. Develop a risk ledger that highlights all identified risks.

    C. Recommend that the biggest risks be avoided.

    D. Develop a risk-based strategy that implements changes slowly over an extended period of time.

Answers

1. **C.** Privacy governance is the mechanism through which a privacy strategy is established, controlled, and monitored. Long-term and other strategic decisions are made in the context of privacy governance.

2. **A.** A software startup in an industry like gaming is going to be highly tolerant of risk: time to market and signing up new customers will be its primary objectives. As the organization achieves viability, other priorities such as security will be introduced.

3. **B.** Competency quizzes as a part of training are an effective means for recording knowledge retention.

4. **D.** Privacy responsibilities flow to nearly all positions in IT and IT security. The principle of privacy by design and by default means that all related information systems and supporting processes and procedures need to align with privacy policy.

5. **B.** When building a new privacy operation, it is first necessary to understand what activities and characteristics are required of the organization. This will come from the text of applicable security and privacy regulations and other legal obligations such as privacy contracts. Legal counsel should be on hand to interpret these regulations and other obligations correctly.

6. **B.** A strategy is the plan to achieve an objective. An objective is the "what" that an organization wants to achieve, and a strategy is the "how" the objective will be achieved.

7. **A.** Without executive support, a privacy leader may struggle to obtain the necessary resources to develop and execute a strategy for building a privacy program.

8. **D.** By itself, privacy policy tells someone little about an organization's privacy practices. An organization's policy is only a collection of statements; without interviewing personnel and examining business processes and records, a privacy professional cannot develop any conclusions about an organization's privacy practices.

9. **A.** An organization that does not have a privacy or security incident log probably lacks the capability to detect and respond to an incident. It is not reasonable to assume that the organization has had no incidents, since minor incidents occur with regularity. Claiming that the organization has effective controls is unreasonable, because it is understood that incidents occur even when effective controls are in place (because not all types of incidents can reasonably be prevented).

10. **D.** Governance is the process that permits senior management to exert strategic control over business functions in an organization.

11. **B.** A process that is performed consistently but is undocumented is generally considered to be managed.

12. **C.** There are no rules that specify that the maturity levels of different processes need to be the same or at different values relative to one another. In this example, each process may already be at an appropriate level based on risk appetite, risk levels, and other considerations.

13. **C.** The security operations team is the best choice for monitoring a DLP system. Such a system would probably be sending alerts to a SIEM, which a security operations team would be routinely monitoring.

14. **A.** Organizational culture is powerful, as it reflects how people think and work. In this example, there is no mention that the strong culture is bad, only that it is casual. Punishing people for their behavior may cause resentment, a revolt, or the loss of good employees who decide to leave the organization. The best approach here is to conduct focus groups to try to understand the culture and work with people in the organization to figure out how a culture of privacy and security can be introduced successfully.

15. **D.** A privacy strategist needs to understand an organization's capacity to spend its way to lower risk. Developing a risk-based strategy that implements changes slowly over an extended period of time is the correct response because it is unlikely that an organization with low profit margins is going to agree to an aggressive improvement plan. Developing a risk ledger that depicts these risks may be a helpful tool for communicating risk, but by itself, it involves no action to change anything. Similarly, recommending risk avoidance may mean discontinuing the very operations that bring in revenue.

Privacy Program Framework

In this chapter, you will learn about
- Components of a privacy program framework
- Privacy policy, standards, processes, controls, and guidelines
- Well-known control frameworks
- Significant privacy laws and regulations
- Data governance and data management
- Data classification, data retention, and data loss prevention
- Data minimization and de-identification
- Working with data subjects
- Privacy metrics
- Tracking technologies and countermeasures

This chapter covers the Certified Information Privacy Manager job practice II, "Privacy Program Framework." The domain represents approximately 14 percent of the CIPM examination.

When properly implemented, *governance is a process* whereby senior management exerts strategic control over business functions through policies, objectives, delegation of authority, and monitoring. Governance is management's continuous oversight of an organization's business processes that is intended to ensure that these processes effectively meet the organization's business vision and objectives.

Organizations often establish governance through a committee or formalized position that sets long-term business strategies and makes changes to ensure that business processes continue to support business strategies and the organization's overall needs. Effective governance is enabled through the development and enforcement of documented policies, standards, requirements, and various reporting metrics.

Develop the Privacy Program Framework

The framework of a program such as a privacy program comprises the structure and organization of all of its parts. These parts are represented by artifacts, including

- **Privacy program charter**   This describes the program and its purpose, scope, objectives, roles and responsibilities, and budget.
- **Privacy policy**   A typical privacy program includes an external privacy policy that pertains to customers, employees, or constituents; an internal privacy policy informs the workforce of expectations regarding the protection and handling of personal information.
- **Privacy standards**   These are prescribed practices, methods, protocols, and vendors to be used in privacy and security processes and systems.
- **Privacy processes**   These are business processes in the privacy program that apply to normal day-to-day operations as well as to incident response and other unplanned (but expected) events.
- **Privacy guidelines**   This information helps personnel better understand how to comply with privacy policies and standards.
- **Controls**   These formal statements of expected activities or outcomes ensure that privacy policies and processes are correctly followed.

Privacy Charter

A charter is a formal document used in some organizations to define and describe a major business activity and/or department. Typically, a privacy program charter will contain these elements:

- Program name
- Program purpose
- Executive sponsorship
- Roles and responsibilities
- Policies (often referring to one or more external privacy policy documents)
- Primary business processes
- Budget and other resources

 NOTE   Organizations that don't typically use charters can include this information in an internal privacy policy instead of in a charter. More details are discussed in the upcoming "Internal Privacy Policy" section.

Developing Privacy Policies

Privacy policies are statements that describe the collection and use of personal information, as well as the actions that persons can take to inquire and make requests about their personal information. If the organization collects personal information only from its internal workers, this policy may not be publicly available. If the organization collects information from customers and constituents who are external to the organization, its privacy policy will most likely be published externally, often on a public web site. Similarly, at organizations that collect information from customers in person, especially in healthcare organizations, the privacy policy is often visibly posted in business locations, and clients may be asked to sign statements indicating that they have read and understand the policy.

Organizations that collect personal information from persons outside the organization often also have internal, nonpublic privacy policies that affect their employees and other workers. Such policies, like cybersecurity policies, describe the required characteristics and expectations of staff members as well as information systems used by the organization.

If an organization that processes personal information employs any service providers that also store, process, or have access to the personal information used by the organization, the organization will also impose requirements upon those service providers. This aspect is discussed in Chapter 3.

Internal Privacy Policy

Virtually all organizations possess and use information about their employees and other workers. In many countries, these organizations are required to disclose to their employees that the organization has a policy of confidentiality and to inform workers that their personal information is used only in its role as employer to carry out activities required by law.

Organizations lacking a formal privacy program often stop there and make no further attempts to define the meaning or enforcement of "for sanctioned business purposes only." This can, however, lead to improper use of personal information through tactical decisions made by nearly any staff members who may have little or no awareness about applicable laws on this topic.

Organizations with more mature privacy and security programs will have detailed privacy policies that define expected behaviors of their workers and the required characteristics of their information systems. In many cases, their privacy policies will exist as a part of their information security policies for the protection of said information. On the minimum side, privacy or security policies will include general statements about sensitive or personal information that shall be used "for sanctioned business purposes only" without further detail.

Whether a part of an organization's information security policy or separate, an internal privacy policy should include content on the following topics:

- *Roles and responsibilities for the organization's privacy program.* This should include
  - Those who have data management responsibilities
  - Those who approve and review access to personal information
  - Those who review and approve of new uses for personal data

- Those who receive and process subject data requests
- Those who have responsibility for monitoring uses of personal data
- Those who have responsibility for responding to incidents that represent the misuse of personal information
- Those who review privacy business processes
- Those who audit privacy business processes

- *Business processes governing the use of personal information.* This should include periodic reviews of business processes to ensure that they remain compliant with applicable laws and regulations.
- *Language regarding the protection of personal information.* Generally, this will fall back to the organization's information security policy. However, this language can be included in its privacy policy (organizations are cautioned against duplicating this language, because it will require care to keep both policies in sync).
- *Consequences for violations of privacy policy.* Like an information security policy and other policies, this will describe the range of possible outcomes when persons are found to violate privacy policy. Typically, this ranges from verbal warnings to written warnings and even termination of employment.
- *Provisions for the review and audit of privacy business processes.* This will describe reviews that take place within privacy business processes, as well as audits of privacy business processes. Reviews will typically be performed by process owners to confirm that all necessary actions take place as required. Audits of privacy business processes will be performed by persons outside of the organization's privacy office.
- *Descriptions of measurements of privacy business processes.* Any statistics, metrics, key performance indicators (KPIs), key risk indicators (KRIs) and leading or trailing indicators required in the privacy program will be described here.
- *Citations of applicable regulations and other obligations.* Applicable laws, regulations, and other obligations (such as terms and conditions in contracts with other organizations) may be cited in an organization's privacy policy.

External Privacy Policy

Organizations that collect personal information about persons outside the organization should develop privacy policies accessible by those persons. For organizations that sell products or services to the general public, the privacy policy will often be publicly available on a public web site. It may also be posted on the premises where these products or services are rendered.

Privacy laws enacted in many regions of the world have brought about the near universality of public-facing privacy policies posted on web sites or in the form of visible notices at business locations. Driven by these privacy laws, public-facing privacy policies generally include the following:

- Descriptions of the methods used to collect personal information
- Descriptions of the methods used to protect personal information

- Descriptions of primary and secondary uses of personal information
- Descriptions of any international transfers of personal information
- Descriptions of any third parties that may store or process personal information on behalf of the organization
- Descriptions of any tracking or logging activities performed by the organization, such as the use of web browser cookies
- Any procedures that may be available to explain how personal information has been used or is being used
- Statements describing the legal rights of data subjects concerning the organization's use of their personal data, often including several subsections for specific regions or localities
- Contact information or procedures for persons who want to initiate subject data requests or inquiries or lodge complaints regarding the organization's use of their personal information
- Contact information or procedures for regulators or other authorities to whom persons can make inquires or lodge complaints regarding the organization's collection or use of their personal information
- The date that the privacy policy was last updated

Some privacy laws require that an organization inform employees, customers, and/ or constituents if the organization changes its privacy policy. Organizations required by law to collect an acknowledgment stating that data subjects have received a copy of the privacy policy will be required to collect a new acknowledgment for the updated privacy policy. In business applications, this often comes in the form of a brief statement that reads, "Continued use of this application constitutes consent to our updated privacy policy," with a link to the online privacy policy content. Alternatively, organizations may send e-mail notices to users of a system regarding the updated privacy policy; often, the policy itself is not included in the message, but means are provided to access the policy.

 NOTE Like other aspects of service and service levels, organization privacy practices may soon become competitive differentiators.

Privacy Standards

Policies define *what* is to be done, and standards define *how* policies are to be done. For instance, a policy may stipulate that strong passwords are to be used for end-user authentication. A password standard, then, would be more specific by defining the length, complexity, and other characteristics of a strong password.

Where policies are designed to be durable and long-lasting, they do so at the expense of being somewhat unspecific. Standards that are more specific may be frequently affected by change, because they are closer to the technology and are concerned with the details of the implementation of policy.

Standards need to be developed carefully, so that

- They properly reflect the intent of one or more corresponding policies.
- They can be implemented.
- They are unambiguous.
- Their directives can be automated, where large numbers of systems, endpoints, devices, or people are involved, leading to consistency and uniformity.

Several types of standards are in use, including the following:

- **Protocol standards** Examples include Transport Layer Security (TLS) 1.2 for web server session encryption, Advanced Encryption Standard (AES) 256 for encryption at rest, Institute of Electrical and Electronics Engineers (IEEE) 802.11ac for wireless networking, and Security Assertion Markup Language (SAML) 2.0 for authentication.
- **Vendor standards** For example, cloud storage will be implemented through Box.com.
- **Configuration standards** For instance, a server-hardening standard would specify all of the security-related settings to be implemented for each type of server operating system in use.
- **Programming language standards** Examples include C++, Java, and Python. Organizations that do not establish and assert programming language standards may end up with programs written in dozens of different languages, which may drive up the cost of maintaining them.
- **Methodology standards** Examples include the use of Factor Analysis of Information Risk (FAIR) risk analysis techniques; Operationally Critical Threat, Asset, and Vulnerability Evaluation (OCTAVE) for security assessments; and SMART (specific, measurable, attainable, relevant, and timely) for the development of strategic objectives.
- **Control frameworks** These include National Institute of Standards and Technology (NIST) Privacy Framework, Payment Card Industry Data Security Standard (PCI DSS), Health Insurance Portability and Accountability Act (HIPAA), and ISO/IEC 27701.

As the organization develops its privacy framework, it may discover that one or more of its standards are impacted by new requirements or that new standards need to be developed. Because regulations, practices, and technologies change so rapidly, standards are often reviewed and updated more frequently than policies. New privacy strategies are not the only reason that standards are reviewed and updated; other reasons include the enactment of new or updated privacy laws, new techniques for data protection, and the acquisition of new network devices and applications.

Privacy Laws

Laws passed by governments at national, state, and provincial levels impose data collection, handling, and retention requirements on organizations that store or process personal information about natural persons. These laws have been enacted to respond to citizens' outcry at the abuse of their personal information and violations of their desire for privacy as the use of technology and the Internet has become part of our daily lives. Activities such as telemarketing and tracking people's locations and habits have been the focus of growing concerns by citizens and privacy advocates. Advances in the capabilities of information systems and data mining of large databases containing personal information have enabled practices that many private citizens find inappropriate and even intrusive. Abuses of such capabilities would allow for the creation of a new and very invasive form of a surveillance police state, which is not difficult to imagine, as some governments in the world are already there. Legislators in many countries have sought to counterbalance these capabilities by defining the rights of natural persons concerning the data that is collected about them and used in various ways.

The most influential privacy laws include the European Union General Data Protection Regulation (EU GDPR), HIPAA, the US Fair Credit Reporting Act (FCRA), the US Electronic Communications Privacy Act (ECPA), the Canadian Personal Information Protection and Electronic Documents Act (PIPEDA), the California Consumer Privacy Act (CCPA) and California Privacy Rights Act (CPRA), and the Chinese Cybersecurity Law (CCSL). These and other laws are discussed in the remainder of this section. This is not intended to be an exhaustive or authoritative list, but is instead a sampling of better-known privacy laws.

 TIP Because privacy and data protection laws are being rapidly enacted and changed, organizations must devise a way to remain fully aware of new and changing laws and legal precedents.

EU General Data Protection Regulation

One of the most notable modern privacy laws, the GDPR enacts sweeping requirements upon organizations within and beyond the European Union that store, process, or transmit personal data about EU citizens and residents. The GDPR was passed in April 2016 and became effective in May 2018. The main privileges enacted by the GDPR include the following:

- **Rights of data subjects** Any organization collecting information about EU citizens and residents is required to operate with transparency in collecting and using their personal information. Chapter III of the GDPR defines eight data subject rights that have become foundational for other privacy regulations around the world:
  - *Right to access personal data.* Data subjects can access the data collected on them.
  - *Right to rectification.* Data subjects can request a modification of their data to correct errors and the updating of incomplete information.

- *Right to erasure.* Also referred to as the right to be forgotten, data subjects can request that their personal data be erased from an entity's processing activities.
- *Right to restrict processing.* In certain circumstances, data subjects can request that processing of their personal data be stopped.
- *Right to be notified.* Data subjects must be notified about what information is being collected at or before collection, and the use of that information.
- *Right to data portability.* Data subjects can request that their personal data be provided in a commonly used, machine-readable format.
- *Right to object.* Data subjects can object to processing of their data when a controller attempts to argue legitimate grounds for the processing that override the interests, rights, and freedoms of the data subject or for legal purposes.
- *Right to reject automated individual decision-making.* Data subjects can refuse the automated processing of their personal data to make decisions about them.

- **Definitions of data controller and data processor**   The GDPR defines a *data controller* as an organization that directs the use of personal data. A *data processor* is an organization that processes personal data as directed by a data controller. Controllers and processors are required to maintain records regarding the processing of personal information.

- **Data protection and privacy by design and by default**   Organizations are required to design, operate, and maintain their business processes and information systems with privacy and security as a part of their default design.

- **Cybersecurity**   Organizations that process personal information are required to enact cybersecurity capabilities to protect that data.

- **Breach notification**   Organizations are required to notify supervisory authorities and affected data subjects in the event of a privacy or security breach of personal data.

- **Data protection impact assessment (DPIA)**   The DPIA is a formal process to identify and minimize the data protection risks of a data processing activity. Organizations are required to perform DPIAs whenever they are implementing new, or making significant changes to, business processes or information systems.

- **Data protection officer (DPO)**   An organization is required to appoint a DPO if it processes personal data on a large scale. The DPO is expected to have expert knowledge of data protection law and practices.

- **Certification**   The GDPR permits the creation of certification authorities and voluntary certifications of organizations that process personal data.

NOTE   At the time of this writing, no GDPR certification has been approved by the national supervisory authorities or the European Data Protection Board.

- **Cross-border data transfers**   The GDPR contains rules regarding the transfer of personal data out of the European Union.

- **Binding corporate rules**   The GDPR accommodates the use of binding corporate rules that multinational organizations may enact to ensure the protection and appropriate use of personal data when transferred outside the European Union to their overseas systems.

- **Supervisory authority**   Each EU member state establishes a supervisory authority that is responsible for monitoring GDPR compliance.

- **Penalties**   The GDPR provides supervisory authorities to enact fines against organizations that violate any terms of the GDPR. Administrative fines can be as high as €20 million or 4 percent of global turnover, whichever is greater.

The GDPR claims to have extraterritorial jurisdiction over companies not based in the European Union that provide services to EU citizens in EU member states. In November 2019, the European Data Protection Board issued its final guidelines on the territorial scope of the GDPR. The guidelines are designed to assist both companies and regulators in assessing whether certain data processing activities are within the scope of the GDPR. While claims of jurisdiction beyond its own borders have yet to be seriously tested in courts, the final guidelines provide some clarity for data processing activities of a non-EU entity. For organizations offering goods or services in the EU to become subject to the GDPR, these activities should result from intentional actions rather than inadvertently or incidentally.

NOTE   EU data protection authorities fined Marriott £99 million for a 2018 breach and Google €50 million for alleged abuses of privacy settings. Ultimately the penalty to Marriott was settled at £18.4 million. Subsequent appeals of these and other fines against non-EU companies should begin to reveal the law's true reach over the next several years.

US Health Insurance Portability and Accountability Act

Enacted in 1996, HIPAA includes two rules that are concerned with the protection of protected health information (PHI) and electronic protected health information (ePHI). Covered entities are organizations that store or process medical information and are subject to one or both of these rules:

- **Security Rule**   This part of HIPAA requires that organizations enact several administrative, physical, and technical safeguards to protect ePHI. Many of these controls are compulsory, while others are "addressable" (an organization can rationalize their disuse).

- **Privacy Rule**   Effective in 2003, this part of HIPAA requires that organizations protect PHI, mainly in hard copy form.

Note that additional provisions of HIPAA are not related to security or privacy.

HIPAA defines various civil and criminal penalties for organizations that violate the law. Covered entities are required to enact business associate agreements (BAAs) with all third parties that store or process ePHI on behalf of covered entities.

Health Information Technology for Economic and Clinical Health Act   Enacted in 2009, HITECH extends the Security Rule and Privacy Rule in HIPAA by expanding security breach notification requirements and expanding the disclosures of the use of a patient's PHI.

US Fair Credit Reporting Act

Enacted in 1970, the FCRA provides visibility, remedies, and assurances through civil liability that the information contained in consumers' credit history is accurate. Since credit reports are used by banks and other financial institutions (as well as employers in many states for making hire/no-hire decisions), FCRA provides a means for consumers to obtain copies of their credit reports and procedures for making corrections to erroneous information contained in those credit reports.

FCRA is an early example of a privacy law that provides persons with the ability to know what personal information is being stored, how it is used, and what methods can be used for obtaining copies and requesting corrections.

If consumers' rights are violated, they may recover damages, attorney fees, and court costs, and punitive damages may be awarded if actions against them were willful.

Canadian Personal Information Protection and Electronic Documents Act

PIPEDA went into effect in 2000 and seeks to ensure consumer data privacy in the context of e-commerce. In part, PIPEDA was enacted to provide assurances to European countries and consumers that their personal information present in Canadian companies' information systems would be safe and free from abuses.

PIPEDA also gives Canadians the right to know why organizations collect, use, or disclose their personal information, and the assurance that their information will not be used for any other purpose. They can further know who within the organizations are responsible for protecting their information. They can contact the organizations to ensure that their personal data is accurate and can lodge complaints if they believe their privacy rights have been violated. Canadian companies must obtain consent for the collection of personal information, and they cannot refuse to provide service to a Canadian citizen if the citizen refuses to provide such consent.

California Consumer Protection Act and California Privacy Rights Act

Made effective on January 1, 2020, CCPA is a state law designed to improve California residents' privacy rights. Provisions of CCPA give California residents certain rights, including the following:

- Knowledge of what personal information is being collected
- Notification of whether such personal information is subsequently transferred or disclosed to another party

- The ability to prohibit an organization from transferring or selling personal information
- The ability to examine the personal information held by organizations, with the right to request that the information be corrected or removed
- The freedom from discrimination should individuals choose to exercise their privacy rights

Californians can sue for damages when unencrypted and unredacted personal information is subject to unauthorized access and exfiltration, theft, or disclosure as a result of a business's violation of the duty to implement and maintain reasonable security procedures.

Like the EU GDPR, the CCPA claims jurisdiction over companies not located in California if they collect personal information about California residents. And like the GDPR, this provision has yet to be tested in court.

Approved by ballot measure in 2020 and effective in 2023, the CPRA expands the CCPA's provisions, including

- Triples the fines imposed on violators
- Permits civil penalties for theft of login information
- Creates the California Privacy Protection Agency that will implement and enforce California privacy laws

 NOTE   The CCPA is expected to change significantly, and enforcement actions have yet to begin as of the writing of this book. Organizations subject to CCPA should watch this law, updates, enforcement, and resulting case law carefully.

Chinese Cybersecurity Law

Enacted in 2016 and effective in 2017, the CCSL consists of three main parts:

- **Data protection**   Organizations holding personal information about Chinese citizens must take measures to protect that information.
- **Data localization**   Organizations collecting information about Chinese citizens must keep such data within the country of China. Organizations that want to transfer data out of China must undergo a data assessment by the Chinese government.
- **Cybersecurity**   Organizations are required to enact controls to prevent malware, intrusions, and other attacks. The law includes mandatory standards, assessments, and certifications for network devices.

CCSL's data protection principles resemble those of the GDPR. Both laws require that citizens be informed if an organization holds their personal data; the organization must explain the use of their personal data, identify collection methods, and obtain consent for continued use.

Brazilian General Data Protection Law

Enacted in 2019 and effective in August 2020, Brazil's Lei Geral de Proteção de Dados (LGPD) is similar to the EU GDPR. The LGPD establishes a National Data Protection Authority that is designated as the federal agency responsible for overseeing the data protection regulation.

The LGPD establishes a number of individual rights over personal data, many of which are similar to what is provided by the GDPR. However, some additional rights are provided by the LGPD, including access to information about entities with which an organization has shared the individual's personal data.

Like the GDPR and the CCPA, the LGPD claims jurisdiction over companies not located in Brazil if one of the following criteria are met:

- The processing operation is carried out in Brazil.
- The purpose of the processing activity is to offer or provide goods or services to individuals located in Brazil.
- The personal data was collected in Brazil.

Similar to the GDPR and the CCPA, this provision has yet to be tested in court.

Privacy Laws Enforced by the FTC

In the United States, the Federal Trade Commission (FTC), the agency that monitors consumers' rights, has brought legal action against scores of companies in alleged violation of consumer protection laws, including violations of posted privacy policies, deceptive practices with regards to US-EU Safe Harbor registration, breaches of personal information, improper collection of personal data without consent, and failures to protect personal information.

The FTC enforces more than 70 laws, including the following:

- Federal Trade Commission Act, which protects consumers from unfair and deceptive practices
- Children's Online Privacy Protection Act (COPPA), which protects children's online privacy, particularly those under age 13
- Do-Not-Call Implementation Act, which provides for consumers to opt out of all telemarketing calls
- Controlling the Assault of Non-Solicited Pornography and Marketing Act (CAN-SPAM), which prevents misleading advertising and requires consumer opt out
- Gramm–Leach–Bliley Act (GLBA), which protects and secures the privacy of consumer personal information by financial institutions
- HITECH, which extends the scope of HIPAA
- Identity Theft and Assumption Deterrence Act, which provides a central clearinghouse of identity theft complaints

- Fair Credit Reporting Act (FCRA), which protects personal information collected by consumer credit bureaus, medical information companies, and tenant screening services
- Clayton Antitrust Act, which prevents illegal contracts, mergers, and acquisitions

International Data-Sharing Agreements

Multinational organizations, as well as organizations doing business with citizens in many countries, need to be aware of the presence of and requirements imposed by international data-sharing agreements. These agreements between governments serve as implementation requirements that organizations must follow.

These international data-sharing agreements have a history of changing more frequently than privacy laws. Case in point: International Safe Harbor Privacy Principles (known to most in the privacy business as Safe Harbor) were developed in the late 1990s. In 2015, the European Court of Justice invalidated Safe Harbor. In 2016, the EU-US Privacy Shield was developed, but through US court decisions it was weakened, until the EU-US Umbrella Agreement was approved in 2017. In 2020, the EU Court of Justice struck down EU-US Privacy Shield. The uncertainty continues.

International organizations are able to make use of Binding Corporate Rules, now known as Standard Contractual Clauses, that define international transfers and protection of data within organizations. This approach most often applies to employment and human resources records of an organization's workforce.

 NOTE International data-sharing agreements have proven to be volatile; hence, organizations should monitor developments concerning these agreements and be able to respond accordingly.

Works Councils

Organizations in Europe and other places are often required to engage with local works councils, which are groups not unlike labor unions that represent organization workers regarding matters of collection and use of their personal information. Unlike US-based organizations, which are less constrained on the collection and use of personally identifiable information (PII), European organizations, and European branches and subsidiaries of non-European organizations, must make a business case with local works councils to win approval for data collection as well as various types of information systems monitoring and recordkeeping.

Other Legal Obligations

In addition to abiding by applicable laws and regulations, organizations may negotiate additional terms and conditions regarding the protection of personal information. Such obligations may be related to specific services rendered by third-party service providers that store or process personal information on behalf of other organizations. For instance, a service provider may comply with all applicable laws, agree to specific protective measures, undergo periodic audits or examinations, or provide specific reporting regarding the storage or use of personal data.

Establishing Legal Basis for Processing

Within the context of data privacy and privacy regulations, organizations must identify specifically the legal basis under which they are collecting and/or processing personal information. Simply put, it must be lawful for the organization to collect and use data subjects' personal information, and the organization must be able to cite specifically how it is lawful.

Article 6.1 of the GDPR provides five possible avenues of legal basis (quoting directly from GDPR):

- *processing is necessary for the performance of a contract to which the data subject is party or in order to take steps at the request of the data subject prior to entering into a contract;*

- *processing is necessary for compliance with a legal obligation to which the controller is subject;*

- *processing is necessary in order to protect the vital interests of the data subject or of another natural person;*

- *processing is necessary for the performance of a task carried out in the public interest or in the exercise of official authority vested in the controller;*

- *processing is necessary for the purposes of the legitimate interests pursued by the controller or by a third party, except where such interests are overridden by the interests or fundamental rights and freedoms of the data subject which require protection.* [This does not apply to public authorities in the performance of their duties.]

Individual EU member states are permitted to include additional provisions.

The CCPA does not treat this in the same way as the GDPR. Instead, entities subject to CCPA must follow the law in general. Certain use cases, such as healthcare and employment, with specific provisions are cited.

Establishing Legitimate Interest

The term *legitimate interest* is used in the GDPR as one of five bases for legal collection and processing of personal information. One might consider legitimate interest a loophole, but it is the author's opinion that this provision was included so that GDPR did not need to enumerate every possible use of personal information (which would soon be out of date, requiring frequent updates to the law).

Legitimate interest gives organizations a basis for collecting and processing personal information if they benefit from doing so. But it doesn't end there: the real issue of legitimate interest lies in the fact that organizations must balance their interests with those of the data subject.

Online advertising is an interesting case to consider. Advertisers have an interest in serving advertising content to readers and viewers. To stay in business and earn advertising revenue (which is the business model for a considerable number of web sites), advertisers claim that readers and viewers benefit by advertising that is aligned with topics of interest to them (the readers' and viewers' interest). Thus, there is an argument that online advertising benefits the advertiser (and web site operator) as well as the viewer (the data subject).

 CAUTION Organizations are cautioned not to lean upon legitimate interest too readily. Some long-established industry and business practices may be forever altered as a result of GDPR, CCPA, and other privacy laws.

Controls

Before we dive into the topic of technical privacy controls, we first need to discuss the concept and application of controls in general. This section contains a brief discussion of controls; a comprehensive discussion of controls and control frameworks can be found in *CISM Certified Information Security Manager All-In-One Exam Guide*.

Controls are statements that define required outcomes. Controls are often implemented through policies, procedures, mechanisms, systems, and other measures designed to reduce risk. An organization develops controls to ensure that its business objectives will be met, risks will be reduced, and errors will be prevented or corrected. Controls are used for two primary purposes in an organization: they are implemented to ensure desired outcomes and to avoid unwanted outcomes. In the context of privacy and information security, controls should be defined and implemented to ensure the protection and proper handling of personal information.

Control Objectives

Control objectives are statements of desired states or outcomes from business operations to mitigate risks. When building a security program, and preferably before selecting a control framework, you need to establish high-level control objectives. Example control objective subject matter includes the following:

- Confidentiality and privacy of personal and sensitive information
- Proper and sanctioned use of personal information
- Protection of IT assets
- Accuracy of transactions
- Availability of IT systems
- Controlled changes to IT systems
- Compliance with corporate policies
- Compliance with applicable regulations and other legal obligations

Control objectives are the foundation for one or more controls. For each control objective, one or more control activities will exist to ensure the realization of the objective.

For example, the "availability of IT systems" control objective could be implemented via several control activities, including these:

- IT systems will be continuously monitored, and any interruptions in availability will result in alerts sent to appropriate personnel.
- IT systems will have resource-measuring capabilities.
- IT management will review capacity reports monthly and adjust resources accordingly.
- IT systems will have antimalware controls that are monitored by appropriate staff.

Together, these four (or more) controls contribute to the overall control objective of IT system availability. Similarly, other control objectives will include one or more controls that will ensure their realization.

After establishing control objectives and defining the control activities that will support the objectives, the next step is to design controls. This can be a considerable undertaking when done in a vacuum. A better approach is to utilize one of several high-quality, industry-accepted control frameworks as a starting point.

If an organization elects to adopt a standard control framework, its next step is to perform a risk assessment to determine whether controls in the control framework adequately meet each control objective. Where there are gaps in control coverage, additional controls must be developed and put in place.

 NOTE An IT organization supporting many applications and services will generally have some controls that are specific to each application. However, IT will also have controls that apply across all applications and services. These are usually called IT general controls (ITGC).

Privacy Control Objectives

Privacy control objectives resemble ordinary control objectives but are set in the context of privacy and information security. Following are some examples of privacy control objectives:

- Protection of personal information from unauthorized personnel
- Protection of personal information from unauthorized modification
- Integrity of personal information
- Controlled use of personal information
- Operational compliance with the privacy policy

An organization will probably create several additional information systems control objectives on other basic topics such as malware, availability, and resource management, many of which directly or indirectly contribute to the protection and proper use of personal information.

Control Frameworks

While every organization may have unique missions, objectives, business models, tolerance for risk, and so on, organizations need not invent governance frameworks from scratch to manage their privacy and security objectives.

In the context of strategy development, some organizations may already have suitable control frameworks in place, while others may not. Although it is not always necessary for an organization to select an industry-standard control framework, it is advantageous to do so. Industry-standard control frameworks have been used in thousands of companies, and they are regularly updated to reflect changing business practices, emerging threats, and new technologies.

Information security is a somewhat more mature profession than privacy. Thus, organizations developing privacy programs and privacy controls are often overlaying privacy controls over an existing information security framework. Doing this is the expected approach, and this idea is reinforced with the recent publication of privacy-specific control frameworks that are extensions of existing information security and risk management frameworks.

It is often considered a mistake to select a control framework because of the presence or absence of a small number of specific controls. Usually, such selection is made on the assumption that control frameworks are rigid and inflexible. Instead, the strategist should take a different approach: select a control framework based on industry alignment and then institute a risk management process for developing additional controls based on the results of risk assessments. This is precisely the approach described in ISO/IEC 27701, as well as in the NIST Privacy Framework. Start with a well-known control framework and then create additional controls, if needed, to address risks specific to the organization. When assessing the use of a specific framework, you may find that a specific control area is not applicable. In those cases, do not just ignore the section; instead, document both the business and technical reasons why the organization chose not to use the control area. If a question about the decision is raised in the future, this information will indicate why the decision was made not to implement the control area. The date and those involved in the decision should also be documented.

Several standard privacy and security frameworks are discussed in the remainder of this section:

- ISO/IEC 27701
- NIST Privacy Framework
- NIST SP 800-122
- HIPAA
- NIST Cybersecurity Framework (CSF)
- ISO/IEC 27001
- NIST SP 800-53
- Center for Internet Security Critical Security Controls (CIS CSC)
- PCI DSS

EXAM TIP CIPM candidates are not expected to memorize the contents of any privacy or security control frameworks for the exam, but you should be generally aware of them and their purposes.

ISO/IEC 27701

ISO/IEC 27701:2019, *Security techniques – Extension to ISO/IEC 27001 and ISO/IEC 27002 for privacy information management – Requirements and guidelines,* is an international standard that directs the formation and management of a Privacy Information Management System (PIMS), including the controls and processes to ensure privacy by design and proper ongoing monitoring and management of personal information. The first version of this standard was published in August 2019.

ISO/IEC 27701 follows a similar structure to ISO/IEC 27001 and is divided into three main sections: requirements, guidance, and controls.

Requirements This section describes required activities included in effective PIMS. The structure of the section uses the same seven sections used in ISO/IEC 27001.

Guidance This section provides direction on how privacy programs can utilize ISO/IEC 27002 within the PIMS and provides specific considerations for controllers and processors. The section is divided into three groups: PIMS-specific guidance related to ISO/IEC 27002, additional ISO/IEC 27002 guidance for PII controllers, and additional ISO/IEC 27002 guidance for processors.

PIMS-specific guidance related to ISO/IEC 27002 expands on the 14 control categories to enable an organization to evaluate the control objectives and controls in the context of risks to information security as well as risks to privacy. The sections on additional ISO/IEC 27002 guidance for PII controllers and additional ISO/IEC 27002 guidance for processors create specific guidance on privacy management for controllers and processors.

Controls This section contains a baseline set of controls for controllers and processors that can be used in context with ISO/IEC 27001. The controls for controllers and processors in ISO/IEC 27701 are described in these four categories:

- Conditions for collection and processing
- Obligations to PII principals
- Privacy by design and privacy by default
- PII sharing, transfer, and disclosure

 NOTE ISO/IEC 27701 is available from www.iso.org/standard/71670.html.

NIST Privacy Framework

The NIST Privacy Framework is a guide for organizations that need to protect and properly handle personal information. The Privacy Framework is deliberately organized similarly to the NIST CSF to facilitate the parallel use of both tools. The framework consists of three parts:

- **Core**   This set of privacy protection activities facilitates the communication of protection activities. There are five core activities: Identify, Govern, Control, Communicate, and Protect.

- **Profile**   This is an organization's current set of activities used to protect personal information. You can think of the profile as a baseline that can be referenced at a future date to gauge progress, as well as a foundation for defining the desired future state of a privacy program.

- **Implementation Tiers**   These are maturity levels, from least to most mature: Partial, Risk Informed, Repeatable, and Adaptive.

Similar to the extension of ISO/IEC 27001 with ISO/IEC 27701, the integration with the NIST CSF is highlighted in the Privacy Framework Core with a key that identifies whether control objectives are identical to the CSF or they align with the CSF, but the descriptions have been adapted for privacy programs. This approach reinforces the idea that an effective privacy program requires integration with information security and risk management programs.

Organizations seeking to adopt the framework will find a wealth of information, including crosswalks (mappings to other standards), profiles, guidance, and tools to build and improve their privacy practices.

NOTE   The NIST Privacy Framework is available at www.nist.gov/privacy-framework.

NIST SP 800-122

NIST SP 800-122, *Guide to Protecting the Confidentiality of Personally Identifiable Information (PII),* contains directives for protecting personal information. Although the guidelines are required of US government agencies, many other organizations employ them, as they are considered good practices.

NOTE   NIST SP 800-122 is available from http://csrc.nist.gov/publications/PubsSPs.html.

HIPAA

HIPAA established requirements for the protection of ePHI. These requirements apply to virtually every corporate or government entity (known as a *covered entity*) that stores or processes ePHI. HIPAA requirements fall into three main categories.

- Administrative safeguards
- Physical safeguards
- Technical safeguards

Several controls reside within each of these three categories. Each control is labeled as Required or Addressable. Required controls must be implemented by every covered entity. Addressable controls are considered optional in each covered entity, meaning the organization does not have to implement an Addressable control if it does not apply or if there is negligible risk if the control is not implemented.

 NOTE HIPAA is available from www.gpo.gov/fdsys/pkg/CRPT-104hrpt736/pdf/CRPT-104hrpt736.pdf.

NIST Cybersecurity Framework

The NIST CSF is a risk-based life-cycle methodology for assessing risk, enacting controls, and measuring control effectiveness, not unlike ISO/IEC 27001. The components of the NIST CSF are as follows:

- **Framework Core** This set of functions—Identify, Protect, Detect, Respond, and Recover—makes up the life cycle of high-level functions in an information security program. The Framework Core includes a complete set of controls (known as *references*) within the four activities.
- **Framework Implementation Tiers** These are maturity levels, from least mature to most mature: Partial, Risk Informed, Repeatable, and Adaptive.
- **Framework Profile** This is an alignment of elements of the Framework Core (the functions, categories, subcategories, and references) with an organization's business requirements, risk tolerance, and available resources.

Organizations implementing the NIST CSF would first perform an assessment by measuring its maturity (Implementation Tiers) for each activity in the Framework Core. Next, the organization would determine the desired levels of maturity for each activity in the Framework Core. The differences found would be gaps that would need to be filled through several means, which could include the following:

- Hiring additional resources
- Training resources
- Adding or changing business processes or procedures

- Changing system or device configuration
- Acquiring new systems or devices

 NOTE The NIST CSF is available from www.nist.gov/cyberframework.

ISO/IEC 27001

ISO/IEC 27001, *Information technology – Security techniques – Information security management systems – Requirements,* is an international standard for information security and risk management. This standard contains a requirements section that outlines a properly functioning information security management system (ISMS) and a comprehensive control framework.

ISO/IEC 27001 is divided into two sections: Requirements and Controls. The Requirements section describes required activities found in effective ISMSs. The Controls section contains a baseline set of controls that serve as a starting point for the organization. The standard is updated periodically; the latest version is known as ISO/IEC 27001:2015. The requirements in ISO/IEC 27001 are described in seven sections: Context of the Organization, Leadership, Planning, Support, Operation, Performance Evaluation, and Improvement.

Although ISO/IEC 27001 is a highly respected control framework, its adoption has been modest, partly because a single copy of the standard costs more than US $100. Unlike NIST standards, which are free of charge, it is unlikely that students or professionals will pay this much for a standard just to learn more about it. Despite this, ISO/IEC 27001 is growing in popularity in organizations throughout the world.

 NOTE ISO/IEC 27001 is available from www.iso.org/standard/54534.html (registration and payment required).

NIST SP 800-53 and NIST SP 800-53A

NIST SP 800-53, *Security and Privacy Controls for Federal Information Systems and Organizations,* is one of the most well-known and adopted security control frameworks. NIST SP 800-53 is required for all US government information systems, as well as all information systems in private industry that store or process information on behalf of the US government.

Even though the NIST 800-53 control framework is required for US federal information systems, many organizations that are not required to employ the framework have utilized it, primarily because it is a high-quality control framework with in-depth implementation guidance and because it is available without cost.

NIST SP 800-53A, *Assessing Security and Privacy Controls in Federal Information Systems and Organizations: Building Effective Assessment Plans,* is the companion standard to NIST SP800-53 that defines techniques for auditing or assessing each control in NIST SP 800-53.

NOTE NIST SP 800-53 and NIST SP 800-53A are available from https://csrc .nist.gov/publications/PubsSPs.html.

Center for Internet Security Critical Security Controls

The CSC framework from CIS, or CIS CSC, is a control framework that traces its lineage to the SANS Institute. The framework is still commonly referred to as the "SANS Top 20" or "SANS 20 Critical Security Controls."

NOTE CIS CSC Controls are available from www.cisecurity.org/critical-controls/ (registration and terms of use agreement required).

PCI DSS

PCI DSS is a global control framework specifically for the protection of credit card numbers and related information when stored, processed, and transmitted on an organization's networks. The PCI DSS was developed by the PCI Standards Council, a consortium of the world's dominant credit card brands, namely Visa, MasterCard, American Express, Discover, and JCB.

PCI DSS is mandatory for all organizations that store, process, or transmit credit card data. Organizations with larger volumes of card data are required to undergo annual onsite audits. Many organizations use the controls and the principles in PCI DSS to protect other types of financial and personal data such as account numbers, Social Security numbers, and dates of birth.

NOTE PCI DSS is available from www.pcisecuritystandards.org (registration and license agreement required).

Mapping Control Frameworks

Frequently, organizations find themselves in a position where more than one control framework needs to be selected and adopted. The primary factors driving this are as follows:

- Multiple applicable regulatory frameworks
- Multiple operational contexts

Organizations with multiple control frameworks often crave a simpler framework for their controls. Often, organizations will "map" their control frameworks together, resulting in a single control framework with controls from each framework present. Mapping control frameworks together is time-consuming and tedious, although in some instances, the work has already been done. For example, Appendix H in NIST SP 800-53 contains a forward and reverse mapping between NIST SP 800-53 and ISO/IEC 27001. Other controls mapping references can be found online. Some must be built manually.

Working with Control Frameworks

Once an organization selects a control framework and multiple frameworks are mapped together (if the organization has decided to undertake that), security managers will need to organize a framework of activities around the selected/mapped control framework.

Risk Assessment   Before a control can be designed, the privacy or security manager needs to have some idea of the nature of risks that a control is intended to address. In a running risk management program, new risks may have been identified during a risk assessment that led to the creation of additional controls. In this case, information from the risk assessment is needed so that the controls will be properly designed to handle these risks.

If an organization is implementing a control prior to a risk assessment, it may not design and implement the control properly. Here are some examples:

- A control may not be rigorous enough to counter a threat.
- A control may be too rigorous and costly (in the case of a moderate or low risk).
- A control may not counter all relevant threats.

In the absence of a risk assessment, the chances of realizing one or more of these undesirable outcomes are quite high. If an organization is implementing a control, a risk assessment needs to be performed. If an organization-wide risk assessment is not feasible, then a risk assessment that is focused on the control area should be performed so that the organization will know what risks the control will be intended to address.

Control Design   An early step in control use is its design. In a standard control framework, the control language itself appears, as well as some degree of guidance. The privacy or security manager, together with personnel who have responsibility for relevant technologies and business processes, need to determine what activities should occur. In other words, they need to figure out how to operationalize the control.

Proper control design will potentially require one or more of the following:

- New or changed policies
- New or changed business process documents
- New or changed information systems
- New or changed business records

Control Implementation   After a control has been designed, it needs to be put into service. Depending upon the nature of the control, this could involve operational impact in the form of changes to business processes and/or information systems. Changes with greater impact will require greater care so that business processes are not adversely affected. For instance, an organization may implement a control that requires production servers and other devices to be hardened from attack to comply with recognized standards such as CIS Benchmarks. After the hardening standards are developed (no easy task, by the way), they need to be tested and implemented. If a production environment is affected, it could take quite a bit of time to ensure that none of the hardening standard items adversely affects the performance, integrity, or availability of affected systems.

 NOTE Further detailed discussion on control development and assessment is included in Chapter 6 in *CISM Certified Information Security Manager All-In-One Exam Guide*. Detailed discussion on audits of controls is included in *CISA Certified Information Systems Auditor All-In-One Exam Guide*.

Control Monitoring   After an organization has implemented a control, it needs to monitor the control. For this to happen, the control needs to have been designed so that monitoring can occur. In the absence of monitoring, the organization will lack the methodical means for observing the control to determine whether it is being operated correctly and whether it is effective.

Some controls are not easily monitored. For instance, a control addressing abuse of intellectual property rights includes the enactment of new acceptable use policies (AUPs) that forbid employees from violating intellectual property laws and copyrights. There are many forms of abuse that cannot be easily monitored.

Control Assessment   Any organization that implements controls to address risks should periodically examine those controls to determine whether they are working as intended and as designed. There are several available approaches to control assessment:

- **Security review**   One or more information security staff members examine the control along with any relevant business records.
- **Control self-assessment (CSA)**   Control owners answer questions and provide any relevant evidence that demonstrates a control's operation.
- **Internal audit**   The organization's internal auditors (or information security staff) perform a formal examination of the control.
- **External audit**   An external auditor formally examines the control.

An organization will select one or more of these methods, guided by any applicable laws, regulations, legal obligations, and results of risk assessments.

Data Inventory

A nearly worn-out but still highly relevant cliché in information security is this: *you cannot protect what you don't know you have.* This statement underscores the need for effective asset management at all levels, because only specifically identified information can be managed and protected.

For a privacy program to be effective, organizations must have a complete and accurate inventory of *all* the personal information it has collected. Although an inventory of structured information (data residing in application database management systems) will remain fairly static, the transient nature of unstructured data creates additional challenges.

Somehow, organizations must identify means for knowing about all structured and unstructured data, particularly when it contains personal information that is in scope of relevant privacy laws. Proactive data discovery, discussed later in this chapter in the section "Data Loss Prevention Automation," can be put in place to provide visibility into the creation and use of unstructured data.

For an organization's data inventory to remain current, three activities need to be included in business-as-usual processes:

- Change management processes must require updates to data inventory whenever an addition or change to an information system impacts the data inventory.

- Business processes that interact with personal information must be documented.

- Periodic reviews of the data inventory should be performed to confirm its accuracy.

Periodic data inventory reviews should not only catalog existing instances of sensitive and personal information, but they should also determine in each instance whether data *should* exist where it is found. By understanding the business processes that interact with personal information, you can better identify where personal information is collected, processed, and stored. Thus, a data inventory should be thought of less as a census and more of a gap analysis. Every instance of sensitive information should be examined through the lens of the business processes and data management policy to determine whether each instance should exist and whether current protective controls are adequate.

Organizations with lower process maturity are more likely to use unstructured means for performing procedures and completing tasks. Often this will result in a greater use of e-mail for process workflow and a greater use of unstructured data stores for storing data. E-mail, file servers, and cloud storage services represent the majority of unstructured data in many organizations.

When inventorying data, you should include the following information in each catalog entry:

- Name of the file(s) or directory/directories

- Description of the contents, including PII data fields

- Date of last update (this will aid in the removal of old data)

- Access permissions

- Data owner

This information will be useful for the development of data flow diagrams, as discussed later in the section "Data Flow and Usage Diagrams."

 NOTE Automation in larger organizations will ease the burden of otherwise manual and time-consuming processes to keep data inventories up to date.

Data Classification

Many types of information reside in an organization's information systems. Some of this information is highly sensitive because it contains personal information, intellectual property, and internal financial information; some information is important but not sensitive at all; and some is not very important. Because resources are required to protect information, it doesn't make much sense to apply equal rigor to protect both unimportant data and highly secretive or sensitive information. To this point, former US national security advisor McGeorge Bundy is attributed to have said, "If we guard our toothbrushes and diamonds with equal zeal, we will lose fewer toothbrushes and more diamonds."

Data Classification Levels

A *data classification policy* is a formal and intentional way for an organization to define levels of importance or sensitivity of information. A typical data classification policy will define two or more (but rarely more than five) data classification levels, such as the following:

- Registered
- Restricted
- Confidential
- Public

Along with defining levels of classification, a data classification policy will include examples that show the classification levels that should be assigned to various datasets. Table 2-1 provides examples of this concept.

Classification Level	Examples of Information at this Level
Registered	Merger and acquisition proceedings, pre-announcement
Restricted	Customer PII Employee PII Program source code Unpublished financial records
Confidential	Internal e-mail messages Marketing plans Policies
Public	Web site content Released marketing brochures Social media postings Published financial reports

Table 2-1 Examples of Information at Varying Data Classification Levels

Classification Level	Datasets at this Level
Registered	Merger and acquisition proceedings, pre-announcement User and service account passwords
Restricted	Customer Relationship Management system database Human Capital Management system database Program source code repositories Unpublished Enterprise Resource Management system records Unpublished annual report, 10-K, 10-Q IT network diagrams IT data flow diagrams Contents of internal HR and legal investigations All legal contracts
Confidential	Internal e-mail messages Internal memos Contents of an internal intranet site, including policy and benefit information Marketing plans
Public	www.company.com web site content Released marketing brochures Official @Company social media postings on LinkedIn, Facebook, and Twitter Public 10-K and 10-Q filings, when published Annual report, when published

Table 2-2   Examples of Official Data Classification Levels

NOTE   Data classification policies need to be as simple as possible so that workers will be able to understand the classification of data easily and handle it accordingly.

Data classification policy can go still further and emphatically state the classification levels that are, by policy, assigned to specific datasets. This is shown in Table 2-2.

Data Handling Standards

Because so much information is handled by personnel on a daily basis, data classification policy goes still further to define acceptable handling procedures for data at various levels of classification and in numerous types of situations. Often called *data handling standards,* these procedures provide real-world guidance that workers can easily follow and use. Because information can be used and moved in many different ways, data handling standards should clearly state what is expected of personnel when handling sensitive data.

Data handling standards usually take the form of a matrix, with various levels of classification as the columns and different data handling situations as rows. Each individual cell defines the standard for handling data at a given classification level in a certain way. Table 2-3 shows a part of such a matrix.

	Public	Confidential	Restricted	Registered
Laptop storage	Permitted	Must be encrypted	Must be encrypted	NOT permitted
USB drive storage	Permitted	Secure drive only	Secure drive only	NOT permitted
File server storage	Permitted	"Mars" server only	"Mars" server only	"Ares" server only
Cloud storage	Permitted	OneDrive only	OneDrive only	NOT permitted
E-mail, internal	Permitted	Permitted	Permitted	Must be encrypted
E-mail, external	Permitted	Must be encrypted	Must be encrypted	NOT permitted
Fax	Permitted	Attended destination only	Attended destination only	NOT permitted
Courier	Permitted	Permitted	Must be encrypted	Must be encrypted

Table 2-3 Example Data Handling Standards Matrix

To help the workforce better understand handling standards, organizations should develop training content or tutorials to explain in detail their meanings and to introduce appropriate procedures.

EXAM TIP CIPM candidates need to understand the typical structure of roles and responsibilities regarding the protection of data. While a data protection officer, general counsel, or CISO is responsible for establishing the organization's data classification policy, it is usually the responsibility of a document owner to classify and mark a document correctly. It is then the responsibility of any party who uses a document to handle it according to its classification level.

The Data Handling Culture Shift

Privacy professionals in organizations introducing data classification, handling standards, training, and automation must understand that such an undertaking may represent a significant culture shift. It's potentially a tall order to expect a workforce that formerly took data handling for granted to become data-aware and to understand and follow new procedures. Such a change does not happen overnight. Even when executives lead by example and in the presence of an internal marketing plan, many workers' responses will range from confusion to resistance and outright evasion. It is, therefore, important for the workforce to understand the purpose of data classification.

Data Loss Prevention Automation

Along with defining levels of classification, a data classification policy will define policies and procedures for handling information in various settings at these levels.

For instance, a data handling standard will state the conditions at each level in which sensitive information may be e-mailed, faxed, stored, transmitted, and shipped. Note that some methods for handling may be forbidden—such as e-mailing a registered document over the Internet.

Relying on an organization's workers to apply data handling standards consistently is chancy at best—not because of the lack of good intentions, but because workers simply will not have safe data handling on their minds all of the time. This situation is not unlike workers who click a link on the occasional phishing message despite having attended effective security awareness training. People are simply not "on their guard" all of the time.

Data loss prevention (DLP) systems can greatly aid in the effort to provide visibility and even control over the use of personal and other sensitive information. Approaches to the implementation of DLP capabilities fill the remainder of this section.

Static DLP   Static DLP tools scan static data stores to identify files containing data matching specific patterns. Most often, static DLP scanning is performed on file servers—both the on-premises and cloud varieties. DLP scanning can also be performed on database management systems, either by scanning specific tools or by scanning flat-file exports of databases.

Organizations undertaking static DLP scanning for the first time may find an abundance of files containing PII and other sensitive data. Privacy managers need to keep in mind that such data may have been accumulated over a long period of time, and it may represent current practices or former activities that are no longer practiced.

A careful analysis of the results of an initial DLP scan should be undertaken to determine the following:

- The age of files containing PII found in file stores
- The extent to which files containing PII are still being deposited in file stores
- The access rights of files containing PII
- Which users actively access the files (available in some DLP static scanning tools)
- Whether current use is following sanctioned policies, procedures, and practices

Privacy managers should not be overly hasty in the quest to "solve" any or all of the discovered instances of PII in static data stores. Some uses may be a part of key business processes along with adequately restricted access controls. Often, privacy managers will find that files containing PII in file stores are the result of one-time or ad hoc activities. For instance, a business analyst may be asked to perform a research task on the demographics of customers; the business analyst would perform a query or run a report on the customer relationship management (CRM) system, export the report to a spreadsheet, and save the spreadsheet on a file server. After completing the task, the business analyst will keep the file there in case questions are asked about it later. Soon the existence of the spreadsheet containing PII is forgotten, and there it will reside in perpetuity unless some purge, cleanup, or DLP scan is performed that discovers its existence.

EXAM TIP CIPM candidates need to understand the detective nature of static DLP tools. These tools merely scan file stores to determine whether sensitive data is present; they indicate data handling behavior but do nothing to alter it.

Data Tagging Through the process is similar to static DLP analysis, data files can be tagged, or marked in some way, if they are found to contain PII or other sensitive information. Such tagging can take on several forms, including these:

- **Metadata tagging** The metadata of a data file can be updated to include a specially coded tag that will be recognized by DLP tooling.
- **Watermarking** Visible or invisible watermarks can be added to data files.
- **Marking** According to data file-marking policy, a human-readable word or phrase can be added to the header, footer, or other location in a data file (such as "XYZ Company restricted to internal use only").

Including human-readable watermarks or other markings on documents provides a visual reminder to workers using data files about the sensitivity of the files. The main purpose of including machine-readable marks or tags in a data file is to facilitate appropriate action by dynamic DLP tools, discussed next.

Dynamic DLP Dynamic DLP represents a variety of technologies used to detect and even intervene in the transfer of PII and other sensitive information. Dynamic DLP tools can take the form of network devices or tools running on operating systems with the ability to observe data in motion in many different circumstances. These tools can be configured to identify the specific sensitivity of data files in motion by reading their contents to determine whether they contain specific PII or other sensitive information, or they can be configured to look for previously applied tags.

There are several common forms of dynamic DLP:

- **E-mail DLP** DLP tools can examine the contents of an outgoing e-mail message to determine whether it contains specific sensitive information. E-mail–based DLP will consider whether the information is being sent to internal or external recipients.
- **USB storage control** Host-based DLP tools restrict USB usage to company-approved (and usually encrypted) USB drives only, or they block USB storage entirely.
- **Local file storage control** Host-based agents observe and optionally block actions violating policy, such as local storage of highly classified documents.
- **File server storage control** Host- or server-based agents observe and optionally block actions violating policy, such as storage of highly classified documents on shares with broad access.

- **Cloud server storage control**   DLP capabilities in cloud storage services are configured to mimic local or file server DLP controls to monitor and optionally block actions violating policy.
- **Network DLP**   Network devices, or DLP modules in next-generation firewalls, observe the content of data in motion.

Most of these forms of dynamic DLP, when operating in the context of an interactive user, can present the following to the user:

- Silently note the occurrence.
- Block the action and inform the user.
- Warn the user that the intended action is forbidden by policy, and give the user the ability to permit the action anyway after providing a user-entered business justification to complete the action.

Other tools may be used to assist in dynamic DLP efforts:

- **Firewall**   Blocks access to/from specific networks or systems
- **IDS/IPS**   Blocks access to/from networks and systems thought to be hazardous
- **Web content filter**   Blocks browser access to sites based on policy
- **Cloud access security broker (CASB)**   Monitors and controls access to cloud-based service providers based on organization policy
- **NetFlow**   Monitors network traffic and produces alerts when anomalous traffic is seen on the network

EXAM TIP   CIPM candidates need to understand the role of Dynamic DLP as a detective control, a preventive control, or both.

Dynamic DLP controls, in any of the forms discussed, can be highly valuable for preventing the mishandling of sensitive information. Unfortunately, dynamic DLP is also adept at interfering with legitimate business processes by blocking activities approved by management (including the privacy or security manager). Legitimate activities are blocked either because the DLP system is misconfigured or because of a "false positive" situation where the DLP system misidentifies data. Examples of such false positives include strings of numerals that are mistaken for social insurance numbers, bank account numbers, phone numbers, or credit card numbers.

TIP   Privacy and security personnel should identify "friendly" departments or groups when first implementing the preventive features of a DLP system to increase confidence in the system and work out any remaining configuration problems.

Run in Learn Mode First   Despite what readers may be told by experienced users of DLP systems or DLP vendors themselves, readers are *highly* recommended to run any dynamic DLP system in "learn" mode first for an extended period of time. The best way to do this is to configure the DLP system to silently log occurrences that are thought to be file-handling policy violations. This enables privacy and security personnel to see whether the DLP system properly identifies the actual motion of private and other sensitive information.

Another highly useful benefit of running DLP in learn mode is similar to that of running static DLP scans: to determine what data movement currently takes place in the organization to help personnel better understand existing business processes, as well as those occasional (hopefully infrequent) actions that represent actual violations of policy.

When privacy and security personnel become confident in their dynamic DLP system's ability to identify sensitive data movement correctly without false positives, they can proceed to begin activation of preventive actions to be performed by the DLP system. It is suggested that organizations proceed slowly as they build their confidence in the proper operation of the system. Additionally, once a DLP system is in preventive mode, there is an expectation that alerts corresponding to blocked actions will be properly investigated and addressed.

Develop Response and Exception Procedures   Before activating any rules in a dynamic DLP system that will block file handling actions, privacy and security personnel— preferably in cooperation with the IT service desk—should develop a playbook of response procedures when end users encounter DLP systems blocking their intended actions. Rather than be caught by surprise, IT service desk personnel (or others designated to work with end users) must have clear procedures in place for handling users who insist that the DLP system is blocking legitimate actions. Often, IT service desk personnel will need to contact privacy or security personnel who can look into these matters to determine the best course of action. The response will often require that a privacy or security manager approve exceptions and direct the configuration of the DLP system to permit specific activities that are contrary to policy. Recordkeeping of all such exceptions is important, whether as a part of an existing change control, incident management, or policy exception, or as part of another process.

Data Security Has Arrived

As far back as computers have existed and have been used to store and process personal information, data security has been on the minds of management. For decades, data security has come in the form of firewalls and other network access controls, system hardening, event monitoring, and other measures—most of which protected the information enclave while virtually ignoring access to and use of personal information.

Emerging privacy laws, as well as emerging capabilities such as DLP, have created the first real opportunity for organizations to enact actual data security capabilities focused on the data itself instead of merely keeping intruders out and preventing workers from removing data. There is much progress yet to be made, but the capabilities exist today for organizations to focus specifically on data they intend to protect and manage.

Data Use Governance

One could say that privacy laws are "sunshine laws" that pertain to organizations' use of personal information. They have sparked lively debate in organizations that were accustomed to doing "whatever they wished" with personal information they collected from customers and others, with little or no scrutiny. Indeed, prior to modern privacy laws, organizations had little accountability regarding creative uses of the personal information they held. Privacy leaders often face an uphill battle as they compel organizations to rein in and control uses of personal information.

Organizations need to include governance structures to provide visibility and control on the topic of data usage. Such a structure would include the following:

- Internal policies stating permitted use of personal information
- External privacy policy accessible by relevant parties that describes all such uses
- Establishment of controls to ensure these outcomes
- Monitoring of these controls to verify their effectiveness
- Corrective action to remedy all deviations
- Metrics that measure all of the foregoing

The following sections discuss various privacy principles that privacy leaders need to transform into intentional practices.

Data Use Limitation

A key tenet of the GDPR and other privacy laws is the concept of limiting the use of personal information. Following numerous abuses of PII by private organizations, privacy laws now restrict how organizations can use the personal information they collect.

Article 5(1)(b) of the GDPR reads,

> Personal data shall be collected for specified, explicit and legitimate purposes and not further processed in a manner that is incompatible with those purposes; further processing for archiving purposes in the public interest, scientific or historical research purposes or statistical purposes shall, in accordance with Article 89(1), not be considered to be incompatible with the initial purposes ("purpose limitation").

Title 1.81.5 of the CCPA states,

> A business that collects a consumer's personal information shall, at or before the point of collection, inform consumers as to the categories of personal information to be collected and the purposes for which the categories of personal information shall be used. A business shall not collect additional categories of personal information or use personal information collected for additional purposes without providing the consumer with notice consistent with this section.

Privacy leaders face challenges on the topic of data use limitation. Organizations that are accustomed to a freewheeling "we do anything we want with customer information" attitude are now seeing constraints in the form of privacy laws and changing social norms.

These constraints often include data governance councils or other bodies to oversee the uses of personal information to ensure that organizations don't run afoul of privacy laws or their own stated privacy policies.

Data Minimization

The concept of *data minimization* refers to the practice of collecting and retaining only those specific data elements necessary to perform agreed-upon functions. In other words, organizations should be careful to collect or accept only those specific PII details required to perform whatever services they provide.

Historically, organizations have retained business records containing personal information for long periods of time. Privacy laws counter this tendency, which leads many privacy leaders to enact changes in organizational processes and systems to minimize the collection and retention of personal information.

In the same way that double-entry accounting describes each item on a balance sheet as both asset and liability, personal and sensitive information can provide value to an organization as an asset, but it also represents a liability. Although the asset value aspect of personal and sensitive information may be clear, organizations are slower to realize that accumulating and retaining personal and sensitive information also represents a liability.

Unfortunately, the financial liability portion of retained personal information rarely shows up on an organization's financial balance sheet. And yet it is indeed a liability: the impact upon an organization if cybercriminals steal that information or if the information is misused is real, in the form of breach response costs, the costs related to reducing harm inflicted on affected parties (think of credit monitoring services that are a frequent remedy for stolen credit card numbers), the costs of fines from governmental regulators, and the occasional class-action lawsuit.

Data minimization has multiple dimensions:

- Collect only required data items.
- Collect only required records.
- Retain only as long as is needed.
- Pseudonymize or anonymize as soon as possible.
- Reduce accessibility.

These and other concepts are discussed in the remainder of this section.

Collecting Only Required Data Items When collecting personal information directly from data subjects, organizations should collect only data items that are required for the organization to fulfill the intended purpose for the collection. Every item collected must be rationalized and the reason for collecting it documented. Data items that cannot be justified as necessary should not be collected.

Any data item proposed to be collected that does not have a present business purpose should not be collected. Such collection would introduce liability to the organization with no corresponding benefit. For example, suppose an e-commerce company that sells books developed a customer portal where a customer can select favorite categories of books and save a shipping address, so the customer does not need to enter them in for each order. An analyst is proposing that the organization collect the date of birth (including year) for each customer so that a birthday discount code can be sent during the month of their birthday. The privacy officer successfully argues that this function does not require the day or year of the customer's birth but only the month. The organization decides not to collect the birth year and day for its customers because there was no purpose identified that would require it (such as selling adult-only merchandise).

Though in the preceding example a valid decision was made, more is required. Organizations need to create a business record in the form of a detailed inventory of data items collected, including the collection purpose(s). This way, months or years later, a privacy professional can examine business records and understand the reasons for specific data collection decisions without relying upon the memory of people who may not even be employed in the organization any longer.

There remains some inferred responsibility for providing personal information that falls on data subjects who are providing it. Data subjects should be aware of the information they provide to an organization or government and attempt to withhold any information they believe is unnecessary for the organization to fulfill the intended purpose. For example, most e-commerce sites should not require a data subject's date of birth to complete transactions (the sale of products prohibited for minors is one exception; applying for a credit card is another). If an e-commerce site requests a date of birth, a data subject should avoid providing it unless some clear purpose is stated that the data subject agrees with.

Collecting Only Required Records Organizations that acquire personal information in bulk (such as purchasing from a data broker) should collect only those records required to fulfill the intended business purpose. The collection of unneeded records brings only liability to an organization when unneeded records provide no value or benefit. If, for example, an intruder breaks in and steals this information, the organization that collected the data may need to make reparations to all persons whose records were collected.

Organizations that purchase data about citizens in bulk must ensure that they obtain only the records they need to meet their business objectives. Sometimes, only large datasets are available when just certain records are needed. In such cases, organizations should remove unneeded records as soon as it's practical to do so.

NOTE One option for record removal is pseudonymization or anonymization of selected records, discussed later in this section.

On a record-by-record basis, organizations should devise options to enable choices when collecting individual records. One example is e-commerce; many online shopping sites permit customers to "check out as a guest," where buyers provide only enough information to complete the purchase, instead of being required to create a persistent user account that requires collection of additional information such as a credit card number, billing address, shipping address, and other information. For customers who opt for guest checkout, the organization collects only what is necessary to complete the transaction.

Discarding Data When No Longer Needed   Organizations collecting and retaining personal data should understand their uses of personal data fields to determine whether long-term retention is appropriate. For instance, an e-commerce web site accepting a credit card payment may collect the CVV (card verification value) from the customer and discard the CVV as soon as the transaction has been approved or rejected. Or a web site providing services to adults who are 21 or older may require evidence of the customer's age before they can conduct business. This practice may involve the uploading of a government-issued ID or some other identification means. Once the organization has verified that the subject is at least 21 years old, the organization can discard the PII collected to prove the subject's age and simply indicate that their age has been verified.

Minimizing Access   Data minimization is all about risk reduction by limiting the amount of data available for various functions. In risk-speak, data minimization reduces the impact of improper data usage or a breach of personal information. An organization can achieve effective data minimization through access controls in several ways:

- *Reduce access volume.* Organizations can limit the number of records that a worker can access, extract, or download in bulk operations. In B2C (business-to-customer) organizations, few persons in the organization genuinely need access to the entire customer database, and access could be limited by various means.

- *Reduce the number of personnel with data access.* Organizations can limit access to customer data to those workers whose jobs require it.

- *Reduce access to sensitive fields.* Organizations can limit the data fields accessible by their workers. For instance, if a worker doesn't need to access customers' birthdays or full credit card numbers, their ability to see these or other sensitive fields should be reduced.

Data masking can be used to protect the contents of personal information from personnel who do not need to see it. A typical example is the display of credit card or social insurance numbers. Although an information system may store the full contents of these values, some of the characters can be masked so that personnel cannot see them. Most often, programs will display only the last four digits of a credit card or social insurance number.

 NOTE   Encryption is another form of access control that may be applicable in some situations for limiting access to personal information.

Minimizing Storage   Organizations can significantly enhance the security of sensitive and personal information by limiting where and how workers can store such data. When workers work with downloads or extracts from business applications, organizations can enact controls that limit where that data can be stored. Primarily, organizations should limit the storage of personal information about their customers, constituents, and employees to organization-managed systems.

Organizations can enact policies that state that all sensitive and personal information must be stored only on organization file servers, and not on laptop or desktop computers, mobile devices, removable storage devices, or personal cloud-based storage services. Further, sensitive and personal information can be blocked from being sent via company or personal e-mail. These controls are typically implemented with DLP controls, but web content filtering systems and CASB capabilities can supplement DLP solutions.

The ultimate objective is to limit the storage of personal information to locations permitted by policy and controlled through tooling. Privacy and security professionals need to tread carefully, however, to prevent disruption of sanctioned business processes. This topic is explored further in the section "Developing and Running Data Monitoring Operations," later in this chapter.

Minimizing Availability   A common approach to minimizing the availability of information is to migrate data on widely accessed systems to archival systems that few personnel can access. For example, suppose a regional hospital's patient care and billing systems contain medical records and billing records for the past 15 years. To reduce the risk of exposure, the hospital migrates all records more than two years old to an archival system that few hospital personnel can access. This permits the hospital to comply with minimum data retention requirements while reducing risks associated with hospital personnel having access to large volumes of medical and financial information. Further, since the data archival system is accessible only from internal networks and by few personnel, there is a correspondingly lower risk of a break-in by intruders.

Organizations can implement additional controls to further protect the archival system and reduce risk, including DLP, end user behavior analytics (EUBA), and NetFlow.

Minimization Through Retention Practices   Organizations are accustomed to retaining data for very long periods, often in perpetuity. For generations, the risks associated with long-term data retention have been quite low. Digital transformation has changed all of that: datasets that contain more details about data subjects (more fields with sensitive information, and more records) are considered high-value targets by cybercriminal organizations. Privacy professionals often call highly sensitive information "toxic data," since its theft can have dire consequences on the organization.

Although the accumulation of sensitive data may bring value to the organization, it increases liability as well: the theft of a large trove of sensitive data will incur greater costs than the theft of a smaller dataset. For example, suppose each of two similar e-commerce organizations has about 5 million customers. One of the organizations keeps only two years' worth of transaction data and moves dormant customer data to an offline storage system. The other organization keeps all customer data online, even for customers who have not patronized the organization for years. If each organization's customer database was stolen, the organization that reduced its customer database size would incur fewer costs than the organization that kept all of its customer data online.

The approach to data retention involves the development of a data retention schedule, a chart that specifies the minimum and maximum periods that specific types or sets of data will be retained by the organization. A data retention schedule is considered policy, and organization departments are expected to comply. Security and privacy personnel may perform reviews or audits periodically to determine whether the organization complies with its data retention policy, and corrective actions may result when violations are found.

Enacting the purging of older records is not always easy. Several challenges may present themselves:

- **Database referential integrity**   The design of relational databases may make the prospect of removing records a bit tricky. Primarily, a record cannot be removed if another record elsewhere in the database refers to that record through a foreign key. The referential integrity concept refers to the restriction where a record (or row) cannot be removed if another table has a row whose foreign key points to the record to be removed. The other table's row would first have to be modified or removed. This is typically a problem in older databases that were not designed with data retention in mind.

- **Comingling of data**   Some storage media cannot be modified once created. For instance, magnetic tape is an "all-or-nothing" medium; it is impossible to remove specific data from a magnetic tape while retaining other data. If, for example, a system to be backed up to magnetic tape contains specific data that must be purged after two years, along with other data that must be retained for ten years, storing all of this data on magnetic tape will create a conflict, and the organization will not be able to conform to both of these retention requirements.

- **Unstructured data**   Because data can be extracted and further manipulated by users' workstations, it can become difficult to know whether individual workbooks contain information that has exceeded its retention. The date stamp on a workbook does not indicate the transaction dates of rows in the workbook, which could be recent or quite old. Variations in the ways that data can be represented in workbooks make it infeasible to enforce transaction-level data retention effectively in unstructured file stores.

- **Third parties**   Organizations outsourcing business applications to third parties (through platform as a service or software as a service models) may find that one or more of the third parties cannot remove older records from their systems. They may have referential integrity issues in their databases, or they may simply lack the tools to remove older records from selected customers' databases. This kind of situation often arises when an organization, after selecting and using third-party applications, enacts data retention policy only to discover that one or more third parties cannot comply.

- **E-mail**   In some organizations, workers send sensitive and personal information to one another via e-mail. Searching for and removing specific e-mail messages that contain sensitive information may not be feasible; this problem is similar to the unstructured data problem discussed earlier. Removing all older e-mail messages may be a viable approach. Still, the organization needs to fully understand the nature of the organization's use of e-mail so that purging older e-mail messages does not introduce unintended consequences such as the destruction of other records that should be retained for longer periods.

Data retention does not require an "all-or-nothing" approach that requires the organization to delete all older records. Instead, organizations can define storage locations for business records that can be tightly managed and establish a generic retention schedule for other storage locations. Additionally, records that have reached their expiration date can be pseudonymized or anonymized, thereby removing personal information from records but retaining other aspects of the records for historical purposes. Pseudonymization and anonymization are discussed in the next subsection.

Minimization Through De-identification   Depending upon the purpose of acquiring personal information, organizations can consider de-identification as a method for minimizing the amount of PII that they retain. For instance, if an organization acquires personal information for statistical purposes, it can pseudonymize or anonymize the records to remove their association with specific persons, while still providing statistical value.

When implemented correctly and from the perspective of privacy, de-identification is as effective as the outright removal of records. When de-identification is implemented correctly, an organization will continue to derive value from de-identified data through analytical value. For instance, after a database of user transactions has been de-identified, the organization won't know precisely who performed individual transactions, but it will still be able to understand the details of sales trends and other big-picture insights.

Two primary techniques are used in de-identification: pseudonymization and anonymization. While these techniques differ, the results are similar.

    NOTE   From a privacy perspective, de-identifying a record is equivalent to its removal.

Pseudonymization   *Pseudonymization* is the substitution of data in sensitive data fields with alternate values to de-identify data records with specific persons. Article 4 of the GDPR defines pseudonymization as "the processing of personal data in such a manner that the personal data can no longer be attributed to a specific data subject without the use of additional information, provided that such additional information is kept separately and is subject to technical and organisational measures to ensure that the personal data are not attributed to an identified or identifiable natural person." Here, specific identifying fields such as name, address, phone number, e-mail address, and financial account numbers are removed and replaced with pseudonyms. Pseudonymization is generally a reversible substitution technique: field values that identify actual persons are replaced with pseudonym values. Here are some examples:

- *Peter Gregory* becomes *Qoem Rebnurvo*
- *118 Elm Street* becomes *539 Tlo Uepv*
- *peterhgregory@mail.com* becomes *juwnfodpwlrmg@drep.tld*

The substitution technique permits software to function correctly, while substitutions eliminate the association of the record from the actual person. Pseudonymization differs from anonymization because pseudonymization still may enable an individual's data to be singled out and linkable across different datasets.

Anonymization   *Anonymization* is the process of irreversibly altering or removing sensitive data fields from records so that an individual can no longer be identified directly or indirectly. ISO 25237 (*Health Informatics – Pseudonymization*) defines anonymization as any "process by which personal data is irreversibly altered in such a way that a data subject can no longer be identified directly or indirectly, either by the data controller alone or in collaboration with any other party." PII fields can be removed or hashed so that the data cannot be associated with specific data subjects. Anonymization can involve a simple removal technique in which data fields that could associate a record with a specific person are removed. Here are some examples:

- *Peter Gregory* becomes (blanks)
- *118 Elm Street* becomes (blanks)
- *peterhgregory@mail.com* becomes (blanks)

Note that anonymization may cause software to behave in unexpected ways. Further, database management systems may resist anonymization, because this could endanger referential integrity. For anonymization by removing field data to work correctly, it may be necessary to copy records in a database to a separate database whose structure lacks the removed fields.

NOTE   The challenge with de-identification is to ensure that data records can no longer be associated with natural persons while retaining the information's value for other purposes. Put another way, if de-identified data can be re-identified through reasonable means, the de-identification is considered inadequate.

Data Quality and Accuracy

In the context of data privacy, data quality or data accuracy is a gauge of the care that an organization places on the fidelity of its stores of personal data. Since the reality of data usage includes personal information being passed from organization to organization, the task of maintaining the accuracy of PII is an important one. Privacy leaders building and implementing privacy programs need to determine where in an organization's business processes and information systems the means to ensure data quality and accuracy reside.

In addition, the organization must ensure that, at a minimum, the quality and accuracy of stored data complies with the requirements of applicable privacy laws. Article 5(1)(d) of the GDPR, for example, reads, "Personal data shall be accurate and, where necessary, kept up to date; every reasonable step must be taken to ensure that personal data that are inaccurate, having regard to the purposes for which they are processed, are erased or rectified without delay ('accuracy')." Once just a good idea, data accuracy is now required by law.

Data quality and accuracy are more than just the completeness and accuracy of data fields for data subjects; it also includes whether records for specific data subjects should even reside in an organization's database at all. Data subjects' information sometimes ends up in an organization's database simply by accident, often because of a matching error. Here are some examples:

- **Matches by name**   Some organization databases key off a subject's name only, resulting in snafus of every sort. In a real-life instance, this book's author and another person of the same name were in the Seattle job market at the same time, applying for some of the same jobs. Communications between companies and the two applicants were frequently crossed-up.

- **Matches by characteristic**   Some organizations use ancillary information to associate people. In a real-life instance from decades ago, parking tickets in Reno, Nevada, were entered into a computer system; if there was no license plate on the offending vehicle, the word "none" was entered. After a citizen ordered a vanity plate that read, "NONE," he was charged tens of thousands of dollars in unpaid parking tickets that had been issued over a period of many years (all predating the existence of the issued vanity plate).

- **Data entry errors**   These are certainly the most common reason that things get fouled up. With literally billions of people using e-mail today, countless errors occur because e-mail addresses are miskeyed, resulting in messages being sent to the wrong persons. This book's author regularly receives e-mails intended for a physician located in the US Northeast, as well as e-mails intended for the owner of a private jet aircraft maintenance company in Southeast Asia. This problem goes way beyond e-mail addresses: miskeying dates of birth and other personal characteristics can result in communications and records being crossed-up, as well as many intended actions not being carried out because some of the information is incomplete or incorrect.

Prior to the introduction of modern privacy laws such as GDPR, many private sector organizations had little reason to care about the accuracy of personal information, unless the accuracy had a direct monetary impact on them. For instance, an automobile manufacturer's database of vehicle owners is surely going to have incorrect mailing addresses for customers who move and do not inform the manufacturer. The result is twofold: marketing materials sent by mail are no longer reaching the customer, and neither are safety recall notices that represent cost-per-vehicle repairs.

Data Flow and Usage Diagrams

The efforts undertaken to build and maintain data inventories do not end when it is known where all data is stored, who the owners are, and what access permissions are granted. An essential aspect of data inventory is the knowledge of two additional data characteristics: data flow and data usage.

Understanding data flow requires a deeper study of the information systems where data resides to understand how data arrives in the system and where data is sent from the system. Interviews with business users with regard to the business process and IT personnel at the application layer as well as in system and network layers are needed to build a complete picture. The term "picture" is used deliberately: it's often useful to build a visual schematic of data flows, as this can help privacy and security professionals, as well as business leaders, better understand the usage of personal information in an organization. A *data flow diagram* (DFD), like the one shown in Figure 2-1, is a visual depiction of the flow of information between systems.

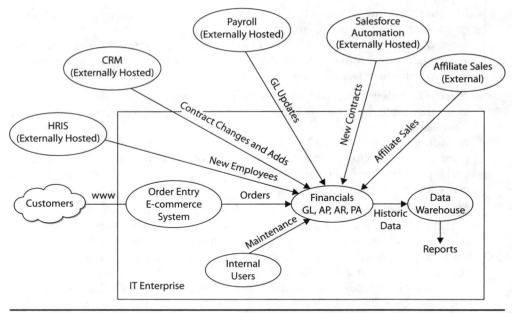

Figure 2-1   A high-level DFD depicts general data flow between IT applications.

In this effort, privacy professionals need to understand that data flow implies usage, and data usage implies flow. One is often perceived with the other.

 NOTE   Privacy professionals mapping data flow and usage will discover both sanctioned and unsanctioned uses of data.

Discovering Data Flow and Usage

Prior to the passage of privacy laws, including the GDPR and the CCPA, many organizations simply had no idea of the extent of the movement of their data. In many organizations, a common first step in working toward GDPR compliance was the development of a data inventory, along with the creation of data flow diagrams and the discovery of data usage. Amazing as it sounds, in many organizations, nobody was responsible for knowing these things.

The next step in most organizations is the development of data governance, providing management with visibility and control over the storage and use of personal information. It's as though there were no real rules for the management of personal information prior to GDPR.

Data Analytics

Mainstream organizations have access to advanced data management and data analytics capabilities that can provide them with additional insight into their businesses. Indeed, monetization is a primary impetus for an organization to mine its own data to improve how it can exploit its customers' buying preferences to increase revenues. Data analytics techniques have other purposes as well, including the discovery of new potential customers and improved insight into the use of an organization's products and services.

Data Aggregation

Marketing departments in organizations frequently embark on targeted marketing and advertising, whether it's by e-mail, postal mail, online ads, or other means. To reach their target markets with the right message at the right time, organizations often purchase lists of targeted individuals from data brokers and merge that data into their marketing databases. *Data aggregation* is the practice of combining databases to enrich available data. For instance, suppose a marketing department wants to send out flyers about a new line of luxury vehicles to wealthier persons (who are more likely to buy than those with lower incomes), and it purchases data from a data broker that includes household income and other details. The organization merges this information into its database and then selects those wealthy persons as targets for their campaign.

This sort of activity occurs far more frequently than most people realize. There exists an entire industry of organizations with vast dossiers on virtually all adults in the United States and many other countries. This data is traded, bought, sold, merged, sorted, culled, updated, and recirculated in an endless cycle. Most of this occurs in companies most people have never heard of until a breach occurs—and, even then, personal notices are rarely sent to affected parties.

Returning to the main point of data aggregation and embellishment, another activity that frequently takes place is this: organizations seeking to aggregate customer data purchase additional data from data brokers in order to add specific data to their databases. Sometimes they receive additional data fields that are also retained, resulting in the organization having more details about its customers and prospects than it really wants or needs. This phenomenon is an example of *data sprawl.*

Aggregation works in other ways. Organizations with large customer and prospect databases can purchase data from data brokers in attempts to keep their data up to date. For instance, a motor vehicle manufacturer can purchase data from data brokers in an attempt to obtain up-to-date mailing addresses for its customers so that its safety recalls will actually reach these people.

Citizens are most concerned about the potential for data aggregation among various government agencies. One can only imagine the abuses that could occur if data from one agency were accessible by malevolent persons in other agencies. To this end, citizens need to be aware of whether privacy laws apply to government agencies as well as private businesses. For example, while the GDPR applies both to government agencies as well as private businesses, the CCPA applies only to private businesses, and government agencies are exempt.

Implement the Privacy Program Framework

The implementation of a privacy program involves numerous activities. The opening move is the creation of the privacy program charter (or internal privacy policy—whichever defines the privacy program with objectives, roles and responsibilities, and so on) that has been completed and ratified by executives. This is followed by the development or update of internal and external privacy policies and the development of privacy processes. Because privacy is inexorably linked to cybersecurity, the boundaries of roles, responsibilities, business processes, and uses of any automation need to be clearly defined.

Building a Privacy Operation

A privacy operation consists of activities that ensure that the collection and use of personal information comply with privacy policies and applicable regulations. Privacy operations are often implemented in an oversight capacity or as an "overlay" in an organization. Often, this is implemented through the formation of a privacy office, led by the organization's privacy leader (often, but not always, the chief privacy officer [CPO] or DPO), and a team of one or more analysts. The privacy office functions as a catalyst to ensure that the intake, processing, and disposal of personal information throughout the organization is done properly—according to the organization's privacy policy, which should align with applicable privacy laws as well as other contractual and legal obligations.

It is said that, similar to information security, privacy is "everyone's job." This means that the procedures and practices followed by all persons involved in the processing of personal information include steps to ensure that personal information is used only in officially sanctioned ways. The main function of the privacy office is to ensure this ongoing outcome.

An organization establishing a privacy office needs to define the scope of its responsibilities. In smaller organizations, the scope would typically include all business operations in all locations. In larger organizations, particularly those with a presence in one or more countries with strict privacy laws (such as the GDPR), the organization may appoint local privacy personnel in each local country. This can help better align local business operations with local laws and requirements.

NOTE   There is no single approach to implementing privacy operations in an organization. Some organizations will designate separate staff, while others will appoint existing staff with various privacy-related responsibilities.

Identifying Privacy Requirements

Before the privacy office can begin enforcing privacy-related activities in an organization, it must first identify and document requirements that define the specifics regarding the collection, protection, and use of personal information.

Culture and Values   At the risk of implying a "motherhood and apple pie" sentiment, it's necessary to start with an understanding of the organization's culture and stated values. Culture and values define the personality and uniqueness of an organization; the way that the organization values its assets, including the personal information of its customers, constituents, and employees, should be reflected in its policies and requirements.

Applicable Regulations   All regulations that apply to the organization need to be identified. This includes industry-specific regulations such as GLBA and HIPAA, as well as geographically related regulations such as PIPEDA, CCPA, CPRA, and GDPR. These and other regulations are cited and described earlier in this chapter.

Privacy regulations are developing and changing at high velocity. Organizations need to have an established system in place to keep them informed about new and changing regulations on the topics of information privacy and cybersecurity. Cybersecurity professionals and lawyers, for example, have particular industry news sources; at present, the best sources appear to be newsletters and paid subscriptions from legal sources that keep their subscribers up to date on new laws and related developments. It is recommended that organizations keep an official inventory of applicable laws and regulations related to cybersecurity and privacy; depending upon the organization's industry sector, this inventory may extend to other industry-specific topics as well.

Legal Interpretation   It's a wise practice to employ internal or outside legal counsel to provide an interpretation of privacy and cybersecurity laws. Legal counsel experienced in these fields should first provide guidance on the applicability of these laws. For laws deemed applicable, legal counsel should guide the organization on the meaning of applicable portions and how they should be implemented.

As the de facto risk officer, an organization's legal counsel is responsible for identifying legal and regulatory requirements and risks. It is in this capacity that legal counsel determines which laws are applicable and what the organization should do to comply with them. Like individuals in other professions, legal counsel will often confer with their industry peers and outside experts to get an idea of the consensus of opinion on the applicability and compliance approach to new and existing laws.

NOTE   Legal interpretation of applicable regulations is a key function that organizations need to acquire with in-house or external legal counsel.

Cybersecurity Policies, Requirements, and Regulations   As is often cited in this book, it's impossible to implement privacy successfully without also implementing effective cybersecurity. For the protective aspect of information privacy, organizations also need to identify their cybersecurity practices, policies, requirements, and applicable regulations and do their best to implement them in the form of cyber-risk management and cybersecurity operations. If the protective side of privacy is unable to succeed, the proper handling side of privacy will be in danger of failure.

Developing and Running Data Protection Operations

The protection of personal data is one of the primary responsibilities of an organization's information security function. In most organizations, this function is separate from the privacy office or privacy operations. Generally speaking,

- Data protection operations are generally built upon a framework of security controls. Security control frameworks are discussed in Chapter 1.
- Data protection technologies are typically operated by the IT department, although in some organizations, a separate security operations function will manage these. The technology of data protection is discussed fully in *CISM Certified Information Security Manager All-In-One Exam Guide*.
- Decisions regarding the ongoing development of security privacy and controls are a part of the larger risk management life cycle, described in Chapter 3.

 NOTE The management of information security is discussed in great detail in the *CISM Certified Information Security Manager All-In-One Exam Guide*.

Developing and Running Data Monitoring Operations

Monitoring the use of personal data is at the core of many organizations' privacy programs. Since privacy is concerned with the protection and use of personal information, privacy operations are uniquely different from operational security processes.

Data Discovery Scanning

To determine whether personnel are complying with privacy and data classification and handling policies, organizations will conduct data discovery scans of their data storage systems. Typically performed by automated DLP scanning tools, these scans generally target file shares and other structured and unstructured repositories and employ rules to identify the presence of specific types of information.

Examples of scan targets include account numbers, credit card numbers, medical records, and government-issued identification numbers, in an attempt to discover whether files containing personal information have been stored on file shares in violation of policy. Scans can also include nonpersonal information such as source code, financial information, and intellectual property.

Upon receiving the results of discovery scans, security or privacy analysts will investigate the presence of these files and attempt to determine why those files are there, who put them there, and when. Where such files are used as a part of sanctioned business processes, security or privacy analysts will confirm that access rights comply with access policies, including least privilege and need-to-know principles. Where such files are not a part of legitimate business processes, corrective action should be taken to prevent such security or privacy issues from recurring.

Data discovery often identifies undocumented procedures as well as improper behaviors. Over time, corrective actions will gradually lift the maturity of related business processes and inform staff of proper data handling policies and procedures.

 CAUTION Privacy regulations are not always explicitly clear on which data fields are considered personal information. Legal counsel may be needed to clarify this, so that privacy operations can be sure to monitor effectively.

Data Movement Monitoring

Information systems can be supplemented with DLP tooling that will monitor the movement of sensitive and personal information in real time. Monitoring agents placed in key information systems can detect the creation, movement, and deletion of specific information and generate alerts that are sent to security or privacy personnel for investigation and follow-up.

Following are examples of data movement monitoring:

- **E-mail** Agents on e-mail servers and endpoints can detect sensitive information in the contents of incoming or outgoing e-mail.

- **Endpoint storage** Agents on endpoints can detect the local storage of information.

- **File servers** Agents on file servers and other storage systems can detect the creation and movement of information.

- **USB storage** Agents on endpoints can detect the movement of information to and from external USB storage devices,

- **Internet ingress/egress** Agents on endpoints and network ingress/egress points (including Internet connections) can monitor data movement.

In all of these cases (and more that are not mentioned here), alerts can be sent to security or privacy analysts who would investigate these events to determine whether the data movement is legitimate (in which case, alerts can be adjusted to reduce the number of false positives) or whether corrective action is warranted.

In addition to monitoring the movement of sensitive information, DLP monitoring agents can be configured to intervene and prevent the data movement that is attempted. When implementing these DLP systems, organizations often configure them initially to operate in passive monitoring mode to help them understand and distinguish legitimate business processes from activities that violate policy. Then, carefully, organizations can configure DLP agents to intervene in circumstances where data movement is a clear policy violation.

On end-user systems, in many cases, DLP agents can display a window to the end user that asks for confirmation of the intended data movement. Though the agents do not overtly block such data movement, asking for confirmation can remind users that some data movement may violate policy. Still, users can be empowered in some circumstances to confirm that the intended data movement is legitimate. This action will still produce an event or an alert that can be investigated to determine whether the user is abusing policy. If the movement is legitimate, privacy and security analysts can determine whether they want users to continue to confirm such data movement or whether the movement can be permitted without intervention.

DLP systems, whether used to perform discovery scans or monitor data movement, require a good deal of "tuning" to ensure that they do not interfere with legitimate business processes but properly alert personnel when potential violations of data classification or privacy policies occur. Because business processes typically change slowly over time, the task of tuning DLP is never finished and is an ongoing activity.

Working with Data Subjects

Modern data privacy laws require that organizations provide transparency with regard to the collection and use of personal data, but they must also provide one or more means for data subjects to make inquiries and requests about the use of their personal information. The procedures for making such subject data requests are typically included in an organization's privacy policy (laws such as GDPR require that the privacy policy describe this). Occasionally, this information may be included in a user guide or in system documentation. Working with data subjects is considered a core privacy operations activity and must be implemented properly.

Inquiries for Data Usage

A data subject may send an inquiry regarding the presence and usage of his personal information. Their request may be general or quite specific. For instance, a data subject may ask whether any of his personal information is present in the organization's systems. Or a data subject may ask about specific personal information, such as a home address.

Smaller organizations may provide only an inquiry form, an e-mail address, a telephone number, or a surface mail address where such inquiries may be sent. These organizations must train personnel to manage these inquiries properly and respond to data subjects within specific timeframes (which are sometimes spelled out in regulations). Personnel who handle the requests must have access to systems and applications containing personal information so that they may respond accurately.

Larger organizations automate inquiries in some cases. For instance, a data subject with an existing account on an organization's systems can log in and click a link to learn how and where personal information is used. Often, such tools provide the means for data subjects to make changes to some of their information. This is discussed more fully in the next section.

Organizations must maintain a log of inquiries, including the subject's name (or other identifying information), so that management can better understand the frequency of requests and the workload incurred. Privacy personnel will recognize that these logs themselves may also contain personal information.

Requests for Corrections

In some circumstances, a data subject may ask for changes in personal information held by an organization. For instance, a data subject may change residences and need to update a mailing or shipping address, or a data subject may request a correction in the spelling of their name. Or they may make changes in a payment method, family status, or service provider such as insurance. Finally, sometimes personal information has been mistyped, so spelling and other corrections are needed.

Organizations are required to provide one or more means through which data subjects can request these corrections. Data subjects often can make these changes through self-service programs, but sometimes they must request that personnel in the organization make the changes on their behalf.

Privacy policies often provide one or more methods that can be used by data subjects to make these requests. Whether the means are automated or manual, organizations typically log these events as a part of routine systems and activity measurements. Like other mature business processes, this logging will sometimes compel management to make changes or improvements to systems and processes. For example, if the organization is receiving numerous requests that personnel must deal with manually, the organization may provide more self-service tools for data subjects to make some changes themselves.

Requests for Removal

The GDPR made famous the notion of "the right to be forgotten," meaning the outright removal of a data subject's information from an organization's records. Data subjects often want to opt out of an activity a particular organization may be conducting. As with other subject data requests, privacy policy will provide specific means for such requests to be made.

To respond to data removal requests appropriately, organizations must understand the full range of legal obligations regarding the use and retention of specific information. For example, laws regarding the financial records of public companies require that detailed financial records be kept for many years; requests by a current or former employee to have their data removed from these records would violate those financial recordkeeping laws: the organization would have to respectfully deny the request and give the reason for doing so. Also, some privacy laws provide specific exclusions, such as denying a request to remove one's criminal history from criminal records.

Complaints

Data subject requests should include the ability for persons to file a general complaint regarding the use of their personal information. At times, complaints will involve one or more provisions of applicable privacy laws, and at times they will involve other matters. Customers and constituents are not experts in privacy law and should not be expected to know their rights in detail. Organizations should effectively and respectfully respond to all such complaints, whatever their nature, and without being tossed back and forth between departments in internal "not my problem" handoffs.

Collecting Consent

In the context of data privacy, *consent* is a distinct action taken by a data subject to grant an organization permission to collect and/or process his or her personal information. There are several ways in which consent is given and obtained, including the following:

- **At the time of data collection** When providing one or more items of personal information to an organization, the data subject also provides consent for the collection and processing of that information. In an online context, consent often involves a checkbox with words citing agreement with a privacy policy that can be read in its entirety. On a paper form, consent often requires a signature.

- **Prior to data collection** When a data subject is establishing a relationship with an organization, a part of the agreement may include the collection of consent for instances of data collection that will take place in the future.

- **Consent obtained through a third party** In some instances, it is not feasible for an organization to collect consent directly from a data subject. For example, an organization displaying advertising that is specifically chosen for and delivered to a data subject will have collected consent "for other uses" including advertising. The advertiser will have been assured that consent has been obtained from all data subjects to whom the advertiser is displaying ad content.

Regardless of the method used to collect consent, it is obligatory for organizations to record the specific date, time, stipulations, and circumstances in which that consent was collected. It is important for organizations to be quite specific with regard to this collection. For instance, if an organization collects items of personal information for use in a specific context or event, and consent for the use of that information is for that context or event only, the organization cannot later use that information for other contexts or events.

 NOTE The GDPR and the CCPA treat consent somewhat differently. The GDPR requires explicit consent prior to the collection and processing of personal information, meaning that data subjects must opt in for any collection and use of their personal data. On the other hand, the CCPA permits the collection and processing of personal information but requires that data subjects be able to opt out of all such processing.

Working with Authorities

Some privacy laws, such as GDPR and CPRA, provide for the creation of government authorities that act in a supervisory capacity as a part of the enforcement of these laws. (Although this book does focus on organizations that will, from time to time, work with supervisory authorities, details on work performed by these authorities are beyond its scope.)

Organizations need to understand the nature of their relationships with any supervisory authorities and treat their requests not unlike data subject requests from customers and constituents: specific personnel should be identified and trained in response procedures. But unlike DSRs, it is suggested that management also be informed of supervisory authorities' inquiries and requests upon receipt if special treatment is required.

To respond effectively to supervisory authority requests, organizations need to maintain complete and up-to-date business records, including processes and procedures, data flow diagrams, and complete business records. Supervisory authorities are more likely to want to dig deeper into companies that appear disorganized or out of control. Such inquiries may consume more time and result in "damage control" responses.

Working with supervisory authorities should be considered a two-way street. For instance, organizations may be required by law to notify authorities when certain types of privacy incidents and breaches occur. Again, these proceedings should be organized and consistent, giving authorities confidence in organizations' ability to respond effectively.

Privacy Program Metrics

Metrics are the means through which management can measure key processes and determine whether their strategies are working. Metrics are used in many operational processes, but in this discussion, metrics in the privacy governance context are the emphasis. In other words, there is a distinction between tactical privacy metrics and those that reveal the state of the overall privacy program.

Metrics and stats are also used in operations to ensure that processes and machinery are operating correctly. Often, these metrics and stats are not reported up, but are monitored by operations personnel to ensure that processes and systems are running as expected.

Privacy metrics are often used to observe technical privacy controls and processes to determine whether they are operating correctly. This helps management better understand the impact of past decisions and can help drive future decisions. Here are some examples of technical metrics:

- Number of personal information records received
- Number of personal information records purged
- Number of personal information records anonymized
- Number of personal information records accessed
- Number of subject data requests received
- Number of privacy impact assessments performed, and their results
- Number of workers trained in information privacy and information security

While useful, these metrics do not address the bigger picture of the effectiveness or alignment of an organization's overall privacy program. They do not answer key questions that boards of directors and executive management often ask, such as the following:

- How much security is enough?
- How should security resources be invested and applied?
- What is the potential impact of a threat event?
- Is our privacy policy aligned with applicable privacy laws?
- Are our privacy practices aligned with customer or constituent expectations?

These and other business-related questions can be addressed through the appropriate metrics, discussed in the remainder of this section.

Privacy strategists sometimes think about metrics in simple categorizations such as these:

- **Key risk indicators (KRIs)**　These metrics are associated with the measurement of risk.
- **Key goal indicators (KGIs)**　These metrics represent the attainment of strategic goals.
- **Key performance indicators (KPIs)**　These metrics are used to show the efficiency or effectiveness of privacy- or security-related activities.

Effective Metrics

For metrics to be effective, they need to be measurable. A common way to ensure the quality and effectiveness of a metric is to use the SMART method. A metric that is SMART is

- Specific
- Measurable
- Attainable
- Relevant
- Timely

 NOTE　You can find more information about the development of security metrics in NIST SP 800-55 Revision 1, *Performance Measurement Guide for Information Security,* available at www.nist.gov.

Risk Management Metrics

Effective risk management is the culmination of the highest order activities in information privacy and security programs; these include risk analyses, the use of a risk ledger, formal risk treatment, and adjustments to the suite of privacy and security controls.

Although it is difficult to measure the success of a risk management program effectively and objectively, it is possible to take indirect measurements—much like measuring the shadow of a tree (and some applied trigonometry) to gauge its height. Thus, the best indicators of a successful risk management program would be improving trends in metrics involved with the following:

- The number of privacy impact assessments (PIAs) performed and their results
- Reduction in the number of privacy and security incidents
- Reduction in the impact of privacy and security incidents
- Reduction in the time to remediate privacy and security incidents
- Reduction in the time to remediate vulnerabilities
- Reduction in the number of new unmitigated risks

Regarding the reduction in the number of privacy and security incidents, a privacy and security program improving its maturity from low levels should first expect to see the number of incidents increase. This would be not because of lapses in privacy or security controls but because of the development of—and improvements in—mechanisms used to detect and report privacy and security incidents. If a tree falls in the forest, it will be heard if microphones are installed in key locations. Similarly, as a privacy and security program is improved and matures over time, the number of new risks will, at first, increase and then will later decrease.

 NOTE Risk management is discussed fully in Appendix A.

Data Subject Engagement Metrics

Metrics concerning the various forms of data subject engagement help the organization understand the extent to which personal information is being collected, as well as communications of various sorts from data subjects. Some of the metrics that may be reported include

- Number of data collections
- Number of opt-ins and opt-outs
- Number of data subject requests, broken out by inquiries, requests for correction, and requests for deletion
- Amount of time spent processing data subject requests

Data Governance Metrics

Metrics in the realm of data governance and data management enable company management to understand whether the management of data, including personal information, is proceeding as expected. Examples of data governance metrics include

- Data retention activities, including purges and exceptions found
- Data usage activities, including approvals for new uses and policy violations
- Changes and activities regarding data sent to and received from other organizations
- Coverage of automated tools, and where the blind spots may be
- Changes in data inventory, particularly that which contains personal information
- Changes in the numbers and types of data collection and data input and output points

Program and Process Maturity

Privacy leaders schooled in the concepts and practices of process maturity will be familiar with the need to bring the processes in a privacy program (and the many related processes in IT, cybersecurity, and business unit) to target maturity levels. When a business process achieves a given maturity level, management will be more confident that the process has an expected degree of consistency, an established business record, and perhaps even measurements to ensure continuous improvement of the process over time.

Capability maturity models are used to measure and plan the maturity level of a business process. Maturity models are discussed in detail in Chapter 1.

Performance Measurement

Metrics on the performance of privacy information security provide measures of timeliness and effectiveness. Generally speaking, performance measurement metrics provide a view of tactical privacy and security processes and activities. As discussed earlier in this section, performance measurements are often the operational metrics that need to be transformed into executive-level metrics for those audiences.

Performance measurement metrics can include any of the following:

- Time to detect privacy and security incidents
- Time to remediate privacy and security incidents
- Time to provision user accounts
- Time to deprovision user accounts
- Time to respond to subject access requests
- Time to discover vulnerabilities
- Time to remediate vulnerabilities

Nearly every operational activity that is privacy- or security-related and measurable is a candidate for performance metrics.

Resilience Metrics

The objective of a business resilience program is the planned continuation of key business activities when challenged by interruption events such as natural disasters, including earthquakes, floods, and weather events, as well as man-made or man-caused disasters, such as utility outages, riots, and fires.

The keystone of business resilience is the business impact analysis (BIA) that identifies the organization's most critical business processes and the resources required to operate and support them.

Privacy leaders should be involved in creating BIAs and in an organization's resilience program to ensure that contingency and emergency response plans do not run afoul of applicable privacy laws. These laws, and the regulators enforcing them, rarely give a free pass to an organization that fails to comply with applicable privacy laws just because it had a disaster event that required drastic action to continue business operations.

Business resilience metrics include these:

- Business impact analyses performed and their results
- Business contingency plans developed
- Business contingency training sessions held
- Privacy and security reviews of business contingency plans
- Audits of the business resilience program
- Reviews of the presence and effectiveness of business resilience programs in key supplier organizations

Convergence Metrics

Larger organizations with multiple business units, geographic locations, privacy functions, or security functions (often as a result of mergers and acquisitions) may be experiencing issues related to overlaps or gaps in coverage or activities. For instance, an organization that recently acquired another company may have some duplication of effort in the asset management and risk management functions. In another example, local privacy personnel in a large, distributed organization may be performing privacy functions that are also being performed on their behalf from other personnel at headquarters.

Metrics in the category of convergence will be highly individualized, based on specific circumstances in an organization. Categories of metrics may include these:

- Gaps and overlaps in asset coverage
- Gaps and overlaps in data management tools coverage
- Consolidation of licenses for privacy and security tools
- Gaps or overlaps in skills, responsibilities, or coverage

Resource Management Metrics

Resource management metrics are similar to value delivery metrics: both convey an efficient use of resources in an organization's privacy program. But because the emphasis here is on program efficiency, resource management metrics may be developed in these ways:

- Standardization of privacy-related processes—because consistency drives costs down
- Privacy and security involvement in every procurement and acquisition project
- Percentage of personal information records protected by privacy and security controls

Developing Metrics in Layers for Audience Relevance

When embarking on the quest for privacy and security metrics development, a common pitfall is the development of a one-dimensional metrics framework that publishes a single set of metrics to all audiences. For instance, a metrics program may publish figures on vulnerabilities discovered, vulnerabilities remediated, privacy incidents, security incidents, and internal audits and their exceptions. Publishing this or a similar set of metrics to various stakeholders will be of little value to some audiences and of no value to others.

A better approach is the development of operational metrics, which are usually easily discovered and measured. The next step is to transform those operational metrics into different metrics, stated in business terms, for particular business audiences. In a given organization, a privacy program may employ two, three, or more layers of metrics, usually related to one another and stated in relevant technical or business terms for each respective audience.

Though it may be a good starting point to ask business leaders what kinds of metrics they want to see, in many cases, privacy and security leaders will be asked what metrics *they* want to see. This can be a challenge at times, but by understanding the business, culture, compliance climate, and individuals involved at the stakeholder level, the privacy and security leader can start with a set of metrics that shows success in investments made or use metrics as a call to action for the leadership team.

Online Tracking and Behavioral Profiling

The Web and mobile applications are the engines of commerce in many industries. Today, measuring business is all about measuring what happens in information systems. In their zeal for insight, some of these measurements intrude into people's privacy. This section describes a variety of techniques used to track individual users' activities, as well as ways in which tracking can be limited.

Privacy leaders need to revisit the organization's visitor, customer, and employee tracking practices to ensure they are performing only the tracking necessary for business operations, and that all tracking mechanisms are compliant with applicable laws.

NOTE The 2020–21 COVID-19 pandemic, with its lockdowns and work-from-home (WFH) shift, has accelerated the transformation of many organizations into digital businesses, resulting in the proliferation of usage tracking data.

Advertising Tracking

An old joke in the advertising business goes like this: "Did you hear about the marketer who could not sleep at night? He was worried that he was wasting half of his advertising budget, but he didn't know which half." Cue rim shot.

In the traditional advertising world, when companies purchased ad space on billboards and buses, at airports, and in radio and television commercials, they had no direct way of knowing whether their ads were influential, never mind which individuals were responding to those ads. The Internet and the Web have changed all of that. With ads served to individuals on their laptops, tablets, and smartphones, it is now fairly simple to distinguish individuals from one another, deliver data-driven targeted advertising, and know the outcomes with more certainty based on shared tracking data.

This leap in technology has resulted in citizens saying "Enough!" and in laws to curb this tracking and its uses and potential abuses. Indeed, the existence of this book, and your interest in it, is a result of tracking, plus the accumulation and abuse of personal information that has gone too far in many cases.

Tracking Techniques and Technologies

Numerous techniques and technologies are used to track the activities and locations of Internet-connected devices and their owners. Information systems log various types of events that give system owners better insight into how, how much, and by whom their systems are used. Some of this logging is highly detailed and often includes, directly or indirectly, the identities of the persons using these devices; this may be considered unnecessary and can represent an invasion of privacy.

IP Addresses

Every endpoint—smartphone, tablet, laptop, or desktop computer, or connected device such as home surveillance camera, voice assistant, printer, and more—has an IP address. An IP address is a unique numeric value assigned to each of the devices connected to a wired or wireless network.

Most web sites, as well as many mobile applications, log basic activities such as authentication and meaningful transactions. Because IP addresses on the public Internet are unique and provide approximate geographical location information (sometimes no better than an entire country), IP addresses are often a part of these log entries.

In techniques such as network address translation, a public IP address will represent an organization's network or a residential network, but not the individual devices within that network. This means that in a single network, separate individuals using their own devices and visiting the same web site will have the same public IP address associated with them. To the uninformed, these could appear as a single user, unless log entries include some other uniquely identifying information.

 NOTE In some jurisdictions, a media access control (MAC) address and/or an IP address is considered an element of PII.

Device Identifiers

Individual devices such as laptop computers, tablet computers, and smartphones have internal device identifiers that uniquely identify them. Device serial numbers are stamped on these devices and are also available electronically. Also, mobile phones have an IMEI (International Mobile Equipment Identity) number that mobile network service providers use to identify devices throughout the world. Some of the activity tracking performed by mobile network operators and Internet service providers include identifiers like these. Often, these identifiers can be associated with their owners, giving network operators unique insight into the detailed usage of their devices.

Building Visitor Tracking

Retail stores and other organizations use a variety of technologies to record the number of visitors who visit a store or office. Video surveillance is a mainstay, but with improved camera resolution, facial recognition is now possible.

Some organizations also implement Wi-Fi–based tracking technology, which counts visitors but also knows their exact location and whether they are unique or repeat visitors. Device Wi-Fi MAC addresses, which are unique for every device in the world, are the bases for visitor tracking.

Web Tracking

Web tracking refers to general practices associated with measuring and observing users who visit web sites. Web site operators track individual user sessions on their sites for three primary reasons:

- **Session integrity**   The nature and design of Internet protocols and multiuser applications require that each user's session be uniquely identified. This is necessary to distinguish each user from every other. For instance, e-commerce sites need to identify individual user sessions properly and uniquely, so that each user is able to browse through and purchase products and services. This session integrity also gives each user a relative feeling of privacy, knowing that no other user is able to know what products they are viewing and purchasing.

- **Usage statistics**   Web sites and applications want to accumulate analytics regarding their use: how many users are visiting (and at what times of the day, what days of the week, and so on), what pages are they viewing in what sequence, and how long are they remaining on individual pages. This information helps organizations design web sites and applications that are easier and simpler to use.

- **Advertising tracking** Advertising and its revenue fuel a significant portion of the Internet. Thus, advertisers and web site operators track not only the numbers of visitors, but they track and uniquely identify visitors to distinguish one from another. The technologies in play here give rise to the "creepy factor"— for example, after a person does an Internet search for a specific thing, for days afterward, on every page she visits, she sees advertisements from various companies for those very things.

NOTE Many of the tracking techniques used by web servers and browsers are also used by mobile apps, sometimes without the user's awareness or consent.

Cookies *Cookies* are small pieces of data that web sites create and store in a user's browser. Generally, a cookie is used by the web site to distinguish users from one another and also to remember unique users' preferences such as language and display or usage settings. Several types of cookies are used for various purposes:

- **Session cookies** These are used to identify a unique user's session. A session cookie is assigned when a user logs in to a web site and is removed when the user logs off or closes the browser.

- **Persistent cookies** These cookies remain on a user's browser and are sometimes used to remember users' preferences such as language, country, and landing page. Persistent cookies are also known as advertising cookies because they are used to distinguish users from one another.

- **First-party cookies** These cookies are placed by the domain the user is visiting and identified with that domain. For instance, if a user is visiting www.company .com, a first-party cookie will be associated with the domain company.com.

- **Third-party cookies** These cookies are placed by the domain the user is visiting, where the cookie is associated with a different domain. For example, if a user is visiting www.company.com, that web server could attempt to place a cookie from www.cooltrackinging.com for advertising purposes.

- **Super cookies** These are cookies with an origin of a top-level domain such as .com or .co.uk. They are used for tracking users across many domains.

- **Flash cookies** The once-popular Adobe Flash program has a feature, Flash Local stored object, that functions much like a cookie.

- **Zombie cookies** These cookies are created by various means and designed to be difficult or impossible to detect or delete; they regenerate themselves when possible.

- **HTML5 web storage** The now popular HTML5 standard includes specifications for local storage of information. One such use mimics the function of cookies.

Web Beacons   A *web beacon* is a technique used by web servers to track the viewing of web pages and e-mail messages. Web beacons generally take the form of a 1×1 pixel image that is essentially invisible to users. Because web servers log details of the downloading of every object, including images, web beacons can function much like cookies and can enable the collection of information, such as whether the recipient has opened an e-mail and whether it was opened by others (presumably after being forwarded). This is particularly true if a web site utilizes uniquely named web beacon image files that are each sent only to a specific user.

Location   On devices with GPS or similar device location capabilities, web servers may request specific device location via the user's web browser. In modern operating systems, web sites are not permitted to obtain a device's location unless the user specifically consents to it. These consents are generally persistent, and it may be difficult for a user to view the web sites for which she has approved for sending location information.

NOTE   Many mobile apps also have the ability to request a device's location and report it to the apps' central servers.

Device Information and Name   When a user visits a web site, the site's web servers can obtain a limited amount of information about the user's device, including

- **Device name**   For a personally owned device, usually the name that the user assigned to the device when she purchased it and set it up
- **Browser**   The name and version of the browser used to visit the site
- **Operating system**   The name and version of the operating system
- **Viewport width**   The width of the device's display in pixels

With location tracking enabled, some apps and web sites accumulate a detailed location history for users. This becomes a point of contention with citizens who believe that this constitutes overreach—perhaps this information could be used against them in some way. Many also believe that the manufacturers of mobile devices likewise accumulate detailed location history that includes an excessive amount of personal information that could lead to misuse or abuse.

Eavesdropping

A growing concern among privacy and security professionals is the increase in consumer devices and mobile apps that eavesdrop on their users in various ways. Many mobile apps access sensitive data on users' mobile devices, often for no good reason, and many "smart" consumer devices collect more information from us than may seem reasonable. For instance, there is no reason for a camera or photo-editing app to access a user's contact list; when installing such an app, users often "click through" the permission dialog without thinking about what they're being asked to permit.

Similarly, some apps are able to sneak around a mobile device's controls to obtain such information anyway. The operators of mobile app stores (primarily Apple and Google) do a pretty good job of preventing illicit eavesdropping, but some app developers are clever and find ways around the controls.

Some consumer devices are designed to eavesdrop on their customers, with only vague clues in the standard terms and conditions that indicate what is really going on. For instance, one brand of smart TVs advises that customers should not have conversations on sensitive topics in the presence of the television!

Applications can access and abuse users' privacy and security in the following ways:

- **Camera** Many apps for both mobile devices and laptops request access to the device's camera. For "honest" applications, it's evident when the camera is being used, but apps could access the camera at other times as well. On many laptop computers, a small indicator light illuminates when the camera is in use, but not all mobile devices have this feature. (Personally, I am suspicious about whether new smart televisions have built-in cameras in their bezels.)

- **Photos** Many apps request access to stored photos on mobile devices. Although this is a legitimate need for photo-editing apps and social media apps for purposes of posting photos or updating profile pictures, users should pay attention to permission requests to access stored photos.

- **Microphone** Apps that need to record a user's voice or other sounds will need to request access to a device's microphone. This includes videoconferencing and audio calling applications. Others, such as health apps (for observing sleep, for example), may also request mic access. Remember that any voice-activated product has a built-in microphone that is essentially listening all the time (likely even when the product is switched off).

- **Location** Some applications need to know the location of the device in order to be useful to users. While mapping, navigation, and travel-related applications obviously require location services, others may not.

- **Contacts** Mobile device users will sometimes be asked if certain applications are allowed to access stored or cloud-based contact lists. Users should be especially careful with this permission, as unscrupulous vendors' applications may harvest others' contact information for marketing purposes.

- **Voice assistant** Many mobile devices and laptop computers are equipped with "Siri," "Alexa," and "Hey Google" voice assistants. Users need to be aware of whether these voice assistants, when activated, are listening and potentially uploading all speaking that takes place within range of the device.

- **Local and cloud storage** Mobile device users should be wary of applications that request permission to access local and cloud-based storage. Miscreant apps may attempt to exfiltrate those contents for who knows what purposes.

- **Social media accounts** Many mobile apps provide "value add" services as an adjunct to popular social media services such as Facebook, Twitter, LinkedIn, and Instagram. Those apps request permission to log in to users' social media accounts to provide their services. Sometimes this access is misused or abused, with more personal information being sent to these other services than most users would consider reasonable.

- **Paste buffer (clipboard)**   The paste buffer (known as the clipboard) on Apple mobile devices can, at times, contain highly sensitive information such as passwords, URLs, e-mail addresses, and phone numbers. Apps in some mobile devices have free access to the paste buffer on mobile devices, resulting in leakage of sensitive information.

 NOTE   Mobile apps often have the ability to access personal information such as contacts and photos, sometimes without the user providing consent.

Is Big Tech the New Big Brother?

Companies like Apple, Google, Microsoft, FaceBook, Twitter, Samsung, Vizio, and scores of others have designed numerous high-tech products that are revolutionary in the ways in which they make our work lives and personal lives easier and richer. But in recent years, we're learning of some of the practices that may represent overreach in their capabilities. Here are some examples:

- It was revealed that Google Nest thermostats are equipped with secret microphones.

- Samsung suggests that the owners of their smart televisions should take sensitive conversations away from the television lest voice-recognition software hears what's said.

- Several brands of children's smart toys, including toys from Mattel and Genesis Toys, eavesdrop on children and their families' conversations—by design.

- Google keeps a detailed dossier about the specific movements of users who use Android devices or who use Google Maps and other navigation apps.

- Employees of Amazon's Ring doorbell and ADT's security systems have been caught eavesdropping on customers' homes.

- Apple and Android smartphones have controls to restrict installed apps' access to location, voice, contacts, and data usage, but the manufacturers themselves are often exempt from these restrictions.

- And, finally, voice assistants hear everything.

Consumers are growing wary of big tech and the potential for overreach. Privacy professionals have long been concerned. The pendulum of acceptable tracking versus intrusions into privacy continues to swing, even as new technologies reveal even more about the lives of the people using them.

Facial Recognition

Combined with advancements in mobile device and CCTV optical capabilities, facial recognition software is going mainstream. Many products from Apple, Microsoft, and others utilize facial recognition for logging in to mobile devices. Commercial facial recognition products are also enabling corporations and law enforcement to recognize people, such as wanted criminals.

Privacy rights advocates are rigorously opposing facial recognition capabilities in public places such as airports, shopping malls, and city streets out of concerns that it could be abused by authorities aspiring to create a surveillance state. Some cities, states, provinces, and countries are passing laws forbidding the use of facial recognition capabilities in public places, and some larger technology organizations are refusing to sell these capabilities to governments. Public-setting facial recognition cannot be "uninvented," however, and it is likely to continue to be used secretly by corporations and governments despite regulations forbidding its use.

Biometrics

Aside from facial recognition, other forms of biometrics have been in use for years and even decades. Numerous companies manufacture fingerprint and palm scan readers for use on mobile devices, as well as for building and secure zone entrance control. Iris scanning is also fairly common, as high-resolution cameras can obtain a quality image from a few feet away.

Static signature recognition, which is the task of verifying whether a signed document is genuine, has been used for centuries and is still used in banking to confirm signatures on checks. More intrusive biometric techniques such as voice recognition, retinal scan, and dynamic handwriting scanning are no longer in common use.

Contact Tracing

Contact tracing has been used for disease control for decades. Historically, contact tracing has been a manual process consisting of interviews with confirmed case patients to learn about their recent contacts with other individuals. Being highly manual, it has not been the most efficient tool to assist in reducing the spread of disease. However, the proliferation of smartphones that can provide proximity information may prove useful for contact tracing. As a result of the COVID-19 pandemic, Apple and Google introduced support for "COVID-19 apps" that could use their smartphone's Bluetooth radio signals to notify a user who comes into close proximity with someone who is also using a "COVID-19 app" and has recorded in the app as testing positive for an infectious disease.

While health authorities view contact tracing as a valuable tool for infectious disease control, privacy advocates consider it an overly intrusive process that is subject to abuse by police states. Indeed, contact tracing can be used to discover associations between people who meet only face-to-face. Critics of contact tracing point to numerous "false positives" that would result. For instance, two hotel guests sleeping in adjacent hotel rooms might be identified as being in close proximity for several hours.

In mid-2020, Apple and Google included contact tracing as a standard feature of the iOS and Android operating systems; this feature is not activated by default and must be explicitly turned on (see Figure 2-2), or so it appears.

Figure 2-2
Contact tracing is
built into Apple
mobile devices.
(Source: author)

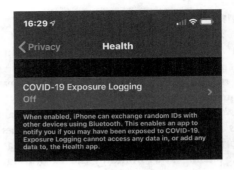

Tracking in the Workplace

Organizations that conduct part or all of their business through the use of computers need to enact a variety of controls to reduce the likelihood and impact of attacks. Indeed, this is the whole point of cybersecurity, as well as a substantial portion of information privacy. Some of the controls associated with cybersecurity involve the management and logging of activities on computing devices (laptops, desktops, tablets, and smartphones) used by its workers. After all, anomalous behavior on any of these devices may be signs of an attack. To detect and prevent such attacks, organizations must track and centrally log many types of user activities on computers, including the following:

- Web sites visited
- Files created, viewed, updated, transferred to other media, and deleted
- E-mail messages sent and received
- Contents of network communications
- Location of said devices (for device theft detection and remote data destruction)

Organizations with more mature cybersecurity programs will track and log most or all of these activities and use analytics of these records to detect anomalies that may be indications of security or privacy breaches.

Organizations undertaking such tracking and recording often include notices on these devices and in company policy, stating that such measures are taken in the name of data protection, and that any personal use of these devices (or networks) is subject to these practices, resulting in "no expectation of privacy."

NOTE In many countries, security tracking must be approved by works councils and similar employment bodies, even if the organization claims legitimate interest for the protection of its information.

Internet Access History

Web content filtering is used to prevent users from visiting web sites whose subject matter is not business related (such as weapons, gambling, and pornography sites), or to prevent users from visiting certain web sites that are known to have malicious content.

When users visit these sites, malware or spyware may be installed on visitors' computers. Many web content filtering systems log the web sites and web pages viewed by organization personnel, often associating web activity with specific workers by name. This log data can prove invaluable in a security or privacy breach investigation. CASBs are implemented to prevent the use of unauthorized cloud services. The logging capabilities in these systems are frowned upon or even illegal in some countries.

SSL Decryption

To detect and prevent leakage of sensitive information, some organizations undertake a practice known as *SSL (Secure Sockets Layer) decryption*, in which encrypted network traffic is decrypted so that the contents of the traffic can be examined for evidence of a security or privacy breach. Because so much Internet traffic is encrypted, organizations lacking SSL decryption are blind to many types of threats.

Legal problems with SSL decryption arise when workers occasionally use organization-issued computers to conduct personal business, such as accessing personal e-mail, making personal purchases, accessing healthcare services, conducting personal banking, and so on. Though a small number of organizations prohibit and actively block all such personal uses, most permit a minimal amount of personal use and will make an effort not to decrypt traffic from sites believed to be low business risk that could transmit personal information; however, they warn workers that all activities, whether business or personal, are monitored for security and privacy purposes.

Some organizations "whitelist" the use of personal banking and other, similar, activities so that an employee's personal use of organization-issued computers is not examined in some cases. Indeed, personal banking is an unlikely path for exfiltrating sensitive data and represents a low risk for security and privacy breaches.

E-mail Archiving

Internal e-mail represents an ongoing conversation in most organizations. For this reason, many organizations continuously archive all e-mail communication on separate e-mail archive servers. If the organization receives a legal request for specific e-mail messages, search capabilities on e-mail archive servers streamline the data collection effort. Any personal uses of organization e-mail accounts are naturally going to be included in such archiving. Again, employees are generally cautioned through visible notices that monitoring is taking place.

Tracking Prevention

Users of mobile devices and smart products have limited abilities to prevent tracking and eavesdropping. Various tracking prevention remedies are discussed in this section.

Cookie Opt-Out

Visitors to web sites are often informed of the use of cookies for tracking their preferences, and users are free to decline the use of these cookies. Sometimes this will mean that a user's preferences won't be remembered between visits; if the cookie opt-out includes the use of session cookies, however, a visitor may be unable to conduct transactions with the organization from their browser. Although many browsers provide a function to remove all cookies, some browsers permit users to remove individual cookies.

Cookie Blocking

Most browsers always permit users to reject third-party cookies. This will sometimes break the normal function of some web sites, depending upon their architecture. Some browsers enable users to permit and/or block cookies by specific domain, which gives users more granular control over cookie-based web tracking.

Cookie Removal

Web browsers on mobile devices and laptop computers enable users to remove all cookies from their browser. This will result in all logged in sessions being effectively logged out, and any web site preferences such as preferred language or postal code will be removed.

Do Not Track

The Do Not Track web browser setting can be used to disable web server tracking for a user. Note that Do Not Track is a request that lacks specific controls for enforcement; web site operators must voluntarily implement features that result in the user's visits not being tracked. Do Not Track has not been widely adopted by the industry, in part because of the lack of legal mandates for its use. Do Not Track is the web version of the US Do-Not-Call legislation that was enacted in 2003 as a result of the scourge of annoying telemarketing calls.

Privacy Mode Browsing

Many browsers have a privacy mode, sometimes called incognito mode, in which the tracking of web site visits is not included in a user's browsing history. This may be useful on shared computers if a user does not want other users to know about their browsing history. Many people are unaware of the fact that privacy mode browsing does not diminish or affect the full logging that web content filters, CASBs, and web sites themselves perform. Indeed, web sites make no distinction regarding privacy mode browsing in their activity logs.

Tor Browsers

Users who don't want their locations to be tracked online can use a Tor browser, which employs network routing through the Tor network. The Tor network is designed to conceal the IP address and, thus, the physical location of the device using the Tor browser. Tor browsers also do not retain cookies or browsing history. Use of the Tor network is limited to the Tor browser. Users who want to anonymize their IP addresses for other programs turn to the use of private virtual private network (VPN) services.

 NOTE It is generally believed that the details of many of the "exit nodes" of the Tor network have been identified by government law enforcement or intelligence agencies, resulting in Tor use not being as anonymous as it once was.

Private VPN Services

Persons who are concerned with the protection of their network traffic or who want to anonymize their IP address can use a private VPN service. These services, available on mobile devices as well as laptop and desktop computers, enable users to "hide" behind a relatively anonymous IP address, which will help to conceal their location.

VPN services do not anonymize a user's web browser. For instance, if an e-mail user logs in to his webmail service and then activates a VPN, his webmail session will probably continue uninterrupted, since the user's identity is asserted through session cookies. That said, web sites with better security regimens may alert users or even block access if the users are seen to be logging in from faraway countries. In a similar vein, the online banking app on my smartphone blocks VPN function because the GPS location and the VPN IP address location contradict each other.

Faraday Bags

Users of mobile phones and other small devices can purchase Faraday bags, which are small pouches that include a metallic material that blocks radiofrequency (RF) signals. Placing a mobile device into a Faraday bag essentially causes it to "disappear" from cellular, Wi-Fi, and Bluetooth networks.

Mobile device Faraday bags can also be used for building access cards to prevent them from being cloned by attackers. Smaller versions of Faraday bags are made for key fobs used to lock, unlock, and remotely start automobiles. Because of the relatively poor security associated with key fobs, people concerned with automobile theft utilize these bags. Figure 2-3 shows Faraday bags for a mobile device and for a key fob. A disadvantage of a Faraday bag is that the mobile device is unavailable for any use while inside the bag.

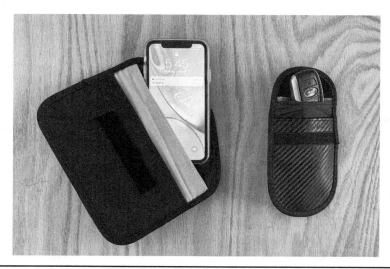

Figure 2-3 Faraday bags protect mobile devices and key fobs from eavesdropping and tracking. (Source: author)

Chapter Review

A privacy program framework consists of a program charter, privacy policy, privacy standards, privacy processes, privacy guidelines, and controls.

Privacy policies are statements that describe the collection and use of personal information, as well as actions that persons can take to inquire and make requests about their personal information. Organizations generally should have both external and internal privacy policies.

Organizations that collect personal information about persons outside the organization should develop privacy policies accessible by those persons. In the case of organizations that sell products or services to the general public, the privacy policy will often be publicly available on a public web site. It may also be posted on the premises where these products or services are rendered.

Privacy standards are prescriptive statements that inform the workforce of how privacy policies are to be carried out.

Privacy laws passed by governments at national, state, and provincial levels impose data collection, handling, and retention requirements on organizations that store or process personal information about natural persons.

Multinational organizations, as well as organizations doing business with citizens in many countries, need to be aware of the presence of and requirements imposed by international data-sharing agreements. These agreements between governments serve as implementation requirements that organizations must follow.

Within the context of data privacy and privacy regulations, organizations must identify specifically the legal basis under which they are collecting and/or processing personal information.

Controls are statements that define required outcomes. Controls are often implemented through policies, procedures, mechanisms, systems, and other measures designed to reduce risk.

For a privacy program to be effective, organizations must have a complete and accurate inventory of all personal information. Although an inventory of structured information (data residing in application database management systems) will remain fairly static, the transient nature of unstructured data creates additional challenges.

A data classification policy is a formal and intentional way for an organization to define levels of importance or sensitivity to information. A typical data classification policy will define two or more (but rarely more than five) data classification levels.

Static and dynamic data loss prevention (DLP) systems can greatly aid in the effort to provide visibility and even control over the use of personal and other sensitive information.

Data use limitation is the privacy-oriented concept that states that organizations should use personal information only for purposes required for organizations to perform their services.

Data minimization refers to the practice of collecting and retaining only those specific data elements necessary to perform agreed-upon functions. Those elements should be discarded as soon as they are no longer needed. Only authorized personnel should have access to this information.

De-identification is the means through which PII is removed from business records. Two primary techniques of de-identification are anonymization and pseudonymization.

Privacy laws place emphasis on the concepts of data quality and data accuracy; organizations need to enact processes to ensure these outcomes.

Periodic data discovery scanning enables an organization to monitor the presence of personal information in unstructured data stores.

Information systems can be supplemented with DLP tooling that will monitor the movement of sensitive and personal information in real-time. Monitoring agents placed in key information systems can detect the creation, movement, and deletion of specific information and generate alerts that are sent to security or privacy personnel for investigation and follow-up.

A key part of an organization's privacy program is the implementation of an intake function to receive inquiries and requests from data subjects. The incoming requests are known as data subject requests (DSRs). Requests will include inquiries about data usage, corrections, complaints, opt-ins, opt-outs, and requests for removal of personal information.

Organizations must identify relevant regulatory authorities and understand how they should interact with them.

Organizations must have a complete understanding of all of the methods of personal information input and intake, and ensure that consent is directly or indirectly collected from data subjects in every case.

Metrics are the means through which management can measure key processes and determine whether their strategies are working. Metrics are used in many operational processes, but in this discussion, metrics in the privacy governance context are the emphasis.

An organization's privacy program may have one or more key risk indicators (KRIs), key goal indicators (KGIs), and key performance indicators (KPIs) that inform management of the effectiveness and progress of the program.

Privacy leaders need to revisit the organization's visitor, customer, and employee tracking practices to ensure they are performing only the tracking necessary for business operations, and that all tracking mechanisms are compliant with applicable laws.

Quick Review

- Because privacy and data protection laws are being rapidly enacted and changed, organizations must devise a way to remain fully aware of new and changing laws and legal precedents.

- The CCPA/CPRA is expected to change significantly, and enforcement actions have yet to begin as of the writing of this book. Organizations subject to CCPA/CPRA should watch this law, updates, enforcement, and resulting case law carefully.

- International data-sharing agreements have proven to be volatile; hence, organizations should monitor developments concerning these agreements and be able to respond accordingly.

- An IT organization supporting many applications and services will generally have some controls that are specific to each application. However, IT will also have controls that apply across all applications and services. These are usually called its IT general controls (ITGC).

- Although it is not always necessary for an organization to select an industry-standard control framework, it is advantageous to do so. Industry-standard control frameworks have been used in thousands of companies, and they are regularly updated to reflect changing business practices, emerging threats, and new technologies.

- Organizations with multiple control frameworks often crave a simpler organization for their controls. Often, organizations will "map" their control frameworks together, resulting in a single control framework that includes controls from each framework.

- Organizations with lower process maturity are more likely to use unstructured means for performing procedures and completing tasks. Often this will result in a greater use of e-mail for process workflow and a greater use of unstructured data stores for storing data. E-mail, file servers, and cloud storage services represent the majority of unstructured data in many organizations.

- Organizations should strive to keep their data classification schemes simple, so that the workforce will be more likely to understand and comply with them.

- Organizations are cautioned to proceed slowly with the implementation of intervention DLP tools so as not to disrupt sanctioned business processes and activities.

- Organizations implementing data retention will encounter obstacles such as database referential integrity, comingling of data on backup media, sensitive data in e-mail, and unstructured data on data stores and stored on end user devices.

- The challenge with de-identification is to ensure that data records can no longer be associated with natural persons while retaining the information's value for other purposes.

- Organizations need to ensure, through privacy controls, that data aggregation is performed only when approved by management.

- Qualified legal counsel is needed to confirm the applicability of privacy laws and to interpret their meaning.

- For a privacy program to be effective, an organization needs to implement an effective cybersecurity program, which provides the data protection aspects of a privacy program.

- Privacy regulations are not always explicitly clear on which data fields are considered personal information. Legal counsel may be needed to clarify this, so that privacy operations can be sure to monitor effectively.

- Various privacy laws are based on potentially unique philosophies and treat consent somewhat differently. For instance, GDPR requires explicit consent prior to the collection and processing of personal information, meaning that data subjects must opt in for any collection and use of their personal data. On the other hand, CCPA permits collection and processing of personal information but requires that data subjects be able to opt out of all such processing.

- Privacy leaders need to understand the distinction between tactical privacy metrics and those that reveal the state and health of the overall privacy program.

- In some jurisdictions, a MAC address and/or IP address is considered an element of PII.

- Organizations in some jurisdictions must carefully plan any tracking of employee computer usage to ensure that they do not run afoul of privacy laws or works councils.

Questions

1. Privacy governance is most concerned with:

   A. Privacy policy

   B. Security policy

   C. Privacy strategy

   D. Security executive compensation

2. A privacy leader is reviewing a document that explains the purpose of the privacy program, along with roles and responsibilities and descriptions of business processes. What document is the privacy leader viewing?

   A. Program charter

   B. External privacy policy

   C. Control framework

   D. Audit results

3. An organization's board of directors wants to see quarterly metrics on risk reduction. What would be the best metric for this purpose?

   A. Number of data subject requests received

   B. Viruses blocked by antivirus programs

   C. Packets dropped by the firewall

   D. Time to patch vulnerabilities on critical servers

4. Which of the following metrics is the best example of a leading indicator?

   A. Average time to mitigate security incidents

   B. Increase in the number of attacks blocked by the intrusion prevention system (IPS)

   C. Increase in the number of attacks blocked by the firewall

   D. Percentage of critical servers being patched within service level agreements (SLAs)

5. The term *legitimate interest* refers to what privacy activity?

   A. The basis for a user access request

   B. Whether data collection is allowed by law

   C. The legal basis for processing personal information

   D. An alternative to lawful processing of personal information

6. The purpose of an internal privacy policy is:

   A. Define system specifications

   B. Define workforce behavior expectations

   C. Describe business processes

   D. Describe the next potential external privacy policy

7. The primary factor related to the selection of a control framework is:

   A. Industry vertical

   B. Current process maturity level

   C. Size of the organization

   D. Compliance level

8. Which of the following is the best definition of control objectives?

   A. Detailed statements of desired outcomes

   B. High-level statements of desired outcomes

   C. Elements of a control audit procedure

   D. Mapping of controls to applicable laws

9. The applicability of the NIST Privacy Framework is:

   A. Any organization that is building a privacy program

   B. US government agencies

   C. US government agencies and their key suppliers

   D. Key suppliers to US government agencies

10. One primary difference between GDPR and CCPA is:

   A. GDPR requires an opt-out while CCPA requires an opt-in.

   B. Only GDPR asserts extraterritorial jurisdiction.

   C. Only CCPA asserts extraterritorial jurisdiction.

   D. GDPR requires an opt-in while CCPA requires an opt-out.

11. A privacy strategist has examined a business process and has determined that personnel who perform the process do so consistently, but there is no written process document. The maturity level of this process is:

 A. Initial

 B. Repeatable

 C. Defined

 D. Managed

12. After examining several business processes, a privacy strategist found that their individual maturity levels range from Repeatable to Optimizing. What is the best future state for these business processes?

 A. All processes should be changed to Repeatable.

 B. All processes should be changed to Optimizing.

 C. There is insufficient information to determine the desired end states of these processes.

 D. Processes that are Repeatable should be changed to Defined.

13. In an organization using HIPAA as its control framework, the conclusion of a recent risk assessment stipulates that additional controls not present in HIPAA but present in ISO/IEC 27001 should be enacted. What is the best course of action in this situation?

 A. Adopt ISO/IEC 27001 as the new control framework.

 B. Retain HIPAA as the control framework and update process documentation.

 C. Add the required controls to the existing control framework.

 D. Adopt NIST SP 800-53 as the new control framework.

14. The best sequence for implementing DLP is:

 A. Static, detective dynamic, preventive dynamic

 B. Detective dynamic, preventive dynamic, static

 C. Administrative, prevention, detection

 D. File shares, networks, end user devices

15. An organization has written a program that substitutes data subject names and various PII fields with other values. What specific practice does this represent?

 A. Masking

 B. De-identification

 C. Anonymization

 D. Pseudonymization

Answers

1. **C.** Privacy governance is the mechanism through which a privacy strategy is established, controlled, and monitored. Long-term and other strategic decisions are made in the context of privacy governance.

2. **A.** A program charter generally includes an overall description of a program (in this case, a privacy program), strategic objectives, roles and responsibilities, and primary business processes.

3. **D.** The metric on time to patch critical servers will be the most meaningful metric for the board of directors. The other metrics, while potentially interesting at the operational level, do not convey business meaning to board members.

4. **D.** The metric of percentage of critical servers being patched within SLAs is the best leading indicator because it is a rough predictor of the probability of a future security incident. The other metrics are trailing indicators because they report on past incidents.

5. **C.** Legitimate interest refers to a legal basis for the collection and processing of personal information where the interests of the organization collecting and processing personal information are balanced with the data subject's interests.

6. **B.** An internal privacy policy states expectations of the workforce, often in terms of information protection as well as the use of personal information of employees and customers.

7. **A.** The most important factor influencing the selection of a control framework is the industry vertical. For example, a healthcare organization would likely select HIPAA as its primary control framework, whereas a retail organization may select PCI DSS.

8. **B.** Control objectives are high-level statements of desired outcomes. In a typical control framework, multiple detailed controls will be included in each control objective.

9. **A.** Any organization may use the NIST Privacy Framework as a guide for designing, building, and implementing a privacy program.

10. **D.** GDPR requires that organizations provide data subjects an opportunity to opt in to be included in the collection and use of personal information. CCPA requires organizations to provide an opportunity to opt out for data subjects who no longer want their personal data used by organizations.

11. **B.** A process that is performed consistently but is undocumented is generally considered to be Repeatable.

12. **C.** There are no rules that specify that the maturity levels of different processes need to be the same or at different values relative to one another. In this example, each process may already be at an appropriate level based on risk appetite, risk levels, and other considerations.

13. **C.** An organization that needs to implement new controls should do so within its existing control framework. It is not necessary to adopt an entirely new control framework when a few controls need to be added.

14. **A.** The best approach for implementing a DLP environment is to start with static DLP scanning, which detects PII on data stores. This is followed by dynamic DLP that works in detective mode to learn more about data movement. Finally, dynamic DLP in preventive mode will block disallowed data movement.

15. **D.** Pseudonymization is the practice of substituting fictitious values for actual values in data records, as a way of de-identifying those records.

Privacy Operational Lifecycle: Assess

3

In this chapter, you will learn about

- Baselining a privacy program to gauge future progress
- Assessing service providers as a part of a third-party risk management program
- Performing physical assessments of work centers and processing centers
- Protecting physical records, devices, and media
- Dealing with mergers, acquisitions, and divestitures
- Incorporating privacy impact assessments into business processes

This chapter covers Certified Information Privacy Manager job practice III, "Privacy Operational Lifecycle: Assess." The domain represents approximately 22 percent of the CIPM examination.

"Trust but verify" is a Russian proverb that is commonly used by privacy and cybersecurity industry professionals. The complexity of information processing and management, which includes layers of underlying business processes and information systems, invites seemingly minor changes that can bring disastrous consequences.

This chapter covers a variety of privacy assessment and privacy management topics:

- Baseline assessments of privacy programs help privacy leaders understand the initial state of an organization's privacy program so that progress can be more easily measured over time.
- Third-party risk management, or TPRM, is a business practice of growing concern, given that the majority of organizations now outsource a growing proportion of IT services to outside organizations.
- Physical assessments include reviews of work center and processing center protective measures and environmental controls, as well as document protection, media destruction, and device and media security.

- Mergers, acquisitions, and divestitures involve numerous considerations on a privacy program that privacy leaders need to influence and manage.
- Privacy impact assessments need to be incorporated into existing business change processes to ensure continuous and effective compliance with privacy laws and other legal obligations. The chapter includes discussions of privacy threats, vulnerabilities, and countermeasures.

Monitoring and auditing of a privacy program are covered in Chapter 5.

Privacy Program Baseline

It can be difficult to know whether we have made progress unless we know where we began. When building, reinvigorating, or improving a privacy program, the act of developing a baseline will result in an important business record that will help privacy leaders and management understand in tangible terms the progress that has been made since the baseline was created. The development of a baseline involves documenting the current state of a program so that a later analysis of a future state will highlight the progress made. Privacy programs need to make progress to keep up with rapidly emerging privacy laws and changing societal norms.

The remainder of this section is focused on the functional areas of a privacy program that should be included in a baseline.

Process Maturity

When baselining a program of any kind, whether privacy, security, information management, or other programs, the organization must include the concept of process maturity as an important measurement tool. The maturity of a process gauges its health on a chaos–order continuum: maturity is a measure of how organized a process is, whether it is performed consistently, whether it is documented, whether it is measured, and whether measurements are examined from time to time to make improvements in the process.

Maturity is not the only measure to be used, however, and maturity can be misleading if we do not understand what each process is intended to achieve. A process can be well designed and highly mature, but its absence outside of its intended scope could bring serious harm to the organization if its scope is too narrow. For example, an organization may have a nicely designed and managed security awareness program for headquarters employees that the remote salesforce is not required to use. Or a business continuity program may be too confined and may not include parts of the organization that are more vital than realized.

The gold standard for process maturity is the Capability Maturity Model Integration (CMMI), originally developed at Carnegie Mellon University and now owned by ISACA. CMMI is discussed in detail in Chapter 1.

Baselining Program Elements

The following functions should be examined and documented when baselining an organization's privacy program:

- **Education and awareness**   Examine privacy and security training at each employee's time of hire and periodically after that. See if training includes competency scores and if a minimum score is required. Determine whether training is required before an employee is granted access to business applications. Look for a variety of messaging on privacy and security awareness such as e-mails, intranet pages, posters, and management reiterating the importance of privacy and security in the organization.

- **Monitoring regulatory developments and incorporating change**   Determine whether the corporate legal team has subscription or advisory services to alert them to new laws and developments in privacy and security. See if the legal team has formally documented all of the laws and regulations the organization is required to comply with. Sometimes, smaller legal teams will retain outside counsel on specific subject matter, including cybersecurity and privacy.

- **Internal compliance to policy**   Determine whether the organization tracks the organization's compliance with internal and external privacy policies. Further, it is important to know whether the privacy policy is compliant with applicable privacy laws, regulations, standards, and other obligations such as legal agreements with customers and other organizations. See if policy compliance is tracked and deficiencies are followed up.

- **Data management practices**   Determine whether the organization has data classification policy and handling procedures, and whether the workforce is aware of these procedures. See if there are any automatic controls such as data loss prevention (DLP) that scan, monitor, or intervene in data storage and data movement activities warranting action. Determine whether procedures are in place to follow-up with data movement alerts. Identify whether the organization maintains data inventories and data flow diagrams (DFDs).

- **Risk management and risk assessments**   See if the organization has a formal privacy and security risk management program, including the performance of risk assessments to identify privacy and cybersecurity risks. Also, look for a risk register and a risk treatment process with business records to see who is making business-level decisions about privacy and security and whether risk assessment findings are properly addressed.

- **Incident response and remediation**   Determine whether the organization has a formal privacy and security incident response process that includes severity levels, escalations, recordkeeping, after-action reviews, periodic tabletop testing, and training. Examine the incident record to understand the history of privacy and security incidents in the past. The absence of an incident record often suggests that the organization is not equipped to recognize and respond even to minor incidents.

- **Audits**   See if there have been internal or external audits of the organization's privacy and security programs. If so, determine who was apprised of the results and whether significant issues were remediated and confirmed. See how often audits occur and whether they are performed by qualified (such as CISA [Certified Information Systems Auditor] or ISO 27001 Lead Auditor–certified) personnel. Determine the frequency and scope of audits and whether they have adequately revealed weaknesses in the organization's privacy and security programs.

- **Staff competence and capability**   Identify all of the organization's privacy and security staff and active stakeholders and participants in existing business processes to understand the organization's ability to operate sound programs. Privacy and security programs cannot succeed without qualified and competent staff.

- **IT service management**   Benchmark the IT organization's service management processes to understand the integrity of IT business processes and systems. An effective privacy program requires a sound cybersecurity program, which depends upon the integrity of IT service management.

- **Business continuity and disaster recovery planning**   Determine whether the organization has business continuity and/or disaster recovery planning programs. If so, see if they adequately address privacy and security issues so that contingency plans do not compromise privacy or security compliance requirements. See how often a business impact analysis (BIA) is performed and how frequently it is updated.

- **Program metrics and reporting**   Investigate the metrics gathered, analyzed, and reported in the organization's privacy and security programs. Determine to whom reporting is delivered, notably what is reported to the board of directors.

A program baseline can be used as a basis for a compliance gap analysis between the organization's current state and requirements in applicable privacy regulations, industry practices, and customer and societal expectations. As detailed in Chapter 2, the privacy leader can develop roadmaps to close the capability gaps to bring the program to the desired state.

Third-Party Risk Management

Third-party risk management (TPRM) refers to activities used to discover and manage risks associated with external organizations performing operational functions for an organization. Many organizations outsource some of their information processing to third-party organizations, often in the form of cloud-based software as a service (SaaS) and platform as a service (PaaS), and often for economic reasons: it is less expensive to pay for software in a leasing arrangement than to develop, implement, integrate, and maintain software internally. Similarly, many organizations prefer to lease server operating systems using infrastructure as a service (IAAS) versus purchasing their own hardware.

TPRM involves the extension of techniques used to identify and treat privacy and security risk within the organization. The same risks present in third parties' services are present within an organization's processing environment. The discipline of third-party risk exists because of the complexities associated with identifying risks in third-party organizations, as well as risks inherent in doing business with specific third parties. At its core, TPRM is similar to other risk management; the difference lies in acquiring relevant information to identify risks outside of the organization's direct control.

NOTE Organizations lacking a mature TPRM program should implement a process that asserts both security and privacy requirements to relevant service providers.

Cloud Service Providers

Organizations moving to cloud-based environments often assume that their cloud service providers have taken care of many or all information security functions, when generally this is not the case at all. This often results in security and privacy breaches, because each party believes that the other was performing critical data protection tasks. Many organizations are unfamiliar with the shared responsibility model that delineates which party is responsible for specific operations and security functions. Tables 3-1 and 3-2 depict shared responsibility models in terms of operations and security, respectively.

NOTE The specific responsibilities for operations and security between an organization and any specific service provider may vary somewhat from these tables. It is vital that an organization clearly understand its specific responsibilities for each third-party relationship, so that no responsibilities that may introduce risks to the organization are overlooked or neglected.

Operation	On-premises	IaaS	PaaS	SaaS
Applications	Org	Org	Org	Provider
Data	Org	Org	Org	Provider
Runtime	Org	Org	Provider	Provider
Middleware	Org	Org	Provider	Provider
Operating system	Org	Org	Provider	Provider
Virtualization	Org	Provider	Provider	Provider
Servers	Org	Provider	Provider	Provider
Storage	Org	Provider	Provider	Provider
Networking	Org	Provider	Provider	Provider
Data center	Org	Provider	Provider	Provider

Table 3-1 IT Operational Shared Responsibility Model

Activity	On-premises	IaaS	PaaS	SaaS
Human Resources	Org	Shared	Shared	Provider
Privacy	Org	Org	Org	Shared
Application Security	Org	Org	Shared	Provider
Identity and access management	Org	Org	Shared	Provider
Log management	Org	Org	Shared	Provider
System monitoring	Org	Org	Shared	Provider
Incident response	Org	Org	Shared	Shared
Data Governance	Org	Org	Shared	Shared
Data Encryption	Org	Org	Shared	Provider
Host intrusion detection	Org	Org	Shared	Provider
Host hardening	Org	Org	Shared	Provider
Asset management	Org	Org	Shared	Provider
Network intrusion detection	Org	Org	Provider	Provider
Network security	Org	Org	Provider	Provider
Security policy	Org	Shared	Shared	Provider
Physical security	Org	Provider	Provider	Provider

Table 3-2 Security and Privacy Shared Responsibility Model

The privacy officer should recognize that third-party service providers generally play little or no role in the data-handling aspect of privacy. These functions are wholly the responsibility of the organization using the third-party services, not the third party itself.

TPRM has been the subject of many standards and regulations that compel organizations to be proactive in discovering any security risks present in the services provided by critical third parties. Historically, many organizations were not voluntarily assessing these third parties. Statistical data about breaches over several years has revealed that more than half of all breaches have a nexus in third parties. This statistic has illuminated the magnitude of the third-party risk problem and has resulted in the enactment of laws and regulations in many industries that now require organizations to build and operate effective third-party risk programs in their organizations.

Privacy Regulation Requirements

In GDPR parlance, organizations that use third-party service providers are often, but not always, considered *data controllers,* which are entities that determine the purposes and means of the processing of personal data and that can include directing third parties to process personal data on their behalf. The third parties that process data on behalf of data controllers are known as *data processors.* The CCPA uses the terms *business* and *service provider* like GDPR's *data controller* and *data processor,* respectively. Increasingly, organizations not subject to GDPR or CCPA are also using these and similar terms to identify roles and expectations in contractual relationships.

HIPAA requires that *covered entities* (organizations subject to HIPAA regulations) establish a *business associate agreement* (BAA) with every service provider with access to the covered entity's information or information systems. Sarbanes–Oxley requires that organizations perform up-front and periodic due diligence on financially relevant service providers.

TPRM Life Cycle

The management of business relationships with third parties is a life-cycle process. The life cycle begins when an organization contemplates using a third party to augment or support the organization's operations. The life cycle continues during the third party's ongoing relationship and concludes when the organization no longer uses the third party's services: all connections are severed, and all data stored at the third party is removed or destroyed.

Initial Assessment

Before establishing a business relationship with a third party, an organization will assess and evaluate the third party for suitability. Often this evaluation is competitive, where two or more third parties are vying for the formal relationship. During the evaluation, the organization will require that each third party provides information describing its services, generally in a structured manner through a request for information (RFI) or a request for proposal (RFP) process.

In their RFIs and RFPs, organizations often include sections on privacy and security to help determine how each third party protects the organization's information. This, together with information about the services themselves, pricing, and other information, reveals details that the organization uses to select the third party that will provide services.

Legal Agreement

Before services can begin, the organization and the third party will negotiate a legal agreement that describes the services provided, along with service levels, quality, pricing, and other terms included in typical legal agreements. Based on the details discovered in the assessment phase, the organization can develop a section in the legal agreement that addresses privacy and security and typically covers these subjects:

- **Privacy and/or security program**   Requires the third party to have a formal privacy and/or security program, including but not limited to governance, policy, risk management, annual risk assessment, internal audit, vulnerability management, incident management, secure development, privacy and security awareness training, data protection, and third-party risk.

- **Security and/or privacy controls**   Require the third party to have a controls framework, including linkages to risk management and internal audit.

- **Vulnerability assessments**   Require the third party to undergo penetration tests or vulnerability assessments of its service infrastructure and applications, performed by a competent security professional services firm, with reports made available to the organization upon request.

- **External audits and certifications**   Require the third party to undergo annual SOC 1 and/or SOC 2 Type 2 audits (SOC stands for System and Organization Controls), TrustArc audits, ISO/IEC 27001 certifications, HITRUST certifications, Payment Card Industry Reports on Compliance (PCI ROCs), or other industry-recognized and applicable external audits, with reports made available to the organization upon request.
- **Privacy and security incident response**   Requires the third party to have a formal privacy and security incident capability that includes testing and training.
- **Privacy and security incident notification**   Requires the third party to notify the organization within a specific timeframe in the event of a suspected and confirmed breach—typically, 24–48 hours. The language around "suspected" and "confirmed" needs to be developed very carefully so that the third party cannot sidestep this responsibility.
- **Right to audit**   Requires the third party to permit the organization to conduct an audit of the third-party organization without cause. If the third party does not want to permit this, one fallback position is to insist on the right to audit in the event of a suspected or confirmed breach or other circumstances. Further, include the right to have a competent security professional services firm perform an audit of the third-party privacy and security environment on behalf of the organization (useful for several reasons, including geographic location; the external audit firm will be more objective).
- **Periodic review**   Requires the third party to permit an annual review of its operations, privacy, and security. This can improve confidence in the third party's privacy and security.
- **Third-party disclosures**   Require the third party to list any contracted parties it uses to perform services along with a suitable third-party due diligence process.
- **Annual due diligence**   Requires the third party to respond to annual questionnaires and evidence requests as a part of the organization's third-party risk program.
- **Cyber insurance**   Requires that the third party carry a cyber-insurance policy with minimum coverage levels. Require that the third party comply with all policy requirements so that the policy will pay out in the event of a privacy or security event. A great option is to have the organization be a named beneficiary on the policy, in the event of a widespread breach that could result in a large payout to many customers being diluted.

Organizations with many third parties may consider developing standard privacy and security clauses that include all of these provisions. When a new third-party service is being considered, the organization's privacy and security teams can perform their upfront examination of the third party's privacy and security environment and then make adjustments to the privacy and security clauses as needed.

During the vetting process, organizations will often find one or more shortcomings in the third party's privacy or security program that the third party is unwilling or unable to remediate right away. There are still options, however: the organization can compel the third party to enact improvements in a reasonable period after starting the business relationship. For example, a third-party service provider may not have had an external audit such as a SOC 1 or SOC 2 audit, but it may agree to undergo such an audit one year later. Or a third-party service provider that has never had external penetration testing could be compelled to begin testing at regular intervals. Alternatively, the third party could be required to undergo a penetration test and remediate all critical- and high-level issues before the organization will begin using the third party's services.

Classifying Third Parties

Organizations utilizing third parties often discover a wide range of risks: Some third parties may have access to large volumes of operationally critical or personal information. In contrast, others may have access to small volumes of personal information. Still others do not access data associated with critical operations at all. Because of this wide span of risk levels, many organizations choose to develop a scheme consisting of risk levels based on criteria important to the organization. Typically, this risk scheme will have two to four risk levels, with a level assigned to each third party.

Organizations need to assess their third parties periodically to ensure that they remain at the right classification level. Third parties that provide a variety of services may initially be classified as low risk. However, in the future, if the third party is retained to provide additional services, this could result in reclassification at a higher level of risk.

The purpose of this classification is explained in the following sections on questionnaires and assessing third parties.

Questionnaires and Evidence

Organizations that utilize third parties need to assess those third parties periodically. Generally, this consists of creating and sending a privacy and/or security questionnaire to the third party, with the request to answer all of the questions and return to the organization within a reasonable amount of time. The organization may choose not to rely simply on the answers provided, but may also request that the third party furnish specific artifacts that serve as evidence that support the responses in the questionnaire. Here are some typical artifacts that an organization will request of its third party:

- Privacy and security policies
- Privacy and security controls
- Privacy and security awareness training records
- New-hire checklists
- Details on employee background checks (not necessarily actual records but a description of the checks performed)
- Nondisclosure and other agreements signed by employees (not necessarily signed copies, but blank copies)
- Vulnerability management process
- Secure development process

- Copy of general insurance and cyber-insurance policies
- Incident response plan and evidence of testing

An organization that uses many third parties may find that it utilizes various services: some store or process large volumes of personal or critical data, others are operationally critical but do not access personal information, and other categories. Often it makes sense for an organization to utilize different versions of questionnaires, one or more for each category of third party, so that the majority of questions asked of each third party are relevant. Organizations that don't utilize different questionnaires risk having large portions of some questionnaires being irrelevant, which could be frustrating to third parties that would rightfully complain of wasted time and effort.

As described earlier on the classification of third parties, organizations often use different questionnaires according to third parties' risk levels. For example, third parties in high-risk categories would be asked to complete very extensive questionnaires that include requests for many pieces of evidence on a regular basis, typically at least annually. In contrast, third parties of medium risk would receive shorter questionnaires and on a less frequent basis, and low-risk third parties would receive very short questionnaires on a much less frequent basis. Although it is courteous to send questionnaires of appropriate length to various third parties (mainly to avoid overburdening low-risk third parties with huge questionnaires), remember that this practice also increases the organization's burden, since someone has to review the questionnaires and attached evidence. An organization that uses the services of hundreds of third parties does not want to overburden itself with the task of analyzing hundreds of questionnaires, each with hundreds of questions, when most of the third parties are lower risk and warrant shorter questionnaires.

Assessing Third Parties

To discover risks, organizations need to assess their third parties, not only at the onset of the business relationship (before the legal agreement is signed, as explained earlier), but periodically after that. Business conditions and operations often change over time, necessitating that third parties be assessed throughout the timespan of the relationship.

Organizations assessing third parties often recognize that IT, privacy, and security controls are not the only forms of risk that require examination. Organizations generally will seek other forms of information about its more critical third parties, including

- Financial risk
- Geopolitical risk
- Inherent risk
- Recent security breaches
- Lawsuits

These and other factors can influence the overall risk to the organization and manifest in various ways, including degradations in overall privacy and security, failures to meet production or quality targets, and even failure of the business.

Because of the effort required to collect information on these other risk areas, organizations often rely on outside service organizations that collect information on companies and make it available on a subscription basis. Of course, these are also third-party organizations that require an appropriate measure of due diligence.

Risk Mitigation

When assessing third parties, organizations that carefully examine the parties' information often discover some unacceptable aspects. In these cases, the organization will analyze the issues and decide on a course of action.

For instance, suppose a highly critical third party indicates that it does not perform annual privacy and security awareness training for its employees and the organization finds this unacceptable. To remedy this, the organization needs to analyze the risk (in a manner not unlike any risk found internally) and decide on a course of action. In this example, the organization contacts the third party and attempts to compel them to institute annual privacy and security awareness training for their employees.

Sometimes, a deficiency problem in a third party is not easily solved. For example, suppose a third party providing services for many years indicates in its annual questionnaire that it does not employ encryption of stored personal information. At the onset of the third-party business relationship, this was not a common practice, but it has become a common practice in the organization's industry over time. The service provider, when confronted with this, explains that it is not operationally feasible to implement encryption of personal information in a manner acceptable to the organization, mainly for financial reasons. Because of the significant impact of cost on its operations, the third party would have to increase its prices to cover these costs. In this example, the organization and the third party would need to discover the most pragmatic course of action to be satisfied with the level of risk and control costs.

Metrics and Reporting

A mature TPRM program will include several operational metrics representing a measure of activities performed within the program. Perhaps the program will also include one or more key risk indicators (KRIs) used to identify trends in risks among key service providers.

As a part of a privacy and security program that manages risk, information from the TPRM program should also flow into the organization's overall risk reporting and any dashboards used for management reporting. After all, third-party service providers are extensions of the organization's business operations.

Physical Assessments

Privacy and security program practices include periodic assessments to identify whether controls are effective and whether the organization is compliant with its policies. The purpose of such assessments is to identify operational risks that could lead to compliance issues and incidents. A variety of assessments used in privacy programs is discussed in this section.

Assessing Processing Centers and Work Centers

In the context of a privacy program, assessments of processing centers and work centers are performed to understand controls that—directly or indirectly—contribute to the protection of personal information. Areas of interest in these assessments include the following:

- **Access controls**   Processing centers and work centers should have access controls in place so that only authorized personnel can enter these facilities. Controls often used include keycard entry systems. Additional entry controls such as biometrics or PIN pads are used for higher security areas such as processing centers. All facilities should have formal visitor procedures that record each visitor, their purpose for visiting, and the name of the work personnel responsible for them.

- **Surveillance**   Work centers and processing centers often employ video surveillance to observe facility ingress and egress points. Processing centers often include video surveillance to observe activities where data processing equipment is located. Modern video surveillance systems include continuous or motion-activated recording, with recordings retained for 90 days or more. Although facial recognition is a controversial capability that is disallowed in some jurisdictions, some organizations may use it.

- **Hazards**   Processing center policy often requires that flammable materials, such as equipment packaging, be removed from facilities to reduce fire risk.

- **Clean desk/screen**   Work and processing centers frequently have "clean desk" and "clean screen" policies that forbid workers from leaving sensitive information in printed form on desks and work surfaces and/or viewable on screens and monitors. Workers in higher traffic areas are often equipped with screen privacy filters to reduce the risk of onlookers viewing sensitive information on displays. Related controls include automatic screen locking and shred bins.

- **Environmental controls**   Processing center equipment requires finely tuned environments with temperature and humidity within a narrow range to ensure prolonged equipment life and the absence of equipment failure due to overheating, static discharge, or condensation. HVAC systems require maintenance and testing that should be documented. Processing centers also require continuous clean power that often includes the use of one or more UPSs (uninterruptible power supplies) and electric generators. These power systems require periodic maintenance and testing that should all be reflected in detailed operational records.

In addition, the cleanliness and orderly placement of furniture and equipment contribute to an overall sense of control and organization in work centers and processing centers. Skilled auditors often look for these less tangible attributes when examining these locations.

Document Storage

Organizations that continue to work with paper records (and those that have switched to electronic records in the past ten years) often have a document management system that functions as a working inventory of paper records. These inventories provide information that can include but is not limited to the types of records being retained, the retention time frame for records, destruction date, where they may be located, and how they should be protected from damage and unauthorized access. All of the preceding should be documented in terms of procedures and records.

Organizations that have paper records often assign one or more employees the role of records manager, who is responsible for maintaining the inventory of paper records, retrieves records when needed, and discards records that have reached their retention end of life. A records manager is also responsible for ensuring that only authorized personnel are permitted to access paper records and ensures appropriate measures are in place to protect paper records from damage from threats such as water or fire.

Document storage controls include periodic reviews to ensure that actual physical records align with inventory records and that documents continue to be properly protected.

Document and Media Destruction

Organizations retaining sensitive and personal information usually have a formal records retention schedule that stipulates the maximum time that various records are retained. When specific records exceed their storage period, those records are discarded. Because such information is often sensitive, an organization will employ secure means for destroying records, so that no one can reconstitute them. Destruction techniques for paper records usually involve shredding, although burning and pulping are sometimes used. Electronic media is generally erased, degaussed, or shredded.

Many organizations utilize shredders for the immediate destruction of sensitive paper records, or they secure shred bins in work centers so that personnel can dispose of printed matter containing sensitive information. Often, external document destruction services periodically collect shred bins' contents and shred these materials onsite or at a centralized location. Personnel should be directed to use shred bins for the disposal of all printed matter, as well as data storage media such as optical discs.

Organizations disposing of older computers and devices should have detailed procedures that outline secure data wipe methods and proper tracking concerning the destruction of sensitive and personal information on internal hard drives, solid-state drives, and optical discs. Data stored in office equipment such as copiers and printers should be wiped using secure data wipe methods as well.

Detailed document and media destruction records are maintained by a records manager or custodian.

Device Security

Because so much of an organization's information is in electronic form, considerable attention to the security of devices and media containing information is required. Several use cases are discussed here:

- **Desktop computers**   The use of desktop computers should be controlled to prevent the loss of sensitive information caused by device loss or attack. Information stored on desktop computers should be encrypted, rendering stored information inaccessible in the case of theft. Desktop computers should be equipped with capabilities to observe and control the use of sensitive information.

- **Laptop computers**   The use of laptop computers should be controlled to prevent the loss of sensitive information through device loss or compromise. All information stored on laptop computers should be encrypted. Laptops should include the full range of security and privacy controls so that the storage and use of personal information are observable and controllable and prevent laptops from attack and compromise. Workers assigned laptops should be required to safeguard them from loss and compromise.

- **Mobile devices**   The use of mobile devices for conducting company business should be controlled so that sensitive information cannot be revealed through device loss or compromise. Often, this involves using a mobile device management (MDM) system used to monitor mobile devices, control the storage and use of sensitive information, and permit remote wiping in the event of loss or theft.

- **Storage media**   Information on backup media such as magnetic tape should be encrypted so that only authorized personnel can recover information. Backup media should be securely stored to prevent loss and stored in locations with appropriate environmental controls to ensure long life. The use of USB external storage devices should be controlled (such as requiring encryption or permitting only company-issued secure devices) or prohibited.

- **Scanners and copiers**   Many types of scanners and copiers have storage devices (hard drives or solid-state drives) where printed, scanned, and copied information persists for potentially extended periods. Safeguards are needed to protect this stored information and ensure its destruction when copiers and printers are maintained and eventually discarded. While it is uncommon for scanners and copiers to include security tools such as antimalware or firewalls, these devices should be protected on and by the network to prevent data loss in the event of an attack.

- **Device forensics**   Organizations need to have device forensics capabilities in the form of trained staff and forensics tools to support investigations of various kinds in determining events and actions on computers and networks. Smaller organizations often outsource forensics services to outside firms in the form of retainers.

Mergers, Acquisitions, and Divestitures

Changes to an organization resulting from mergers, acquisitions, and divestitures have a high potential for disrupting the organization's privacy program. The potential impacts include a change in scope for a program, the gain (or loss) of privacy and security staff, and the addition (or reduction) in regulations, standards, and other compliance obligations.

A privacy leader will be involved in several different ways, in terms of timing and influence. In the best case, the privacy leader is aware in advance of the merger, acquisition, or divestiture—early enough and in a position to influence the details of the transaction. The worst case is when the privacy leader is in the dark until after the action has been completed and announced to the public. Both cases are discussed in this section.

Influencing the Transaction

A privacy leader involved during the development of the terms of a merger, acquisition, or divestiture can play the role of a subject matter expert and advisor to executive management during the transaction's planning and development. The privacy leader has an array of considerations:

- **Change in regulatory scope** A change in the regulations that the post-transaction organization will potentially bring in (or remove) additional privacy regulations. For instance, if a US-based company is acquiring or merging with a company with customers in Europe, it will be required to comply with the GDPR.

- **Post-transaction structure** The privacy leader needs to understand the organization's structure after the transaction has been completed. For instance, in the case of a merger or acquisition, understanding the degree of integration is vital. Will the two pre-transaction organizations function as before, or will some (or all) corporate functions be merged? If they are to remain separate, there may be two similar privacy and security programs that continue long-term after the transaction has closed. Further considerations include how corporate integration will take place—whether all-at-once or through a series of small steps over time.

- **Cultural impact** Engineering a merger, acquisition, or divestiture is challenging, and the impact and influence on corporate culture is a key consideration. From simple considerations, including job security, to longer term issues such as career paths and changing organization charts, the workforce can become distracted by expected, anticipated, and actual changes that affect productivity and morale. Maintaining the integrity and effectiveness of key activities in privacy and cybersecurity can be a significant challenge, particularly when some workers decide to leave the organization for greener pastures. Some mergers and acquisitions represent a clash of different cultures that bring a lot of angst and conflict (or just the fear of it).

- **Divestiture**   In the case of an organization spinning off one or more portions of its business, numerous questions arise, including division of a workforce, assets, and work centers. In many divestitures, one organization may continue providing services to the other until the other can acquire its own capabilities. For instance, one entity may lease data center space and/or some of its IT infrastructure to the other until the other has had an opportunity to acquire its own assets. Some staff members may continue performing services to the other organization until the other can hire its own staff.

 NOTE   Privacy and security leaders can utilize the techniques of third-party risk management to assess organizations targeted for merger and acquisition, to obtain a high-level view of risk in the target organization.

Integrating Programs

After a merger or acquisition, IT, security, and privacy leaders must figure out how their new merged programs will take shape and operate on a day-to-day basis. In many cases, the new organization will have "two of everything." It will need to develop a strategy to return to single processes and solutions that support the new organization's needs. The development of a strategy for a privacy program in the new whole organization after a merger or acquisition is not too different from strategy development in a new program: existing capabilities are cataloged, the new end state is envisioned, a gap analysis is performed, and the roadmap is developed to take the program to its new, merged future state. Program strategy development is discussed in Chapters 1 and 2, and the principles there apply to cases of mergers and acquisitions, and even to divestitures.

Privacy Impact Assessments and Data Privacy Impact Assessments

A privacy impact assessment (PIA), sometimes confused with a data protection impact assessment (DPIA, as coined in the GDPR, Article 35), is a targeted risk assessment undertaken to identify impacts to individual privacy and to an organization's ability to protect information resulting from a proposed change to a business process or information system.

PIAs are not a new concept. They have been required since 2002 for US government electronic services and processes under the E-Government Act of 2002, and the European Union Article 29 Working Party endorsed the requirement to conduct PIAs for radiofrequency identification applications in 2011. However, the GDPR raised the visibility of this process because of the applicability to all businesses that process personal data. Generally, a PIA is conducted for new processes or systems that will collect, store, or transmit personally identifiable information (PII) or a significant modification to a process or system that may create a new privacy risk. The purpose of a PIA is to ensure that personal information collected is used only for the intended purpose. It identifies the impact(s) that any process or system change has on the organization's compliance with its privacy policy and applicable privacy laws and regulations.

One could also say that the purpose of a PIA is to validate the proposed change from a privacy perspective. By "validate," I imply that the proposed change has been well-designed (presumably with privacy and security by design) and that the impact on privacy is neutral or better. A PIA's purpose is the protection of privacy by design principles and practices.

 EXAM TIP CIPM candidates are not expected to memorize PIA procedures. You should, however, be familiar with the concepts, purposes, and approaches for performing PIAs.

Two excellent resources for PIAs and how PIAs achieve these objectives are

- www.gsa.gov/reference/gsa-privacy-program/privacy-impact-assessments-pia
- www.ftc.gov/site-information/privacy-policy/privacy-impact-assessments

Privacy Threshold Analysis

When an organization is considering a change to a business process or an information system, a *privacy threshold analysis* (PTA) is performed. A PTA determines whether the process or system is associated with personal information. If so, the PTA will direct the performance of a PIA. If the process or system does not involve personal information (or influence processes and systems that do), a PIA is unnecessary.

PIA Procedure

Following is the procedure for conducting a PIA:

1. Obtain a description of the project or proposed change, including the purpose of PII data collection and relevant details on business processes or information systems.

2. Identify all changes to data collection, data flows, storage, protection, and use of personal information.

3. Determine whether the proposed change violates any terms of the organization's external privacy policy, internal privacy policy, or security policy. Identify and describe all such violations. Identify any compensating controls or changes that would reduce or eliminate the violations. This determination must include identifying the original purpose of collecting and/or using personal information and whether the proposed change violates or exceeds the purpose.

4. Determine whether the proposed change violates any terms of privacy or security laws, regulations, or related guidelines or codes of conduct.

5. Determine whether the proposed change introduces any new security risks and, if so, what potential alterations to the proposed change may reduce or eliminate those risks.

6. Determine whether the proposed change alters any previously known security risks and, if so, what potential alterations to the proposed change may reduce or eliminate those risks.

7. Develop a list of all such impacts (and possible countermeasures) identified in the preceding steps.

8. Write a formal report describing all of the above.

 NOTE A PIA is nothing more than a risk assessment that focuses on the privacy and security of subject data in some specific context.

Engaging Data Subjects in a PIA

The GDPR, Article 35, Paragraph 9 suggests that the organization consult with data subjects or their representatives to obtain their opinion of proposed changes as part of a PIA. Such engagement could take the form of

- Surveys
- Focus groups
- Announcement of the proposed change with a request for comments

 NOTE The EU GDPR describes the PIA procedure in Articles 35 and 36.

The Necessity of a PIA

Not all regulations explicitly require an analysis of proposed changes to stated or implied data subject rights or the security of their personal information. However, the absence of a specific requirement for a risk assessment does not absolve an organization from performing one. It is a standard business practice to analyze various forms of impact of a proposed change to a business process or supporting information system. A failure to assess the impact of a proposed change could even be seen as negligence: a reasonable person would find such an organization at fault for not seeking to understand the potential impacts of a proposed change upon the security, privacy, or proper use of personal information.

Integrating into Existing Processes

Organizations building their privacy programs need to place "hooks" into three types of existing business processes:

- **Product development**   The PIA is a tool designed to promote privacy by design by ensuring that privacy is considered in technical, organizational, and security measures at the beginning stage of product development and throughout the product life cycle.

- **IT change control**   This process needs to include a security risk assessment and a privacy impact assessment. The data privacy officer must be informed of all changes and counted among the approvers for changes that potentially impact privacy.

- **Business process change control**   This process must include a PIA. The data privacy officer needs to be informed of all changes and counted among the approvers for changes that potentially impact privacy.

CAUTION   Organizations lacking IT change control or business process change control need to implement these processes and ensure that all relevant personnel are aware of, and will comply with, the terms of these processes.

Recordkeeping and Reporting

All PIAs that are performed must be preserved as a part of the organization's recordkeeping. The data protection officer (DPO) is typically assigned this responsibility. The DPO may elect to include statistics about PIAs as a part of regular privacy metrics reported to executive management and the board of directors. Aspects of this reporting may include

- The number of PIAs performed and the level of effort expended

- The projects associated with PIAs that were performed

- The number of exceptions noted where processes or systems required remediation

- The regulations in scope for PIAs (applicable for organizations subject to multiple privacy laws)

- Whether findings for PIAs are placed into a risk register, statistics on the contents of the risk register, including the number of items, aging, time to remediation, and context

Risks Specific to Privacy

To perform an effective PIA, the privacy specialist needs to be aware of privacy-specific threats, vulnerabilities, and attacks. A typical risk assessment considers threats and vulnerabilities in the context of some particular asset. Being familiar with specific threats and vulnerabilities will result in a better PIA.

Privacy Vulnerabilities

During a PIA, the privacy specialist must identify vulnerabilities in an information system, business process, or whatever the PIA is focused upon. A good definition of the term *vulnerability* is "a weakness that may be present in a system that makes the occurrence of one or more threats more likely."

Weaknesses in processes or systems represent opportunities for business processes to deviate from what is expected. The nature of the deviation may be a skipped step in a manual procedure, a software program that behaves unexpectedly when presented with unexpected input, or the ability for a worker to deliberately perform something incorrectly without being detected.

Identifying Vulnerabilities   When the privacy specialist examines business processes, the following may indicate the presence of vulnerabilities:

- Manual steps that rely upon human decision-making
- Steps that require workers to be proactive (such as checking a mailbox for incoming requests)
- Steps that involve data entry (the possibility of miskeying data)
- Steps performed that do not include recordkeeping
- The absence of reconciliation procedures (such as matching the number of incoming requests to the number of outgoing replies)
- Lack of written documentation describing the steps in processes and procedures
- Lack of training for personnel who perform processes and procedures
- Lack of oversight for personnel who perform processes and procedures

When the privacy specialist examines information systems, the techniques performed in typical system vulnerability assessments apply and include the following:

- Misconfiguration
- Missing security patches
- Software vulnerabilities that enable an attacker to cause software to behave in unintended ways (such as script injection, SQL injection, denial of service)
- Poor user access management controls (including easily guessed passwords, failure to remove user accounts for terminated users, password settings that invite brute-force attacks)

Automated tools such as port scanners, vulnerability scanners, and code scanning tools are often used to perform these activities.

Vulnerability Severity   When identifying vulnerabilities, the privacy specialist should also rate the severity of each vulnerability. The severity can be expressed on a high–medium–low scale or a numeric scale such as 1–5 or 1–10. A severity rating is generally associated with the ease of exploiting the vulnerability, the skill level required to exploit it, and the result of exploiting it.

A standard vulnerability rating scale, the Common Vulnerability Scoring System (CVSS), is used in the information security world. The severity of vulnerabilities identified in information systems using CVSS is 0–10, where 10 is the highest. A CVSS score is calculated using several inputs, including attack complexity, whether authentication is required, whether the attacker must be in the physical proximity of the target system, and the impact of exploitation upon the confidentiality, integrity, and availability of information in the system.

Data Storage and Data Flow Vulnerabilities   It's also necessary to understand the flow of personal information in the context of the PIA. The examiner needs to identify all instances of data storage and then examine access control processes and the security of systems associated with stored data. Also, the examiner needs to identify all instances of data movement within the organization and data leaving and entering the organization. For each case, the measures taken to protect the confidentiality and integrity of personal information in transit must be identified.

Application Security Vulnerabilities   Suppose an application is new or is undergoing significant changes. In that case, it should be subjected to various tests to ensure that it is free of vulnerabilities that could be exploited by an attacker to obtain personal information illicitly or cause a malfunction of the application. Testing includes penetration tests, static application security testing (SAST) code reviews, and dynamic application security testing (DAST) code reviews.

Privacy Threats

A privacy analyst should consider reasonable and likely threats that may occur within the business process or system being examined through the performance of a PIA. As mentioned, a PIA is a risk assessment focused on the potential impact on privacy compliance and security, targeted to a process or system undergoing changes. A good definition of the term *threat* is "an event that, if realized, would bring harm to an asset."

In this case, of course, the asset is personal information, but a threat can also include the business process being examined, the underlying information systems that facilitate the operation of the business process, the persons who perform the process, and those who operate and manage the systems. All of these are a part of the *attack surface* that must be considered.

When analyzing a variety of threats, the privacy specialist considers each threat and determines

- Whether the threat is relevant
- How the threat may be carried out (including consideration for any corresponding vulnerabilities that have been identified)
- The likelihood that the threat will be carried out
- The impact on the organization (and the data subject) if the threat were carried out

In a typical PIA, the analyst will create a chart listing all reasonable threats. Each threat is scored in terms of relevance, likelihood of occurrence, and impact of occurrence.

The scoring may be in the form of qualitative values such as high–medium–low or on a numeric scale such as 1–5 or 1–10 (where the highest number in the scale represents the highest probability and impact).

 NOTE The lists of threats found in Appendix E of NIST SP 800-30 and Appendix C of ISO/IEC 27005 represent good starting points for threat analysis.

Privacy Countermeasures

After completing the vulnerability and threat analysis of the process or system being examined, the privacy analyst may conclude that one or more threats or vulnerabilities represent unacceptable conditions and may suggest that one or more countermeasures be enacted to reduce risks considered unacceptable.

Here are some example countermeasures:

- In a data subject request (DSR) process, have a second employee check the contents of the response to be sent back to the data subject.
- Implement a web application firewall (WAF) to offer further protection for a web application that collects and manages personal information.
- Implement automated search tools to ensure more accurate (and timely) results in a DSR.

PIA Case Study

Let's take a look at a case study that represents a likely scenario. An organization in the retail industry has conducted most of its business through a web application. The organization has written a mobile app for Apple and Android devices to make it more convenient for its customers to place orders and check on their order status. The privacy officer was informed of the mobile app late in its development.

As is typical in the organization, a security firm was commissioned to perform a vulnerability analysis on the mobile app. Several vulnerabilities were identified and later remediated by the organization's developers. A retest confirmed that the vulnerabilities were remediated.

The privacy officer determined that the mobile app uses simple user ID and password authentication with no other options. As a result, the privacy officer's PIA made the following recommendations:

- Make multifactor authentication available to mobile app users who prefer to use it.
- Change the system's development life-cycle process so that a PIA can be completed as a new application or system is designed, rather than conducting an analysis of the nearly finished product.
- Include privacy requirements in future systems development projects.

Chapter Review

When an organization is building, reinvigorating, or improving a privacy program, the act of developing a baseline will result in an important business record that will help privacy leaders and management understand in real terms the progress that has been made since the starting point.

Third-party risk management (TPRM) refers to activities used to discover and manage risks associated with external organizations performing operational functions for an organization. Many organizations outsource some of their information processing to third-party organizations, often in the form of cloud-based software as a service (SaaS) and platform as a service (PaaS), and often for economic reasons: it is less expensive to pay for software in a leasing arrangement than to develop, implement, integrate, and maintain software internally.

Because of the wide span of risk levels associated with third-party service providers' services, many organizations choose to develop a scheme consisting of risk levels based on criteria critical to the organization. Typically, this risk scheme will have two to four risk levels, with a level assigned to each third party.

The assessment of work centers and processing centers gives privacy leaders a depiction of potential risks related to protecting personal information and related business processes.

Organizations retaining sensitive and personal information usually have a formal records retention schedule that stipulates the maximum time that various records are retained. When specific records exceed their storage period, those records are discarded.

Devices and media require specialized protection techniques to prevent the compromise of personal information.

Organizational changes in the form of mergers, acquisitions, and divestitures have a high potential for disrupting the organization's privacy program. The potential impacts include a change in scope for a program, the gain (or loss) of privacy and security staff, and the addition (or reduction) in regulations, standards, and other compliance obligations.

A privacy impact assessment (PIA) is a targeted risk assessment that identifies impacts on individual privacy and an organization's ability to protect information resulting from a proposed change to a business process or information system.

A privacy threshold assessment (PTA) determines whether a process or system is associated with personal information. If so, the PTA will direct the initiation of a PIA when an organization is planning changes to a process or system.

Quick Review

- The gold standard for process maturity is the Capability Maturity Model Integration (CMMI), originally developed at Carnegie Mellon University and now owned by ISACA.

- The specific responsibilities for operations and security between an organization and any specific service provider may vary. It is vital that an organization clearly understand its specific responsibilities for each third-party relationship so that no responsibilities that may introduce risks to the organization are overlooked or neglected.

- Organizations need to assess their third parties periodically to ensure that they remain at the right classification level. Third parties that provide a variety of services may initially be classified as low risk. However, in the future, if the third party is retained to provide additional services, this could result in reclassification at a higher level of risk.
- Because personal information is often sensitive, an organization will employ techniques for destroying records so that they cannot be reconstituted.
- Ideally, a privacy leader will be involved in the planning stages of a merger, acquisition, or divestiture to ensure the ongoing integrity of privacy operations in post-transaction organizations.

Questions

1. A privacy leader is documenting the current state of an organization's privacy program so that progress over time can be better understood. The documentation of the current state is known as a(n):
   A. Gap analysis
   B. Risk assessment
   C. Baseline
   D. Audit

2. What is the purpose of the cloud services shared responsibility model?
   A. Defines responsibilities when assigned to a project team
   B. Defines which parties are responsible for which aspects of privacy
   C. Defines which parties are responsible for which aspects of security and privacy
   D. Defines which parties are responsible for which aspects of security

3. An organization that receives and transforms information on behalf of another organization is known as a:
   A. Vendor
   B. Fourth party
   C. Controller
   D. Processor

4. An organization retained a service provider for low-risk services, and the provider was classified at the lowest risk tier in the organization's TPRM program. Later, the organization expanded its use of the service provider, which now collects personal information from customers. What, if any, change is required in the organization's TPRM program?
   A. No change is needed if the vendor's contacts are unchanged.
   B. Inform accounts payable of changes in payment levels.

    C. Issue the questionnaire more frequently.

    D. Reclassify the vendor's risk tier and reassess accordingly.

5. An organization is negotiating a contract with a service provider classified at the highest vendor risk tier. The organization's attorney is contemplating language in the right-to-audit section of the legal agreement. Which of the following is the best term to use?

    A. Right to audit in the event of a new privacy law

    B. Right to audit in the event of a confirmed breach

    C. Right to audit in any circumstance

    D. Right to audit in the event of a suspected breach

6. When assessing a third-party service provider that has been classified at a high-risk tier, which of the following is the best method for confirming the answers provided in a privacy assessment questionnaire?

    A. Require that the service provider attest that the questionnaire is accurate.

    B. Require that the service provider provide specific program artifacts.

    C. Perform a site visit to observe controls.

    D. Require that the service provider be certified to ISO/IEC 27701.

7. A new privacy leader wants to baseline the existing program to help identify improvements over time. Which of the following is NOT required for a baseline?

    A. Format of privacy records

    B. List of applicable regulations

    C. Privacy program metrics

    D. Size and competence of staff

8. An organization has sent a questionnaire to a selected vendor for performing expense management services. The vendor stated in the questionnaire that it does not perform security awareness training. What is the organization's best response?

    A. Accept the risk and proceed.

    B. Contractually require the vendor to begin performing security awareness training.

    C. Select a different service provider.

    D. Create an entry in the risk register.

9. An organization wants to limit the use of USB external storage for the storage of personal information. What is the best first step to accomplish this?

    A. Implement software to detect uses of USB storage of personal information.

    B. Implement software to block uses of USB storage of personal information.

    C. Create a policy that defines the limitations of USB storage.

    D. Disable USB ports on end-user computers.

10. Which of the following represents the best practice for protecting sensitive data on laptop computers?

    A. Encrypted over-the-air backup

    B. User-directed encrypted directories

    C. Encrypted thumb drives

    D. Whole-disk encryption

11. Executive management is considering entering negotiations that, if successful, will result in the acquisition of another organization. What is the best time for the organization's privacy leader to become involved in the acquisition?

    A. During final negotiations

    B. As early as possible

    C. After negotiations have concluded

    D. When the transaction closes

12. Two organizations are planning to merge later in the year. The privacy leader in organization A has determined that the maturity level of the privacy program in organization B is around 2, while the maturity level in the privacy leader's organization is around 3.5. What should be the target maturity of the post-merger organization's privacy program?

    A. 1.5 – the difference between the maturity of the two programs

    B. 3.5 – the highest common denominator of the two programs

    C. 2.75 – an average of the two maturity levels

    D. 2 – the lowest common denominator of the two programs

13. What is the purpose of a privacy threshold analysis (PTA)?

    A. Determine the circumstances in which an organization should perform PIAs.

    B. Determine whether an organization should ever perform PIAs.

    C. Determine whether a full PIA is required in a given situation.

    D. Determine whether the PIA was properly performed.

14. A PIA is:

    A. A risk assessment focused on a proposed business process change

    B. A risk assessment focused on a completed business process change

    C. A vulnerability assessment focused on a new business process

    D. A threat assessment focused on a new business process

15. A privacy strategist wants to eliminate data leakage opportunities in an organization's workforce related to workers' use of laptop and desktop computers. What is the best first step?

  A. Perform a penetration test on a sampling of laptop and desktop computers to identify likely scenarios.

  B. Block access to unsanctioned file storage sites.

  C. Block access to personal webmail.

  D. Perform a risk assessment to identify all data leakage scenarios and potential remedies for each.

Answers

1. C. The documentation of the characteristics of a process or program for later comparison is known as a baseline. Later measurements will reveal changes or improvements.

2. A. The cloud services shared responsibility model is a guide that helps organizations understand the categories of privacy and security and whether the service provider or the organization using the service provider is responsible for each category of activities. Service providers vary somewhat on the details of the privacy and security capabilities they offer.

3. D. A processor is an organization that processes information on behalf of another organization, which is typically known as a controller. The terms controller and processor are defined in the GDPR but used elsewhere by privacy and security professionals.

4. D. When a vendor's role expands and its risk classification changes, the organization will need to reassess the vendor at its new risk classification level. This may involve more frequent assessments, more rigorous assessments, or both.

5. C. The best starting point regarding right-to-audit language in a legal agreement with a service provider is to assert a right to audit in any circumstance. This is a strong opening position that may later be reduced to a right to audit in the event of a suspected or confirmed breach, which often is still an acceptable position.

6. C. A site visit is the best way to verify that controls are effective. However, site visits can be prohibitively expensive, which is why many organizations rely on other means, such as requiring the third party to provide program artifacts such as policy and procedure documents.

7. A. The format of initial state privacy records probably has little bearing on the overall health of the privacy program. However, the slate of applicable regulations, a sampling of program metrics, and the size and competency level of program staff are all relevant starting points for a baseline.

8. B. If the organization has already made a decision to use this provider, the best way forward is to contractually require the service provider to implement a security awareness training program. This is a fundamental activity in an organization's cybersecurity program; the risk should not be accepted.

9. A. The best first step to limiting or blocking the storage of personal information on external USB devices is to implement a tool that provides visibility into the use of USB storage. Then organizations can implement tools that block USB storage with foreknowledge of any issues that may arise. For example, there may be legitimate procedures involving USB storage and personal information that can be altered, or exceptions can be made, so that USB blocking does not disrupt these procedures.

10. D. Whole-disk encryption is the best practice for protecting sensitive data on laptop computers. Whole-disk encryption applies to all files stored on a laptop computer, and in enterprises with central management, end users cannot disable this encryption.

11. B. An organization's privacy leader should be involved in acquisition proceedings as early as possible so that the privacy leader can understand the capabilities and risks associated with the acquired organization's business early, to influence the terms of the acquisition and keep privacy risks as low as possible.

12. B. The maturity level of the new, merged privacy program should be as high as the higher of the two separate pre-merger programs. However, no other information is provided in this scenario that would compel an analysis to determine whether 3.5 is indeed appropriate.

13. C. The purpose of a PTA is to determine the necessity for a PIA in each individual circumstance. Where a PTA determines that a proposed business change has no bearing on personal information, a PIA need not be performed. If, however, a PTA identifies the presence of personal information in a business process that is to be changed, then a PIA will need to be performed to understand the impact of the change on privacy.

14. A. A PIA, or privacy impact assessment, is a risk assessment that is focused on a planned change to a business process. The purpose of the PIA is to identify potential risks of privacy compliance in the business process that would exist after its proposed changes have been completed.

15. D. Before the privacy strategist can make specific recommendations, it is first necessary for the strategist to conduct a risk assessment to identify all reasonable data leakage methods and identify potential remedies for each. After the risk assessment has been completed, specific actions can be taken to reduce data leakage risks.

CHAPTER 4

Privacy Operational Lifecycle: Protect

In this chapter, you will learn about
- Identity and access management
- Security controls
- Privacy by design
- Integrating privacy into business processes
- Data retention and destruction

This chapter covers Certified Information Privacy Manager job practice IV, "Privacy Operational Lifecycle: Protect." This domain represents approximately 20 percent of the CIPM examination.

The protection of personal information is foundational in any privacy program. Customers, employees, and constituents expect organizations to protect their information from compromise, damage, loss, and theft. Although information protection practices are often the role of the cybersecurity leader, privacy leaders also need to be familiar with these practices because they are fundamental to a privacy program.

Information Security Practices

Information privacy is wholly dependent upon cybersecurity for the protection of personal information. Cybersecurity is not generally performed by privacy managers, but they should be familiar with numerous information security practices that support their programs.

At the highest level, information security is governed through an *information security management system* (ISMS), a set of processes that provides management with governance capabilities to manage the entire information security program.

NOTE For a comprehensive discussion of all information security practices, read the *CISM Certified Information Security Manager All-In-One Exam Guide*.

Identity and Access Management

Identity and access management in an organization comprises a collection of activities concerned with controlling and monitoring individuals' access to information systems containing sensitive and personal information. Foundational activities include the following:

- Management of an accurate inventory of workers in the organization, whether full-time employees, part-time employees, temporary workers, contractors, consultants, or employees of other organizations performing services requiring access to networks, systems, or data

- Management of all of these workers' access rights into networks, systems, data, applications, and places where business operations take place

Identity and access management is getting more difficult. As organizations shift from on-premises to cloud-based computing, the traditional fallback controls of building access and network firewalls are no longer relevant. Only identity and access management processes are available to distinguish persons and devices authorized to access systems and data from those who are not.

Part of the duality of privacy is security. Increasingly, identity and access management is becoming central to security and, therefore, to privacy as well.

Access Controls

Access controls are used to determine whether and how *subjects* (usually persons, but also running programs and computers) are able to access *objects* (usually systems and/or data). Logical access controls work two ways:

- **Subject access** A logical access control uses some means to determine the *identity* of the subject requesting access. Once the subject's identity is known and verified beyond a reasonable doubt, the access control performs a function to determine whether the subject should be allowed to access the object. If the access is permitted, the subject can proceed; if the access is denied, the subject cannot proceed. An example of this type of access control is an application that first authenticates a user by requiring a user ID and password before enabling access to the application.

- **Service access** A logical access control is used to control the types of messages that are allowed to pass through a control point. The logical access control is designed to permit or deny messages of specific types (and may possibly permit or deny based upon origin and destination) to pass. Examples of this type of access control include a firewall, a screening router, an intrusion protection system (IPS), a web content filter, and a cloud access security broker (CASB) that makes pass/block decisions based upon the type of traffic, its content, its origin, and its destination.

These two types of access are like a concert hall with a parking garage. The parking garage (the service access) permits cars, trucks, and motorcycles to enter but denies oversized vehicles from entering. Upstairs at the concert box office (the subject access), persons are admitted with photo identification if their names match those on a list of prepaid attendees. Further, certain persons are granted "backstage access" if they possess the required credentials and are not carrying dangerous objects such as weapons.

Access Control Concepts   In discussions about access control, security and privacy professionals often use terms that are not used in other disciplines, including these:

- **Subject, object**   In access control situations, a *subject* is usually a person, but it could also be a running program, a device, or a computer. In typical security parlance, a subject is someone (or some thing) that wants to access something. An *object* (which could be a computer, an application, a database, a file, a record, or another resource) is the thing that the subject wants to access.

- **Fail open, fail closed**   These terms refer to the behaviors of controls when they experience a failure of some kind. For instance, if power is removed from a keycard-based building access control system, will all doors be locked or unlocked? The term *fail closed* means that all accesses will be denied if the access control system fails; the term *fail open* means that all accesses will be permitted upon its failure. Generally, security and privacy professionals prefer that access control systems fail closed because it is safer to admit no one than to admit everyone. But there will be exceptions now and then where fail open might be better—for example, building access control systems may need to fail open to facilitate the emergency evacuation of personnel or entrance of emergency services personnel. Fail open and fail closed can also apply to a manual control. For instance, if a building entrance is manned by a security guard who leaves her post, the control would fail closed if the guard is responsible for unlocking the entrance door to admit personnel. It would fail open if the guard merely observes people coming and going.

- **Least privilege**   An individual user should have the lowest (or least amount of) privilege possible that will still enable him or her to perform required tasks.

- **Segregation of duties**   One individual should not have combinations of *privileges* that would permit him or her to conduct high-value operations alone. The classic example is a business accounting department, where the functions of creating a payee, requesting a payment, approving a payment, and making a payment should rest with two or more separate individuals to prevent any one person from being able to embezzle funds from the organization without notice. In the context of information technology, functions such as requesting user accounts and provisioning user accounts should reside with two different persons so that one individual could not request and provision user accounts alone.

- **Split custody**   This is the concept of splitting *knowledge* of a specific object or task between two or more persons. One example is splitting the password for a critical encryption key between two parties: one person has the first half, and the other has the second half. Similarly, the combination to a bank vault could be split so that two persons have the first half of the combination and two others have the second half. In some industries, this practice is known as *dual control*.

Access Control Threats   Because access controls are often the only means of protection between protected assets and users, they are often vigorously attacked. Indeed, the majority of attacks against computers and networks containing valuable assets are against access controls in attempts to trick, defeat, or bypass them. A *threat* represents the intent and ability to do harm to an asset. In the context of privacy, threats represent the desire for an adversary to access personal information to steal it, expose it, corrupt it, or destroy it.

Threats against access controls include social engineering, malware, eavesdropping, logic bombs, back doors, and vulnerability scanning.

NOTE   The potency and frequency of threats on a system are directly proportional to the perceived value of assets that the system contains or protects.

Social Engineering Is the Preferred Initial Attack Vector

Research and numerous surveys reveal that more than 90 percent of successful cyberattacks begin with social engineering—when personnel in an organization are tricked into performing actions that enable an adversary to attack the organization successfully. The most common form of social engineering is phishing, but several other techniques are used as well. Attacks are almost always aided by an initial social engineering attack that gives the adversary the beachhead needed to break into the environment.

Access Control Vulnerabilities   *Vulnerabilities* are the weaknesses present in a system that enable a threat to be more easily carried out or to have greater impact. Vulnerabilities alone do not bring about actual harm. Instead, threats and vulnerabilities work together. Most often, a threat exploits a vulnerability, because it is easier to attack a system at its weakest point. Following are some common vulnerabilities:

- **Unpatched systems**   Security patches are designed to remove specific vulnerabilities. A system that is not patched still has vulnerabilities, some of which are easily exploited. Attackers can easily enter and take over systems that lack important security patches.

- **Default system settings**   Default settings often include unnecessary services that increase the chances that an attacker can find a way to break into a system. The practice of *system hardening* removes all unnecessary services and changes system security configurations to make the system as secure as possible.

- **Default passwords**   Some systems are shipped with default administrative passwords that make it easy for a new customer to configure the system. Often, the organization fails to change these default passwords. Hackers have access to extensive lists of default passwords for practically every kind of computer and device that can be connected to a network.

- **Incorrect permissions settings** If the permissions for access to files, directories, databases, application servers, or software programs are incorrectly set, this could permit access—and even modification or damage—by persons who should not have access.

- **Vulnerabilities in utilities and applications** System utilities, tools, and applications that are not a part of the base operating system may have exploitable weaknesses that could enable an attacker to compromise a system successfully.

- **Faulty application logic** Software applications—especially those that are accessible via the Internet—that contain inadequate session management, resource management, and input testing controls can potentially permit an intruder to take over a system and steal or damage information.

Remote Access

Remote access is defined as the means of providing remote connectivity to a corporate LAN through a logical data link. Remote access is provided by many organizations so that employees who are temporarily or permanently working offsite can access internal LAN-based resources from their remote locations.

Remote access was initially provided using dial-up modems that included authentication. Although remote dial-up is still provided in some instances, most remote access is provided over the Internet and typically uses an encrypted tunnel, or *virtual private network* (VPN), to protect transmissions from any eavesdroppers. VPNs are so prevalent in remote access technology that the terms *VPN* and *remote access* have become synonymous. Remote access architectures are depicted in Figure 4-1.

Two security controls are essential for remote access:

- **Authentication** It is necessary to know *who* is requesting access to the corporate LAN, and with *what* device. Authentication may consist of the same user ID and password that personnel use when working onsite, or multifactor authentication may be required. Authentication may also include a digital certificate or other means for authenticating the device, thereby preventing remote access from assets not owned by the organization.

- **Encryption** Many onsite network applications do not encrypt sensitive traffic because it is all contained within the physically and logically protected corporate LAN. However, because remote access provides the same function as the corporate LAN, and because the applications themselves sometimes do not provide encryption, the remote access service itself usually provides encryption. Encryption may use Secure Sockets Layer (SSL), Internet Protocol security (IPsec), Layer 2 Tunneling Protocol (L2TP), or Point-to-Point Tunneling Protocol (PPTP).

These controls are needed because they are substitutes (or *compensating control*) for the physical access controls that are usually present to control which personnel may enter the building to use the onsite corporate LAN. When personnel are onsite, their identities are confirmed through keycards or other physical access controls. Because the organization cannot "see" offsite personnel who gain remote access, the authentication used is the next best thing.

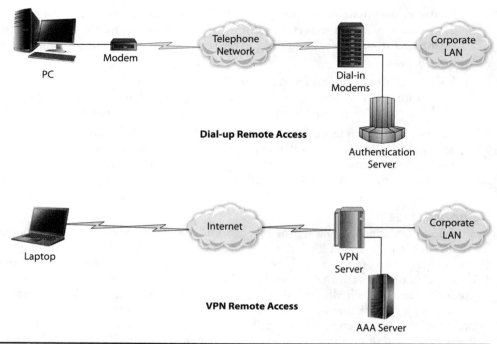

Figure 4-1 Remote access architectures

The migration of corporate resources from internal networks to cloud-based networks is changing the notion of remote access. Organizations are incorporating multifactor authentication for access to the organization's cloud-based resources, regardless of the users' location—whether they are on a corporate LAN, at home, in the field, or traveling.

The New Remote Access Paradigm

As organizations migrate their business applications to colocation centers and XaaS providers, and after the last internal resource is moved to the cloud, what is the point of remote access? Remote access to *what*?

If we think about this in terms of VPNs and the protection afforded through encryption, VPNs still make good business sense for protecting network traffic from potential eavesdroppers (whether the human or malware variety). For this reason, it's preferred to say "VPN" instead of saying "remote access."

Organizations still need to address several subtopics when considering their VPN architectures in light of cloud migration, such as split tunneling and Internet backhauling, and whether VPN should always automatically activate on workstations away from internal corporate networks.

Identification, Authentication, and Authorization   Access to computing resources is protected by mechanisms that ensure that only authorized subjects are permitted to access protected information. Generally, these mechanisms first identify who (or what) wants to access the resource, and then they determine whether the subject is permitted to access the resource and either grant or deny the access.

Several terms, including *identification*, *authentication*, and *authorization*, are used to describe various activities and are explained here.

Identification   *Identification* is the act of asserting an identity without providing any proof of it. This is analogous to one person walking up to another and saying, "Hello, my name is _____." Because it requires no proof, identification is not usually used alone to protect high-value assets or functions.

Identification is often used by web sites to remember someone's profile or preferences. For example, a bank's web application may use a cookie to store the name of the city in which the customer lives. When the customer returns to the web site, the application will display some photo or news that is related to the customer's location. But when the customer is ready to perform online banking, this simple identification is insufficient to prove the customer's actual identity.

Identification is just the *first* step in the process of gaining entry to a system or application. The next steps are authentication and authorization.

Authentication   *Authentication* is similar to identification, where a subject asserts an identity. In identification, no proof of identity is requested or provided, but with authentication, some form of proof of the subject's identity is required. That proof is usually provided in the form of a secret password or some means of higher sophistication and security, such as a token, biometric, smart card, or digital certificate. Each of these is discussed later in this section.

When the user presents a user ID plus a second factor, whether a password, token, biometric, or something else, the system will determine whether the login request will be granted or denied. Regardless of the outcome, the system will record the login event in an event log.

 NOTE   Multifactor authentication is quickly becoming the norm for human subjects who request access to networks and systems containing sensitive information.

Authorization   After a subject has been authenticated, the next step is *authorization*. This is the process by which the system determines whether the subject should be permitted to access the requested resource in the requested manner. To determine whether the subject is permitted to access the resource, the system will perform some type of lookup or other reference to a business rule. For instance, an access control table associated with the requested resource may have a list of users who are permitted to access it. The system will read through the table, and if the user subject's identity in included (and if the type of requested access matches the type permitted in the table), the system will permit the subject to access the resource. If the user's identity is not listed in the table, he or she will be denied access. Whether the login is successful or not, a record of the access attempt (and its disposition) is recorded in an event log.

Typically, permissions are centrally stored by the operating system and administered by system administrators, although some environments enable the owners of resources to administer user access.

EXAM TIP The terms "identification," "authentication," and "authorization" are often misused by business professionals, who may not realize the differences between them. These terms may be used in the exam, and for the exam and in your professional capacity you need to understand the differences.

User IDs and Passwords   User IDs and passwords are the most common means for users to authenticate to a resource—whether a network, a server, or an application. In most environments, a user's ID will not be a secret; in fact, user IDs may be a derivation of the user's name or an identification number. Some of the common forms of a user ID include combinations of the user's first and last name or an employee ID number.

CAUTION   Confidential numbers such as social insurance (Social Security in the United States) or driver's license numbers should not be used as user IDs, because these identifying numbers are generally meant to be kept confidential.

Whereas a user ID is not necessarily kept confidential, a password *always* is kept confidential. A password, also known as a *passphrase,* is a secret combination of letters, numbers, and other symbols known only to the actual user. End users are typically advised the following about passwords:

- Select a strong password or passphrase that is easy to remember but difficult for others to guess.
- Passwords must never be shared or used by others.
- Passwords must never be transmitted over any network.
- Passwords should be stored in a secure password vault.
- Each system should have a unique password.
- Passwords used for personal accounts should not be used for any work-related account.

User Account Provisioning   When a user is issued a new computer or system user account, he or she needs to know the password to access the resource. Generating and transmitting an initial password to a user can be tricky, because passwords should never be sent in an e-mail message. A sound practice for initial user account provisioning would involve the use of a limited time, one-time password that would be securely provided to the user; upon first use, the system would require that the user change the password to a value that no one else would know.

NOTE Ideally, users will be required to change their passwords after their user accounts are set up, but some systems don't permit this. Privacy and security professionals should understand an environment's capabilities as well as the risks and value of the assets being protected. Any recommendations should reflect system capabilities, data sensitivity, applicable laws and standards, and asset value.

Risks with User IDs and Passwords   Password-based authentication is among the oldest in use in information systems. Although password authentication is still quite prevalent, a number of risks are associated with its use because of the different ways in which passwords can be discovered and reused by others, and include the following:

- Eavesdropping
- Keylogging
- Phishing
- Finding a password written down
- Finding a stored password
- Exploiting a browser's password store

These follow the same theme: user IDs and passwords are static and, if discovered, can be used by others. For this reason, other, more secure means for authentication have been developed, including biometrics, tokens, smart cards, and certificates, all of which are collectively known as *multifactor authentication.*

Multifactor Authentication   Multifactor authentication (MFA) is so-called because it relies not only on "something you know" (namely, a user ID and password), but also "something you have" (such as a key card or smart card) and/or "something you are" (such as a fingerprint). MFA requires a user ID and password, but the user must also possess something or use a biometric to form a part of the authentication. Several technologies are used for MFA, including tokens, soft tokens, SMS tokens, smart cards, digital certificates, and biometrics.

Users of MFA systems need to be trained on their proper use. For example, they need to be told not to store their tokens or smart cards with their computers and to keep their smartphones or mobile devices locked except when in use.

NOTE MFA using short message service (SMS) is increasingly being considered unsafe because of risks associated with SIM fraud and other threats. Other methods are preferred as a result.

Biometrics   A number of different biometrics authentication technologies have a common theme: all use some way of measuring a unique physical characteristic of the person who is authenticating. Some of the technologies in use are

- Fingerprint
- Handprint
- Voice recognition
- Iris scan
- Facial scan

Reduced Sign-On   In a reduced sign-on environment, several applications use a centralized directory service such as LDAP (Lightweight Directory Access Protocol), RADIUS (Remote Authentication Dial-in User Service), Diameter protocol, or Microsoft Active Directory for authentication. The term comes from the result of changing each application's authentication from stand-alone to centralized and the resulting reduction in the number of user ID–password pairs that each user is required to remember.

 EXAM TIP   The terms "reduced sign-on" and "single sign-on" are often used interchangeably, and you may see questions in the exam that expect you to know the difference between the two. Many times, a reduced sign-on environment is labeled as single sign-on. For the exam, and in your professional practice, be aware that they are not the same.

Single Sign-On   In a single sign-on (SSO) interconnected environment, applications are logically connected to a centralized authentication server that is aware of the logged-in/logged-out status of each user. At the start of the workday, when a user logs in to an application, he or she will be prompted for login credentials. When the user logs in to another application, the application will consult the central authentication server to determine whether the user is logged in, and, if so, the second application will not require the user's credentials. The term refers to the fact that a user needs to log in only one time, even in a multiple-application environment.

SSO is more complicated than reduced sign-on. In an SSO environment, each participating application must be able to communicate with a centralized authentication controller and act accordingly by requiring a new user to log in, or not.

Access Control Lists   *Access control lists* (ACLs) are a common means to administer access controls. ACLs are used by many operating systems and other devices such as routers as a simple means to control access to a resource such as a server or a network.

On many devices and systems, the list of packet-filtering rules (which give a router many of the characteristics of a firewall) is known as an ACL. In the Unix operating system, for instance, ACLs can control which users are permitted to access files and directories and run tools and programs. ACLs in these and other contexts are often simple text files that can be edited with a text editor.

Access Control Processes   Sound business processes must be in place for access controls to manage user access effectively and protect critical systems and sensitive information. These business processes should be documented and detailed business records kept that document all related activities. Formal roles and responsibilities must be defined so that only authorized persons may perform various functions.

Access control processes generally fall into two categories: the processing of access requests and periodic access reviews.

Access Requests   Formal access request processes should be used to control the provisioning of user access. Using the principle of separation of duties, the actions of requesting access, approving access, and providing access should be performed by three different individuals.

Each step in an access request process should be recorded. These business records permit audits of access request processes to confirm that only properly issued and processed access requests result in the granting of user access.

NOTE   The approver of an access request should be the system owner, typically an individual in a business unit or department. IT personnel who act as stewards for information systems should not be approvers of access requests.

Access Reviews   The rate of change in organizations creates the need for periodic reviews of access rights to ensure that all subjects that have access to systems and sensitive data still require that access. Several types of reviews ensure that provisioning and deprovisioning processes are effective, accurate, and timely.

Reviews are warranted even in organizations with automation and workflow in their identity and access management processes. Reviews are even more critical in organizations that use manual processes. The objectives of access reviews ensure that access management processes remain effective and accurate and that access rights remain valid and justified.

Several types of access reviews are performed:

- **Access certifications**   System owners review access rights for subjects and confirm that each subject still requires access rights. Any subjects that no longer require access rights are flagged and their accesses are removed.

- **Provisioning certifications**   Access management personnel examine subjects' access rights and confirm that there is valid evidence of properly executed requests, reviews, approvals, and execution for each.

- **Deprovisioning certifications**   Security personnel obtain lists of terminated personnel from human resources and confirm that deprovisioning was properly and timely executed for each.

- **Activity reviews**   Security personnel examine systems to determine whether subjects have logged into them recently. Inactive user accounts can be flagged for removal if subjects have not logged into them for extended periods of time, which indicates that they probably do not require access.

- **Segregation of duties (SOD) matrix reviews**   Periodic reviews of SOD matrices help to determine whether all disallowed combinations of access are represented in SOD matrices. This is a review of the roles themselves, not the persons who have the roles.

- **Segregation of duties reviews**   Reviews of subject accesses to detect SOD exceptions confirm whether any persons have access rights that violate the segregation of duties policy.

- **Temporary worker reviews**   In organizations lacking centralized management of temporary workers, additional reviews will be needed to ensure that no active user accounts exist for temporary workers who are no longer active in the organization.

- **Privileged account reviews**   All of the reviews listed here should be performed at a higher frequency for privileged accounts. This is warranted because of the additional powers associated with privileged accounts and the greater damage that may result in cases of abuse and compromise.

- **Service account reviews**   These reviews determine whether service accounts are still being used, where and how they are used, and who manages them to ensure that there is no unauthorized use of service accounts.

In the absence of access governance tools, some of these reviews may be labor intensive. Because of this, organizations will perform these reviews on a risk basis, in which reviews of more critical systems will be performed more frequently than others.

Access Monitoring   Because many cyberattacks begin with attempts to compromise individual user and system accounts, continuous monitoring of user and system account activity is considered an essential practice in cybersecurity. This monitoring is typically achieved through the real-time transmission of user account events to a centralized log server, or better yet to a security information and event management (SIEM) system, so that alerts on suspicious behaviors can be created and such matters investigated.

The events that should be sent to a log server or SIEM include the following:

- **All successful logins**   Should include the originating IP address and geolocation of the login event

- **All unsuccessful logins**   Also needs to include IP address and location

- **All user account permission changes**   Should include the IP address and/or user account that performed the change

- **All user account creations**   Should include IP address and user account performing the change

- **Privileged account changes**   Includes permission changes and password changes.

- **Service account changes**   Includes the creation of and modification of any service account

Organizations need to develop "use cases" in their SIEM systems to alert security personnel of events that warrant investigation and action. For instance, if a user account logs in from the United States, and then a short time later there is a login for the same user account in another country, an investigation should immediately commence to determine whether the user account has been compromised, resulting in an adversary logging into the account from the foreign location.

Technical Security Controls

While identity and access management is a critical activity with dire consequences for mismanagement, several other controls are also considered foundational to information security.

Vulnerability Management

Vulnerability management is the practice of periodically examining information systems (including but not limited to operating systems, subsystems such as database management systems, applications, and network devices) for the purpose of discovering exploitable vulnerabilities, conducting related analysis, and making decisions about remediation. Organizations employ vulnerability management as a primary activity to reduce the likelihood of successful attacks on their IT environments.

Often, one or more *scanning tools* are used to scan target systems in the search for vulnerabilities:

- Network device identification
- Open port identification
- Software version identification
- Exploitable vulnerability identification
- Web application vulnerability identification
- Source code defect identification

Security managers generally employ several of these tools for routine and nonroutine vulnerability management tasks. Routine tasks include scheduled scans of specific IT assets, while nonroutine tasks include troubleshooting and various types of investigations.

A typical vulnerability management process includes these activities:

- **Periodic scanning**   One or more tools will be used to scan assets in the organization in the search for vulnerabilities.
- **Analysis of scan results**   A security manager will examine the results of a vulnerability scan to ensure there are no false-positive results. This analysis often includes a risk analysis to understand an identified vulnerability in the context of the asset, its role, and its criticality. Scanning tools generally include a criticality level or score for an identified vulnerability so that personnel can begin to understand the severity of the vulnerability. Most tools utilize the common vulnerability scoring system (CVSS) method.

After noting the CVSS score of a specific vulnerability, a security manager will analyze the vulnerability to establish the contextual criticality of the vulnerability. For example, a vulnerability in the service message block (SMB) service on Microsoft Windows servers may be rated as critical. A security manager may downgrade the risk in the organization if SMB services are not accessible over the Internet. In another example, a security manager may raise the severity of a vulnerability if the organization lacks detective controls that would alert the organization that the vulnerable component has been attacked and compromised.

- **Delivery of scan results to asset owners**   The security manager will deliver the report to the owners or custodians of affected assets so that those people can begin planning remediation activities.

- **Remediation**   Asset owners will make changes to affected assets, typically through the installation of one or more security patches or through the implementation of one or more security configuration changes. Often, risk analysis is performed to determine the risks associated with proposed remediation plans.

Organizations often establish service level agreements (SLAs) for the maximum amounts of time required for remediation of identified vulnerabilities. Table 4-1 shows a typical SLA example.

NOTE   One of the most important security operations processes, vulnerability management comprises scanning, patching, and security configuration.

Common Vulnerability Scoring System   The CVSS is an open framework that is used to provide a common methodology for scoring vulnerabilities. CVSS employs a standard methodology for examining and scoring a vulnerability based on the exploitability of the vulnerability, the impact of exploitation, and the complexity of the vulnerability. The CVSS has made it possible for organizations to adopt a consistent approach for the analysis and remediation of vulnerabilities. Specifically, organizations can develop SLAs that determine the speed by which an organization will remediate vulnerabilities.

CVSS Score	Internet-Facing Assets	Internal Assets
8.01 to 10.0	5 days	10 days
4.01 to 8.0	10 days	15 days
2.01 to 4.0	30 days	45 days
0 to 2.0	90 days	180 days

Table 4-1   Typical Vulnerability Management Remediation SLA

Vulnerability Identification Techniques   Several techniques are used for identifying vulnerabilities in target systems:

- **Security scan**   This involves the use of one or more vulnerability scanning tools to help identify easily found vulnerabilities in target systems. A security scan will identify a vulnerability in one or two ways: by confirming the version of a target system or program that is known to be vulnerable, or by making an attempt at proving the existence of a vulnerability by testing a system's response to specific stimuli.

- **Penetration test**   This test involves the use of a security scan plus additional manual tests that security scanning tools do not employ. A pen test is considered a realistic simulation of an attacker who intends to break into a target system. A pen test of an organization's production environment may fall somewhat short of the techniques used by an actual attacker. A pen tester is careful not to exploit vulnerabilities that could result in a malfunction of the target system. Often, an actual attacker will not take this precaution unless he or she wants to attack a system without being noticed. For this reason, it is sometimes desirable to conduct a pen test of nonproduction infrastructure; however, nonproduction environments are often not identical to their production counterparts.

- **Social engineering assessment**   This is an assessment of the judgment of personnel in the organization to see how well they are able to recognize various ruses used by attackers in an attempt to trick users into performing tasks or providing information. Several means are used, including e-mail, telephone calls, and in-person encounters. Social engineering assessments help organizations identify training and improvement opportunities.

  Social engineering attacks can have a high impact on an organization. A particular form of social engineering known as *business e-mail compromise* (BEC), *CEO fraud*, or *wire transfer fraud* consists of a ruse where an attacker sends an e-mail that pretends to originate from a CEO to the chief financial officer (CFO), claiming that a secret merger or acquisition proceeding requires a wire transfer for a significant sum be sent to a specific offshore account. According to the Federal Bureau of Investigation (FBI), aggregate losses resulting from BEC fraud in the year 2019 are estimated to exceed $1.7 billion.

Patch Management   Closely related to vulnerability management, *patch management* ensures that IT systems, tools, and applications have consistent version and patch levels. In all but the smallest organizations, patch management can be successful only through the use of tools that are used to automate the deployment of patches to target systems. Without automated tools, patch management is labor intensive and prone to errors that are often unnoticed, resulting in systems that remain vulnerable to exploitation even when IT and security staff believe they are protected.

Patch management is related to other IT processes, including change management and configuration management, which are discussed later in this chapter.

EXAM TIP Be mindful of the fact that vulnerability management and patch management address information protection only, and they do not address information usage. On the exam, you may see questions that misidentify the objectives of these management techniques.

Event Monitoring and Anomaly Detection

Event monitoring is a set of activities that focus on the collection of security- and privacy-related events, the correlation of events, and the generation of alerts when actionable events occur. Like vulnerability management, event monitoring and anomaly detection are critical to an organization's defenses.

NOTE Event monitoring is discussed in detail in Chapter 5.

Incident Response

Incident response represents a set of activities that are initiated when certain events or conditions occur. The practice of incident response includes the creation of a formal incident response plan, with detailed playbooks to be used when specific types of events occur and training and exercises to ensure that incident responders are familiar with the plans and playbooks.

NOTE Incident response is discussed in detail in Chapter 6.

IT Service Management

IT service management (ITSM) activities ensure that the delivery of IT services is efficient and effective through active management and the continuous improvement of processes. ITSM is defined in the IT Infrastructure Library (ITIL) process framework, a well-recognized standard managed by AXELOS. ITSM processes can be audited and registered to the ISO/IEC 20000:2011 standard, the international standard for ITSM.

ITSM consists of several distinct activities:

- IT service desk
- Incident management
- Problem management
- Change management
- Configuration management

- Release management
- Service-level management
- Financial management
- Capacity management
- Service continuity management
- Availability management
- Asset management

Each of these activities is described in detail in this section.

Why ITSM Matters to Privacy and Security

At first glance, ITSM and information risk may not appear to be related. However, information risk and information security rely a great deal on effective ITSM for the following reasons:

- In the absence of effective change management and configuration management, the configuration of IT systems will be inconsistent, in many cases resulting in exploitable vulnerabilities that could lead to security incidents.

- In the absence of effective release management, security defects may persist in production environments, possibly resulting in vulnerabilities and incidents.

- In the absence of effective capacity management, system and application malfunctions could occur, resulting in unscheduled downtime and data corruption.

- Without effective financial management, IT organizations may have insufficient funds for important security initiatives.

IT Service Desk   Often known as the help desk, the IT service desk function handles incidents and service requests on behalf of customers by acting as a single point of contact. The service desk performs end-to-end management of incidents and service requests (at least from the perspective of the customer) and is also responsible for communicating status reports to customers.

The service desk can also serve as a collection point for other ITSM processes, such as change management, configuration management, service-level management, availability management, and other ITSM functions. A typical service desk function consists of frontline analysts who take calls from users and perform basic triage, and they are often trained to perform routine tasks such as resetting passwords, troubleshooting hardware and software issues, and assisting users with questions and problems with software programs. When frontline analysts are unable to assist a user, the matter is typically escalated to a subject-matter expert who can provide assistance.

Incident Management   ITIL defines an *incident* as "an unplanned interruption to an IT service or reduction in the quality of an IT service. Failure of a configuration item that has not yet affected service is also an incident—for example, failure of one disk from a mirror set." ISO/IEC 20000-1:2011 defines an incident as an "unplanned interruption to a service, a reduction in the quality of a service or an event that has not yet impacted the service to the customer."

Thus, an incident may be any of the following:

- Service outage
- Service slowdown
- Software bug

Regardless of the cause, incidents are a result of failures or errors in any component or layer in IT infrastructure.

In ITIL terminology, if the incident has been seen before and its root cause is known, this is a *known error*. If the service desk is able to access the catalog of known errors, this may result in a more rapid resolution of incidents and less downtime and inconvenience. The change management and configuration management processes are used to modify the system to fix it temporarily or permanently. If the root cause of the incident is not known, the incident may be escalated to a *problem*, which is discussed in the next section.

Problem Management   When several incidents have occurred that appear to have the same or a similar root cause, a problem is occurring. ITIL defines a *problem* as "a cause of one or more incidents." ISO/IEC 20000-1:2011 defines a problem as the "root cause of one or more incidents" and continues, "the root cause is not usually known at the time a problem record is created and the problem management process is responsible for further investigation."

The overall objective of problem management is the reduction in the number and severity of incidents. Problem management can also include some proactive measures, including system monitoring to measure system health and capacity management that will help management to forestall capacity-related incidents.

Examples of problems include the following:

- A server that has exhausted available resources that result in similar, multiple errors (which, in ITSM terms, are known as *incidents*)
- A software bug in a service that is noticed by and affecting many users
- A chronically congested network that causes the communications between many IT components to fail

Similar to incidents, when the root cause of a problem has been identified, the change management and configuration management processes will be enacted to make temporary and permanent fixes.

Change Management   *Change management* is the set of processes that ensures all changes performed in an IT environment are controlled and performed consistently. ITIL defines change management as follows: "The goal of the change management process is to ensure that standardized methods and procedures are used for efficient and prompt handling of all changes, in order to minimize the impact of change-related incidents upon service quality, and consequently improve the day-to-day operations of the organization."

The main purpose of change management is to ensure that all proposed changes to an IT environment are vetted for suitability and risk and to ensure that changes will not interfere with each other or with other planned or unplanned activities. To be effective, each stakeholder should review all changes so that every perspective of each change is properly reviewed.

A typical change management process is a formal "waterfall" process that includes the following steps:

- **Proposal or request**   The person or group performing the change announces the proposed change. Typically, a change proposal contains a description of the change, the change procedure, the IT components that are expected to be affected by the change, a verification procedure to ensure that the change was applied properly, a back-out procedure in the event the change cannot be applied (or failed verification), and the results of tests that were performed in a test environment. The proposal should be distributed to all stakeholders several days prior to its review.

- **Review**   This is typically a meeting or discussion about the proposed change, where the personnel who will be performing the change can discuss the change and answer stakeholders' questions. Since the change proposal was sent out earlier, each stakeholder should have had an opportunity to read about the proposed change in advance of the review. Stakeholders can discuss any aspect of the change during the review. The stakeholders may agree to approve the change, or they may request that it be deferred or that some aspect of the proposed change be altered.

- **Approval**   When a change has been formally approved in the review step, the person or group responsible for change management recordkeeping will record the approval, including the names of the individuals who consented to the change. If, however, a change has been deferred or denied, the person or group that proposed the change will need to make alterations to the proposed change so that it will be acceptable, or they can withdraw the change altogether.

- **Implementation**   The actual change is implemented per the procedure described in the change proposal. Here, the personnel identified as the change implementers perform the actual change to the IT systems identified in the approved change procedure.

- **Verification**   After the implementers have completed the change, they will perform the verification procedure to make sure that the change was implemented correctly and that it produces the desired result. Generally, the verification procedure will include one or more steps that include the gathering of evidence (and directions for confirming correct versus incorrect change) that shows the change was performed correctly. This evidence will be filed with other records related to the change and may be useful in the future if there is any problem with the system where this change is suspected as part of the root cause.

- **Post-change review**   Some or all changes in an IT organization will be reviewed after the change is implemented. In this activity, the persons who made the change discuss the change with other stakeholders to learn more about the change and whether any updates to future changes may be needed.

These activities should be part of a *change control board* (CCB) or *change advisory board* (CAB), a group of stakeholders from IT and every group that is affected by changes in IT applications and supporting infrastructure.

 NOTE   The change management process is similar to the systems development life cycle (SDLC) in that it consists of activities that systematically enact changes to an IT environment.

Change Management Records   Most or all of the activities related to a change should include updates to business records so that all of the facts related to each change are captured for future reference. In even the smallest IT organization, there are too many changes taking place over time to expect that anyone will later be able to recall facts about each change. Records that are related to each change serve as a permanent record.

Emergency Changes   While most changes can be planned in advance using the change management process described here, there are times when IT systems need to be changed right away. Most change management processes include a process for emergency changes that details most of the steps in the nonemergency change management process, but they are performed out of order. The steps for emergency changes are as follows:

- **Emergency approval**   When an emergency situation arises, the staff members attending to the emergency should seek management approval for the proposed change. This approval may be done by phone, in person, or in writing (typically, e-mail). If the approval was by phone or in person, e-mail or other follow-up is usually performed. Certain members of management should be designated in advance who can approve these emergency changes.

- **Implementation**   The staff members perform the change.

- **Verification**   Staff members verify that the change produced the expected result. This may involve other staff members from other departments or end users.

- **Review**   The emergency change is formally reviewed. This review may be performed alongside nonemergency changes with the CCB, the same group of individuals who discuss nonemergency changes.

Like nonemergency changes, emergency changes should have a full set of records available for future reference.

Configuration Management   *Configuration management* (CM) is the process of recording and maintaining the configuration of IT systems. Each asset being configured is known in ITSM parlance as a *configuration item* (CI). CIs usually include the following:

- **Hardware complement**   This includes the hardware specifications of each system (such as CPU speed, amount of memory, firmware version, adapters, and peripherals).

- **Hardware configuration**   Settings at the hardware level may include boot settings, adapter configuration, and firmware settings.

- **Operating system version and configuration**   These includes versions, patches, and many operating system configuration items that have an impact on system performance and functionality.

- **Software versions and configuration**   Software components such as database management systems, application servers, and integration interfaces often have many configuration settings of their own.

Organizations that have many IT systems may automate the CM function with tools that are used to record and change configuration settings automatically. These tools help to streamline IT operations and make it easier for IT systems to be more consistent with one another. The database of system configurations is called a *configuration management database* (CMDB).

Release Management   *Release management* is the ITIL term used to describe the portion of the SDLC where changes in applications are made available to end users. Release management is used to control the changes that are made to software programs, applications, and environments.

The release process is used for several types of changes to a system, including the following:

- **Incidents and problem resolution**   Casually known as *bug fixes,* these types of changes are made in response to an incident or problem, where it has been determined that a change to application software is the appropriate remedy.

- **Enhancements**   New functions in an application are created and implemented. These enhancements may have been requested by customers, or they may be a part of the long-range vision on the part of the designers of the software program.

- **Subsystem patches and changes**   Changes in lower layers in an application environment may require a level of testing similar to testing used when changes are made to the application itself. Examples of changes are patches, service packs, and version upgrades to operating systems, database management systems, application servers, and middleware.

The release process is a sequential process—that is, each change that is proposed to a software program will be taken through each step in the release management process. In many applications, changes are usually assembled into a "package" for process efficiency purposes: it is more effective to discuss and manage groups of changes than it would be to manage individual changes.

The steps in a typical release process are preceded by typical SDLC process steps, which are as follows:

- **Feasibility study**   This includes activities that seek to determine the expected benefits of a program, project, or change to a system.

- **Requirements definition**   Each software change is described in terms of a feature description and requirements. The feature description is a high-level description of a change to software that may explain the change in business terms. Requirements are the detailed statements that describe a change in enough detail for a developer to make changes and additions to application code that will provide the desired functionality. Often, end users will be involved in the development of requirements so that they may verify that the proposed software change is actually what they desire.

- **Design**   After requirements have been developed, a programmer/analyst or application designer will create a formal design. For an existing software application, this will usually involve changes to existing design documents and diagrams, but for new applications, designs will need to be created from scratch or copied from similar designs and modified. Regardless, the design will have a sufficient level of detail to permit a programmer or software engineer to complete development without having to discern the meaning of requirements or design.

- **Development**   When requirements and design have been completed, reviewed, and approved, programmers or software engineers begin development. This involves actual coding in the chosen computer language with approved development tools, as well as the creation or update to ancillary components, such as a database design or application programming interface (API). Developers will often perform their own *unit testing*, where they test individual modules and sections of the application code to make sure that it works properly.

- **Testing**   When the developers have finished coding and unit testing, a more formal and comprehensive test phase is performed. Here, analysts, dedicated software testers, and perhaps end users will test all of the new and changed functionality to confirm whether it is performing according to requirements. Depending on the nature of the changes, some amount of *regression testing* is also performed; this means that functions that were confirmed to be working properly in prior releases are tested again to make sure that they continue to work as expected. Testing is performed according to formal, written test plans that are designed to confirm that every requirement is fulfilled. Formal test scripts are used, and the results of all tests should be recorded and archived. The testing that users perform is usually called *user acceptance testing* (UAT). Often, automated test tools are used, which can make testing more accurate and efficient. After testing is completed, a formal review and approval are required before the process is allowed to continue.

- **Implementation**   When testing has been completed, the software is implemented on production systems. Here, developers hand off the completed software to operations personnel who install it according to instructions created by developers. This could also involve the use of tools to make changes to data and database design to accommodate changes in the software. When changes are completed and tested, the release itself is carried out with these last two steps:

  - **Release preparation**   When UAT and regression testing have been completed, reviewed, and approved, a release management team will begin to prepare the new or changed software for release. Depending upon the complexity of the application and of the change itself, release preparation may involve not only software installation but also the installation or change to database design, and perhaps even changes to customer data. Hence, the software release may involve the development and testing of data conversion tools and other programs that are required so that the new or changed software will operate properly. As with testing and other phases, full records of testing and implementation of release preparation details need to be captured and archived.

  - **Release deployment**   When release preparation is completed (and perhaps reviewed and approved), the release is installed on the target systems. Personnel deploying the release will follow the release procedure, which may involve the use of tools that will make changes to the target system at the operating system, database, or other level; any required data manipulation or migration; and the installation of the actual software. The release procedure will also include verification steps that will be used to confirm the correct installation of all components.

- **Post-implementation**   After the software has been implemented, a post-implementation review takes place to examine matters of system adequacy, security, return on investment (ROI), and any issues encountered during implementation.

Utilizing a Gate Process   Many organizations utilize a "gate process" approach in their release management process. This means that each step of the process undergoes formal review and approval before the next step is allowed to begin. For example, a formal design review will be performed and attended by end users, personnel who created requirements and feature description documents, developers, and management. If the design is approved, development may begin. But if questions or concerns are raised in the design review, the design may need to be modified and reviewed again before development is allowed to begin.

Agile processes utilize gates as well, although the flow of agile processes is often parallel rather than sequential. The concept of formal reviews is the same, regardless of the SDLC process in use.

Service-Level Management   *Service-level management* is composed of the set of activities that confirms whether information services (IS) operations are providing adequate services to customers. This is achieved through continuous monitoring and periodic review of IT service delivery.

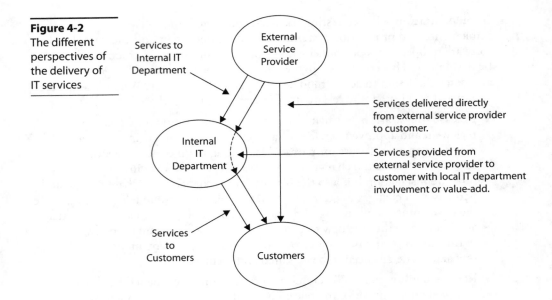

Figure 4-2
The different perspectives of the delivery of IT services

An IS department often plays two different roles in service-level management. As a provider of service to its own customers, the IS department will measure and manage the services that it provides directly. Also, many IT departments directly or indirectly manage services that are provided by external service providers. Thus, many IT departments are both service provider and customer, and often the two are interrelated, as depicted in Figure 4-2.

Financial Management   IT *financial management* is the portion of IT management that takes into account the financial value of IT services that support organizational objectives. Financial management for IT services consists of several activities, including the following:

- Budgeting
- Capital investment
- Expense management
- Project accounting and project ROI

Capacity Management   *Capacity management* is a set of activities that confirms there is sufficient capacity in IT systems and IT processes to meet service needs. Primarily, an IT system or process has sufficient capacity if its performance falls within an acceptable range, as specified in SLAs.

Capacity management is not just a concern for current needs; it must also be concerned about meeting future needs. This is attained through several activities, including the following:

- **Periodic measurements**   Systems and processes need to be regularly measured so that trends in usage can be used to predict future capacity needs.

- **Considering planned changes**   Planned changes to processes and IT systems may have an impact on the predicted workload.

- **Understanding long-term strategies**   Changes in the organization, including IT systems, business processes, and organizational objectives, may have an impact on workloads, requiring more (or less) capacity than would be extrapolated through simpler trend analysis.

- **Changes in technology**   Several factors may influence capacity plans, including the expectation that computing and network technologies will deliver better performance in the future and that trends may influence how end users use technology.

Service Continuity Management   *Service continuity management* includes the activities concerned with the ability of the organization to continue providing services, primarily in the event that a natural or manmade disaster has occurred. Service continuity management is ITIL parlance for the more common terms *business continuity planning* and *disaster recovery planning*.

 NOTE   Business continuity is discussed in detail in *CISM Certified Information Security Manager All-In-One Exam Guide*.

Availability Management   The goal of availability management is the sustainment of IT service availability in support of organizational objectives and processes. The availability of IT systems is governed by the following:

- **Effective change management**   When changes to systems and infrastructure are properly vetted through a change management process, changes are less likely to result in unanticipated downtime.

- **Effective application testing**   When changes to applications are made according to a set of formal requirements, review, and testing, the application is less likely to fail and become unavailable.

- **Resilient architecture**   When the overall architecture of an application environment is designed from the beginning to be highly reliable, it will be more resilient and more tolerant of individual faults and component failures.

- **Serviceable components**   When the individual components of an application environment can be effectively serviced by third-party service organizations, those components will be less likely to fail unexpectedly.

NOTE Organizations typically measure availability as a percentage of uptime of an application or service.

Asset Management *Asset management* is the collection of activities used to manage the inventory, classification, use, and disposal of assets. Asset management is a foundational activity, without which several other activities could not be effectively managed, including vulnerability management, device hardening, incident management, data security, and some aspects of financial management.

In information security, asset management is critical to the success of vulnerability management. If assets are not known to exist, they may be excluded from processes used to identify and remediate vulnerabilities. Similarly, it will be impossible to harden assets if their existence is not known. And if an unknown asset is attacked, the organization may have no way of directly knowing this in a timely manner; instead, if an attacker compromises an unknown device, the attack may not be known until the attacker pivots and selects additional assets to compromise. This time lag could prove crucial to the impact of the incident.

EXAM TIP Remember that asset management is a prerequisite IT activity that is critical for the success of security processes such as vulnerability management and event monitoring. You may be questioned about what is required to manage these security processes successfully.

Asset Identification A security management program's main objective (whether formally stated or not) is the protection of the organization's assets. These assets may be tangible or intangible, physical, logical, or virtual. Here are some examples of assets:

- **Buildings and property** These assets include real estate, structures, and other improvements.
- **Equipment** This includes machinery, vehicles, and office equipment such as copiers, printers, and scanners.
- **IT equipment** This includes computers, printers, scanners, tape libraries (the devices that create backup tapes, not the tapes themselves), storage systems, network devices, and phone systems.
- **Virtual assets** In addition to the tangible IT equipment cited, virtual assets include virtual machines and software running on them.
- **Supplies and materials** These include office supplies as well as materials that are used in manufacturing.
- **Records** These include business records, such as contracts, video surveillance tapes, visitor logs, and far more.
- **Information** This includes data in software applications, documents, e-mail messages, and files of every kind on workstations, servers, and in the cloud.

- **Intellectual property**   This includes an organization's designs, architectures, patents, software source code, processes, and procedures.

- **Personnel**   In a real sense, an organization's personnel *are* the organization. Without its staff, the organization cannot perform or sustain its processes.

- **Reputation**   One of the intangible characteristics of an organization, reputation is the individual and collective opinion about an organization in the eyes of its customers, competitors, shareholders, and the community.

- **Brand equity**   Similar to reputation, this is the perceived or actual market value of an individual brand of product or service that is produced by the organization.

Asset Data Sources   An organization that is building or improving its security management program may need to build its asset inventory from scratch. Management will need to determine where this initial asset data will originate. Sources include the following:

- **Financial system asset inventory**   An organization that keeps all of its assets on the books will have a wealth of asset inventory information. However, it may not be entirely useful: asset lists often do not include the location or purpose of the asset and whether it is still in use. Correlating a financial asset inventory to assets in actual use may consume more effort than the other methods for creating the initial asset list. However, for organizations that have a relatively small number of highly valued assets (for instance, an ore crusher in a gold mine or a mainframe computer in a small company), knowing the precise financial value of an asset is highly useful because the actual depreciated value of the asset is used in the risk analysis phase of risk management. Knowing the depreciated value of other assets is also useful, because this will figure into the risk treatment choices that will be identified later.

 NOTE   Financial records that indicate the value of an asset do not include the value of information stored on (or processed by) the asset.

- **Interviews**   Discussions with key personnel for purposes of identifying assets are usually the best approach. However, to be effective, several people usually need to be interviewed to ensure that all relevant assets are included.

- **IT systems portfolio**   A well-managed IT organization will have formal documents and records for its major applications. Although this information may not encompass every IT asset in the organization, it can provide information on the assets supporting individual applications or geographic locations.

- **Online data**   An organization with a large number of IT assets (systems, network devices, and so on) can sometimes utilize the capability of online data to identify those assets. An organization with cloud-based assets can use the asset management portion of the cloud services dashboard to determine the number and type of assets in use there. Also, a systems or network management system often includes a list of managed assets, which can be a good starting point when creating the initial asset list.

- **Security scans** An organization that has security scanning tools can use them to identify network assets. This technique will identify authorized as well as unauthorized assets.
- **Asset management system** Larger organizations may find it more cost-effective to use an asset management application dedicated to this purpose rather than rely on lists of assets from other sources.

None of these sources should be considered accurate or complete. Instead, as a formal asset inventory is being assembled, the security manager should continue to explore other sources of assets.

Note that it is rarely possible to take (or create) a list of assets from a single source. Rather, more than one source of information is often needed to be sure that the risk management program has identified at least the important, in-scope assets that it needs to worry about.

 NOTE As part of IT governance, management needs to determine which person or group is responsible for maintaining an asset inventory.

It is usually useful to organize or classify assets. This will help to get identified assets into smaller chunks that can be analyzed more effectively. There is no single way to organize assets, but here are a few ideas:

- **Geography** A widely dispersed organization may want to classify its assets according to their location. This will aid risk managers during the risk analysis phase, since many risks are geographic-centric, particularly natural hazards.
- **Service provider** An organization utilizing one or more infrastructure as a service (IaaS) providers can group its assets by service provider.
- **Business process** Because some organizations rank the criticality of their individual business processes, it can be useful to group assets according to the business processes they support. This helps the risk analysis and risk treatment phases because assets supporting individual processes can be associated with business criticality and treated appropriately.
- **Organizational unit** In larger organizations, it may be easier to classify assets according to the organizational unit they support.
- **Sensitivity** Usually ascribed to information, sensitivity relates to the nature and content of that information. Sensitivity usually applies in two ways: to an individual, where the information is considered personal or private, and to an organization, where the information may be considered a trade secret. Sometimes sensitivity is somewhat subjective and arbitrary, but often it is defined in laws and regulations.

- **Regulation**   For organizations that are required to follow government and other legal obligations regarding the processing and protection of information, it will be useful to include data points that indicate whether specific assets are considered in scope for specific regulations. This is important because some regulations specify how assets should be protected, so it's useful to be aware of this during risk analysis and risk treatment.

There is no need to choose which of these methods will be used to classify assets. Instead, an IT analyst should collect several points of metadata about each asset (including location, process supported, and organizational unit supported). This will enable the security manager to sort and filter the list of assets in various ways to understand which assets are in a given location or which support a particular process or part of the business.

   TIP   Organizations should consider managing information about assets in a fixed-assets application.

Why Asset Management Is Control #1
The well-known control framework Critical Security Controls, produced by the Center for Internet Security (commonly known as the *CIS 20*), lists hardware asset inventory as the first control. I believe there is a specific purpose to this: an organization cannot protect assets that it does not know about.

Administrative Safeguards
Within an information security program, administrative safeguards take the form of information security policy, security and IT standards, and other statements that define security-related roles, responsibilities, and other expected outcomes.

Security Policy
Information security policy is a foundational component of any organization's security program and a necessary prerequisite to an organization's privacy program. Security policy defines the principles and required actions for the organization to protect its assets and personnel properly.

The audience for security policy is the organization's personnel—not only full-time and part-time employees, but also temporary workers, including contractors and consultants. Security policy must be easily accessible by all personnel so that they can never offer ignorance as an excuse for violating policy. To this point, many organizations require all personnel to acknowledge the existence of, and their understanding of, the organization's security policy at the time of hire and annually thereafter.

Security policy cannot be developed in a vacuum. Instead, it needs to align with a number of internal and external factors. The development of policy needs to incorporate several considerations, including the following:

- Applicable laws, regulations, standards, and other legal obligations
- Risk tolerance
- Controls
- Organizational culture

Alignment with Controls   Security policy and controls need to be in alignment. This is not to say that there must be a control for every policy or a policy for every control. However, policies and controls must not contradict each other. For example, if one control states that no personally owned mobile devices may connect to internal networks, then another policy cannot state that those devices may be used provided no corporate information is stored on them.

 NOTE   An extensive discussion of controls is included in *CISM Certified Information Security Manager All-In-One Exam Guide.*

Alignment with the Audience   Security policy needs to align with the audience. In most organizations, this means that policy statements need to be understood by the majority of workers. A common mistake in the development of security policy is the inclusion of highly technical policies such as permitted encryption algorithms or statements about the hardening of servers. Such topics are irrelevant to most workers. The danger of including policies that are irrelevant to most workers is that they are likely to "tune out" and not pay attention to those policies that *are* applicable to them. In other words, security policy should have a high signal-to-noise ratio.

In organizations with extensive technology use, one avenue is to create a general security policy intended for all workers (technical and nontechnical) and a separate policy for technical workers who design, build, and maintain information systems. Another alternative is to create a general security policy for all workers that includes a policy stating that all controls are mandatory. Either approach would be sufficient by aligning messages about policy with various audiences.

Security Policy Structure   Several different topics are included in a security policy, including the following:

- Acceptable use of organization assets
- Mobile devices
- Protection of information and assets
- Access control and passwords
- Personally owned devices

- Security incidents
- E-mail and other communications
- Social media
- Ethics and applicable laws
- Workplace safety
- Visitors
- Consequences of noncompliance
- Cloud computing
- Data exchange with third parties

Security managers are free to choose how to package these and other security policies. For example, they may exist in separate documents or all together in one document. There is no right or wrong here: a security manager should figure out what would work best in the organization by observing how other policies are structured and published.

Security policy statements should be general in nature and not cite specific devices, technologies, or configurations. Policy statements should state *what* is to be done (or not done) but not *how*. This way, security policies will be durable and will need to be changed infrequently. On the other hand, security standards and procedures may change more frequently as practices, techniques, and technologies change.

Policy Distribution and Acknowledgment   Security policy—indeed, all organization policy—should be well known and easily accessible by all workers. It may be published on a corporate intranet or other online location where workers go to obtain information about internal operations.

All workers need to be informed of the presence of the organization's security policy. The best method in most organizations is for a high-ranking executive to write a memo or an e-mail to all workers stating the importance of information security in the organization and informing them that the information security policy describes required behavior on the part of all workers. Another effective tactic is to have the senior executive record a message outlining the need for and importance of security policy. Additionally, the message should state that the executive leadership team has reviewed and fully supports the policies.

Executives need to be mindful that they lead by example. If executives carve out exceptions for themselves (for example, if an executive insists on using a personal tablet computer for company business when policy forbids it), other workers are apt to notice and take their own shortcuts wherever they're able. If executives visibly comply with security policy, others will too. Organizational culture includes behavior such as compliance to policy or a tendency for workers to skirt policy whenever possible.

Security and IT Standards

An organization's security and IT standards describe, in detail, the methods, techniques, technologies, specifications, brands, and configurations to be used throughout the organization.

As with the security policy, it is important that the privacy and security managers understand the breadth of coverage, strictness, compliance, and last review and update.

These tell the managers the extent to which an organization's security standards are used—if at all.

In addition to the aforementioned characteristics, it is important to know how the organization's standards were developed and how good they are. For instance, if there are device-hardening standards, and whether they are aligned to or derived from industry-recognized standards such as CIS, National Institute for Standards and Technology (NIST), European Union Agency for Network and Information Security (ENISA), Defense Information Systems Agency Security Technical Implementation Guides (DISA STIG), or others.

Similarly, it is important to know whether standards are highly detailed (configuration item by configuration item) or whether they are principle-based. If they are the latter, engineers may exercise potentially wide latitude when implementing these standards. You should understand that highly detailed standards are not necessarily better than principle-based standards; their worth depends on the nature of the organization, its risk tolerance, and its maturity.

Guidelines

Guidelines are statements that help organization personnel better understand how to implement or comply with policies and standards. Although an organization's guidelines are not "the law" per se, the presence of guidelines may signal a higher than average maturity. Many organizations don't get any further than creating policies and standards, so the presence of proper guidelines means that the organization may have (or had, in the past) sufficient resources or prioritization to make documenting guidance on policies important enough to do.

According to their very nature, guidelines are typically written for personnel who need a little extra help on how to adhere to policies.

Like other types of security program documents, guidelines should be reviewed and updated regularly. Because guidelines bridge rarely changing policy with often-changing technologies and practices, a strategist examining guidelines should find them being changed frequently—or they may be found to be irrelevant. That, too, is possibly evidence of an attempt to improve maturity or communications (or both) but with the absence of long-term commitment.

Privacy and Security by Design

Privacy and security by design is a concept that reinforces the need to incorporate privacy and security considerations into systems and applications as a standard practice. In other words, the product is designed with privacy and security as a priority, along with whatever other functional purposes the product delivers.

Privacy by design is based on seven foundational principles:

- **Proactive, not reactive; preventive, not remedial**   The privacy by design approach is characterized by proactive rather than reactive measures. It anticipates and prevents privacy-invasive events before they happen. Privacy by design does not wait for privacy risks to materialize, and it does not offer remedies for resolving privacy infractions once they have occurred; instead, it aims to prevent them from occurring.

- **Privacy embedded into design**   Privacy by design is embedded into the design and architecture of IT systems as well as business practices. It is not bolted on as an add-on, after the fact. The result is that privacy becomes an essential component of the core functionality being delivered. Privacy is integral to the system without diminishing its functionality.

- **Privacy as the default setting**   Privacy by default seeks to deliver the maximum degree of privacy by ensuring that personal data is automatically protected in any given IT system or business practice. If an individual does nothing to protect her privacy, it should still remain intact. No action should be required on the part of the individual to protect her individual privacy.

- **Full functionality—positive-sum, not zero-sum**   Privacy by design seeks to accommodate all legitimate interests and objectives in a positive-sum "win-win" manner, not through a dated, zero-sum approach, where unnecessary trade-offs are made. Privacy by design avoids the pretense of false dichotomies, such as privacy versus security, demonstrating that it is possible to have both.

- **End-to-end security—full life-cycle protection**   Privacy by design, having been embedded into the system prior to the first element of information being collected, extends securely throughout the entire life cycle of the data involved— strong security measures are essential to privacy, from start to finish. This ensures that all data is securely retained and then securely destroyed at the end of the process, in a timely fashion. Thus, privacy by design ensures cradle-to-grave, secure life-cycle management of information, end to end.

- **Visibility and transparency—keep it open**   Privacy by design seeks to assure all stakeholders that whatever the business practice or technology involved, it is, in fact, operating according to the stated promises and objectives, subject to independent verification. Its component parts and operations remain visible and transparent to users and providers alike.

- **Respect for user privacy—keep it user-centric**   Privacy by design requires architects and administrators to keep the interests of the individual uppermost by offering such measures as strong privacy defaults, appropriate notice, and user-friendly empowerment options.

It is essential that business application architectures, designs, data flows, and configurations all contribute to and support privacy and security. The SDLC represents the business processes used to develop, maintain, and operate business applications, and it must include steps to ensure that new information systems and changes to existing information systems do not impact security and privacy in unexpected ways. Policies and standards must also contribute to and support security and privacy principles to ensure that personal information is adequately protected and properly used. Ongoing operations must likewise ensure that the security and privacy of systems are not compromised and that continuous monitoring is employed to detect security and privacy incidents early so that they may be contained.

Integrating Privacy into Organization Operations

Privacy principles and practices need to permeate throughout the organization in the form of a lifestyle of awareness and protection of personal information. While privacy plays a dominant role in IT and information security functions, it's vital elsewhere as well. This section describes privacy practices throughout the organization.

 NOTE These are examples of organization functions where privacy awareness and practices are important. This should not be considered a complete list.

Information Security

Information security is a foundation piece of privacy. Without it, privacy has only the "proper use" principle without the "information protection" principle.

Information security must be privacy-aware in the following key areas:

- **Logging and monitoring** Event logs created by applications, database management systems, business applications, and operating systems should not contain full data subject information except where specifically required. For instance, full bank account or credit card numbers should not be included in security event alerts sent to a SIEM.

- **Software and systems development** Privacy requirements derived from applicable laws and privacy policy should be included in functional and nonfunctional requirements. Like other requirements, privacy requirements should be verifiable through systematic testing.

- **Security incident response** Incident response proceedings and records should not contain full data subject details except where required by law; otherwise, the business records created in the security incident response process would themselves be subject to privacy requirements.

- **Identity and access management** Data at the core of identity and access management systems contains names and other details about data subjects, whether employees, customers, or constituents. All this data should be considered in scope for applicable privacy laws and internal privacy policy. Identity and access management practices are described in more detail earlier in this chapter.

IT Development and Operations

IT is the core of information processing in organizations. Although the IT department itself may be distributed, and though there may be a degree of shadow IT and citizen IT, business rules in the form of privacy and security requirements must be a core tenet of the development and operations of all IT systems. If privacy and security by design are not a part of IT culture, then IT will either be using significant resources to retrofit systems or the organization is going to be in a sorry state of noncompliance to privacy laws, security laws, and societal norms.

Security and privacy requirements must align with applicable laws and other legal obligations, and they must be a part of every systems acquisition and development effort. Doing any less will send the organization on a slippery backslide into noncompliance and its consequences.

Business Continuity and Disaster Recovery Planning

Business continuity and disaster recovery (BCDR) planning work hand-in-hand to ensure the organization's survival despite minor or major disruptive events. At its heart, BCDR ensures business resilience through the implementation of resilient infrastructure and emergency response and operations plans to keep key business processes operating before, during, and after a disaster.

BCDR requirements and operations cannot surrender ground when it comes to the protection and proper use of personal information. Although key business processes and information systems may operate with reduced capacity or features during a disaster, the protection of personal information cannot be reduced. Audits of BCDR plans and records will help to confirm whether BCDR plans ensure the protection of personal information as they should.

Mergers, Acquisitions, Divestitures

Mergers, acquisitions, and divestitures (MAD) are transactions in which one organization is combining with another (in the case of a merger or acquisition) or breaking into two or more organizations (in the case of a divestiture). These transactions are generally orchestrated by the organization's most senior executives and board members. Privacy and security leaders are often not involved until later in transaction negotiations, and they are sometimes not informed until the transaction has closed.

Privacy and security leaders need to be in a position of influence in all MAD transactions. Doing so requires a high level of trust among other executives.

 NOTE This topic is discussed in more detail in Chapter 3.

Human Resources

Human resources, or HR, is a corporate function responsible for the administration of hiring, internal transfers, and termination of employees. HR departments generally perform the roles of performance review, salary administration, benefits administration, career development, and training. All of the records for these and other activities are managed by HR in one or more systems known as a human resources information system (HRIS) or a human capital management (HCM) system.

Sensitive Employment Data

Whether stored piecemeal or in an HRIS or HCM, human resources has under its control a significant amount of sensitive information about all of the employees in an organization, including

- **Contact information**   Residential address, phone numbers, personal e-mail
- **Government IDs**   Driver's license or passport number
- **Financial**   Compensation information, bank account numbers
- **Behavioral**   Records concerning performance and discipline
- **Medical**   Records concerning healthcare benefits and possibly the healthcare records themselves
- **Background**   Records concerning education, prior employment, financial history, references, and criminal activity

Organizations must take great care to protect these records from misuse and compromise.

Prior to the enactment of modern privacy laws, many organizations implemented protection and proper-use principles concerning their HR records that were not unlike the provisions of privacy laws. In many cases, organizations need look no further than HR to observe privacy principles in practice.

NOTE   In the United States, the records concerning healthcare benefits are considered in scope for the Health Insurance Portability and Accountability Act (HIPAA).

Support of Information Security

The accuracy, completeness, and integrity of HR information are key for information security, primarily its identity and access management processes and systems. Information security considers the HRIS or HCM system as the official system of record for the organization's workforce and will often integrate HRIS/HCM systems with identity management systems for efficiency and accuracy.

At the time of hire and periodically thereafter, an organization's HR department will administer employees' written acknowledgment of key policies, including ethics, harassment, privacy, and security. Information security and privacy leaders also count on HR to carry out disciplinary action when security, privacy, and other policies are violated in order to maintain a practice of consistent and fair policy enforcement. HR generally maintains discipline-related records.

EXAM TIP   Accurate human resource recordkeeping is critical for identity and access management processes, to ensure that only authorized personnel are able to access data subjects' personal information. You're expected to know of the forms and importance of recordkeeping for the exam.

Temporary Workers

On account of the 1999 Microsoft Contingent Worker's Lawsuit, HR organizations often refuse to be the steward of business records concerning temporary workers, contractors, and other workers that are not full-time employees. This complicates security-related processes such as identity and access management and policy enforcement.

HRIS and HCM systems are now capable of managing temporary workers separately from employees. As a result, HR departments are once again considering managing the temporary workers' records. Because a generation of HR leaders have worked under the regime of temporary workers being managed outside of HR, the adoption is slowly gaining ground.

Compliance and Ethics

Compliance and ethics functions in organizations intersect in two ways. First, the compliance function is often the driving force that facilitates efforts to comply with various laws and regulations, including privacy and information security. Second, the ethics function often maintains an information store that includes the record of employees' acknowledgment to ethics or "code of conduct" policies, as well as recordkeeping for "whistleblower" events. All such records are highly sensitive (sometimes meeting the definition of personally identifiable information) and must be closely managed.

Audit

The audit function in an organization examines selected business processes to ensure that they are being managed properly and that they are effective. An organization's audit leader will determine which business processes to examine in any given year based upon several factors, primarily compliance and risk. The compliance driver is associated with ensuring that an organization is compliant with specific industry-related regulations, and the risk driver brings audit scrutiny to those business processes that warrant more attention.

Audit records are almost always considered highly sensitive, and often they contain personally identifiable information when auditors are collecting business records' evidence in the course of their audits. Auditors generally maintain audit records on purpose-built information systems or on tightly controlled storage systems.

 NOTE Audit is explored in detail in Chapter 5.

Marketing

An organization's marketing function undertakes various efforts, called campaigns, to inform persons and organizations of its goods and services. A marketing department will perform many activities, including

- Development of product or service names and descriptions
- Determining product or service pricing and terms
- Creating advertising content

Marketing and privacy intersect where marketing is developing direct marketing campaigns in which the organization sends information to selected individuals. Direct marketing involves several channels, including but not limited to telephone, texts, e-mail, web site advertisements, flyers, and postal mail.

The recipients of direct marketing messaging consist of current customers and other individuals that have been preselected. Current customers generally provide their contact information as a part of purchase transactions.

To reach individuals who are not current customers, organizations generally obtain lists of desired customers from information brokers that sell these lists based on targeted characteristics of individuals, such as age, address, income, and others.

Prior to the enactment of privacy laws, marketing departments had nearly carte blanche autonomy to develop any and every kind of direct marketing campaigns. Because privacy laws in part target direct marketing, organizations need to review applicable privacy laws and their own privacy policies carefully to ensure the compliance of all direct marketing activities.

NOTE Abuses in direct marketing practices have led to the enactment of today's privacy laws.

Business Development

An organization's business development function is tasked with identifying and developing new business opportunities in the form of relationships and partnerships to ensure the continued growth of the organization. Business development often performs feasibility studies to determine the potential benefit of a new product or service developed internally or with an external party.

Privacy and security leaders should be involved in the development or review of feasibility studies to ensure that privacy and security risks are identified. Involving privacy and security early reduces the probability of privacy- or security-related surprises that may influence or invalidate a business case.

Privacy and security leaders need to earn a high level of trust in order to be involved in business development. Successful involvement in business development comes in the form of collaboration and exploration to figure out how to ensure the success of a new business endeavor. This is opposed to the reputation of privacy and security professionals who instead attempt to halt specific business development efforts because of the presence of privacy- or security-related risks.

NOTE In business development, privacy and security leaders should assume the role of facilitators rather than that of gatekeepers.

Public Relations

An organization's public relations (PR) function is tasked with keeping customers, regulators, partners, and the general public informed of activities and developments in the organization. The mission of PR is to influence the perception of the organization.

A PR department often maintains a list of contacts to which communications are directed. Such a list would include journalists, regulators, and other interested parties. Often these lists will be considered in scope of privacy laws, requiring their protection and management of their use.

Public relations may play a role in privacy and security incident response in situations where communications to outside parties are required. Often this is in the form of established relationships with key parties as well as prewritten press releases and other material. Contact lists curated by PR should be considered in scope for privacy policy and controls and treated accordingly.

Procurement and Sourcing

An organization's procurement and sourcing functions are responsible for managing the acquisition of products and services. These functions perform a number of activities, including the following:

- **Issuing requests for information and requests for proposals**   Requests for information (RFIs) and requests for proposal (RFPs) are solicitations to product and service providers to help the organization better understand the providers' products and services. Procurement and sourcing will often include functional and nonfunctional requirements on many topics, including information security and privacy.

- **Management of requirements**   As discussed earlier, procurement and sourcing will collect and manage requirements on many topics to be used when tasked with acquiring new products and services. Privacy and security requirements should align with applicable privacy and security laws, as well as with internal policies and controls, so that new products and services contribute to the organization's compliance.

- **Contract negotiations**   Procurement and sourcing is often involved in the parts of contract negotiations that are related to product or service terms, conditions, pricing, and compliance with privacy and security requirements. The legal department usually takes the lead on contracts and will manage all other components of a contract.

Legal and Contracts

An organization's legal department consists of one or more attorneys and has responsibility for several important functions, including these:

- **Interpretation of laws and regulations**   A primary role of a legal department is the interpretation of laws and regulations, including the determination of applicability.

- **Policy**   The legal department generally approves all corporate policies developed by different departments. In the contact of privacy, this will include security policy as well as internal and external privacy policies.

- **Legal contracts**   The legal department takes the lead on all contracts between the organization and outside parties. Procurement and sourcing, when involved, will have managed pricing as well as terms and conditions related to the product or service being acquired.

- **Insurance**   The legal department often leads efforts related to insurance policies, including cyber-risk policies.

- **Compliance**   Through its involvement with policy, contracts, and insurance, a legal department is often considered a key role in an organization's overall compliance.

- **Business risk**   The legal department is often thought of as an organization's business risk manager, through the management of policies, contracts, and insurance.

- **Incident response**   The legal department plays a key role in privacy and security incident response, primarily in decisions on whether and when (and how) to involve external parties, including regulators, law enforcement, and affected persons.

Many organizations lack legal expertise on all relevant topics. A common approach involves the establishment of legal retainer relationships with outside legal counsel with expertise in areas of occasional concern to the organization.

Security and Emergency Services

An organization's security and emergency services department is concerned with the protection of work centers and processing centers, as well as response to security-related matters that occur there. Generally, the nexus of privacy with these services is related to two main areas: contact information for security and emergency response personnel, and business records containing incident descriptions and the names of involved persons. Although the volume of information related to these activities may be low in comparison to the organization's workforce and its customers, the personal information held in security and emergency services business records must be kept confidential and used for no other purposes.

Finance

An organization's financial records will contain the names of accounting department personnel as well as outsiders, including persons to whom payments are sent and those who work in vendor organizations. As is the case with business records in other parts of an organization, the identities of persons whose names and other information appears in financial records should be kept confidential and used for no other purposes.

In most circumstances, organizations are required by law to retain detailed financial records for many years. The names of persons are a part of these records. Subject data requests concerning financial records may request corrections or even removal; in most cases, these requests cannot be granted as doing so would violate laws concerning the completeness, integrity, and retention of financial records.

Other Functions

Organizations often have business activities in areas or functions not listed in this section. Business records throughout the organization may contain subject names for one reason or another. In all cases, the principles of privacy and security apply: protection and proper use. An organization's security and privacy policies should apply to information created or used in all departments regardless of its use. All such data stores should be included in an information catalog so that privacy, security, and information management personnel include them in routine data management and protection activities.

Other Protection Measures

Privacy managers need to understand the full range of information protection techniques. A key tenet of data protection is the concept of keeping data for the shortest possible period of time, thereby reducing overall risk in terms of the numbers of records present at any given time. And when information is no longer needed, destruction techniques ensure that data cannot be reconstituted by anyone.

This section follows with discussions about organizations and individuals sharing data with others and the need for visibility and control of these sharing events. This section concludes with a discussion on quantifying the costs of information protection.

Data Retention and Archiving

Organizations are accustomed to retaining data for very long periods, often in perpetuity. For generations, the risks associated with long-term data retention have been quite low. Digital transformation has changed all of that: with business functions implemented in a workflow and records retained online, sensitive data such as personal information can be used, misused, abused, stolen, and subsequently monetized in numerous ways by cyber-criminals, bringing potential and real harm to affected persons. The practice of data retention involves the management of a data retention schedule that determines the amount of time that various types of business records should be retained in an organization.

Today, the liability of excess data retention is being felt: executives are beginning to understand that retaining certain types of records represents risk. This realization results in a greater emphasis on establishing data retention schedules to limit how long organizations retain sensitive information.

Industry Data Retention Laws

Privacy and security professionals need to work with business unit leaders and legal counsel to determine appropriate data retention periods for various data types. Often, there are laws on the context of said data that need to be identified and understood.

For instance, nation, state, or provincial laws specify that organizations must retain employment HR records throughout an employee's length of employment, plus several years afterward. Financial services and banking laws similarly have similar requirements for minimum retention periods for retaining financial transaction data.

Right to Be Forgotten

The General Data Protection Regulation (GDPR), California Consumer Privacy Act (CCPA), and other privacy laws give data subjects a "right to be forgotten." Generally, data subjects can request that their data be removed. Still, such requests can be granted only to the extent that an organization can remove such information without violating other laws that specify that information be retained. For example, Fred was unceremoniously fired from his job at Best State Bank. Thinking he could improve his employment prospects elsewhere, Fred asked Best State Bank to remove his employment record data under the "right to be forgotten" concept in applicable privacy laws. However, Best State Bank refused to fulfill the request, citing employment laws that require that all employment records be retained for the length of employment, plus seven years after the end of employment relationships.

Data Archiving

In the early years of computing, archiving meant that data was copied to magnetic tapes, and those tapes were kept in a vault for many years. Nowadays, with low data storage costs, organizations are apt to retain some data in perpetuity, particularly business transactions and records about employees and customers. However, the risks associated with long-term retention have compelled organizations to consider alternatives, including *data archiving,* the process of preparing data for long-term storage.

In instances where organizations are bound by specific laws to retain data for many years, archiving is a viable opportunity for removing data from online transaction systems to other systems or media.

The terms "online," "nearline," and "offline" connote approaches to archiving. Data that is online remains in a primary processing system along with current records. Data that is nearline may exist in a different system such as a data warehouse and can be accessed in the data warehouse or even returned to the primary transaction processing and storage system for a time. Offline data generally resides in another form such as backup media, whether tapes, a virtual tape library (VTL), or disk storage of some sort—but not in a form that is immediately available for normal processing.

Archiving may be a viable option for risk-averse organizations that want to be rid of their older records systems but where applicable laws require long-term storage of original records. In this case, techniques such as pseudonymization and anonymization may not be available options, since organizations are generally obligated to retain original information in business transactions, including subject names and other personal information.

The Data Retention Tug of War

Privacy professionals and business leaders are sometimes at odds with one another, particularly on data retention. The core of the conflict is this: Business leaders want to keep information for as long as possible, to mine every last inkling of value from collected information. On the other side, privacy professionals want data retained for the shortest possible time, if it is retained at all.

Neither side is entirely correct. Instead, business leaders and privacy professionals need to understand the facts, applicable laws, use cases, and options available to enable the organization to derive maximum value from its information, while applying techniques to reduce risks as much as possible.

Data Destruction

For all of an organization's efforts to ensure data availability, an equal amount of effort is required when it no longer needs to retain data even in adverse conditions. Data destruction is the purposeful act of destroying data so that it cannot be recovered. Data destruction is invoked as a part of two processes: data classification and handling, and data retention.

Data destruction policy should include directives for the safe removal of data in numerous use cases, including

- Electronic storage on a laptop computer, desktop computer, tablet computer, smartphone, or USB drive
- Electronic storage on a server
- Electronic storage on a file server
- Electronic storage on a hard disk drive (HDD) or a solid-state drive (SSD)
- Stored as a record in a database management system
- Stored as a record in a business application
- Stored on backup media
- Stored on printed paper

The rigor used to destroy data safely should depend upon the sensitivity of the data being destroyed and a risk or threat assessment that helps determine the extent to which an adversary would attempt to reconstitute discarded or destroyed data.

Data Sharing and Disclosure

It is said that sensitive information does not provide value until it is collected, used, and reused. The use and reuse of information occur when it is shared and subsequently used. However, privacy laws and emerging privacy practices are putting controls around the sharing and subsequent use of information. It is still possible and often profitable to share and reuse information, but in light of privacy laws, this sharing and reuse is monitored and controlled so that management has a say in these activities.

Data sharing takes place on two levels:

- **Sharing unstructured data in a storage system**   Individuals in an organization share the contents of individual files and directories with others in the organization, and sometimes with persons outside the organization. The ability for individuals to share data needs to be restricted to persons familiar with these responsibilities. Further, sharing activities need to be logged and acted upon when they exceed norms or violate policy. Every organization must define these thresholds based on numerous factors, such as the sensitivity and volume of data being shared, security and privacy policy, and management's risk tolerance. Many variables need to be sorted out so that reasonable and actionable business rules can be developed and managed.

- **Sharing structured data in intra- and inter-company arrangements** Management makes business decisions to share specific data sets within the organization or externally to other organizations. These decisions are often motivated by monetization objectives to contribute to an organization's bottom line. Intercompany data sharing is a prime focus of privacy laws, so all such arrangements should require approval at the highest levels.

Costs of Technical Controls

Management may, at times, wonder about the costs expended to protect information and ensure its proper handling: Is our security or privacy program worth its cost? What does it cost our organization to comply with specific privacy or security laws? These questions are often easier asked than answered for reasons that include the following:

- **Blended costs**   Any given software as a service (SaaS) application includes privacy and security features and controls such as event monitoring, forensics, and response. The trouble is that SaaS services rarely, if ever, break out the costs of privacy and security in their fees. If they did, would you use those figures or other arbitrary amounts?

- **Bundled features**   Numerous IT products, including but not limited to network devices, operating systems, and database management systems, include capabilities that facilitate privacy and security capabilities. However, like SaaS applications, the proportion of total cost that represents privacy or security is elusive.

- **Feature utilization**   Continuing the preceding point, if it were possible to know the proportion of the cost of a product allocated to security or privacy, the next hurdle in this thought experiment is related to the use of security and privacy features in IT products. For example, if an organization arbitrarily allocates 20 percent of the cost of a network router to security, and the organization emphasizes security in its network, then should the 20 percent figure be increased to some higher value?

- **Privacy and security controls**   Another thought experiment targeting the costs allocated to privacy and security is related to the effort expended to operate privacy and security controls. Take, for example, controls related to identity and access management. As an extreme example, an organization that believes that it spends zero dollars on security still has to spend time creating and managing user accounts, because information systems are designed in a way that requires identity and access management efforts to create user accounts. Thus, can an organization that has applications with user accounts really say it spends no money on security?

- **Staff compensation**   Measuring the time that IT and other personnel spend on privacy and security is an achievable endeavor, but it requires effort to reach the correct conclusions. This is partly because security and privacy are parts of many workers' jobs, whether or not "security" and "privacy" are mentioned in their job descriptions. For instance, security is probably not 100 percent of a security engineer's job, nor is security 0 percent of a system engineer's job. Realistic estimates are only a little better than outright guesses and may be clouded by biases as well as arbitrary statements about which activities are security-related or privacy-related.

- **Benchmarking**   Many organizations wonder what percentage of total IT spend is devoted to security or to privacy. In the past, it was easier to answer this. Nowadays, with organizations using SaaS and other cloud services, many IT costs aren't included in IT's budgets, and many security and privacy costs are even harder to identify and allocate. Today, many organization departments "do IT" but don't have an IT budget per se. Instead, their IT work is buried (not intentionally) within other operational budgets.

What is possible in an organization is the tracking of costs for specific activities and services, including tracking spending from one budget year to the next. It may be possible to understand whether the costs of security and privacy measures are increasing if consistent means are used to track different kinds of costs.

Management can also ask the opposite question: What is the potential cost if we don't implement privacy or security in the organization? This is no easier determined than the costs of controls, because when estimating the consequences for the lack of controls, it is also necessary to estimate the probability of costly events that their lack would permit. For instance, what is the statistical probability for a ransomware attack to occur in different types of organizations? The risk factors are numerous and difficult to quantify.

It should be clear by now that privacy is not just an IT and information security function. Management and execution of a privacy program and activities require buy-in and support from all levels of an organization. As the speed of business continues to accelerate with the use of technology and privacy regulations continue to evolve, the ability to identify and control personal information will continue to be at the forefront of business concerns so that organizations can build sustainable privacy and security programs that can adapt to future requirements.

Chapter Review

Information privacy is wholly dependent upon cybersecurity for the protection of personal information. While cybersecurity is generally performed by others, privacy managers should be familiar with numerous information security practices that support their programs.

Identity and access management comprises a collection of activities in an organization that is concerned with controlling and monitoring individuals' access to information systems containing sensitive and personal information.

Vulnerability management is the practice of periodically examining information systems to discover exploitable vulnerabilities, related analyses, and decisions about remediation.

The practice of *patch management,* a part of vulnerability management, ensures that IT systems, tools, and applications have consistent version and patch levels.

Incident response represents a set of activities focused on activities that are initiated when certain events or conditions occur.

IT service management (ITSM) is the set of activities that ensures that the delivery of IT services is efficient and effective, through active management and the continuous improvement of processes.

Information security policy is a foundational component of any organization's security program and a necessary prerequisite to an organization's privacy program. Security policy defines the principles and required actions for the organization to protect its assets and personnel properly.

An organization's security and IT *standards* describe, in detail, the methods, techniques, technologies, specifications, brands, and configurations to be used throughout the organization.

Guidelines are statements that help organization personnel better understand how to implement or comply with policies and standards.

Privacy and security by design is a concept that reinforces the need to have privacy and security considerations incorporated into systems and applications as a standard practice.

Key areas where information security must be privacy-aware include logging and monitoring, software and systems development, security incident response, identity and access management, and business continuity and disaster recovery planning.

Privacy principles and policies should be integrated into many facets of organizations and their activities, including human resources, compliance and ethics, audit, marketing and business development, public relations, procurement and sourcing, legal and contracts, security and emergency services, finance, and mergers, acquisitions, and divestitures.

The practice of *data retention* involves the management of a *data retention schedule* that determines the amount of time that various types of business records should be retained in an organization.

Data destruction is the purposeful act of destroying data so that it cannot be recovered.

Organizations should develop the ability to monitor and control data sharing and data disclosure events.

Quick Review

- More than 90 percent of successful cyberattacks begin with social engineering, when personnel in an organization are tricked into performing actions that enable an adversary to attack the organization successfully.

- Vulnerabilities are the weaknesses that may be present in a system and that enable a threat to be more easily carried out or to have greater impact.

- Privacy managers need to understand the differences in meaning among the terms *identification, authentication,* and *authorization.*

- The *common vulnerability scoring system* (CVSS) is an open framework that is used to provide a common methodology for scoring vulnerabilities.

- Privacy principles and practices need to permeate throughout the organization in the form of a lifestyle of awareness and protection of personal information. Though privacy plays a dominant role in IT and information security functions, it's vital elsewhere as well.

- Organizations need to reconcile data retention and data minimization practices.

- Determination of the cost of privacy and security controls is difficult because information systems and business processes blend privacy, security, and operations activities in varying proportions.

Questions

1. The purpose of vulnerability management is to:
   A. Identify and remediate vulnerabilities in all systems.
   B. Transfer vulnerabilities to low-risk systems.
   C. Identify exploitable vulnerabilities in all systems.
   D. Transfer vulnerabilities to third parties.

2. A privacy manager has written a procedure in which the password for a system has been divided into two parts, each given to separate persons. This practice is an example of:
   A. Split custody
   B. Dual control
   C. Segregation of duties
   D. Twin secrecy

3. All of the following threats are reduced through the use of multifactor authentication except:
   A. Dictionary attacks
   B. Password replay attacks
   C. Keyloggers
   D. User ID replay attacks

4. In an organization whose IT environment is entirely cloud-based, what purpose does a VPN serve?

   A. Blocks command-and-control traffic

   B. Prevents malware from executing

   C. Provides defense in depth authentication

   D. Protects traffic from eavesdroppers

5. When logging in to an application, a user has provided a user ID and clicked the Next button. What has the user performed at this point?

   A. Assertion

   B. Authentication

   C. Identification

   D. Captcha

6. The activity consisting of the use of tools to identify security defects on systems is known as:

   A. Vulnerability management

   B. Vulnerability scanning

   C. Patch management

   D. Penetration testing

7. The IT process concerned with the review and approval of alterations to IT systems is known as:

   A. Change management

   B. Problem management

   C. Configuration management

   D. Defect management

8. The IT process that is often considered the cornerstone of tactical security management is:

   A. Change management

   B. Asset management

   C. Configuration management

   D. Incident management

9. All of the following are deemed administrative safeguards except:

   A. Privileged access controls

   B. Security policy

   C. Privacy policy

   D. Security standards

10. The practice of incorporating security and privacy into business processes is known as:

   A. Security and privacy requirements development

   B. Security and privacy awareness training

   C. Security and privacy policy

   D. Security and privacy by design

11. By integrating privacy and security into business continuity planning, an organization ensures that:

   A. Processes related to personal information are given priority for restoration.

   B. Personal information protection and valid use continues to be the norm.

   C. Processes related to personal information are more resilient.

   D. Privacy and security are the most important characteristics of business processes.

12. Which of the following statements regarding information in an HRIS is true?

   A. Data in an HRIS system should be classified at the lowest level.

   B. Data in an HRIS system should be classified at the highest level.

   C. Data in an HRIS system is generally considered in scope for privacy laws.

   D. Data in an HRIS system is generally considered out of scope for privacy laws.

13. In the context of privacy laws, the purpose of data retention schedules is:

   A. Develop means for automatic removal of personal information.

   B. Retain personal information for the longest possible time.

   C. Retain personal information for the shortest possible time.

   D. Develop procedures for manual removal of personal information.

14. Which of the following techniques is most suitable for the removal of expired records in a large database management system?

   A. Removal of specific rows

   B. Degaussing

   C. Shredding

   D. Deleting

15. In a large multiuser file storage system, instances of directories and files shared by users with other parties should be:

   A. Permitted

   B. Investigated

   C. Prohibited

   D. Monitored

Answers

1. **A.** The purpose of vulnerability management is to identify vulnerabilities in information systems and devices and to remediate vulnerabilities on a schedule according to risk.

2. **A.** Split custody is an arrangement whereby one person controls part of a password, and another person controls another part. Each person is required to perform a procedure that completes the entire password.

3. **D.** Multifactor authentication does not reduce the threat of user ID replay attacks. It reduces or eliminates the threats of dictionary attacks, password replay attacks, and keyloggers.

4. **D.** A VPN connection is encrypted, thus preventing any party from eavesdropping on the connection.

5. **C.** When a user has presented only a user ID, the user is said to have identified himself. The user is not authenticated until he successfully presents a correct password and potentially performs an additional step of multifactor authentication.

6. **B.** Vulnerability scanning is the use of tools to perform scans to identify security defects—often in the form of missing patches and configuration errors—on systems in a network.

7. **A.** Change management is the IT process whereby changes to IT systems are proposed, reviewed, analyzed, approved, performed, verified, and recorded.

8. **B.** Asset management is considered a cornerstone process, without which other processes such as vulnerability management, event management, and change management cannot be effective.

9. **A.** Privileged access controls are considered detective and/or preventive safeguards. Security policy, privacy policy, and security standards (among others) are considered administrative safeguards.

10. **D.** Security and privacy by design is the culture of including security and privacy in business processes, particularly those in which innovation occurs.

11. **B.** When privacy and security are incorporated into business continuity and disaster recovery planning, the protection of personal information and safeguards to enforce proper use of personal information will be a part of business contingency and disaster recovery procedures.

12. **C.** Data in a human resources information system (HRIS) includes numerous types of personal information about an organization's workforce. For the most part, privacy laws consider this personal information to be subject to those laws.

13. **C.** Data retention schedules specify the period of time that various types of business records should be retained. Generally, data containing personal information should be kept for only as long as necessary and no longer.

14. A. The only practical way to remove expired data from a large database management system is to delete the rows that have expired. Other techniques are ineffective or not applicable.

15. D. File and directory sharing actions in a file storage system should be logged and monitored for violations of policy. Many sharing actions will be considered appropriate, but some may warrant investigation.

Privacy Operational Lifecycle: Sustain

In this chapter, you will learn about
- Privacy and security program and systems monitoring
- Data loss prevention–based privacy monitoring
- Control self-assessment
- External development monitoring
- Privacy programs and practices auditing

This chapter covers the Certified Information Privacy Manager job practice V, "Privacy Operational Lifecycle: Sustain." The domain represents approximately 9 percent of the CIPM examination.

Sustainment of a privacy program requires continuous observation and periodic examination of privacy and security business processes. Continuous observation comes in the form of process and system monitoring. The nature of privacy and security also requires that monitoring of external developments be instituted.

Examinations of privacy and security processes take the form of audits performed internally or by external parties that conform to audit practices and standards. Organizations can take their destinies into their own hands by instituting control self-assessments, in which control owners take a more active role in the assurance of control effectiveness.

Monitoring and audits of privacy and security programs help to reveal weaknesses and deficiencies in business processes and information systems that can be subsequently corrected.

Monitoring a Privacy Program

Privacy program monitoring represents a continual observation of the program's business processes and supporting information systems to ensure that they perform as expected. Because privacy depends heavily upon information security, and in turn, that information security relies upon IT service management, all of these fundamental components must be monitored.

Business Process Monitoring

Monitoring business processes consists of the collection of statistics created by business processes, subsequently examining these statistics, transforming statistics into key risk and key performance indicators, and reporting these indicators to management.

To determine what needs to be monitored, you need look no further than to the slate of privacy business processes. Each and all processes must be measured so that management can know how many different types of events—those that are expected and those that are not—may occur in a given reporting period.

Privacy Program Monitoring

Some of the types of program- and process-level monitoring that can be monitored include

- Privacy impact assessments, discussed in detail in Chapter 3
- Data subject requests, discussed in detail in Chapter 3
- Privacy incidents, discussed in detail in Chapter 6
- Privacy policy violations, discussed in Chapter 6
- Privacy awareness training, including subjects trained and their competency quiz scores
- Audits completed and the numbers and types of findings, discussed later in this chapter
- Risk assessments and the numbers and types of findings, discussed in Chapter 3 and Appendix A; results of risk assessments will determine where monitoring should focus
- Privacy and security event monitoring, discussed in the next section

Privacy leaders need more than just the numbers—they need to elicit meaning from the numbers. For instance, if the number of completed data subject requests is trending downward, this could be the result of a shortage of privacy analysts to process them, or the trend could be attributed to staff training; however, it may actually represent backlash of upset customers over a change in privacy practices.

Some metrics can be transformed into key risk indicators (KRIs) or key performance indicators (KPIs). For instance, a downward trend in data subject requests may be considered a leading risk indicator that could be a harbinger of a decrease in customer renewals. Or the time required for the organization to detect and respond to a privacy incident may be used as a key performance indicator (KPI) that should trend down over time as the organization improves its detection and response capabilities.

Because many privacy processes are supported by information systems, numerous privacy process statistics can be derived from those systems. The next section delves into this topic.

Privacy and Security Event Monitoring

The logging of privacy- and security-related events, the centralized collection of these logs, and the proactive monitoring of these logs with correlation engines are considered essential cybersecurity and privacy practices. These activities help an organization detect an array of activities, from misbehavior by an employee to an active attack by a cyber-criminal organization.

Monitoring activities related to data access can help an organization identify improper uses of personal information. This monitoring activity is historically practiced by highly regulated organizations; however, more organizations are implementing this type of capability on account of new privacy laws such as the General Data Protection Regulation (GDPR), California Consumer Privacy Act (CCPA), and California Privacy Rights Act (CPRA).

Event monitoring is the practice of examining the events occurring on information systems—including applications, operating systems, database management systems, end-user devices, file servers, and every type and kind of network device—and being aware of what is going on throughout the entire operating environment. The types of events of interest to privacy and security managers include the following:

- Successful and unsuccessful logins
- Unexpected system or device reboots
- Changes made to security configurations
- Changes made to operating system files
- Queries to databases
- Changes made to access permissions of sensitive files containing personal information on a file server
- Anomalous movement of sensitive files containing personal information

Historically, it was considered sufficient to review system event logs on a daily basis. Mainly this entailed a review of yesterday's events (or the weekend's events on a Monday) to ensure that no privacy or security incidents warranted further investigation. Those days are mostly gone, however. Today, most organizations perform *real-time event monitoring*. This means organizations need to have systems in place that will immediately inform them if events are occurring anyplace in the environment that warrant attention.

Although the technology available today that enables real-time event monitoring is impressive, the vast amounts of information that are collected and analyzed can create meaningless alerts if the systems are not correctly tuned. Staff must understand the logs that are being collected and take the time to define the use cases that warrant alerts and investigation. Organizations that do not invest the time and resources required to tune the system will experience teams overwhelmed with alerts, many of which will often be ignored.

Log Reviews

A *log review* is an examination of an event log in an information system to determine whether any privacy, security, or operational incidents have occurred in the system. A log review is an examination of yesterday's activities in a system. Most organizations, however, conduct *continuous log reviews* by sending log data into a security information and event management (SIEM) system.

Centralized Log Management

Centralized log management involves sending event logs on various systems over the network to a central collection and storage point, called a *log server*. There are two primary uses for a log server: for archival storage of events that may be used at a later date in an investigation, and for storage of events to be reviewed on a daily basis or in real-time. Generally, real-time analysis is performed by a SIEM system.

Security Information and Event Management

A SIEM system collects and analyzes log data from many or all systems in an organization and produces alerts to inform personnel of specific events. A SIEM has rules to correlate events from one or more devices to provide additional details about an incident. For instance, a worker busy exfiltrating sensitive data files containing personal information may be moving a large number of files to a location where they can be exfiltrated. A SIEM would portray the incident using events from these and possibly other systems and devices to give personnel a richer depiction of the incident.

For a SIEM to be effective, the timestamps in log entries from various devices must be accurate. The SIEM must be able to discern the actual sequence of events, which is based on each log entry's timestamp. Because computer time clocks are notoriously inaccurate on their own, configuring computers to synchronize their clocks with an authoritative *time source,* or time server, is an essential practice.

 EXAM TIP Despite its name (*security* information and event management), CIPM candidates need to understand that a SIEM system is often used not only to inform personnel of security events, but also to inform them of operational- and privacy-related events. Security and privacy event visibility that a SIEM brings is a foundation capability that should be present in every organization.

Orchestration

In the context of SIEM systems, *orchestration* refers to a scripted response that is automatically or manually triggered when specific events occur. Orchestration systems can be stand-alone systems or may exist as part of the SIEM.

For example, suppose an organization has developed "run books," or short procedures for personnel who manage the SIEM for actions to perform when specific types of events occur. The organization, desiring to automate some of these responses, implements an orchestration tool that includes scripts that can run automatically when specific events occur. The orchestration system can be configured to run some scripts immediately, while other scripts can be set up and run when an analyst "approves" them.

The advantage of orchestration is twofold: First, repetitive and routine tasks are automated, relieving personnel of boredom and improving accuracy. Second, response to some types of events can be performed much quicker, thereby blunting the impact of certain types of incidents.

Data Loss Prevention

Organizations intent on proactively protecting sensitive information, including personal information about customers, constituents, and employees, may implement one or more types of data loss prevention (DLP) systems. For many organizations, policy alone is an insufficient means for protecting personal information. Instead, any of several types of controls can be introduced to protect specific data containing personal information, sensitive information, and intellectual property. Several tools and techniques are available for passive (detective) or active (preventive) DLP:

- **Document scanning**   Tools can be used to scan stores of unstructured data to determine the extent of the presence of sensitive and personal information.

- **Document tagging**   During document scanning, DLP tools tag files if they contain data matching specific patterns such as social insurance numbers, credit card numbers, financial account numbers, and others.

- **Document marking**   Once tagged, documents can be marked or watermarked, which introduces human-readable content into files to remind people that these files contain sensitive information of some type.

- **E-mail restrictions**   DLP tools can be integrated into an organization's e-mail system to monitor and block the practice of e-mailing files containing sensitive information. These tools can be configured to read files' tags or scan the contents of the files themselves to determine whether they violate e-mail policy. When violations occur, users can be alerted; optionally, they can be given a choice on whether to proceed with their intended activity.

- **Storage restrictions**   DLP tools can be integrated into end-user devices to monitor their handling of sensitive data files. These tools can merely observe data movement or intervene when specific policies are violated. Users can be warned against or forbidden from storing sensitive files or using external storage devices and/or cloud-based storage and messaging services.

All of these forms of DLP tools can be configured to send their events to the organization's log servers or SIEM so that privacy and security personnel can be alerted when data handling policy violations occur.

 CAUTION   DLP tools should be used carefully, because false positives can occur, which could disrupt legitimate business activities. Also, false negatives represent a failure to detect forbidden activities.

DLP, the Cornerstone of Automated Privacy Controls

Arguably, DLP tools represent the new cornerstone of automatic controls that have the ability to detect the movement and use of sensitive information. When these tools are properly tuned, privacy analysts and leaders can know, on a case-by-case basis, exactly when and how data containing personal information is used, where it is stored, and where it is sent. Often, DLP controls can block any of these actions, resulting in a previously unknown level of visibility and control—just in time for emerging privacy laws.

DLP systems can be integrated with orchestration tools. For instance, if a worker is performing anomalous activities related to large amounts of personal information, orchestration can automatically limit the worker's access to sensitive information—effectively halting the current activities—until an analyst can look into the matter to see what is going on.

Threat Intelligence

Modern SIEMs can ingest threat intelligence feeds from various external sources. This enables the SIEM to correlate events in an organization's systems with various threats experienced by other organizations.

Organizations can subscribe to one or more machine-readable threat intelligence sources that help the organization better understand which security events in its environment may represent intrusions. Some of these sources are open source, while others are fee-based commercial services. For example, suppose another organization is attacked by an adversary from a specific IP address in a foreign country. This information is included in a threat intelligence feed that arrives in your organization's SIEM. This helps your SIEM be more aware of activity of the same type or from the same IP address. This can alert the organization to incidents occurring elsewhere that could occur in the organization's network.

 EXAM TIP CIPM candidates should understand the concept of threat intelligence feeds that help organizations better anticipate malicious events perpetrated by cybercriminal organizations and lone actors.

Threat Hunting

For many organizations, it's no longer sufficient to wait for attacks to manifest themselves in their SIEMs or other monitoring systems. Instead, organizations go on the offensive to look for clues of possible intrusions in their environments. *Threat hunting* is the practice of conducting searches—typically in SIEM logs and configuration management databases—to determine whether traces of intrusions are present in their systems.

For example, an organization may have received an advisory from a national law enforcement organization with specific intelligence on a new strain of malware. The advisory contains the filenames of some of the malware's artifacts. Threat hunters in the organization can scan log files or configuration management databases (CMDBs) in a search for the presence of those files on their systems to determine whether a similar attack in their own network may be occurring.

 NOTE   The author envisions a future form of threat hunting that looks for signs of anomalous behavior, suggesting the misuse of personal information. Such a proactive effort can potentially thwart misbehavior and breaches in their early stages.

User Behavior Analytics

User behavior analytics (UBA), sometimes known as end user behavior analytics (EUBA), represents a detective capability wherein each user's actions are recorded and a profile of normal behavior is established. When a user's conduct falls outside the norms, an alert or a report can be generated that privacy and security personnel can examine to determine whether policy violations are occurring.

UBA capabilities exist in the form of agents on endpoints and servers, as well as analytical capabilities in a SIEM.

Input Controls

Privacy leaders focused on the use, and potential misuse, of personal information can enact input controls and input authorization controls. These safeguards work on different levels but contribute to the same objective: to act as a detective control to alert privacy managers of incoming personal information that may be an indicator of unauthorized activity. For instance, the detection of sensitive information coming into the organization could represent the unauthorized acquisition of information from a data broker as a part of an embellishment operation to monetize personal information in violation of privacy policy.

Input controls come in the form of DLP capabilities watching for incoming personal information, alerting personnel of incoming data that is unexpected. *Input authorization* represents policy that states that new sources of information are permitted only upon management approval.

Security Advisories

Numerous organizations, including law enforcement, publish human-readable advisories on various cybersecurity events. Security teams in companies often subscribe to one or more of these advisories to be better informed on events occurring around the world. Sometimes these advisories compel security teams to request that their IT departments take action, which could include any of the following:

- Blocking specific IP addresses on external firewalls
- Installing specific security patches

- Making configuration changes to systems or devices
- Threat hunting to look for signs of intrusion
- Blocking e-mail from specific domains, IP addresses, or accounts
- Blocking access to specific web sites
- Issuing advisories to the workforce to be on the lookout for signs of suspicious activities

Organizations should actively subscribe to security advisories from the manufacturers of the hardware and software products they use in their environments. Organizations should also subscribe to two or more nonvendor advisory sources.

Privacy Responsibilities

The practice of monitoring privacy responsibilities helps an organization confirm that personal information is being properly collected, used, protected, and then discarded when no longer needed, and that subject requests are being handled timely and correctly. There is no single approach, but several activities provide information to management, including the following:

- **Controls and internal audit**   Developing one or more controls around specific responsibilities increases management's ability to direct key activities. An internal audit of privacy and security controls provides an objective analysis of the controls' effectiveness.
- **Metrics and reporting**   Developing metrics for routine activities helps management better understand work output and quality.
- **Work measurement**   This structured activity is used to measure routine tasks carefully to help management better understand the volume of work performed.
- **Performance evaluation**   This traditional qualitative method is used by management to evaluate employee performance.
- **360 feedback**   Soliciting structured feedback from peers, subordinates, and management helps subjects and management better understand characteristics related to specific responsibilities.
- **Position benchmarking**   This technique is used by organizations that want to compare job titles and people holding them with equivalent roles in other organizations. Benchmarking does not involve direct monitoring of responsibilities, but it helps an organization determine whether the appropriate positions are in place and ensure that the positions are staffed by competent and qualified personnel. This may be useful for organizations that are troubleshooting employee performance.

External Monitoring

In addition to monitoring several aspects of internal business and system operations, privacy leaders cannot neglect to monitor external developments. Areas of external monitoring include

- **New privacy laws and regulations**   States, provinces, nations, and regions have been busy developing and enacting privacy laws. There should be no expectation that the pace of passage of new privacy laws will slow down any time soon. Privacy legislation developments also need to be monitored—that is, bills in committee that help legal counsel understand what lawmakers are considering enacting into future laws. An organization's legal department generally is responsible for this monitoring.

- **Developments in case law and other legal precedents**   As new laws are enacted, they are tested by the courts, leading to precedents that help organizations better understand how laws are enforced and, thus, what organizations need to do to comply with them.

- **Changes in societal norms**   Organizations need to pay attention to the shifting opinions of their customer base and of society as a whole. Organizations can organize their own focus groups to understand how their customers (and others) feel about privacy, security, and other matters. Research papers on these topics are available as well.

- **Emerging industry privacy practices**   As laws and societal norms evolve, organizations innovate and continue to improve practices and techniques.

- **Emerging threats and threat actors**   Security leaders need to stay abreast of developments in threats, threat techniques, and threat actors, as well as the defensive techniques that develop as a result. This will, at times, require changes in tooling, detective, and responsive processes in an organization's security program.

 NOTE   Organizations often rely on outside counsel with expertise in privacy for guidance on the applicability and applicability of privacy laws.

Control Self-Assessment

Control self-assessment (CSA) is a methodology used by an organization to review key business objectives, risks related to achieving these objectives, and the key controls designed to manage those risks. The primary characteristic of a CSA is that the organization takes the initiative to self-regulate rather than engage outsiders, who may be experts in auditing but not in the organization's mission, goals, and culture.

Examples of CSA include

- **Sarbanes–Oxley mandated internal audit**   US public companies are required to implement an internal audit function that examines financial controls. CSA further extends internal auditors' reach by providing additional telemetry about selected internal controls.

CIPM Certified Information Privacy Manager All-in-One Exam Guide

226

- **PCI Self-Assessment Questionnaire (SAQ)**   The Payment Card Industry requires all merchants and service providers to comply with the PCI DSS; organizations whose transaction volumes are below set thresholds are allowed to self-assess with the PCI's Self-Assessment Questionnaires.
- **Voluntary internal audit**   Better organizations that realize that privacy and security controls are essential to protect their ongoing business undertake voluntary internal audits, not because a law or regulation requires them to, but because they understand that audits ensure that their controls continue to be effective.

CSA Advantages and Disadvantages

Like almost any business activity, CSAs have some advantages and disadvantages that privacy leaders, security leaders, internal auditors, and others should be familiar with. These pros and cons will help the organization make the most of this process and avoid some common problems.

The advantages of a CSA include

- Risks can be detected earlier because subject matter experts are involved earlier.
- Control owners can improve their internal controls promptly.
- CSA leads to greater ownership of controls through involvement in their assessment and improvement.
- CSA leads to improved employee awareness of controls through involvement in their improvement.
- With limited resources in internal audit departments, CSA extends visibility into control effectiveness.
- CSA may help improve relationships between departments and auditors.

Control self-assessments are not a panacea. The disadvantages of a CSA include

- CSA could be mistaken by employees or management as a substitute for an internal audit.
- CSA may be considered extra work and dismissed as unnecessary.
- Control owners may attempt to cover up shoddy work and misdeeds.
- CSA may be considered an attempt by the auditor to shrug off responsibilities.
- Lack of employee involvement could translate to little or no process improvement.

The CSA Life Cycle

Like most continuous-improvement processes, the CSA process is an iterative life cycle with several phases:

- *Identify and assess risks.* Operational risks are identified and analyzed.
- *Identify and assess controls.* Controls to manage risks are identified and assessed. If any controls are missing, new controls are designed and implemented.

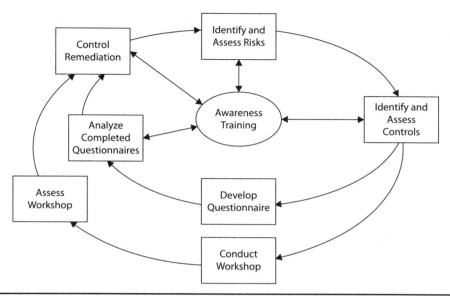

Figure 5-1 The control self-assessment life cycle

- *Develop a questionnaire or conduct a workshop.* An interactive session is conducted for discussion of risks and possible controls. If attending personnel are distributed across several locations, a conference call can be convened, or a questionnaire may be developed and sent to them.

- *Analyze completed questionnaires or assess workshop results.* If a workshop occurred, the workshop results are assessed to determine what good ideas for remediation emerged. If a questionnaire was distributed, the results are analyzed for ideas for risk remediation.

- *Undergo control remediation.* Using the best ideas culled from the workshop or questionnaire, controls are designed or altered to manage specific risks more effectively.

- *Conduct awareness training.* This activity is carried out through every phase of the life cycle to keep personnel informed about the activities in the various phases.

The CSA life cycle is illustrated in Figure 5-1.

CSA Objectives

The primary objective of a CSA is to transfer some of the responsibility for oversight of control performance and monitoring to the control owners. The internal auditor's role is not diminished; although internal audit or an external firm may still need to test control effectiveness periodically, control owners will play active roles in audits of their controls.

Another objective of CSA is the long-term reduction in exceptions. As control owners assume more responsibility for their controls' performance, they will strive to avoid situations where internal auditors identify exceptions. The CSA gives control owners an opportunity and a process for cleaning house and improving audit results.

 NOTE Privacy leaders, security leaders, and internal auditors should be involved in CSAs to ensure that the CSA process is not hijacked by efficiency zealots who try to remove the controls from processes because they do not understand their significance.

Management, Internal Audit, and Self-Assessments

Privacy and security leaders should be involved in the CSAs that their departments conduct. If the organization has an internal audit department, it should assume the role of an objective subject matter expert. Internal audit can guide discussions in the appropriate direction so that controls will receive the appropriate kind of development over time.

Internal audit should resist taking too large a role in CSAs, however. Responsibility for control development and maturation should lie within the department that owns the CSA. However, if a department is new at conducting a CSA, it may take some time before they are confident and competent enough to take full ownership and responsibility for the process.

Auditing Privacy Programs

The purpose of any audit is to confirm, using objective means, the effectiveness of controls and processes. An audit may be performed by a customer, a regulator, an audit firm, or internal audit staff. An audit of an organization's privacy processes and underlying information system will be performed using established audit practices.

This section contains a summary of audit practices in the context of information privacy. For more detailed information about audit planning and audits, refer to *CISA Certified Information Systems Auditor All-In-One Exam Guide, Fourth Edition,* particularly Chapter 3, "The Audit Process." (Be sure to use the latest edition.)

Privacy Audit Scope

An audit is planned for good reason. Because audits are disruptive and often expensive, one or more compelling business drivers should be identified to help management determine whether an audit is needed and what the desired outcome of the audit is likely to be.

For privacy, the *scope* of a privacy audit is likely to be the controls, processes, and systems used to protect personal information, or the controls, processes, and systems used to collect, process, and use personal information. Just as privacy itself has two perspectives (the *protection* of personal information and the *use* of personal information), a privacy audit is likely to focus on one or both of these perspectives.

Privacy Audit Objectives

Privacy audit *objectives* are the specific goals for a privacy audit. Generally, these objectives will determine whether privacy controls exist and are effective in some specific aspect of business operations in an organization. Typically, a privacy audit is performed to comply with applicable privacy regulations or related legal obligations. An audit may also be performed as the result of a recent privacy incident or event.

Depending on the subject and nature of the audit, the auditor may examine privacy controls and related evidence herself, or she may instead focus on the business content that is processed by the controls. For example, if the focus of a privacy audit is an organization's subject data request process, the auditor may focus on requests in the system to see if they comply with the organization's privacy policy or applicable regulations. Or the auditor could focus on the information systems processes that support the processing of personal information. Formal audit objectives should make such a distinction so that the auditor has a sound understanding of the objectives: objectives tell the auditor what to examine during the audit. Of course, knowing the type of audit to be undertaken helps too; this is covered in the next section.

Types of Privacy Audits

The scope, purpose, and objectives of a privacy audit will determine the type of audit that will be performed. Auditors need to understand each type of audit, including the procedures that are used for each:

- **Operational audit**   This involves an examination of privacy controls, security controls, or business controls to determine the controls' existence and effectiveness. The focus of the audit is usually the operation of one or more controls, and it could concentrate on the management of a business process or on the business process itself.

- **Information systems (IS) audit**   This involves a detailed examination of an IT department's operations related to the storage and processing of personal information. An IS audit looks at IT governance to determine whether the IT department is aligned with overall organization goals, objectives, privacy policy, security policy, and applicable regulations. The audit may also look closely at all of the major IT processes, including service delivery, change and configuration management, security management, systems development life cycle (SDLC), business relationship and supplier management, and incident and problem management. The integrity of a privacy process ultimately depends upon the integrity of the underlying IT systems and processes. This audit will determine whether each control objective and control is effective and operating correctly.

- **Integrated audit**   This audit combines an operational audit and an information systems audit to help the auditor fully understand the entire environment's integrity. The audit will closely examine privacy operations processes, procedures, and records, as well as the IT applications used to store and process personal information.

- **Administrative audit**   This involves an examination of the operational efficiency of privacy-related business processes.

- **Compliance audit**   This audit is performed to determine the level and degree of compliance with one or more applicable privacy regulations, other legal requirements, or internal policies and standards. If a particular privacy law requires an external audit, the compliance audit may be required to be performed by approved or licensed external auditors and/or be performed using specific audit standards. If, however, the law does not explicitly require audits, the organization may still decide to perform one-time or regular audits to determine the level of compliance with the law. Internal or external auditors may perform this type of audit, typically to give management a better understanding of the level of compliance risk.

- **Forensic audit**   This audit is usually performed by an IS auditor or a forensic specialist in support of an anticipated or active legal proceeding and is typically part of the investigation of a privacy breach. To withstand cross-examination and avoid having evidence being ruled inadmissible, a forensic audit must follow strict procedures, including the preservation of evidence and a chain of custody of evidence.

- **Service provider audit**   Because many organizations outsource parts of their operations, third-party service organizations will undergo one or more external audits to increase customer confidence in the integrity of the third-party's services. In the United States, the Statement on Standards for Attestation Engagements No. 18, *Reporting on Controls at a Service Organization* (SSAE 18), can be performed on a service provider's operations and the audit report transmitted to customers of the service provider.

Privacy Audit Planning

The auditor must obtain information about the privacy audit that will enable her to establish the audit plan. Information needed includes

- Location or locations that need to be visited
- A list of the business processes and supporting applications to be examined
- The personnel to be interviewed
- The technologies supporting each application
- Privacy policies, security policies, standards, and data flow diagrams that describe the environment and the personal data stored and processed there

This and other information will enable the auditor to determine the resources and skills required to examine and evaluate privacy-related business processes and information systems. The auditor will be able to establish an audit schedule and a good idea of the types of evidence needed. The auditor may be able to make advance requests for certain other types of evidence even before the onsite phase of the audit begins.

For an audit with a risk-based approach, the auditor has a couple of options:

- Precede the audit itself with a risk assessment to determine which privacy processes or controls warrant additional audit scrutiny.
- Gather information about the organization and historical events to discover risks that warrant additional audit scrutiny.

Audit Statement of Work

For an external audit, the auditor may need to develop a statement of work or engagement letter that describes the audit purpose, scope, duration, and costs. The auditor may require written approval from the client before audit work can officially begin.

Establish Audit Procedures

Using information obtained regarding audit objectives and scope, the auditor can develop procedures for the audit. For each privacy process, control, and objective to be tested, the auditor can specify the following:

- A list of people to interview
- Inquiries to make during each interview
- Documentation (policies, procedures, and other documents) to request during each interview
- Audit tools to use
- Sampling rates and methodologies
- How and where evidence will be archived
- How evidence will be evaluated
- How findings will be reported

Communication Plan

The auditor will develop a communication plan to keep the auditor's management, and the auditee's management, informed throughout the audit project. The communication plan may contain one or more of the following:

- A list of evidence requested, usually in the form of a PBC (provided by client) list, which is typically a worksheet that lists specific documents or records and the names of personnel who can provide them (or who provided them in a prior audit)
- Regular written status reports that include activities performed since the last status report, upcoming activities, and any significant findings that may require immediate attention
- Regular status meetings where audit progress, issues, and other matters may be discussed in person or via conference call
- Contact information for both auditor and auditee so that both parties can contact each other quickly if needed

Report Preparation

The auditor needs to develop a plan that describes how the audit report will be prepared. This will include the format and the content of the report, as well as how findings will be established and documented. The auditor should ensure that the audit report complies with all applicable audit standards, including applicable regulations and ISACA IS audit standards.

Wrap-Up

The auditor must perform some tasks at the conclusion of the audit, including the following:

- Deliver the report to the auditee.
- Schedule a closing meeting so that the results of the audit can be discussed with the auditee and so that the auditor can collect feedback.
- For external audits, send an invoice to the auditee.
- Collect and archive all work papers. Enter their existence in a document management system so that they can be retrieved later if needed and to ensure their destruction when they have reached the end of their retention life.
- Update PBC documents if the auditor anticipates that the audit will be performed again in the future.
- Collect feedback from the auditee and convey it to audit staff as needed.

Post-Audit Follow-Up

After a given period (which could range from days to months), the auditor should contact the auditee to determine what progress has been made to remedy any audit findings. This establishes a tone of concern for the auditee organization and helps to establish a dialogue whereby the auditor can help auditee management work through any needed process or technology changes as a result of the audit.

Privacy Audit Evidence

Evidence is the information collected by the auditor during the course of the audit project. The contents and reliability of the evidence obtained are used by the auditor to reach conclusions on the effectiveness of privacy controls and control objectives. The auditor needs to understand how to evaluate various types of evidence and how (and if) it can be used to support audit findings. The auditor will collect many kinds of evidence during an audit, including observations, written notes, correspondence, independent confirmations from other auditors, process and procedure documentation, and business records.

When examining the evidence, the auditor should consider several characteristics that will contribute to its weight and reliability, including the following:

- **Independence of the evidence provider**   Evidence provided by the process owner may be tainted (to influence audit results); an independent evidence provider may be preferred.

- **Qualifications of the evidence provider**   The evidence provider should be a person qualified to represent the process or system being audited.
- **Objectivity**   The evidence should be objective. Digital evidence is more objective than the opinion of a process owner, for instance.
- **Timing**   The evidence should be timely and appropriate to the issue at hand. Some evidence, such as system logs, may be available only for a short period.

NOTE   Evidence collected in a privacy audit is likely to contain personal information. The auditor and auditee should understand the protective measures required to protect this evidence, whether it can be anonymized, and how long it must be retained.

Gathering Evidence

The privacy auditor must understand and be familiar with the methods and techniques used to gather evidence during an audit. The methods and techniques used most often in audits include reviews of the organization chart, department and project charters, third-party contracts and service level agreements (SLAs), policies and procedures, risk registers, incident log, standards, system documentation, interviews of personnel, re-performance (where auditors will confirm that the organization's processes and systems calculate results properly), and passive observation.

NOTE   The privacy auditor should pay attention to what department charters, policies, and procedure documents *do* say, as well as what they *don't* say, and should perform corroborative interviews to determine whether these documents define the organization's behavior or if they're just window dressing. This will help the auditor understand the maturity of the organization, a valuable insight that will be helpful when writing the audit report.

Sampling

Sampling refers to a technique used when it is not feasible to test an entire population of privacy events or transactions. The objective of sampling is to select a portion of a population so that the characteristics observed will reflect the characteristics of the entire population. Several methods are used for sampling, including the following:

- Statistical sampling
- Judgmental sampling (also known as nonstatistical sampling)
- Attribute sampling
- Variable sampling
- Stop-or-go sampling
- Discovery sampling
- Stratified sampling

EXAM TIP CIPM candidates are not expected to memorize specific sampling techniques or their purposes, although it is crucial that you understand the general concept.

Relying on the Work of Other Auditors

Audit departments and external auditors, like other IT service organizations, are challenged to find qualified audit professionals who understand all aspects of organizations' technologies in use. Increased specialization in IT is resulting in auditors who have advanced technical knowledge in certain areas and fewer auditors with all of the necessary expertise to perform an audit. Third-party service providers usually do not permit customers to audit them but instead rely on external auditors to perform audits, and they then make those audit reports available to the customer. These and other factors are putting increasing pressure on organizations to outsource some auditing tasks (or entire audits) to third-party organizations and to rely upon audit reports from other sources.

For example, it's unlikely that Amazon Web Services or Microsoft Azure will permit any customer to audit them. Amazon and Microsoft will instead commission a number of types of external audits and certifications, such as SOC 1, SOC 2, ISAE 3402, ISO/IEC 27001, or PCI DSS, and make those audit reports (or summaries) available to their customers upon request. The auditors in customer organizations often have little choice but to rely upon them.

Reporting Privacy Audit Results

The work product of a privacy audit project is the *audit report,* a written report that describes the entire audit project, including audit objectives, scope, controls evaluated, opinions on the effectiveness and integrity of those controls, and recommendations for improvement.

Although an auditor or audit firm will generally use a standard format for an audit report, some privacy laws and standards require that an audit report regarding those laws or standards contain specific information or be presented in a particular format. Still, there will be some variance in the structure and appearance of audit reports created by different audit organizations.

The auditor is typically asked to present findings in a closing meeting, explaining the audit and its results and being available to answer questions about the audit. The auditor may include an electronic presentation to guide discussions of the audit.

Auditing Specific Privacy Practices

An organization's privacy audit is likely to focus on one or more key aspects of its privacy policy and operations. Several are discussed here.

Auditing Privacy Policy

A privacy policy audit will focus on one or more of these:

- **Compliance with applicable privacy regulations** Does the organization's privacy policy align with privacy regulations that the organization is required to comply with?

- **Compliance with privacy policies**   Does the organization's practices align with its internal and external privacy policies? For example, if the organization's external privacy policy claims that the organization does not sell personal information, the auditor will determine whether this is really true.

- **Alignment with security policy and practices**   Is the organization's security policy content adequate for protecting personal information? And do the organization's practices align with its policies?

Auditing Data Management

An organization's data management audit, which should include the protection and management of personal information, is likely to focus on one or more of these:

- **Data classification**   The auditor will examine the organization's data classification policy and handling procedures. Because most organizations lack automation, auditors will want to interview workers to see if there is a pervasive awareness of the classification policy and to determine how often it is applied in practice. If automation is present in the form of DLP or other solutions, the auditor will examine those systems to understand their capabilities and how they are managed.

- **Data protection**   The auditor will examine one or more facets of information security to see how effectively the organization protects personal information. This potentially covers a large variety of topics, from system hardening to identity and access management.

- **Data flows**   The auditor will examine data flow diagrams and supporting documentation to determine whether the organization truly knows where personal information flows and resides in its environment.

- **Data loss prevention**   The auditor will examine any DLP systems to determine whether they effectively identify the presence and flows of personal information.

Auditing Data Collection

Auditors looking at an organization's practice of collecting personal information will examine several aspects of data collection:

- **Security**   The auditor will look for secure protocols to ensure the protection of personal information in transit and upon arrival on the organization's systems.

- **Alignment with privacy policy**   The auditor will compare data collection practices with privacy policy to determine whether they align. For instance, if privacy policy states that only names, addresses, and phone numbers are collected, the auditor will compare that policy with systems that collect data to confirm that these are the only items collected from data subjects.

- **Alignment with applicable regulations**   The auditor will confirm whether data collection practices are compliant with specific privacy regulations.

- **Consent**   The auditor will examine privacy policy and data collection practices to understand how the organization obtains consent from the data subject at the time of collection. Note that an absence of consent is not necessarily a violation of policy or regulations, as there are circumstances in which it is infeasible or unnecessary for an organization to obtain consent.

- **Data aggregation**   The auditor will seek to understand the organization's practices for aggregating personal information collected from the data subject with data obtained from other sources.

Auditing Data Subject Requests

The auditor will examine business processes and supporting information systems to understand how the organization receives data subject requests (DSRs) and how the organization responds to them. Aspects of an audit will include the following:

- **Data subject authentication**   The auditor will examine the procedures used by the organization to authenticate the user. The authentication process itself may involve the collection of data that authenticates the user; the auditor will need to understand how that information is used, whether it is retained, and if that information is disclosed in subsequent requests.

- **Effectiveness of response**   The auditor looks for the procedures undertaken by the organization to determine whether they identify all areas where a subject's data resides and whether all instances are disclosed to the data subject.

- **Accuracy of response**   The auditor examines procedures to determine whether the organization correctly processes the request, including changes or corrections.

- **Completeness of response**   The auditor checks to see whether the organization's response to a data subject includes all instances of storage and use of personal information.

- **Timeliness of response**   The auditor examines records to see how long the organization takes to respond to requests.

- **Recordkeeping**   The auditor examines business records to see what information about the data subject request is retained.

- **Compliance with policy and applicable regulations**   Finally, the auditor will confirm whether the organization's processing of data subject requests aligns with its privacy policy and applicable regulations.

Auditing Data Minimization

The auditor will examine data collection and aggregation practices and compare those with the organization's services to determine whether the organization is collecting more items of personal information than are necessary for the organization to provide its services. This will also include a comparison with language in the organization's privacy policy to see if practices are in alignment.

Auditing De-identification, Anonymization, and Pseudonymization

The auditor will examine the organization's de-identification, anonymization, and pseudonymization practices to see if these practices are effective. Here, the auditor will need to "think outside the box" to determine whether anonymized and pseudonymized data can be reconstituted and associated with specific natural persons. Whether through ineptness, simple misconfiguration of a system, or outright deception, some organizations tend to fulfill only the *appearance* of anonymization and pseudonymization, but not the *fact* of anonymization and pseudonymization. For instance, merely removing the name of a person otherwise identified as a "46-year-old male electrical engineer with a family of four living on Main Street" is probably an insufficient practice of de-identification.

Auditing Privacy Incident Management

Auditing privacy-related incident management and investigative procedures requires attention to several key activities, including these:

- **Investigation policies and procedures**   The auditor should determine whether there are any policies or procedures regarding privacy and security investigations. These would include who is responsible for performing investigations, where information about investigations is stored, and to whom the results of investigations are reported. Where subject data is examined in an investigation, the auditor will seek to understand how that subject data is protected and used and whether this aligns with the organization's privacy policy and applicable regulations.

- **Computer crime investigations**   The auditor should look for policies, processes, procedures, and records regarding computer crime investigations. The auditor should understand how internal investigations are transitioned to supervisory authorities, regulators, or law enforcement.

- **Security incident response**   Because security incident response is relevant to privacy in instances where personal data is involved, the auditor should examine security incident response policies, procedures, and plans to determine whether they are up to date. Interviewing incident responders to gauge their familiarity with incident response procedures can indicate the effectiveness of training and tabletop exercises. The auditor should examine some of the records from actual security incidents to determine whether the responses were effective and whether the organization conducted post-incident reviews to identify process improvements.

- **Privacy incident response**   For incidents that involve the misuse of personal information, the auditor will examine incident response plans and incident records to see how the organization responds to these incidents. If any personal information becomes a part of the incident response record, the auditor will determine whether the organization complies with privacy policy and applicable regulations for the storage and use of those records.

- **Computer forensics** The auditor should determine whether there are procedures for conducting computer forensics. The auditor should also identify tools and techniques available to the organization for the acquisition and custody of forensic data. The auditor should determine whether any employees in the organization have received computer forensics training and are qualified to perform forensic investigations. Because some organizations employ outside firms for forensics assistance, the auditor should examine any contract in place to see if this prearranged capability was properly established.

Auditing Privacy Compliance

Auditing privacy compliance is concerned with an organization's practices related to its tracking of applicable privacy laws and case law, and its ability to interpret and apply them correctly. Auditors will examine information sources, correspondence, and other records to gain insight into the organization's analysis techniques that lead to decisions of applicability and guidance on compliance.

Audit Standards

The IT audit organization ISACA has published its Information Technology Assurance Framework in the *ITAF: A Professional Practices Framework for IS Audit* (currently in its fourth edition and available free of charge at https://www.isaca.org/ITAF). The ITAF consists of the ISACA Code of Professional Ethics, IS audit and assurance standards, IS audit and assurance guidelines, and IS audit and assurance tools and techniques. These components are illustrated here:

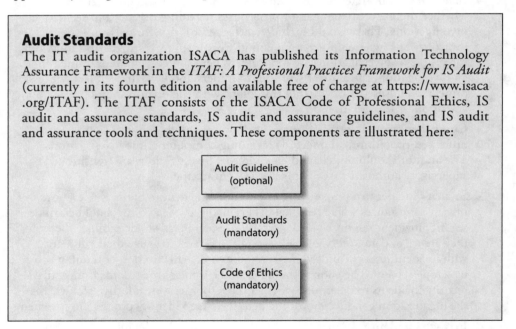

Chapter Review

The monitoring of a privacy program represents a continual observation of the program's business processes and supporting information systems to ensure that they perform as expected. Because privacy depends heavily upon information security, and in turn, that information security relies upon IT service management, all of these fundamental components must be monitored.

Monitoring business processes consist of collecting statistics created by business processes, subsequently examining these statistics, transforming statistics into key risk and key performance indicators, and reporting these indicators to management.

The logging of privacy- and security-related events, the centralized collection of these logs, and the proactive monitoring of the logs with correlation engines are considered essential practices in cybersecurity and privacy.

In addition to monitoring several aspects of internal business and system operations, privacy leaders cannot neglect to monitor external developments. Areas of external monitoring include new privacy laws, developments in case law, changes in societal norms, emerging privacy practices, and emerging threats and threat actors.

Control self-assessment (CSA) is a methodology used by an organization to review key business objectives, risks related to achieving these objectives, and the key controls designed to manage those risks. The primary characteristic of a CSA is that the organization takes the initiative to self-regulate rather than engage outsiders, who may be experts in auditing but not in the organization's mission, goals, and culture.

An audit of an organization's privacy processes and underlying information systems will be performed using established audit practices. A privacy audit is performed to comply with applicable privacy regulations or related legal obligations. An audit may also be performed as the result of a recent privacy incident or event.

An organization's privacy audit is likely to focus on one or more key aspects of its privacy policy and operations. A privacy audit's focus may include data management, data collection, data subject requests, data minimization, anonymization and pseudonymization, privacy incident management, and privacy compliance.

Quick Review

- Metrics obtained from privacy operations may be used for operational process improvement purposes or transformed into key risk indicators (KRIs) and key performance indicators (KPIs).

- While a SIEM is designed for security events, organizations can also use it for privacy events to alert privacy analysts and management of privacy-related events and potential privacy violations.

- Organizations can apply threat-hunting techniques for privacy purposes to detect potential privacy abuses and violations.

- Data loss prevention (DLP) systems hold promise for data-specific information protection and detection of potential privacy abuses.

- Organizations often rely on outside counsel with expertise in privacy for guidance on the applicability and applicability of privacy laws.

- A control self-assessment is not a substitute for an internal or external audit.

- Professional auditors rely on ISACA audit standards published in the IT Assurance Framework, which consists of the ISACA Code of Professional Ethics, IS audit and assurance standards, IS audit and assurance guidelines, and IS audit and assurance tools and techniques.

Questions

1. The examination of log entries present in information systems is known as:
   A. Incident response
   B. Incident monitoring
   C. Event monitoring
   D. Forensics

2. All of the following are examples of information system log entries except:
   A. Data classification
   B. Successful login
   C. Unsuccessful login
   D. Device reboot

3. A system that intakes event data and produces alerts is known as a:
   A. System event and information management system
   B. System event and incident management system
   C. Security event and incident management system
   D. Security information and event management system

4. Which of the following tools is most likely to capture data usage information that could reveal the misuse of personal information?
   A. Web content filter
   B. Firewalls
   C. CASB
   D. DLP

5. The manager responsible for processing data subject requests has been assigned to perform a control self-assessment of the process. What method for sampling should the control owner use to examine the process?
   A. Internal audit to select the samples
   B. Examination of all records
   C. Random sampling
   D. Judgmental sampling

6. The privacy manager of a public company is concerned that some of the privacy controls are not being adequately performed. What activity can be suggested that will compel control owners to take a more significant role in their performance?
   A. Internal audits
   B. Control self-assessment

    C. External audits

    D. A risk assessment

7. The technique of selecting records to examine in an audit is known as:

    A. Sampling

    B. Selection

    C. Randomization

    D. Risk selection

8. An organization uses a privacy records management SaaS application from a large vendor as its primary privacy information system. What is the best method for gaining assurance of the integrity of the SaaS provider's control environment?

    A. SOC 1 audit report

    B. SOC 2 audit report

    C. ISO 27001 certification

    D. Site visit

9. An auditor auditing an organization's data management processes should request all of the following types of information except:

    A. Database schemas

    B. Data flow diagrams

    C. Data management policy

    D. DLP system records

10. In a control self-assessment, to whom should questions about the operation of a control be sent?

    A. Internal auditor

    B. Security control framework owner

    C. Privacy control framework owner

    D. Control owner

11. A team of analysts is being shown how to select items randomly from their business records and follow instructions on examining the detail of their records to determine whether procedures are being followed properly. The analysts are undertaking:

    A. An internal audit

    B. Control self-assessment training

    C. An external audit

    D. Cross-training

12. An organization wants to implement a data loss prevention (DLP) system. Which of the following is considered the best approach for such an implementation?

   A. Employ DLP in passive mode initially.

   B. Employ DLP in active mode initially.

   C. Set DLP in high-sensitivity mode.

   D. Employ DLP on e-mail systems first.

13. An auditor is developing a plan for auditing privacy controls in a retail organization. What type of information should the auditor collect to determine whether data subject requests are correctly recorded?

   A. Interview data subjects.

   B. Interview control owners.

   C. Examine business records.

   D. Examine privacy policy.

14. An auditor is examining an organization's data subject request procedure. Upon asking for the DSR process document, the control owner replies that there is no written procedure. What should the auditor do next?

   A. Continue with the audit by asking the control owner to describe the procedure.

   B. Declare the DSR process as ineffective and halt the audit.

   C. Write down the procedure as described by the control owner.

   D. Contact privacy regulators about this breach of privacy.

15. An organization has hired a privacy manager who has developed a corporate privacy program. Management has told the privacy manager that it wants to monitor the program. What should the privacy manager provide to management?

   A. Operational metrics

   B. A monthly written report

   C. Key risk indicators

   D. Operational metrics and key performance indicators

Answers

1. **C.** Event monitoring is the examination of log entries in information systems.

2. **A.** Data classification is not a system log event. Successful and unsuccessful logins and device reboots are examples of system log events.

3. **D.** A system event and information management system (SIEM) is a system that intakes security events and creates alerts when actionable events occur.

4. **D.** When properly implemented, a data loss prevention (DLP) system is most likely to reveal abuses of personal information by showing which users are accessing files containing personal information.

5. C. The process owner should randomly select samples from the business records, because this will provide the best opportunity for a fair self-assessment. If the control owner judgmentally selects sample records to examine, there could be the appearance of bias.

6. B. A control self-assessment (CSA) involves a control owner in the examination of a control's effectiveness. By pointing out the characteristics that make a control effective, a CSA can help a control owner better understand the concept of control effectiveness.

7. A. Sampling comprises several techniques used to select records from a process or system for examination in an audit.

8. B. A SOC 2 audit report, if available, is the best method for gaining assurance of the integrity of the service provider's control environment. An ISO 27001 certification is a good assurance of an effective security management system but lacks detail on control effectiveness.

9. A. Database schemas are not going to be of much use to an auditor who is auditing an organization's data management processes. The types of information that the auditor will want to examine include data management policies, processes, and records. A data flow diagram will help the auditor better understand the context of the organization's data management.

10. D. In a control self-assessment, questions about a control should be sent to the owner of the control, who will answer questions about its operation. Further, the control owner may be requested to provide evidence, such as control procedures and records.

11. B. The analysts are being shown how to complete a control self-assessment, a procedure in which analysts will select random samples and answer specific questions about the selected samples.

12. A. The best approach to ensure long-term success with a DLP system is to configure it initially in passive mode. This means that the DLP system will not interfere with any access, use, or transmission of personal information, but will instead silently log all such instances. The purpose of this approach is to help security and privacy professionals understand how personal information is used prior to having the DLP system intervene in what could be legitimate business processes.

13. C. To determine whether data subject requests are correctly logged, an auditor should examine business records. Examining privacy policy or interviewing process owners or data subjects would not reveal this information.

14. A. The auditor should continue with the audit by asking how the DSR procedure is conducted and by examining business records. It is likely that the auditor will, at least, find a deficiency because of the lack of a written procedure. It's entirely possible that there would be no other findings.

15. D. Upon management's request to monitor the privacy program, the privacy manager should provide meaningful operational metrics and one or more key risk indicators (KRIs) and key performance indicators (KPIs).

Privacy Operational Lifecycle: Respond

In this chapter, you will learn about
- Data privacy rights
- Responding to data subject requests
- Developing and testing privacy incident response plans
- Aligning response plans to applicable regulations
- Privacy program continuous improvement

This chapter covers the Certified Information Privacy Manager job practice VI, "Privacy Operational Lifecycle: Respond." The domain represents approximately 14 percent of the CIPM examination.

Privacy laws require transparency on the part of organizations that collect personal information about data subjects. Organizations are required to respond to a variety of requests, inquiries, and complaints. Responding to some requests may take time, so organizations should develop procedures or playbooks so that personnel know how to respond properly and in a timely manner.

Organizations need to develop privacy and security incident response plans to help them better recognize and respond quickly to incidents. Privacy incident response can often leverage an existing security incident response plan, since the procedures for both should be similar. It's important to define roles and responsibilities in privacy incident response so that all parties know what is expected of them. Organizations that gather metrics on their incident responses will be able to identify areas for improvement.

Data Subject Requests and Privacy Rights

Modern data privacy laws require transparency not only concerning the collection and use of personal data, but also in providing one or more means for data subjects to make inquiries and requests regarding the use of their personal information. Such requests include enabling data subjects to contact organizations to inquire about the use of their personal data, to enact corrections to their personal information, to lodge complaints, to request that their information be transferred to another similar organization, and to request that their identity be removed from an organization's records. The procedures for making such subject data requests are typically spelled out in an organization's privacy policy—in fact, laws such as the General Data Protection Regulation (GDPR) in the European Union require that privacy policies describe this. Occasionally, procedures may be located elsewhere, such as in a user guide or in system documentation.

Data Subject Requests

The inquiries and requests that persons may lodge with organizations are known as *data subject requests* (DSRs). Organizations generally provide multiple means for making such requests, including

- Postal mail
- Telephone
- FAX
- E-mail
- Web form
- In person

Privacy laws require organizations to disclose specific methods for making such inquiries. In turn, organizations need to develop repeatable business processes and train personnel to manage and respond to these incoming inquiries. Personnel who handle the requests will need access to systems and applications containing personal information to respond accurately.

Organizations typically maintain a log of inquiries, including the subject's name (or other identifying information), so that management can better understand the frequency of requests and the workload incurred. Privacy personnel will recognize that these logs themselves may also contain protected personal information.

Smaller organizations may provide only an inquiry form, an e-mail address, a telephone number, or a surface mail address where such inquiries may be sent. These organizations must respond to DSRs within specific timeframes (which are sometimes spelled out in regulations). Larger organizations automate inquiries in some cases. For instance, a data subject with an existing account on an organization's systems can log in and click a link to learn how and where personal information is used. Often, such tools provide the means for data subjects to make changes to some of their information.

The types of inquiries that data subjects may send are described in the remainder of this section.

Inquiries for Data Usage

Data subjects may send a DSR regarding the presence and usage of their personal information in an organization's records. Such a request may be general or quite specific. For instance, a data subject may ask whether his personal information is present in the organization's systems, or he may ask about specific personal information, such as a home address or telephone number. Depending upon the language of applicable laws and an organization's complexity, an organization receiving a DSR may need to search through multiple business records or systems to create a complete response to the data subject.

Requests for Updates and Corrections

In some circumstances, a data subject may ask for changes in her personal information used by an organization. For instance, a data subject may change residences and need to update a postal mail or shipping address. Or she may make changes in a payment method, family status, or service provider such as insurance. Finally, sometimes personal information is mistyped and spelling and other corrections are needed.

A request for an update or a correction can rise to the level of *redress*. In this case, the organization has made a decision detrimental to the data subject, who is requesting that the situation be corrected to make the data subject whole. For example, suppose an organization, believing it is selling an item to an ethnic minority, has priced the item higher than it would be for others. A customer seeking redress would request a correction to her data as well as a change in the organization's practice.

Organizations are required to provide one or more means through which data subjects can request these corrections. Data subjects often can make these changes through self-service programs, but sometimes they must request that organization personnel make the changes on their behalf.

Privacy policies often provide one or more methods to be used by data subjects to make these requests. Whether the means are automated or manual, organizations typically log these events as routine systems and activity measurements. Like other mature business processes, this logging will sometimes compel management to make changes or improvements to systems and processes. For example, if the organization is receiving numerous requests that personnel must deal with manually, it may provide more self-service tools for data subjects to make some of those changes themselves.

Requests to Opt Out of
Automated Profiling and Decision-Making Processes

In some jurisdictions, data subjects have the right to object to automatic subject profiling and automated decision-making processes. In Articles 13 and 21 of the GDPR, for instance, data subjects may request that they be removed from automated decision-making and profiling processes, regardless of the purpose of such automation. If, for example, an information broker that sells mailing lists to other organizations creates data subject profiles based on demographic information, data subjects can opt out of such activities.

 NOTE Data subjects may have trouble opting out of a data broker's automatic profiling, because these organizations are difficult to track down: they often have a low online profile and are often not identified by name in retail organization literature or in their privacy policies.

Requests for Transfer

A data subject may request that an organization transfer his personal information to another (presumably similar) organization. Article 20 of the GDPR states, "The data subject shall have the right to receive the personal data concerning him or her, which he or she has provided to a controller, in a structured, commonly used and machine-readable format and have the right to transmit those data to another controller without hindrance from the controller to which the personal data have been provided...." An example of such a request includes the transfer of medical records from one physician to another. Some organizations perform these transfers as a courtesy, but they are not required by law to perform them.

Requests for Removal

In Article 17, the GDPR made famous the notion of "the right to be forgotten," meaning the outright removal of a person's data from an organization's records. The California Consumer Privacy Act (CCPA) contains a similar provision in Section 1798.105. This is not a new concept. A data subject may want to opt out of an activity that an organization is conducting that involves the person's data. As with other subject data requests, privacy policy will provide specific means for such requests to be made and dealt with.

Organizations accepting opt-out or data removal requests must understand the nature of such data and any laws requiring the retention of records. For example, suppose a former employee requests that her employment records be removed, but employment law requires that employment records be retained for many years after the end of a person's employment. Similarly, a request made to remove a subject's data from a bank or credit union may conflict with laws requiring the retention of banking transaction records. On the other hand, marketing organizations that facilitate mail or telephone marketing campaigns may have few or no retention requirements and would be compelled to remove a subject's data on request. The same can be said of social networking organizations that have few statutory requirements for retaining subject data. Finally, privacy laws cite specific exclusions to data removal requests: GDPR, for instance, does not require courts or prison systems to expunge a person's criminal history.

Complaints

To improve customer service, organizations may include a means for permitting data subjects to lodge complaints regarding the use of their personal information. A data subject may be venting in the complaint, or the complaint may be an implicit request for a change in the person's relationship with the organization, including an opt-out or outright removal.

Personnel in the organization will need to consider complaints carefully, including whether a complaint describes an activity that could violate the organization's privacy policy. For this reason alone, organizations should pay close attention to data subject complaints, as they may be the only way organizations can become aware of privacy or security incidents.

EXAM TIP CIPM candidates are not expected to memorize the detailed provisions of privacy laws, but they should be familiar with the concepts of provisions such as the right to be forgotten, the ability to opt out of automatic decision-making processes, and requests for corrections.

Working with Authorities

Many privacy laws provide for the creation of government authorities that act in a supervisory capacity as a part of the enforcement of these laws. For instance, Articles 51 through 54 of the GDPR define supervisory authorities and their responsibilities. California Privacy Rights Act (CPRA), passed in 2020 by ballot measure, provides for the creation of the California Privacy Protection Agency to enforce the CCPA and additional privacy provisions in the CPRA itself. (Although this book does focus on organizations that will, from time to time, work with supervisory authorities, details on work performed *by* supervisory authorities are beyond its scope.)

The most important ingredient to successful relationships and encounters with external parties, including auditors, regulators, and supervisory authorities, is the completeness and integrity of business information, including the following:

- Up-to-date process information
- Data-flow diagrams (or detailed descriptions of data flows)
- Effective processes
- Complete and accurate business records

Nothing frustrates these external parties more than an organization that is disorganized and out of control. When such organizations do produce information, it will be regarded with skepticism, as external parties will wonder if the data was conjured up at the last minute or "cooked" (altered in an attempt to avoid accountability). Such disorganization could even be regarded as a lack of cooperation with a supervisory authority. For instance, GDPR Article 31 reads, "The controller and the processor and, where applicable, their representatives, shall cooperate, on request, with the supervisory authority in the performance of its tasks."

Supervisory authorities also do not take kindly the responses of organizations that appear disingenuous. Transparency and cooperation is a far better approach—one that can even result in a level of trust between the parties. That said, organizations with something to hide may continue to be uncooperative until the regulator discontinues the inquiry or the organization is backed into a corner and its dishonesty is no longer concealed. The International Association of Privacy Professionals (IAPP) Code of Ethics does not support such behavior.

Privacy and cybersecurity laws often require organizations that store or process personal information to have privacy and security breach procedures. Further, organizations should identify, in advance of any incident or breach, all applicable laws, regulations, and other obligations, and all instances where notification to regulators, supervisory authorities, and affected parties are required should a breach occur. Then, at the onset of an incident or a breach, the organization simply carries out its procedures, which are known and practiced in advance.

Privacy Incident Response

A *privacy incident* is an event in which one or more data subjects' personal information has been inappropriately used or disclosed in a manner contrary to applicable laws or regulations. A privacy incident is also an event representing a violation of an organization's privacy and/or security policy. For instance, if an organization's privacy policy states that it is not permitted to copy personal information to an external data storage device, the occurrence of such an event would be considered a privacy incident.

NOTE This section focuses primarily on privacy breaches related to data misuse. For a more detailed explanation of data protection breaches, read Chapter 5, "Information Security Incident Management," in *CISM Certified Information Security Manager All-In-One Exam Guide*.

Incident Response Regulations

As they develop their incident response procedures, organizations need to understand applicable regulatory requirements and incorporate them into their plans. Most privacy regulations require that organizations inform affected parties of security and privacy breaches, often when specific conditions occur. For instance, the older California privacy law known as SB 1386 required organizations to notify affected parties of breaches and unauthorized access to their personal information (which was defined in detail); however, if the personal information was in an encrypted state when compromised, no notification was required.

NOTE As with other aspects of privacy law, privacy and security managers should work with legal counsel to ensure that the organization correctly interprets privacy law.

In addition to aligning privacy incident response to applicable regulations, organizations should also be familiar with customer expectations, which may differ from regulations. Acts of goodwill can act as a salve on emotionally or financially harmed customers and the organization's reputation.

Phases of Incident Response

An effective response to a privacy incident is organized, documented, and rehearsed. The phases of a formal incident response plan are explained in this section.

For incident response to be effective, organizations must anticipate that incidents will occur and, accordingly, develop incident response plans, test those plans, and train personnel so that incident response will be effective and timely.

Briefly, the phases of incident response, in order, are

- Planning
- Detection

- Initiation
- Status updates
- Analysis
- Containment
- Eradication
- Recovery
- Remediation
- Closure
- Post-incident review
- Retention of evidence
- Incident reporting

These phases are discussed in detail in the remainder of this section.

 EXAM TIP CIPM candidates are not required to memorize the specific privacy incident response provisions in applicable laws, but they should be familiar with the concepts and procedures of privacy and security incident response.

Planning

This step involves the development of written response procedures that are followed when an incident occurs. These procedures are created once the organization's practices, processes, and technologies are well understood. This helps to ensure that incident response procedures align with the organization's privacy and security policy, applicable regulations, business operations, the technologies in use, and practices in place regarding architecture, development, management, and operations.

Detection

Detection represents the time when an organization is initially aware that a privacy incident is taking place or has taken place. Because of the variety of events that characterize a privacy incident, an organization can become aware of an incident in several ways, including

- Application or network slowdown or malfunction
- Alert from the intrusion detection/prevention system (IDS/IPS), data loss prevention (DLP) system, web filter, cloud access security broker (CASB), and/or other detective and preventive security systems
- Inquiry or compliant in a data subject request (DSR)
- Alert from a security incident and event management system (SIEM)

- Alert from physical security monitoring, including video surveillance and building entrance controls
- Alerts from an external service provider such as a software as a service (SaaS), platform as a service (PaaS), or infrastructure as a service (IaaS) vendor
- Alerts from media outlets and their investigators and reports
- Advisories from open-source intelligence (OSINT) sources
- Notification from an employee or business partner
- Anonymous tip
- Notification from a whistleblower
- Notification from a credit card brand, bank, or other financial institution
- Notification from a regulator
- Notification from law enforcement

Initiation

In this phase, a response to the incident begins. Typically, this will include a declaration of an incident, followed by notifications sent to response team members so that response operations should commence. Notifications are also typically sent to business executives so that they may also be informed.

Many organizations' incident response plans classify incidents by severity or impact, with varying forms and levels of internal communications associated with each classification. At times, the severity level may be changed as more is learned in later stages of incident response.

NOTE Although each organization's privacy incident response plan will vary, an incident is typically confirmed either in the initiation or analysis phases. At that time, organizations may be required to notify regulators, supervisory authorities, or affected parties.

Status Updates

From the onset, the incident response team should have established methodologies, formats, frequencies, and recipients of regular status updates to keep management and others informed as the incident investigation unfolds, progresses, and leads to containment, eradication, recovery, remediation, and closure. Generally, higher severity incidents warrant more frequent status reporting and to higher levels of management. The format of reporting must consider the audience so that the content of status reports is suitable for every audience. Often, this requires multiple layers of status reporting, each targeting respective audiences.

Status updates should be marked or labeled at a sufficiently high classification level to apply the greatest possible protection.

NOTE Some organizations direct all communications and status updates to inside or outside legal counsel, which means that status updates may be protected by attorney–client privilege.

Analysis

In this phase, response team members analyze available data to understand the cause, scope, and impact of the incident. This may involve the use of forensic analysis tools to understand activities on individual systems. Because many organizations lack computer forensics tools and expertise, outside experts are often summoned to perform forensics to understand the full nature and scope of an incident.

NOTE Forensic experts should be chosen carefully, because artifacts of their work could be included in subsequent legal proceedings.

Containment

Incident responders perform or direct actions that halt the progress or advancement of an incident in this phase. The steps required to contain an incident will vary according to the means used by the attacker. Sometimes, outside experts are called upon to assist with containment efforts.

Eradication

In this phase of incident response, responders take steps to remove the source of the incident. This could involve removing malware, blocking incoming attack messages, or changing users' access privileges on one or more systems.

Recovery

When the incident has been evaluated and eradicated, systems or components may need to be restored/recovered to their pre-incident state. This may include restoring data or configurations or replacing damaged or stolen equipment.

Remediation

This phase involves any necessary changes that will reduce or eliminate the possibility of a similar incident occurring in the future. This may take the form of process or technology changes.

Closure

Closure occurs when eradication, recovery, and remediation are completed. Incident response operations are officially closed.

Post-Incident Review

Shortly after the incident closes, incident responders and other personnel will meet to discuss the incident: its cause, its impact, and the organization's response. The discussion will range from lessons learned to possible improvements in technologies and processes to develop better defense and response.

Retention of Evidence

Incident responders and other personnel will direct the retention of evidence and other materials used or collected during the incident. This may include information that may be used in legal proceedings, including prosecution, civil lawsuits, and internal investigations. A chain of custody may be required to ensure evidence integrity.

NOTE Several standards are available that guide organizations toward a structured and organized incident response, including NIST SP 800-61, *Computer Security Incident Handling Guide,* and ISO/IEC 27035, *Information technology — Security techniques — Information security incident management.*

Incident Reporting

Privacy and security leaders should collect metrics on privacy and security incidents large and small, and then report these, together with numerous other metrics, to executive management as an overall part of its governance. Some of the metrics that should be kept and reported include the following:

- Number of incidents at each severity level
- Time required to detect and respond to incidents (this should be measured in minutes, not hours or days)
- Improvements made as a result of post-incident reviews
- Reviews and updates of incident response plans
- Incident responder training
- Improvements in incident detection

EXAM TIP CIPM candidates need to understand both the similarities and the differences between security incident response plans and privacy incident response plans.

Privacy Incident Response Plan Development

Effective incident response plans take time to develop. A privacy manager developing an incident response plan must first thoroughly understand business processes, privacy policy, data flows, and underlying information systems, and then discover resource requirements, dependencies, and failure points. A privacy manager may first develop a high-level incident response plan, which is usually followed by developing several incident response playbooks, the step-by-step instructions to follow when specific incidents occur.

NOTE Because many privacy incidents are also security incidents, the development of a privacy incident response plan should be performed in close cooperation with the information security manager to avoid duplication of effort and to utilize existing response plan resources and practices.

Resources

Before developing privacy incident response procedures, a privacy manager must identify required and available resources for incident detection and response. Perhaps the most important resource is the organization's security incident response plan. A correctly designed security incident response plan will recognize and respond to incidents, including information misuse, theft, and destruction. Two elements are needed to develop a privacy incident response plan:

- Callouts to privacy incident responders, so that they may orchestrate notifications to regulators and affected parties as required by applicable laws and regulations
- Detection and response to incidents of misuse of personal information that are not themselves security incidents

Besides these, other resources that privacy managers need to identify include

- Privacy incident response personnel, beyond those workers identified as security incident responders, who will be responsible for examining information systems to understand the nature of a "misuse of personal information" incident
- Forensics capabilities, including chain of custody procedures, which will ensure that evidence retention is robust if a privacy incident may involve notifications to outside parties
- Attorney–client privilege, to ensure that incident response communications and records are protected
- Contact information and methods for regulators and supervisory authorities
- Prewritten notifications to regulators, supervisory authorities, affected parties, and the public

Roles and Responsibilities

Responding to a privacy or security incident can be complicated; this makes it important for everyone to understand their roles and those of others. Roles and responsibilities should be documented in an organization's privacy and security incident response plans. Here is a typical arrangement:

- **Incident commander**   Coordinate hour-by-hour activities and resources, and identify specific personnel and resources required to work through incident stages. In a longer incident with response occurring over extended hours, this will need to be a "shift" position so that responders do not suffer exhaustion.

- **Incident responder**   Perform the hands-on steps of incident response to identify its cause, contain and eradicate it, and make any adjustments necessary to prevent a recurrence of the incident or a similar one. One or more trained experts in various processes and technologies who are familiar with each incident's processes or technologies can serve as incident responders. They can be employees of the organization or outside experts in incident response or computer and network forensics.

- **Scribe**   Record (generally, note-taking versus actual voice recordings) discussions, decisions, resources used, and outside parties (such as vendors) contacted.

- **Legal counsel**   Interpret and determine the applicability of laws and regulations (during plan development) and make decisions on notifications of external parties. External legal counsel can be retained as required for subject matter expertise and management of attorney–client privilege if used.

- **Privacy officer**   Lead and guide privacy team, possibly including incident responders, and ensure that privacy is upheld during incident response. This could be considered a co-management role alongside the incident commander (the privacy officer could also be the incident commander) and may also be the party to communicate with regulators as directed by applicable laws.

- **Cybersecurity officer**   Lead and guide the security team, possibly including incident responders. Ensure that security is intact during incident response. This could be considered a co-management role alongside the incident commander (the security officer could also be considered for the incident commander role).

- **CIO**   Provide IT staff resources, possibly including incident responders. Lead the continued operation of IT systems during the incident, including potential disaster recovery operations.

- **Business unit leaders**   Manage business unit and department business operations, including those affected by the incident. Carry out business continuity plans as applicable if primary processing systems are unavailable or untrusted.

- **Crisis communications**   Coordinate internal communications as required (generally needed only in larger organizations).

- **Public relations or public information officer (PIO)**   Compose press releases (during plan development), finalize and release tailored press releases, and notify external parties (often through a specialized service).

- **Business continuity and disaster recovery**   The nature of a major privacy or security incident may necessitate the initiation of business continuity and/or disaster recovery plans if primary information systems are unavailable or untrusted.

 NOTE   Privacy and security incident response plans need to define roles and responsibilities clearly, including decision-makers who will handle specific matters such as deciding when to communicate with external parties.

Incident Response Playbooks

More mature organizations will have developed numerous (as many as a dozen or more) playbooks, detailed procedures to be followed when specific types of security incidents occur. Typical playbook scenarios include ransomware, denial of service, a lost or stolen laptop or mobile device, destructive malware, compromise of a user account, and more.

Privacy incident response plans need playbooks as well, since many privacy incidents are not data protection security incidents per se, but instead represent the misuse of personal information. Thus, privacy managers developing privacy incident response plans need to develop additional response playbooks so that privacy incident responders can quickly work through investigation, containment, and recovery steps. A privacy incident is not the time to learn how a specific system works, where its logs reside (and how to read and interpret them), and how to run reports to understand the steps that resulted in the incident. Better organizations develop these playbooks in advance, so that incident responders can quickly determine what happened, why it happened, and who was involved.

Response Plan Tabletop Testing

When privacy incident response plans (and playbooks) have been developed, they need to be tested in one or more *tabletop* exercises. These facilitated discussions are led by an experienced incident responder who walks personnel through a typical privacy incident scenario step by step. At the same time, participants read their privacy incident response plans and discuss the steps they'd be taking if a real incident were taking place.

External Review

Many organizations realize that outside experts should review response plans and other procedures developed internally. Such reviews can draw upon the knowledge and experience of external parties, who can provide objective reviews of privacy and security response plans. Compared to the cost of incident response and subsequent developments, the cost of engaging an expert consultant is nominal.

 EXAM TIP CIPM candidates need to understand the general concepts and sequence of incident response and associated roles and responsibilities, even though each organization's implementation of a response plan will be unique.

Incident Response-able by Design

Just as information systems and business processes must support the concepts of *privacy by design* and *security by design*, so, too, must they be designed with incident response in mind. This includes the use of business records, event logging, and audit logging with sufficient detail to reconstruct an incident with enough clarity to understand how an incident occurred.

(continued)

These requirements need to be imposed on service providers that host many organizations' principal business applications in the form of SaaS services. Organizations need to include forensic analysis in the responsibility model with each SaaS provider to make it clear which parties are to perform which activities when a security or privacy incident occurs.

Privacy Continuous Improvement

The philosophy of *continuous improvement* is a mainstay of quality-oriented organizations. Rather than assume that all of an organization's processes, procedures, controls, and other operations are operating at an optimum level, a more realistic approach is the idea that there is always room for meaningful improvement.

Continuous improvement is primarily concerned with the fact of process and control improvement rather than the appearance of improvement. Still, an organization should consider all of its privacy and security programs' operations as "works in progress," meaning that management and staff recognize that their processes and controls have not achieved a level of perfection, and likely never will.

An organization can improve processes and controls in the following ways:

- **Accuracy** Organization strives to improve its controls and processes so that fewer exceptions and errors occur.
- **Efficiency** Organization will seek opportunities to make controls and processes more efficient, so that they will take less effort or require fewer resources while still maintaining quality objectives.
- **Timeliness** Organization will seek ways to make controls and processes more responsive so that routine and nonroutine tasks take less time to complete.
- **Risk** Organization will look for ways to reduce risks in controls and processes to ensure fewer opportunities for incidents.

Continuous improvement is so important that it is officially a requirement in ISO/IEC 27001:2013. Requirement 10.2 of the standard reads, "The organization shall continually improve the suitability, adequacy and effectiveness of the information security management system." Similarly, ISO/IEC 27701 (*Security techniques – Extension to ISO/IEC 27001 and ISO/IEC 27002 for privacy information management – Requirements and guidelines*) requirement 5.8 extends this to include the privacy information management system.

Chapter Review

Modern data privacy laws require transparency concerning not only the collection and use of personal data, but also concerning the ability to provide one or more means for data subjects to make inquiries and requests regarding the use of their personal information.

Such requests include offering a process by which data subjects can contact organizations to inquire about the use of their personal data, to enact corrections to their personal information, to lodge complaints, to request that their information be transferred to another similar organization, and to request that their identity be removed from an organization's records.

Data subject requests (DSRs) are the inquiries and requests that persons may lodge with organizations. Reasons for DSRs include requests to change information, to understand how personal data is being used, to opt out of one or more functions, or to request their data be removed altogether.

A request for an update or correction can rise to the level of *redress*. In this case, an organization has made a decision detrimental to the data subject, who requests that the organization correct the situation to make the data subject whole.

An organization is obligated to process a "right to be forgotten" request under the GDPR as long as laws forbid the removal of such information.

Many privacy laws provide for the creation of government authorities that act in a supervisory capacity to enforce these laws. For instance, Articles 51 through 54 of the GDPR define supervisory authorities and their responsibilities. The CPRA, passed in 2020 by ballot measure, provides for the creation of the California Privacy Protection Agency to enforce the CCPA and additional privacy provisions in the CPRA itself.

A *privacy incident* is an event in which one or more data subjects' personal information has been inappropriately used or disclosed in a manner contrary to applicable laws or regulations.

The phases of incident response are planning, detection, initiation, status updates, analysis, containment, eradication, recovery, remediation, closure, post-incident review, retention of evidence, and incident reporting. Evidence needs to be retained for a specified period.

Because privacy and security incident response techniques are so similar, it may be prudent to combine them into a single process.

Roles and responsibilities should be documented in an organization's privacy and security incident response plans.

Quick Review

- Depending upon the language of applicable laws and the complexity of the organization, an organization receiving a DSR may need to search through multiple business records or systems to create a complete response to the data subject.

- In some jurisdictions, data subjects have the right to object to automatic subject profiling and automated decision-making processes.

- Most privacy regulations require that organizations inform affected parties of security and privacy breaches, often when specific conditions occur.

- Although each organization's privacy incident response plan will vary, an incident is typically confirmed either in the initiation or analysis phase. At that time, organizations may be required to notify regulators, supervisory authorities, or affected parties.

- Higher severity incidents warrant more frequent status reporting and to higher levels of management. The format of reporting must consider the audience, so that the content of status reports is suitable for every audience. Often, this requires multiple layers of status reporting, each targeting respective audiences.

- Some organizations direct all communications and status updates to inside or outside legal counsel, so that status updates are protected by attorney–client privilege.

- Forensic experts should be chosen carefully, as artifacts of their work could be included in subsequent legal proceedings.

- Because many privacy incidents are also security incidents, the development of a privacy incident response plan should be performed in close cooperation with the security manager to avoid duplication of effort and utilize existing response plan resources and practices.

- More mature organizations will have developed numerous (as many as a dozen or more) *playbooks,* which are detailed procedures to be followed when specific types of security incidents take place. Typical playbook scenarios include ransomware, denial of service, lost or stolen laptop or mobile device, destructive malware, compromise of a user account, and more.

Questions

1. A tabletop exercise is:

   A. A risk analysis to predict an incident

   B. A recap of a recent incident

   C. A simulation of an actual incident

   D. A test of forensic capabilities

2. An organization has received a data subject's request to remove all personal information on file. How should the organization respond?

   A. Pseudonymize the data subject's personal information.

   B. Anonymize the data subject's personal information.

   C. Remove or anonymize the data subject's personal information.

   D. Remove or anonymize the data subject's personal information as permitted by other applicable laws.

3. An organization wants to exempt records for any future security or privacy incidents from discovery requests. What should be included in security and privacy incident response plans to accomplish this?

   A. Change the data retention policy.

   B. Turn off dynamic DLP for the directories where incident records are stored.

   C. Retain outside legal counsel.

   D. Implement attorney–client privilege.

4. Program responsibilities for the activities of managing data subject requests lie with:

   A. Customer support

   B. The chief marketing officer

   C. The chief information security officer

   D. The chief privacy officer

5. In a privacy breach response plan, who should be making decisions on whether (and when) to notify authorities and affected parties?

   A. Privacy officer

   B. Public relations

   C. Legal counsel

   D. Crisis communications

6. The role of privacy incident commander is:

   A. Develop the privacy incident response plan

   B. Coordinate privacy incident proceedings

   C. Decide when authorities should be notified

   D. Determine incident response roles and responsibilities

7. The purpose of a post-incident review is:

   A. Identify improvement opportunities

   B. Identify mistakes made during an incident

   C. Determine how long it took to respond

   D. Review forensic techniques used

8. How long should evidence and records related to a specific privacy incident be retained?

   A. One year

   B. According to the data retention schedule

   C. Seven years

   D. According to the data destruction schedule

9. While gathering and examining various privacy-related business records, the privacy officer has determined that the organization has no privacy or security incident log. What conclusion can the privacy officer make from this?

   A. The organization does not have privacy or security incident detection capabilities.

   B. The organization has not yet experienced a privacy or security incident.

   C. The organization is recording privacy or security incidents in its risk register.

   D. The organization has effective privacy policies.

10. An organization requests that each data subject submit an image of his or her driver's license as a means of authentication when submitting data subject requests. Should subsequent data subject requests cite the driver's license as collected information?

   A. Yes, because authentication data is always subject to data access requests.

   B. No, because the driver's license was collected outside of the collection period.

   C. No, because information submitted as a part of authentication is exempt.

   D. Yes, because the data subject's driver's license was collected by the organization.

11. An incident response team is in the process of responding to an incident. The incident responders have removed the malware and blocked command-and-control traffic. At this stage, the source of the incident has been:

   A. Contained

   B. Eradicated

   C. Remediated

   D. Recovered

12. What is generally the best approach when working with authorities?

   A. Delay for as long as legally permissible.

   B. Slowly and progressively provide requested information.

   C. Cooperate and act with transparency.

   D. Delay for as long as possible.

13. Which of the following methods should an organization provide as means for customers to make inquiries and complaints about privacy matters?

   A. Telephone

   B. E-mail address

   C. Postal mail

   D. All of these

14. What is the best method for ensuring that privacy incident responders are familiar with incident response procedures?

   A. Include incident responders in tabletop testing.

   B. Direct incident responders to develop incident response plans.

   C. Direct incident responders to respond to the next incident.

   D. Direct incident responders to review incident response plans.

15. The best definition of a data subject request is:

   A. A request to be removed from all business records

   B. A request to be added to sales and marketing communication

   C. A request to be removed from sales and marketing communication

   D. An inquiry or request concerning the use of a subject's personal information

Answers

1. **C.** A tabletop exercise is a simulation of a real incident, whether a privacy incident, a security incident, an outage, or a disaster. Tabletop exercises for privacy and security incident response should take place at least once per year.

2. **D.** The organization may proceed with the data subject's data removal request, provided that there are no other laws requiring the retention of this information. For example, banks are typically not permitted to remove financial records for current or former customers.

3. **D.** With guidance from the organization's legal counsel, invoking attorney–client privilege and following certain procedures regarding communications can help to protect incident response records from being discovered in future legal proceedings.

4. **D.** The chief privacy officer has primary responsibility for the organization's receipt of, processing of, and response to data subject requests. Other departments may have operational responsibilities in the management of these requests, but the ultimate accountability lies with the CPO.

5. **C.** Legal counsel should decide when and how regulatory authorities, affected parties, and others should be notified in the event of a privacy or security breach.

6. **B.** A privacy incident commander's role is to coordinate and direct incident response proceedings using the plan that has been documented.

7. **A.** The purpose of a post-incident review is to identify what went well and what improvements can be made—both in terms of incident response procedures as well as with the systems or processes affected.

8. **B.** An organization's data retention schedule (which should align with applicable laws) should determine how long evidence and records from an incident should be retained.

9. **A.** An organization that does not have a privacy or security incident log probably lacks the capability to detect and respond to an incident. It is not reasonable to assume that the organization has experienced no incidents, because minor incidents occur with regularity. Claiming that the organization has effective controls is unreasonable, because it is understood that incidents occur even when effective controls are in place (because not all types of incidents can reasonably be prevented).

10. **D.** Personal information, including the image of a driver's license or other government-issued identification, that is collected by an organization for any reason must be disclosed to a data subject who inquires about what information an organization has collected.

11. **B.** Eradication is the point at which the agent causing an incident (in this case, malware) has been removed from one or more systems.

12. **C.** Cooperation, collaboration, and transparency are generally better approaches when working with regulators, particularly during an inquiry or investigation. Stalling or delaying proceedings may draw suspicion even when none is otherwise warranted.

13. **D.** All of the methods described—telephone, e-mail, and postal mail—are valid means for customers to make inquiries and lodge complaints regarding their privacy.

14. **A.** The best method for incident responders to become familiar with incident response plans is for them to participate in tabletop exercises.

15. **D.** A data subject request (DSR) can be any form of an inquiry, request, or complaint regarding an organization's use of the data subject's personal information.

The Risk Management Life Cycle

In this appendix, you will learn about
- Risk management
- Risk analysis
- Risk treatment
- Threats, vulnerabilities, and assets
- Calculating risk

This appendix covers the risk management life-cycle process that is a vital part of any organization's information security and privacy program. Although risk management is not a core part of the Certified Information Privacy Manager job practice, I have included it in this book because it is considered invaluable for the privacy and security professional. As a privacy professional, you may someday be responsible for privacy risk management, but regardless of your role in the organization, being familiar with risk management will give you additional insight into the process of business risk decision-making.

Like other life-cycle processes, risk management is a cyclical, iterative activity that is used to acquire, analyze, and treat risks. This book focuses on privacy risk, but overall the life cycle for privacy risk is functionally similar to that for information risk or even business risk: a new risk is introduced into the process, the risk is studied, and a decision is made about how to deal with it.

Like other life-cycle processes, risk management is formally defined in policy and process documents that define the scope, roles and responsibilities, workflow, business rules, and business records. Several frameworks and standards from US and international sources define the full life-cycle risk process. Privacy and security managers are generally free to adopt any of these standards, use a blend of different standards, or develop a custom framework.

Both privacy and information risk management rely upon risk assessments that consider valid threats against the organization's information assets, considering any present vulnerabilities. Several standards and models for risk assessments can be used. The results of risk assessments are placed into a risk register, which is the official business record containing current and historic information risk items.

Risk treatment is the activity in which decisions about risks are made after weighing various options. Risk treatment decisions are typically made by a business owner associated with the affected business activity and ratified by an executive steering group.

The Risk Management Process

The risk management process consists of a set of structured activities that enable an organization to manage risks systematically. Like other business processes, risk management processes vary somewhat from one organization to the next, but generally they consist of the following activities:

- **Scope definition**   The organization defines the scope of the risk management process itself. Typically, scope definitions include geographic or business unit parameters. The scope definition is not part of the iterative portion of the risk management process, although scope may be redefined from time to time. In an organization's privacy program, the scope should include
  - Business processes related to the collection, use, and transfer (or sale) of personal information
  - Information systems that support these processes
  - The work centers and processing centers supporting the information systems
  - Information security in support of these systems and processes
  - All of the aforementioned items that are outsourced to third parties

- **Asset identification and valuation**   The organization uses various means to discover and track its stored information (including personal information) and information system assets. A classification scheme may be present that identifies risk and criticality levels. Asset valuation is a key part of asset management processes, and the value of assets is appropriated for use in the risk management process.

- **Risk appetite**   Developed outside of the risk management life-cycle process, risk appetite is an expression of the level of risk that an organization is willing to accept. A risk appetite that is related to information and privacy risk is typically expressed in qualitative means.

- **Risk identification**   This is the first step in the iterative portion of the risk management process, when the organization identifies a risk that comes from one of several sources, including the following:
  - **Risk assessment**   This includes an overall risk assessment or a focused risk assessment.
  - **Privacy impact assessment (PIA)**   This is an analysis of how personally identifiable information (PII) is collected, used, shared, and maintained as part of planned changes to a business process or information system to identify any changes in privacy risk.
  - **Data protection impact assessment (DPIA)**   This is an analysis of how planned changes to a business process or information system will impact an organization's ability to protect specific types of data (such as PII).

- **Vulnerability assessment**   This may be one of several activities, including a security scan, a penetration test, or a source code scan.

- **Threat advisory**   An advisory may be issued from a product vendor, threat intelligence feed, or news story.

- **Internal audit**   A routine internal audit may reveal a weakness in a business process that warrants attention in the risk management process.

- **Control self-assessment (CSA)**   The self-assessment of an internal control may identify a weakness that needs to be managed in the risk management process.

- **Change in regulations**   A new privacy regulation, a change in an existing regulation, or a precedent set in the enforcement or in legal proceedings may compel organizations to see their processes in a new light. Occasionally, this means that a process or control once thought to be compliant (or secure) may need to be revised.

- **Risk analysis**   This analysis is focused on information that may uncover additional risks that require attention.

- **Incident**   A security or privacy incident may reveal risks, whether associated with the incident or not. Though this is sometimes a matter of risk identification in hindsight, such risks cannot be overlooked.

NOTE   Threat events include various aspects of compliance risk, including audits or examinations (with their findings), fines, penalties, sanctions, or notifications to affected parties (employees, customers, or constituents).

- **Risk analysis**   This is the second step in a typical risk management process, including a PIA or DPIA. After the risk has been identified, it is analyzed to determine several characteristics, including the following:

  - **Probability of event occurrence**   The risk analyst studies event scenarios and calculates the likelihood that an event associated with the risk will occur. This is typically expressed as the number of likely events per year.

  - **Impact of event occurrence**   The risk analyst studies different event scenarios and determines the impact of each. This may be expressed in quantitative terms (dollars or other currency) or qualitative terms (high–medium–low or a numeric scale of 1–5 or 1–10).

  - **Mitigation**   The risk analyst studies different available methods for mitigating the risk. Depending upon the type of risk, there are many techniques to choose from, including changing a process or procedure, training staff, changing architecture or configuration, or applying a security patch.

  - **Recommendation**   After studying a risk, the risk analyst may develop a recommended course of action to address the risk. This reflects the fact that the individual performing risk analysis is often not the risk decision-maker.

- **Risk treatment** This is the last step in a typical risk management process. Here, the privacy steering committee (or appropriate authoritative group) makes or approves a decision about a specific risk. The basic options for risk treatment are

  - **Accept** The organization elects to take no action related to the risk.

  - **Mitigate** The organization chooses to mitigate the risk, which takes the form of some action that serves to reduce the probability or impact of a risk event. The actual steps taken may include business process changes, system configuration changes, the enactment of a new control, or staff training.

  - **Transfer** The practice of transferring risk is typically achieved through an insurance policy, although other forms are available, including contract assignment.

  - **Avoid** The organization chooses to discontinue the activity associated with the risk. This is typically selected for an outdated business activity that is no longer profitable or for a business activity that was not formally approved in the first place.

- **Risk communication** This takes many forms, including formal communications within risk management processes and procedures, as well as information communications among risk managers and decision-makers.

In addition to business processes, a risk management process has business records associated with it. The *risk register,* sometimes known as a risk ledger, is the primary business record in most risk management programs. A risk register is a listing of risks that have been identified and typically contains many items, including a description of each risk, the level and type of each risk, and information about risk treatment decisions.

Figure A-1 shows the elements of a typical risk management life cycle.

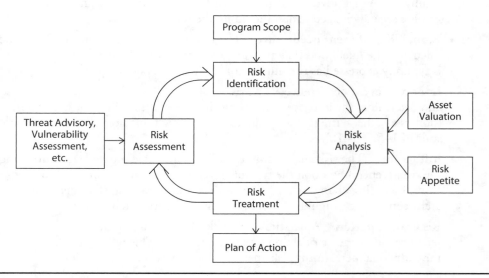

Figure A-1 The risk management life cycle

Risk Management Methodologies

Several established methodologies are available for organizations that want to manage risk using a formal standard. Organizations select one of these standards for a variety of reasons: they may be required to use a specific standard to address regulatory or contractual terms, they may believe that a specific standard better aligns with their overall information risk program or the business as a whole, or they may want to start with a known standard process as opposed to creating one from scratch.

NIST Standards

The National Institute for Standards and Technology (NIST) develops standards for information security and other subject matter. NIST Special Publication (SP) 800-39, *Managing Information Security Risk: Organization, Mission, and Information, System View,* describes the overall risk management process. NIST SP 800-30, *Guide for Conducting Risk Assessments,* is a detailed, high-quality standard that describes the steps for conducting risk assessments. The NIST Risk Management Framework (RMF) is a process framework that encompasses the entire risk management life cycle.

NIST SP 800-39

The methodology described in NIST SP 800-39 consists of multilevel risk management, at the information systems level, at the mission/business process level, and at the overall organization level. Risks are communicated up the levels for overall awareness, while risk awareness and risk decisions are communicated downward for overall awareness. Figure A-2 depicts this approach.

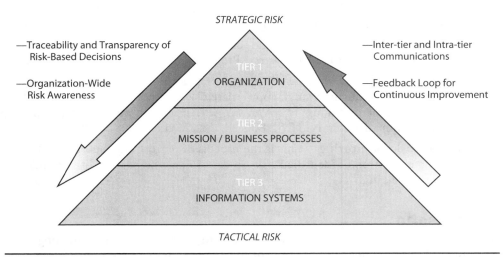

Figure A-2   Multi-tier risk management in NIST SP 800-39 (Source: National Institute for Standards and Technology)

NOTE At first glance, this may appear to be a discussion of cybersecurity risk, but you should know that risk management and risk assessment methodology have wide applications. Organizations practicing risk management can do so in the context of operationally critical information systems, manufacturing assembly lines, biomedical laboratory operations, or the protection and use of personal information. For all these, and more, the methodologies of identifying, analyzing, and treating risk are the same.

The tiers of risk management are described in NIST SP 800-39 in this way:

- **Tier 1: Organization view** This level focuses on the role of governance, the activities performed by the risk executive, and the development of risk management and investment strategies.

- **Tier 2: Mission/business process view** This level is all about enterprise architecture and enterprise security architecture, and ensuring that business processes are risk-aware.

- **Tier 3: Information systems view** This level concentrates on more tactical things such as system configuration and hardening specifications, vulnerability management, and the detailed steps in the systems development life cycle.

Other concepts discussed in NIST SP 800-39 include trust, the trustworthiness of systems, and organizational culture.

The overall risk management process defined by NIST SP 800-39 consists of several steps:

- **Step 1: Risk framing** This consists of the assumptions, scope, tolerances, constraints, and priorities—in other words, the business context that is considered prior to later steps taking place.

- **Step 2: Risk assessment** This is the actual risk assessment, where threats and vulnerabilities are identified and assessed to determine levels and types of risk.

- **Step 3: Risk response** This is the process of analyzing each risk and developing strategies for reducing it through appropriate risk treatment for each identified risk. Risk treatment options are *accept, mitigate, avoid,* and *transfer.* This step is defined in more detail in NIST SP 800-30, described next.

- **Step 4: Risk monitoring** This is the process of performing periodic and ongoing evaluation of identified risks to determine whether conditions and risks are changing.

NIST SP 800-30

NIST SP 800-30 describes in greater detail a standard methodology for conducting a risk assessment. The techniques included in this document are quite structured and essentially involve setting up a number of worksheets where threats and vulnerabilities are recorded, along with the probability of occurrence and impact if they occur.

In this standard, these are the steps for conducting a risk assessment:

- **Step 1: Prepare for assessment**   The organization determines the purpose of the risk assessment. Primarily, it is important to know the purpose of the results of the risk assessment and the decisions that will be made as a result of the risk assessment. Next, the scope of the assessment must be determined and known. This may take many forms, including geographic and business unit boundaries or specific business processes, as well as the range of threat scenarios that are to be included. Also, any assumptions and constraints pertaining to the assessment should be identified. Further, the sources of threat, vulnerability, and impact information must be identified. (NIST SP 800-30 includes exemplary lists of threats, vulnerabilities, and impacts in its appendixes.)

- **Step 2: Conduct assessment**   The organization performs the actual risk assessment. This consists of several tasks.

  a) *Identify threat sources and events.* The organization identifies a list of threat sources and events that will be considered in the assessment. The following sources of threat information are included in the standard and can be used. Organizations are advised to supplement these sources with other information as needed.

    - Table D-1: Inputs—threat source identification
    - Table D-2: Taxonomy of threat sources
    - Table D-3: Assessment scale—characteristics of adversary capabilities
    - Table D-4: Assessment scale—characteristics of adversary intent
    - Table D-5: Assessment scale—adversary targeting
    - Table D-6: Assessment scale—non-adversarial threat effects
    - Table D-7: Template—Identification of adversarial threat sources (organization-specific table to be completed by risk manager)
    - Table D-8: Template—Identification of non-adversarial threat sources (organization-specific table to be completed by risk manager)
    - Table E-1: Inputs—Threat event identification
    - Table E-2: Representative examples—adversarial threat events
    - Table E-3: Representative examples—non-adversarial threat events
    - Table E-4: Relevance of threat events
    - Table E-5: Template—Identification of threat events (organization-specific table to be completed by risk manager)

  b) *Identify vulnerabilities and predisposing conditions.* The organization examines its environment (people, processes, and technology) to determine what vulnerabilities exist that could result in a greater likelihood that threat events may occur. The following sources of vulnerability and predisposing condition information are included in the standard and can be used in a risk assessment.

Like the catalog of threats, organizations are advised to supplement these lists with additional vulnerabilities as needed.

- Table F-1: Inputs—vulnerability and predisposing conditions
- Table F-2: Assessment scale—vulnerability severity
- Table F-3: Template—Identification of organization-specific vulnerabilities
- Table F-4: Taxonomy of predisposing conditions
- Table F-5: Assessment scale—pervasiveness of predisposing conditions
- Table F-6: Template—Identification of predisposing conditions (organization-specific table to be completed by risk manager)

c) *Determine the likelihood of occurrence.* The organization determines the probability that each threat scenario identified will occur. The following tables guide the risk manager in scoring each threat:

- Table G-1: Inputs—determination of likelihood
- Table G-2: Assessment scale—likelihood of threat event initiation (adversarial)
- Table G-3: Assessment scale—likelihood of threat event occurrence (non-adversarial)
- Table G-4: Assessment scale—likelihood of threat event resulting in adverse impacts
- Table G-5: Assessment scale—overall likelihood

d) *Determine the magnitude of impact.* In this phase, the risk manager determines the impact of each type of threat event on the organization. These tables guide the risk manager in this effort:

- Table H-1: Inputs—determination of impact
- Table H-2: Examples of adverse impacts
- Table H-3: Assessment scale—impact of threat events
- Table H-4: Template—Identification of adverse impacts (organization-specific table to be completed by risk manager)

e) *Determine the risk level.* The organization determines the level of risk for each threat event. These tables aid the risk manager in this effort:

- Table I-1: Inputs—risk
- Table I-2: Assessment scale—level of risk (combination of likelihood and impact)
- Table I-3: Assessment scale—level of risk
- Table I-4: Column descriptions for adversarial risk table
- Table I-5: Template—adversarial risk (organization-specific table to be completed by risk manager)
- Table I-6: Column descriptions for non-adversarial risk table
- Table I-7: Template—non-adversarial risk (organization-specific table to be completed by risk manager)

- **Step 3: Communicate results**   When the risk assessment has been completed, the results are communicated to decision-makers and stakeholders in the organization. The purpose of communicating risk assessment results is to ensure that the organization's decision-makers make decisions that include considerations for known risks. Risk assessment results can be communicated in several ways, including the following:
  - Publishing to a central location
  - Briefings
  - Distributing via e-mail
  - Distributing hard copies
- **Step 4: Maintain assessment**   After a risk assessment has been completed, the organization will maintain the assessment by monitoring risk factors identified in the risk assessment. This enables the organization to maintain a view of relevant risks that incorporates changes in the business environment since the risk assessment was completed. NIST SP 800-137, *Information Security Continuous Monitoring (ISCM) for Federal Information Systems and Organizations*, provides guidance on the ongoing monitoring of information systems, operations, and risks.

   NOTE   NIST SP 800-30 is available from https://csrc.nist.gov/publications/sp.

NIST Risk Management Framework (RMF)

The NIST RMF is a high-level, repeatable process for managing the entire risk management life cycle. The methodology described in NIST RMF consists of these seven activities:

- **Prepare**   Participate in activities and take steps to help the organization prepare to identify and manage security and privacy risks.
- **Categorize**   Determine the security categorization of information systems, based upon the nature of the information they store, process, or transmit. This is akin to the concept of *system classification*.
- **Select**   Identify, tailor, and document controls required to protect information and information systems based on risk. These controls may be selected from NIST SP 800-53 or another control framework as needed.
- **Implement**   Implement the controls identified in the Select step. Update security plans accordingly.
- **Assess**   Determine the effectiveness of controls. Often this is accomplished through control self-assessment, internal audit, or an assessment performed by an outside party. Remediation plans are developed and assigned for identified deficiencies.

- **Authorize** This is a formal management sign-off on risks and risk mitigation identified in earlier steps.
- **Monitor** Continually monitor risks, threats, and controls to remain aware of the system's security and privacy postures.

 NOTE NIST RMF is available from https://csrc.nist.gov/Projects/risk-management.

ISO/IEC 27005

ISO/IEC 27005, *Information technology – Security techniques – Information security risk management,* is an international standard that defines a structured approach to risk assessments and risk management. The methodology outlined in this standard is summarized here:

Step 1: Establish Context

Before the risk analyst can perform a risk assessment, a number of parameters need to be established, including the following:

- **Scope of the risk assessment** This includes which portions of an organization are to be included, based on business unit, service, line, geography, organization structure, or other means.
- **Purpose of the risk assessment** Reasons include legal or due diligence or support of an information security management system (ISMS), business continuity plan, vulnerability management plan, or incident response plan.
- **Risk evaluation criteria** Determine the means by which risks will be examined and scored.
- **Impact criteria** Determine how the impact of identified risks will be described and scored.
- **Risk acceptance criteria** Specify the method the organization will use to determine risk acceptance.
- **Logistical plan** This includes which personnel will perform the risk assessment, which personnel in the organization need to provide information such as control evidence, and what supporting facilities are required, such as office space.

Step 2: Risk Assessment

The risk assessment is performed with the following tasks:

- **Asset identification** Risk analysts identify assets, along with their value and criticality.
- **Threat identification** Risk analysts identify relevant and credible threats that have the potential to harm assets, along with their likelihood of occurrence.

There are many types of threats, both naturally occurring and human-caused, and accidental or deliberate. Note that some threats may affect more than one asset. ISO/IEC 27005 contains a list of threat types, as does NIST SP 800-30 (in Table D-2), described earlier.

NOTE A risk analyst should consider additional threats specific to the organization that are not discussed in ISO/IEC 27005 or NIST SP 800-30.

- **Control identification**   Risk analysts identify existing and planned controls. Those controls that already exist should be examined to determine whether they are effective. The criteria for examining a control includes whether it adequately reduces the likelihood or impact of a threat event. The results of this examination will conclude whether the control is effective, ineffective, or unnecessary. Finally, when identifying threats, the risk analyst may determine that a new control is warranted.

- **Vulnerability identification**   Vulnerabilities that can be exploited by threat events that cause harm to an asset are identified. Remember that a vulnerability does not cause harm, but its presence may enable a threat event to harm an asset. ISO/IEC 27005 contains a list of vulnerabilities. Note that a risk analyst may need to identify additional vulnerabilities.

- **Consequences identification**   The risk analyst will identify consequences that would occur for each identified threat against each asset. Consequences may include the loss of confidentiality, integrity, or availability of any asset, as well as the loss of human safety. Depending on the nature of the asset, consequences may take many forms, including service interruption or degradation, reduction in service quality, loss of business, reputation damage, or monetary penalties, including fines. Note that consequences may be a primary result or a secondary result of the realization of a specific threat. For example, the theft of sensitive financial information may have little or no operational impact in the short term, but legal proceedings over the long term could result in financial penalties, unexpected costs, and loss of business.

Step 3: Risk Evaluation
Levels of risk are determined according to the risk evaluation and risk acceptance criteria established in step 1. The output of risk evaluation is a list of risks, with their associated threats, vulnerabilities, and consequences.

Step 4: Risk Treatment
Decision-makers in the organization will select one of four risk treatment options for each risk identified in step 3:

- **Risk reduction (aka risk mitigation)**   The organization alters something in information technology (such as security configuration, application source code, or data), business processes and procedures, or personnel (such as training).

In many cases, an organization will choose to update an existing control or enact a new control so that the risk reduction may be more effectively monitored over time. The cost of updating or creating a control—as well as the impact on ongoing operational costs of the control—will need to be weighed alongside the value of the asset being protected, as well as the consequences associated with the risk being treated. A risk manager remembers that a control can reduce many risks, and potentially for several assets, so the risk manager will need to consider the benefit of risk reduction in more complex terms. Chapter 2 covers a brief discussion of the types of controls. A more complete discussion of controls appears in *CISM Certified Information Security Manager All-In-One Exam Guide*.

- **Risk retention (aka risk acceptance)** The organization chooses to accept the risk and decides not to change anything.

- **Risk avoidance** The organization decides to discontinue the activity associated with the risk. For example, an organization assesses the risks related to the acceptance of credit card data for payments and decides to change the system so that credit card data is sent directly to a payment processor so that the organization will no longer be accepting credit card data.

- **Risk transfer** The organization transfers risk to another party. Common forms of risk transfer are securing insurance and outsourcing security monitoring to a third party. When an organization transfers risk to another party, there will usually be residual risk that is more difficult to treat. For example, although an organization may have reduced the costs of a breach because it had previously secured cyber insurance, the organization may still suffer reputational damage in the form of reduced goodwill.

Decision-makers weigh the costs and benefits associated with each of these four options and decide the best course of action for the organization. These four risk treatment options are not mutually exclusive; sometimes, a combination of risk treatment options may be the best choice for a specific situation. For instance, if a business application was found to accept weak passwords, the chosen risk treatment may be a combination of security awareness training (mitigation) and acceptance (the organization elected not to modify the application because this would have been too expensive).

Further, some treatments can address more than one risk. For example, security awareness training may reduce several risks associated with end-user computing and behavior.

Often, after risk treatment, some risk—known as *residual risk*—remains. When analyzing residual risk, the organization may elect to undergo additional risk treatment to reduce the risk further, or it may accept the residual risk as is. Note that residual risk cannot be reduced to zero—there will always be some level of risk.

Because some forms of risk treatment (mainly, risk reduction and risk transfer) may require an extended period of time to be completed, risk managers usually track ongoing risk treatment activities to completion.

Step 5: Risk Communication

All parties involved in information risk—the chief information security officer (CISO) or another top-ranking information security official, risk managers, business decision-makers, and other stakeholders—need channels of communication throughout the entire risk management and risk treatment life cycle. Examples of risk communication include the following:

- Announcements and discussions of upcoming risk assessments
- Collection of risk information during risk assessments (and at other times)
- Proceedings and results from completed risk assessments
- Discussions of risk tolerance
- Proceedings from risk treatment discussions and risk treatment decisions and plans
- Educational information about security and risk
- Updates to the organization's mission and strategic objectives
- Communication about security incidents to affected parties and stakeholders

Step 6: Risk Monitoring and Review

Organizations are not static, and neither is risk. The value of assets, impacts, threats, and vulnerabilities and the likelihood of risk occurrence should be periodically monitored and reviewed so that the organization's view of risk continues to be relevant and accurate. Monitoring should include

- Discovery of new, changed, and retired assets
- Change in business processes and practices
- Changes in technology architecture
- Presence of new threats that have not been assessed
- Presence of new vulnerabilities that were previously unknown
- Changes in threat event probability and consequences
- Security incidents that may alter the organization's understanding of threats, vulnerabilities, and risks
- Changes in market and other business conditions
- Changes in applicable laws and regulations

NOTE You can search for and access ISO/IEC 27005 at https://www.iso.org/home.html.

Factor Analysis of Information Risk

Factor Analysis of Information Risk (FAIR) is an analysis method that helps a risk manager understand the factors that contribute to risk, the probability of threat occurrence, and an estimation of potential losses. In the FAIR methodology, there are six types of loss:

- **Productivity** Loss of productivity caused by the incident
- **Response** Cost expended in incident response

- **Replacement**   Expense required to rebuild or replace an asset
- **Fines and judgments**   All forms of legal costs resulting from the incident
- **Competitive advantage**   Loss of business to other organizations
- **Reputation**   Loss of goodwill and future business

FAIR also focuses on the concept of asset value and liability. For example, a customer list is an asset because the organization can reach its customers to solicit new business; however, the customer list is also a liability because of the impact on the organization if the customer list is obtained by an unauthorized person.

FAIR guides a risk manager through an analysis of threat agents and the different ways in which a threat agent acts upon an asset:

- **Access**   Threat agent reads data without authorization
- **Misuse**   Threat agent uses an asset differently from its intended usage
- **Disclose**   Threat agent shares data with other unauthorized parties
- **Modify**   Threat agent modifies asset
- **Deny use**   Threat agent prevents legitimate subjects from accessing assets

FAIR is considered to be complementary to risk management methodologies such as NIST SP 800-30 and ISO/IEC 27005.

 NOTE   You can obtain information about FAIR at https://www.fairinstitute.org.

Asset Identification

After a risk assessment's scope has been determined, the initial step in a risk assessment is the identification of assets and a determination of each asset's value. In a typical information risk assessment, assets will consist of various types of information (including intellectual property, internal operations, and personal information), the information systems that support and protect those information assets, and the business processes that are supported by these systems.

Hardware Assets

Hardware assets may include server and network hardware, user workstations, office equipment such as printers and scanners, and Wi-Fi access points. Depending on the scope of the risk assessment, assets in storage and replacement components may also be included.

Because hardware assets are installed, moved, and eventually retired, it is important to verify the information in the asset inventory periodically by physically verifying the existence of the physical assets. Depending upon the value and sensitivity of systems and data, this inventory "true-up" may be performed as often as monthly or as seldom as annually. Discrepancies in actual inventory must be investigated to verify that assets have not been stolen or moved without authorization.

Subsystem and Software Assets

Software applications such as software development tools, drawing tools, security scanning tools, and subsystems such as application servers and database management systems are all considered assets. Like physical assets, these assets often have tangible value and should be periodically inventoried.

Cloud-Based Information Assets

One significant challenge related to information assets lies in the nature of cloud services and how they work. An organization may have a significant portion of its information assets stored by other organizations in their cloud-based services. Unless an organization has exceedingly good business records, some of these assets will be overlooked, mainly because of the ways in which cloud services work. It's easy to sign up for a zero-cost or low-cost service and immediately begin uploading business information to the service. Unless the organization has advanced tools such as a cloud access security broker (CASB), it will be next to impossible for an organization to know all of the cloud-based services that are used.

Virtual Assets

Virtualization technology, which enables an organization to employ multiple, separate operating systems to run on one server, is a popular practice for organizations, whether on their own hardware servers located in their own data centers or in hosting facilities. Organizations employing infrastructure as a service (IaaS) are also employing virtualization technology.

NOTE Though IaaS and virtualization make it far easier to create and manage server assets, maintaining an accurate inventory of virtual server assets is even more challenging than it is for physical assets.

Information Assets

Information assets are less tangible than hardware assets, as they are not easily observed. Information assets take many forms:

- **Personal information** Most organizations store information about people, whether they are employees, customers, constituents, beneficiaries, or citizens. This data may include sensitive information such as contact information and personal details, transactions, order histories, and other items.

CAUTION Organizations need to be mindful of the regulatory definitions of personal information within the context of applicable privacy laws and regulations.

- **Intellectual property** This type of information can take the form of trade secrets, source code, product designs, policies and standards, and marketing collateral.
- **Business operations** This generally includes merger and acquisition information and other types of business processes and records.
- **Virtual machines** Most organizations are moving their business applications to the cloud, thereby eliminating the need to purchase hardware. Organizations that use IaaS have virtual operating systems, which are another form of information. Even though these operating systems are not purchased but instead are rented, there is nonetheless an asset perspective: they take time to build and configure and therefore have a replacement cost. The value of assets is discussed more fully later in this section.

Asset Classification

Asset classification is an activity whereby an organization assigns an asset to a category that represents usage or risk. The purpose of asset classification is to determine, for each asset, its level of criticality to the organization. In an organization with a formal privacy program, asset classification will include one or more classifications for assets related to personal information.

Criticality can be related to information sensitivity. For instance, a database of customers' personal information that includes contact and payment information would be considered highly sensitive and, in the event of compromise, could result in significant impact to present and future business operations.

Criticality can also be related to operational dependency. For example, a database of virtual server images may be considered highly critical. If an organization's server images were to be compromised or lost, this could adversely affect the organization's ability to continue its information processing operations.

These and other measures of criticality form the basis for information protection, system redundancy and resilience, business continuity planning, and access management. Scarce resources in the form of information protection and resilience need to be allocated to the assets that require it the most. It doesn't usually make sense to protect all assets to the same degree—the more valuable, sensitive, and critical assets should be protected more securely than those that are less valuable and critical.

NOTE The best approach to asset classification in most organizations is first to identify and classify *information* assets and then follow this with *system* classification. One area that is often overlooked or not addressed to a satisfactory level is dealing with unstructured data and data that resides outside of the organization's approved systems.

Data Classification

Data classification is a process whereby different sets and collections of data in an organization are analyzed for various types of sensitivity, criticality, integrity, and value. There are different ways to understand these characteristics. These are some examples:

- **Personal information**   This type of information is most commonly associated with natural persons. Examples include personal contact information, employment records, medical records, and personal financial data such as credit card and bank account numbers.

- **Sensitive information**   Information other than personal information can also be considered sensitive, including intellectual property, nonpublished financial records, merger and acquisition information, and strategic plans.

- **Operational criticality**   In this category, information must be available at all times, or perhaps the information is related to some factors of business resilience. Examples of information in this category include virtual server images, incident response procedures, and business continuity procedures. Corruption or loss of this type of information may have a significant impact on ongoing business operations.

- **Accuracy or integrity**   Information in this category is required to be highly accurate. If altered, the organization could suffer significant financial or reputational harm. Types of information include exchange rate tables, product or service inventory data, machine calibration data, and price lists. Corruption or loss of this type of information impacts business operations by causing incomplete or erroneous transactions.

- **Monetary value**   This information may be more easily monetized by intruders who steal it. Types of information include credit card numbers, bank account numbers, gift certificates or cards, and discount or promotion codes. Loss of this type of information may result in direct financial losses.

Most organizations store information that falls into all of these categories, with degrees of importance within them. Although this may result in a complex matrix of information types and degrees of importance or value, the most successful organizations will build a fairly simple data classification scheme. For instance, an organization may develop four levels of information classification, such as Public, Confidential, Regulated, and Secret.

Asset Valuation

A key part of a risk assessment is the identification of the value of an asset. In the absence of an asset's value, it is more difficult to calculate risks associated with an asset, even when qualitative risk valuation is employed. Without a known valuation, the impact of loss is more difficult to determine.

Qualitative Asset Valuation

Because many risk assessments are qualitative in nature (as discussed later in the section "Qualitative Risk Analysis"), establishing asset valuation in qualitative terms is common. Instead of assigning a dollar (or other currency) value figure to an asset, the value of an asset can be assigned to a low–medium–high scale or to a numeric scale such as 1–5 or 1–10.

The objective of qualitative asset valuation is to establish which assets have more value than others. Qualitative valuation enables an organization to determine which assets have greater value and which have less value. This can be highly useful in an organization with a lot of assets, because it can provide a view of its high-value assets without the "noise" of comingled lower valued assets. In a privacy program, qualitative valuation can help identify assets associated with the processing of personal information.

Quantitative Asset Valuation

Many organizations opt to surpass qualitative asset valuation and assign a dollar (or other currency) valuation to assets. This is common in larger or more mature organizations that want to understand the actual costs that may be associated with loss events.

In a typical quantitative valuation, an asset's value may be determined by one of the following:

- **Replacement cost** If the asset is a hardware asset, its valuation may be determined by the cost of purchasing (and deploying) a replacement. If the asset is a database, its cost may be determined by the operational costs required to restore it from backup or the costs to recover it from its source, such as a service provider.

- **Book value** This represents the value of an asset in the organization's financial system, typically the purchase price less depreciation.

- **Net present value (NPV)** If the asset directly or indirectly generates revenue, this valuation method may be used.

- **Redeployment cost** If the asset is a virtual machine, its valuation may be determined by the cost of setting it up again. This is typically a soft cost if it is set up by internal staff, but it could be a hard cost if another company is hired to redeploy it.

- **Creation or reacquisition cost** If the asset is a database, its cost may be determined by the cost of re-creating it. If the asset is intellectual property such as software source code, its valuation may be determined according to the effort required for developers to re-create it.

- **Consequential financial cost** If the asset is a database containing personal information, its valuation may be measured in the form of financial costs that result from its theft or compromise. Although the cost of recovering that database may be relatively low, the consequences of its compromise could cost hundreds of dollars per record. This is a typical cost when measuring the full impact of a privacy breach.

Risk managers must carefully determine the appropriate method for setting the value of each asset. Determining the value may be fairly straightforward or difficult. In many cases, an individual asset will have more than a single valuation category. For example, a credit card database may be valued primarily on its consequential cost (because of the potential fines plus remediation costs associated with consumers who may have been harmed) and also on redeployment costs, although this may be a small fraction of the total valuation.

Risk managers should document their rationale and method of valuation, particularly for sensitive and personal information assets whose valuations could vary widely depending on the method used. Better yet, larger and more mature organizations will have guidelines that specify methods and formulas to be used in information asset valuation.

Threat Identification

Threat identification is a key step in a risk assessment. A *threat* is defined as an event that, if realized, would bring harm to an asset and, thus, to the organization.

In the privacy and cybersecurity industries, the key terms involved with risk assessments are often misunderstood and misused. These terms are distinguished from one another in this way: A *threat* is an actual action that would cause harm, not the person or group (generically called an *actor* or *threat actor*) associated with it. A threat is not a weakness that may permit a threat to occur; this is known as a *vulnerability*.

Threats are typically classified as external or internal, as intentional or unintentional, and as human-made or natural. The origin of many threats is outside the control of the organization but not necessarily outside of its awareness. A good privacy or security manager can develop a list of privacy- and security-related threats that are likely (more or less) to occur to any given asset.

When performing a risk assessment, the risk manager needs to develop a complete list of threats for use in the assessment. Because it's not always possible for a risk manager to memorize all possible threats, the security manager may turn to one or more well-known sources of threats, including the following:

- ISO/IEC 27005, Appendix C, "Examples of Typical Threats"
- NIST SP 800-30, Appendix E, "Threat Events"

Upon capturing threat events from one or both of these sources, the risk manager may well identify a few additional threats not found in these lists. These additional threats may be specific to the organization's location, business model, or other factors. A risk manager will typically remove a few of the threats from the list that do not apply to the organization. For instance, an organization located far inland is not going to be directly affected by tsunamis or hurricanes, so this threat source can be eliminated.

Internal Threats

Internal threats originate within the organization and are most often associated with employees. Quite possibly, internal employees may be the intentional actors behind these threats. This is generally known as an *insider threat*.

Privacy managers need to understand the nature of internal threats and the interaction between personnel and information systems. A wide range of events can take place that constitutes threats, including the following:

- Well-meaning personnel making errors in judgment
- Well-meaning personnel making errors in haste
- Well-meaning personnel making errors because of insufficient knowledge or training
- Well-meaning personnel being tricked into doing something harmful
- Disgruntled personnel being purposefully negligent or reckless
- Disgruntled personnel deliberately bringing harm to an asset
- A trusted individual in a trusted third-party organization doing any of these

After understanding all the ways that something can go wrong, privacy and security managers may sometimes wonder whether things can ever proceed as planned!

A privacy manager must understand this important concept: While employees are at the top of a short list of potential threat actors, employees also need to be given broad access to sensitive data so that they can do their jobs and help the organization function. Although there have been marginal improvements in technologies such as data loss prevention (DLP), employers must trust their employees by giving them access to large sets of valuable information, with the hope that the employees will not accidentally or deliberately abuse those privileges with potential to cause the organization great harm.

Here are some examples of "employees gone rogue":

- A disgruntled internal auditor discloses salary and other personal information relating to 100,000 staff members at a large supermarket chain in an attempt to frame a colleague.
- A consulting firm for a large insurer finds that one of its consultants, who was discovered to be involved in identity theft, has e-mailed a file with more than 18,000 Medicare member details to his personal e-mail account.
- An engineer at a cloud services company breaks into and exposes millions of customer records at a large bank.
- A systems administrator at an intelligence agency acquires and leaks thousands of classified documents to the media.

A significant factor in employees gone rogue is access control policy and access management practices, which result in individual employees having access to more information than is prudent. That said, increasing the granularity of access controls is known to be time-consuming and costly, and it increases the friction of doing business; few organizations tolerate this despite identified risks.

The following list includes internal and external threats caused by humans that may be included in an organization's risk assessment:

Leak data via e-mail

Leak data via upload to unauthorized system

Leak data via external USB storage device or medium

Leak information face-to-face to unauthorized person

Perform programming error

Misconfigure system or device

Shut down application, system, or device

Perpetrate error created by any internal staff

Respond to phishing attack

Respond to social engineering attack

Share login credentials with another person

Install or run unauthorized software program

Copy sensitive data to unauthorized device or system

Destroy or remove sensitive or critical information

Retrieve discarded, recycled, or shredded information

Conduct security scan

Conduct denial-of-service attack

Conduct physical attack on systems or facilities

Conduct credential-guessing attack

Eavesdrop on sensitive communication

Impersonate another individual

Obtain sensitive information through illicit means

Cause data integrity loss through any action

Intercept network traffic

Obtain sensitive information through programmatic data leakage

Perform reconnaissance as part of an attack campaign

Attack via social engineering

Failure or anomaly in power

Failure in communications

Failure in heating, venting, or air conditioning

Degradation of electronic media

Damage via fire

Damage via smoke

Damage via fire retardant

Flood from water main break or drainage failure

Damage via vandalism

Damage from demonstrations/protests/picketing

Attack by terrorist

Damage via electromagnetic pulse

Damage via explosion

Damage via bombing

It may be useful to build a short list of threat actors (the people or groups that may initiate a threat event), but remember that these actors are not the threats themselves. Building such a list may help the security manager identify additional threat events that may not be on the list.

The following list shows internal and external natural threats:

| Forest fire or range fire |
| Smoke damage from a forest fire or range fire |
| River flood |
| Landslide |
| Avalanche |
| Tornado |
| Hurricane |
| Windstorm |
| Hailstorm |
| Earthquake |
| Tsunami |
| Lightning |
| Epidemic |
| Explosion of naturally occurring substances |
| Solar storm |

External Threats

External threats originate outside of the organization. Like internal threats, they can include both deliberate and accidental actions and can be manmade or associated with naturally occurring events.

The security manager performing a risk assessment needs to understand the full range of threat actors, along with motivations. This is particularly important for organizations in which specific types of threat actors or motivations are more common. For example, certain industries such as aerospace and weapons manufacturers attract industrial espionage and intelligence agencies, and certain industries attract hacktivists.

The following lists show external threat actors:

| Former employees |
| Current and former consultants |
| Current and former contractors |
| Competitors |

Hacktivists

Personnel in current and former third-party service organizations, vendors, and suppliers

Government intelligence agencies (foreign and domestic)

Criminal organizations (including individuals)

Terrorist groups (including individuals)

Activist groups (including individuals)

Armed forces (including individuals)

Here are some of their motivations:

Competitive advantage

Economic espionage

Monetary gain

Political gain

Intelligence

Revenge

Ego

Curiosity

Unintentional errors

Activism

In a risk assessment, the assessor must identify all threats that have a reasonable likelihood of occurrence; this is critical. Threats that are unlikely because of geographic and other conditions are usually excluded. For example, hurricanes can be excluded in locations far from oceans, and earthquakes and volcanos can be excluded in locations where these are not known to occur. Threats such as falling meteorites and space debris are rarely included in risk assessments because of the minute chance of their occurrence.

Advanced Persistent Threats

An *advanced persistent threat* (APT) is a particular type of threat actor, so named in the early 2000s to describe a new kind of adversary that worked slowly but effectively to compromise a target organization. Whether perpetrated by an individual or a cybercriminal organization, an APT involves techniques that indicate resourcefulness, patience, and resolve. Rather than employing a "hit-and-run" or "smash-and-grab" operation, an APT actor will patiently perform reconnaissance on a target and use tools to infiltrate the target and build a long-term presence there.

 NOTE   The term *advanced persistent threat* is not often used nowadays, although its definition is largely unchanged. APTs were discussed more often when the technique was new, but now APTs are fairly routine. Today, a multitude of cybercriminal organizations, along with hundreds if not thousands of talented individual threat actors, use techniques that resemble the APTs of a dozen years ago.

APT is defined by NIST SP 800-39 as follows:

> An APT is an adversary that possesses sophisticated levels of expertise and significant resources that allow it to create opportunities to achieve its objectives using multiple attack vectors (e.g., cyber, physical, and deception). These objectives typically include establishing and extending footholds within the IT infrastructure of the targeted organizations for purposes of exfiltrating information, undermining or impeding critical aspects of a mission, program, or organization; or positioning itself to carry out these objectives in the future. The advanced persistent threat: (i) pursues its objectives repeatedly over an extended period of time; (ii) adapts to defenders' efforts to resist it; (iii) is determined to maintain the level of interaction needed to execute its objectives.

Prior to APTs, threat actors primarily conducted operations that ran for short periods of time—a few days at most. But as more organizations put more valuable information assets online, threat actors became craftier and more resourceful; they resorted to longer term campaigns to study a target for long periods of time before attacking it. Once an attack began, it would persist for months or longer. APTs would compromise multiple systems inside the target organization and use a variety of stealthy techniques to establish and maintain a presence using as many compromised targets as possible. Once an APT was discovered (if it is *ever* discovered), the security manager would clean up the compromised target, often unaware that the APT had compromised many other targets using different techniques.

This cat-and-mouse game could continue for months or even years, with the adversary continuing to compromise targets and study the organization's systems—all the while searching for specific targets—while the security manager and others would continually chase the adversary around like the carnival game of "whack a mole."

 NOTE Cliff Stoll's book, *The Cuckoo's Egg: Tracking a Spy Through the Maze of Computer Espionage,* is a true-life story of such an adversary.

Emerging Threats

The cyberwarfare theater of today is constantly changing and evolving. Several forces (see Table A-1) are at work and continually push the envelope in the areas of attack techniques as well as defense techniques.

The subject of emerging threats should be considered a continuing phenomenon of new techniques rather than as a fixed set of techniques. Often, the latest techniques are difficult to detect because they fall outside the span of attack techniques that one expects to observe from time to time. Emerging threats represent the cutting edge of attack techniques that are difficult to detect and/or remediate when they are discovered. But these threats will eventually become routine, and even newer threat techniques will emerge. Privacy and security managers need to understand that, even as defensive technologies improve to help prevent and/or detect attacks of increasing sophistication, attack techniques will continuously improve in their ability to evade detection by even the most sophisticated defense techniques.

Phenomenon	Response
Emerging technologies, including bring-your-own-device (BYOD), cloud computing, virtualization, and Internet of Things (IoT)	New targets of opportunity, many of which are poorly guarded when first implemented
End user behavior analytics (EUBA) that detect anomalous end user behavior	Slower exfiltration of sensitive data in order to stay "under the radar"
Improved technologies (faster processing time)	More rapid compromise of cryptosystems
Improved technologies (faster network speeds)	More rapid exfiltration of larger data sets; easier transport of rainbow tables used to crack hash tables
Improved antimalware controls	Attack innovation—techniques evaded antimalware controls

Table A-1   The Cascade of Emerging Threats

Vulnerability Identification

The identification of vulnerabilities is an essential part of any risk assessment. A *vulnerability* is any weakness in a process or system that permits an attack to compromise a target process or system successfully. In the privacy and security industries, two key terms involved with risk assessments are often misunderstood and misused: vulnerability and threat. These terms are distinguished from one another in this way: A vulnerability is the weaknesses in a system that could permit an attack to occur. A vulnerability is not the attack vector or technique—this is known as a *threat*.

Vulnerabilities usually take one of these forms:

- **Configuration fault**   A system, program, or component with configuration settings has been configured incorrectly, which could provide an attacker with additional opportunities to compromise a system. For example, the authentication settings on a system may permit an attacker to employ a brute-force password-guessing attack that will not be blunted by target user accounts being automatically locked out.

- **Design fault**   The relationship between components of a system may be arranged in a way that makes it easier for an attacker to compromise a target system. For instance, an organization may have placed a database server in its DMZ network instead of in its internal network, making the server easier for an attacker to identity and attack.

- **Business process weakness**   A business process related to the processing of personal information may fail to prevent or detect unwanted activities in certain circumstances. For instance, an end user who extracts a large volume of personal information from a customer application and saves it directly to a personal cloud drive may bypass controls that would detect or prevent this if the file were saved locally.

- **Known unpatched weakness**   A system may have one or more vulnerabilities for which security patches are available but not yet installed. For example, a secure communications protocol may have a flaw in the way that an encrypted session is established, which could permit an attacker to take over an established communications session. A security patch may be available for the flaw, but until the security patch is installed, the flaw exists and may be exploited by anyone who understands the vulnerability and has techniques to exploit it. Sometimes, known weaknesses are made public through a disclosure by the system's manufacturer or a responsible third party. Although a patch may not yet be offered, other avenues may be available to mitigate the vulnerability, such as a configuration change in the target system.

- **Undisclosed unpatched weakness**   A system may have vulnerabilities that are known only to the system's manufacturer and that are not publicized. Until an organization using one of these systems learns of the vulnerability via a security bulletin or a news article, the organization can do little to defend itself, short of employing essential security techniques such as system hardening, network hardening, and secure coding.

- **Undiscovered weakness**   Security managers have long accepted the fact that all kinds of information systems have security vulnerabilities that are yet to be discovered, disclosed, and mitigated. New techniques for attacking systems are constantly being developed, and some of these techniques can exploit weaknesses no one knew to look for. As newly discovered techniques involve examining active memory for snippets of sensitive information, system and tool designers continue to design defense techniques for detecting and even blocking attacks. At one point, for example, new techniques were developed that enabled an attacker to harvest credit card numbers from point-of-sale software programs that were compliant with the Payment Card Industry Data Security Standard (PCI DSS). Unfortunately, effective attacks were soon developed that enabled cybercriminal organizations to steal tens of millions of credit card numbers from global retail companies.

Vulnerabilities exist everywhere—in software programs, database management systems, operating systems, virtualization platforms, business processes, encryption algorithms, business processes, and personnel. As a rule, privacy and security managers should consider that every component of every type in every system has both known and unknown vulnerabilities, some of which, if exploited, could result in painful and expensive consequences for the organization. Table A-2 contains the places where vulnerabilities may exist, together with techniques that can be used to discover at least some of them.

Third-Party Vulnerability Identification

Most organizations outsource at least a portion of their software development and IT operations to third parties. Mainly this occurs through the use of cloud-based applications and services such as software as a service (SaaS) applications and platform as a

Vulnerability Context	Detection Technique
Network device	Vulnerability scanning
	Penetration testing
	Code analysis
	Network architecture review
Operating system	Vulnerability scanning
	Penetration testing
	System architecture review
Database management system	Vulnerability scanning
	Penetration testing
Software application	Vulnerability scanning
	Penetration testing
	Dynamic application scanning
	Static code scanning
	Application architecture review
Physical security	Physical security controls review
	Social engineering assessments
	Physical penetration testing
Business process	Process reviews
	Internal audits
	Control self-assessments
Personnel	Social engineering assessments
	Competency assessments
	Phishing assessments (continual)

Table A-2   Vulnerabilities and Detection Techniques

service (PaaS) and infrastructure as a service (IaaS) environments. Many organizations have the misconception that third parties take care of all security concerns in their services. Instead, organizations should thoroughly understand the security responsibility model for each outsourced service to understand which portions of security are the organization's responsibility and which are managed by the outsourced service.

Whether security responsibilities are the burden of the organization or the outsourcing organization, all vulnerabilities need to be identified and managed. If the organization is responsible for particular aspects of privacy and security, it needs to employ normal means for identifying and managing them. For aspects of privacy and security that are the responsibility of the service provider, the provider needs to identify and manage vulnerabilities. In many cases, a service provider will make these activities available to their customers upon request.

Risk Identification

Risk identification is the activity during a risk assessment in which various scenarios are studied for each asset. Several considerations are applied in the analysis of each risk, including these:

- **Threats**   All realistic threat scenarios are examined for each asset to determine which are reasonably likely to occur.

- **Threat actors**   It is important to understand the variety of threat actors and to know which ones are more motivated to target the organization and for what reasons. This further illuminates the likelihood that a given threat scenario will occur.

- **Vulnerabilities**   Vulnerabilities need to be identified for each asset (both information and information systems), business process, and staff member being examined. Then various threat scenarios are considered to determine which vulnerabilities are most likely.

- **Asset value**   The value of each asset is an important factor to include in risk analysis. As described in the earlier section on asset value, assets may be valued in several ways. For instance, a customer database may have a modest recovery cost if it is damaged or destroyed; however, if that same customer database is stolen and sold on the black market, the value of the data may be much higher to cybercriminals, and the resulting costs to the organization to mitigate the harm done to customers may be higher still. Another way to examine asset value is through the revenue derived from its existence or use. The financial consequences of a ruined reputation are not included here but are a part of the impact, discussed in the next item.

- **Impact**   The risk manager examines vulnerabilities, threats (with threat actors), and asset values, and then estimates the impact of the different threat scenarios. Impact is considered separately from asset value, because some threat scenarios have minimal correlation with asset value and are related to reputation damage instead. Breaches of privacy data, for example, can result in high mitigation costs and reduced business. Breaches in hospital data systems can threaten patient care. Breaches in almost any IoT or industrial control system (ICS) context can result in extensive service interruptions and life-safety issues.

Qualitative and quantitative risk analysis techniques help to distinguish higher risks from lower risks. These techniques are discussed later in this section.

Risks above a certain level are often recorded in a risk register where they will be processed through risk treatment.

Risk, Likelihood, and Impact

During risk analysis in a risk assessment, the risk manager will perform some simple calculations to stratify all of the risks that have been identified. Calculations generally resemble one or more of these:

> *Risk = threats × vulnerabilities*
> *Risk = threats × vulnerabilities × asset value*
> *Risk = threats × vulnerabilities × probabilities*

ISO/IEC Guide 73, *Risk management – Vocabulary,* defines *risk* as "the combination of the probability of an event and its consequence." This is an excellent way to understand risk in simple, qualitative terms. ISO/IEC Guide 73 is available for purchase from https://iso.org/.

Likelihood

In risk assessments, likelihood is an important dimension that helps a risk manager understand several aspects related to the unfolding of a threat event. The likelihood of a serious security incident has less to do with technical details and more to do with the thought process of an adversary.

Considerations related to likelihood include the following:

- **Hygiene**   This is related to an organization's security operations practices. Organizations that do a poor job in vulnerability management, patch management, and system hardening, for example, are more likely to suffer incidents simply because they are making it easier for adversaries to gain access to their systems.

- **Data management**   Relevant in a privacy program, the quality and effectiveness of an organization's data management program will have a bearing on the probability of a privacy breach. If an organization has mature data management capabilities, it likely will be aware of anomalous behavior indicating a potential breach. On the other hand, an organization paying little attention to its data is more likely to have the data compromised without the organization being aware.

- **Visibility**   This factor is related to the organization's standing: how broad and visible the organization is and how much the attacker's prestige will increase as a result of a successfully compromised target.

- **Velocity**   The timing of various threat scenarios and whether there is any warning or foreknowledge are factors. For example, an adversary who is determined to exfiltrate a large volume of data without detection is likely to do so very slowly; on the other hand, ransomware can destroy an organization's information in minutes.

- **Motivation**   It is essential to consider various types of adversaries to understand the factors that would motivate them to attack the organization. It could be about money, reputation, or rivalry.

- **Skill**   For various threat scenarios, what skill level is required to attack the organization successfully? A higher skill level does not always mean an attack is less likely; other considerations such as motivation come into play as well.

Impact

During risk assessments, a risk manager needs to understand the impact of each threat scenario. In the context of privacy, the definition of *impact* is the actual or expected result from some action, such as a breach. Impact is perhaps the most critical attribute to understand for a threat scenario. A risk assessment can describe all types of threat scenarios, the reasons behind them, and how they can be minimized. Still, without understanding the impacts of these scenarios, a risk manager cannot determine the importance of each threat in terms of the urgency to mitigate the risk.

A wide range of impact scenarios is possible:

- Direct cash losses
- Reputation damage
- Loss of business—decrease in sales
- Drop in share price—less access to capital
- Reduction in market share
- Diminished operational efficiency (higher internal costs)
- Diminished operational capacity (lower revenue)
- Civil liability
- Legal liability
- Compliance liability (fines, censures, and so on)
- Interruption of business operations

Some of these impact scenarios are easier to analyze in qualitative terms than others, and the magnitudes of most of these potential impacts are difficult to quantify except in specific threat scenarios.

One of the main tools in the business continuity and disaster planning world, the *business impact analysis* (BIA) is highly useful for privacy and information security managers. A BIA can be conducted as part of a risk assessment or separate from it.

A BIA differs from a risk assessment. Although a risk assessment is used to identify risks and, perhaps, suggested remedies, a BIA is used to identify the most critical business processes, together with their supporting IT systems and dependencies on other processes or systems. The value that a BIA brings to a risk assessment is the understanding of which business processes and IT systems are the most important to the organization. The BIA helps the security manager better understand which processes are the most critical and therefore warrant the most protection, all other considerations being equal.

In qualitative risk analysis, where probability and impact are rated on simple numeric scales, a risk matrix is sometimes used to portray levels of risk based on probability and impact. Figure A-3 shows a risk matrix.

Figure A-3
Qualitative
risk matrix

Probability		Slightly Harmful	Harmful	Extremely Harmful
	Likely	Medium Risk	High Risk	Extreme Risk
	Unlikely	Low Risk	Medium Risk	High Risk
	Highly Unlikely	Insignificant Risk	Low Risk	Medium Risk
		Slightly Harmful	**Harmful**	**Extremely Harmful**
		Consequences		

Risk Analysis Techniques and Considerations

As part of a risk assessment, the risk manager examines assets, together with associated vulnerabilities and likely threat scenarios. The *risk analysis* is the detailed examination that takes place here. Risk analysis considers many dimensions of an asset, including these:

- Asset value
- Threat scenarios
- Threat probabilities
- Relevant vulnerabilities
- Existing controls and their effectiveness
- Impact

Risk analysis can also consider business criticality if a BIA is available.

Various risk analysis techniques are discussed in the remainder of this section.

Information Gathering

A risk manager needs to gather a considerable amount of information so that the risk analysis and the risk assessment are valuable and complete. Several sources are available, including

- Interviews with process owners
- Interviews with application developers
- Interviews with privacy and security personnel
- Interviews with external privacy and security experts, including legal counsel

- Privacy and security incident records
- Analysis of incidents that occur in other organizations
- Prior risk assessments (however, caution is advised to stop the propagation of risk calculation errors from one assessment to the next)

Qualitative Risk Analysis

Most risk analysis begins with qualitative risk analysis. This technique does not seek to identify exact (or even approximate) asset value or impact or the exact probability of occurrence. Instead, these items are expressed on a scale such as high, medium, or low or as a numeric range such as 1 to 5. The purpose of qualitative risk analysis is to understand risks relative to one another so that higher risks can be distinguished from lower risks. This is a valuable pursuit, because it gives an organization the ability to focus on more critical risks, based on impact in qualitative terms.

Semiquantitative Risk Analysis

In qualitative risk analysis, the probability of occurrence can be expressed as a numeric value, such as in the range 1 to 5 (where 5 is the highest probability). Impact can also be expressed as a numeric value, also in the range 1 to 5. Then, for each asset and each threat, risk is calculated as *probability × impact*.

Suppose, for example, that an organization has identified two risk scenarios. The first is a risk of data theft from a customer database; the impact is scored as a 5 (highest), and probability is scored as a 4 (highly likely). The risk is scored as *5 × 4 = 20*. The second is a risk of theft of application source code; the impact is scored as a 2 (low), and probability is scored as a 2 (less likely). This risk is scored as *2 × 2 = 4*. The risk manager understands that the data theft risk is more significant (scored as 20) as compared to the source code theft risk (scored as 4). These risk scores do not indicate that the larger risk is five times as likely to occur; neither do they mean that the larger risk is five times as expensive. They simply indicate that one risk is rated higher than the other. The scores also do not directly indicate whether the probability or the impact alone is high or low—analysis of the detailed scores is necessary to know that.

Note that some risk managers consider this a qualitative risk analysis, because the results are no more accurate in terms of costs and probabilities than the qualitative technique.

Quantitative Risk Analysis

In quantitative risk analysis, risk managers are attempting to determine actual costs and probabilities of events occurring. This technique provides more specific information to executives about the costs they can expect to incur in various security event scenarios.

Two aspects of quantitative risk analysis prove to be a continuing challenge:

- **Event probability**   It is difficult to come up with even an order-of-magnitude estimate on the probability of occurrence for nearly every event scenario. Even with better information from industry sources, the probability of high-impact incidents depends on many factors, some of which are difficult to identify or even quantify.

- **Event cost**   It is difficult to put an exact cost on any given privacy or security incident scenario. Privacy and security incidents are complex events that involve many parties and have unpredictable short- and long-term outcomes. Despite ever-improving information from research organizations on the cost of breaches, event costs are still rough estimates and may not take into account all aspects of the costs.

Because of these challenges, quantitative risk analysis should be regarded as an effort to develop estimates, not exact figures. This is in part because risk analysis is a measure of events that *may* occur, not a measure of events that *do* occur.

Standard quantitative risk analysis involves the development of several figures:

- **Asset value (AV)**   The value of the asset is usually (but not necessarily) the asset's replacement value. Depending on the type of asset, different values may need to be considered.

- **Exposure factor (EF)**   This is the financial loss that results from the realization of a threat, expressed as a percentage of the asset's total value. Most threats do not eliminate the asset's value; instead, they reduce its value. For example, if an organization's $120,000 server is rendered unbootable because of malware, it will still have salvage value, even if that is only 10 percent of the asset's total value. In this case, the EF would be 90 percent. Note that different threats will have various impacts on EF, because the realization of different threats will cause varying amounts of damage to assets.

- **Single loss expectancy (SLE)**   This value represents the financial loss when a threat scenario occurs one time. SLE is defined as $AV \times EF$. Note that different threats have a varied impact on EF, so those threats will have the same multiplicative effect on SLE.

- **Annualized rate of occurrence (ARO)**   This is an estimate of the number of times that a threat will occur per year. If the probability of the threat is 1 in 50 (one occurrence every 50 years), ARO is expressed as 0.02. However, if the threat is estimated to occur four times per year, ARO is 4.0. Like EF and SLE, ARO will vary by threat.

- **Annualized loss expectancy (ALE)**   This is the expected annualized loss of asset value due to threat realization. ALE is defined as $SLE \times ARO$.

ALE is based upon the verifiable values AV, EF, and SLE, but because ARO is only an estimate, ALE is only as good as the ARO. Depending upon the asset's value, the risk manager may need to take extra care to develop the best possible estimate for ARO, based upon whatever data is available. Sources for estimates include the following:

- History of event losses in the organization

- History of similar losses in other organizations

- History of dissimilar losses

- Best estimates based on available data

When the risk manager performs a quantitative risk analysis for a given asset, the ALE for all threats can be added together. The sum of all ALEs is the annualized loss expectancy for the complete array of threats. An unusually high sum of ALEs would mean that a given asset is confronted with a lot of significant threats that are more likely to occur. But in terms of risk treatment, ALEs are better left as separate and associated with their respective threats.

OCTAVE

Operationally Critical Threat, Asset, and Vulnerability Evaluation (OCTAVE) is a risk analysis approach developed by Carnegie Mellon University. The latest version is known as OCTAVE FORTE (**For t**he **E**nterprise) and is used to help organizations identify, evaluate, prioritize, and mitigate privacy and security risks that are relevant to them.

The OCTAVE FORTE methodology consists of ten steps:

1. *Establish risk governance and appetite.* The organization establishes a governance structure that enables determination of how much risk the organization is willing to tolerate and defines policies for how it will manage risk.

2. *Scope critical services and assets.* The organization identifies its in-scope information assets and develops a profile for these assets that describe its features, qualities, characteristics, and value. Noting whether regulated personal information is included is of particular use for an organization's privacy program.

3. *Identify resilience requirements of assets.* The organization identifies the minimum capabilities acceptable to maintain continuity of critical services. This step is concerned with business continuity and managing concepts such as maximum allowable downtime, recovery point objective (RPO), and recovery tie objective (RTO).

4. *Measure current capabilities.* The organization identifies, reviews, and evaluates controls that are currently in place to protect the organization and enable resilience.

5. *Identify risks, threats, and vulnerabilities to assets.* The organization evaluates "what could go wrong" using various techniques such as vulnerability assessments and threat modeling and analyzes the business consequences of an impact.

6. *Analyze risks against capabilities.* The organization creates a risk register to evaluate residual risk based on the organization's capabilities to detect, mitigate, and respond to identified risks.

7. *Plan for response.* The organization identifies how it responds to risks and establishes response plans that are expected to disrupt, reduce, or avoid risk occurrences or consequences.

8. *Implement the response plan.* The organization implements projects and activities to execute the response plans.

9. *Monitor and measure for effectiveness.* The organization defines metrics and performance indicators intended to evaluate how well the program is performing steps 2–8.

10. *Review, update, and repeat.* The organization's risk governance leadership reviews the performance of the risk management program and develops any needed improvement plans.

The OCTAVE FORTE methodology provides many examples for each of the steps described here, making it easy for a person or team to perform a risk analysis based on this technique.

 NOTE Further information about OCTAVE FORTE is available at https://resources.sei.cmu.edu/library/asset-view.cfm?assetid=644636.

Other Risk Analysis Methodologies

Additional risk analysis methodologies provide more complex approaches that may be useful for certain organizations or in selected risk situations:

- **Delphi method** With this method, questionnaires are distributed to a panel of experts in two or more rounds. A facilitator will anonymize the responses and distribute them to the experts. The objective is for the experts to converge on the most critical risks and mitigation strategies.

- **Event tree analysis (ETA)** Derived from the fault tree analysis method (described next), ETA is a logic modeling technique for analysis of success and failure outcomes given a specific event scenario—in this case, a threat scenario.

- **Fault tree analysis (FTA)** This logical modeling technique is used to diagram all the consequences for a given event scenario. FTA begins with a specific scenario and proceeds forward in time with all possible outcomes. A large "tree" diagram can result, which depicts many different chains of events.

- **Monte Carlo analysis** Derived from Monte Carlo computational algorithms, this analysis begins with a given system with inputs, where the inputs are constrained to minimum, likely, and maximum values. Running the simulation provides some insight into actual likely scenarios.

Risk Evaluation and Ranking

Upon completion of a risk assessment, when all risks have been identified and scored, the risk manager, together with others in the organization, will analyze the results and begin to develop a strategy for going forward. Risks can be evaluated singly, but the organization will better benefit from analysis of all the risks together. This is because many risks are interrelated, and the right combination of mitigation strategies can result in many risks being adequately treated.

The results of a risk assessment should be analyzed in several different ways, including the following:

- Looking at all risks by business unit or service line
- Looking at all risks by asset type (in particular, personal information)
- Looking at all risks by activity type
- Looking at all risks by type of consequence

Because no two organizations (or their risk assessment results) are alike, this type of analysis is likely to identify risk treatment *themes* that may have broad implications across many risks. For example, an organization may identify several tactical risks all associated with access management and vulnerability management. Rather than treating individual tactical risks, a better approach may be to improve or reorganize the access or vulnerability management programs from the top down, resulting in many identified risks being mitigated programmatically. Organizations need to consider not just the details in a risk assessment, but the big picture.

Another type of risk to look for is one with a low probability of occurrence and high impact, which is typically the type of risk treated by transfer. *Risk transfer* most often comes in the form of cyber insurance, but it is also relevant to privacy and security monitoring when it includes indemnification.

Risk Ownership

When considering the results of a risk assessment, the organization needs to assign individual risk management tasks to individual people, typically middle- to upper-management leaders. These leaders, who should also have ownership of controls that operate within their span of oversight, use a budget, staff, and other resources in daily business operations. These are the risk owners, and, to the extent that a formal policy or statement is in place on risk tolerance or risk appetite, they should be the people making risk-treatment decisions for risks in their domain. To the extent that these individuals are accountable for operations in their part of the organization, they should also be responsible for risk decisions, including risk treatment, in their operational areas. A simple concept to approach risk ownership is this: if nobody owns the risk, then nobody is accountable for managing the risk, which will lead to a higher probability of the risk becoming an ongoing, unresolved issue with negative impacts on the business, along with the possible identification of a scapegoat who will be blamed if an event occurs.

Risk Treatment

To determine the best risk treatment plan, management can view reports and other information about risks that have been identified, assessed, and analyzed. At this stage, the organization has completed identifying risks and begins to determine what should be done about them. Risk treatment comprises the decisions and the activities that follow. A key element in deciding the appropriate risk treatment is ensuring that the right people at the right level of the organization are actively involved in determining the appropriate risk treatment. This is achieved by having a formalized risk management program that includes all the key elements of an effective program outlined in this appendix.

In a general sense, risk treatment represents the actions that the organization undertakes to reduce risk to an acceptable level. More specifically, for each risk identified in a risk assessment, an organization can consider four responses, or actions:

- Risk acceptance
- Risk mitigation
- Risk avoidance
- Risk transfer

These four actions are explained in more detail in the following sections.

There is a fifth potential action—or, rather, *inaction*—related to risk treatment, known colloquially as *ignoring the risk*. A potentially dangerous undertaking, ignoring a risk amounts to an organization pretending that the risk does not exist. In this case, the organization has unofficially accepted the risk and is responsible if the risk becomes an issue later on. By unofficially accepting the risk and not assigning a risk owner, the organization is possibly increasing the impact and likelihood of the risk evolving into an incident.

Ignoring a *known risk* is different from an organization's ignoring an *unknown risk* and is usually a result of a risk assessment or risk analysis that is not sufficiently thorough in identifying all relevant risks. The best solution for these "unknown unknowns" is to have an external, competent firm perform an organization's risk assessment every few years or examine an organization's risk assessment thoroughly to discover opportunities for improvement, including expanding the span of threats, threat actors, and vulnerabilities so that there are fewer or no unknown risks.

Risk Acceptance

In deciding to accept a risk, the organization determines that the risk requires no reduction or mitigation. If only risk acceptance were this simple!

Further analysis of risk acceptance shows that there are conditions under which an organization will elect to accept risk:

- The cost of risk mitigation is higher than the value of the asset being protected.
- The impact of compromise is low, or the value or classification of the asset is low.

Organizations may elect to establish a framework for risk acceptance, such as the one shown in Table A-3.

Risk Level	Level Required to Accept
Low	Business department leader, plus chief information officer (CIO) or manager of information security
Medium	Business unit leader, plus CISO or director of information security
High	Chief executive officer (CEO), chief operating officer (COO), or organization president
Severe	Board of directors

Table A-3   Framework for Risk Acceptance

When an organization accepts a risk, instead of closing the matter for perpetuity, the organization should review it at least annually for the following reasons:

- The value of the asset may have changed during the year.
- The way that the asset is used may have changed during the year.
- The value of the business activity related to the asset may have changed during the year.
- The potency of threats may have changed during the year, potentially leading to a higher risk rating.
- The cost of mitigation may have changed during the year, potentially leading to greater feasibility for risk mitigation or transfer.

As with other risk treatment activities, detailed recordkeeping helps the risk manager better track matters such as risk assessment review.

Risk Mitigation

In risk mitigation, the organization decides to reduce the risk through some means, such as by changing a process or procedure, by improving a privacy or security control, or by adding a privacy or security control.

Risk mitigation is generally chosen when management understands that performing risk mitigation costs less than the value of the asset being protected. Sometimes, however, an asset's value is difficult to measure, or there may be a high degree of goodwill associated with the asset. For example, a customer database that contains personal information including bank account or credit card information may be of low value to the organization, but the impact of a breach of this database may be substantial because of the fines, loss of business, or adverse publicity that may result.

Risk mitigation may result in a task that can be carried out in a relatively short time. However, risk mitigation may also involve one or more major projects that start in the future, perhaps in the next budget year or many months or quarters in the future. Further, such a project may be delayed, its scope may change, or it may be canceled altogether. Thus, the risk manager needs to monitor risk mitigation activities carefully to ensure that they are completed as originally planned so that the risk mitigation is not forgotten or set aside.

Risk Avoidance

In risk avoidance, the organization decides to discontinue an activity that precipitates the risk. Often, risk avoidance is selected in response to an activity that was not formally approved in the first place. For example, a risk assessment may have identified a department's use of an external service provider that represented a measurable risk to the organization. The service provider may or may not have been formally vetted in the first place. Regardless, after the risk is identified in a risk assessment (or by other means), the organization may choose to end its association with that service provider to avoid the risk.

Risk Transfer

After deciding to transfer a risk, the organization will employ an external organization to accept the risk. In this case, the organization does not have the operational or financial capacity to accept the risk, and risk mitigation is not the best choice. In risk transfer, an organization may have identified a significant financial risk related to a breach of its stores of personal information, for example. The risk transfer decision, in this case, may involve the purchase of cyber insurance that would offset the costs associated with such a breach. A risk transfer decision may also include the purchase of an incident response retainer, which is essentially a pre-purchase of incident response services in the event of a breach.

A risk assessment may reveal the absence of security monitoring of a critical system. Another form of risk transfer involves using an external security services provider to monitor the critical system.

Residual Risk

When an organization undergoes risk treatment for identified risks, the treatment usually does not eliminate the risk but reduces it to some degree. *Residual risk* is what remains after risk treatment is applied.

Some organizations approach risk treatment and residual risk improperly. They identify a risk, apply some risk treatment, and then fail to understand the residual risk and close the risk matter. A better way to approach residual risk is to analyze it as though it were a new risk and apply risk treatment to the residual risk. This iterative process provides organizations with an opportunity to revisit residual risk and make new risk treatment decisions. Ultimately, after one or more iterations, the residual risk will be accepted, and then the matter can be closed.

For instance, suppose a privacy manager identifies a risk in the organization's access management system where multifactor authentication is not used. This is considered high risk, so the IT department implements a multifactor authentication solution. When the privacy manager reassesses the access management system, she finds that multifactor authentication is required in some circumstances but not in others. A new risk is identified, at perhaps a lower level of risk than the original risk. But the organization once again has an opportunity to examine the risk and make a decision about it. This may improve the access management system by requiring multifactor authentication in additional cases, further reducing risk, which should be examined again for further risk treatment opportunities. Finally, the risk will be accepted as is when the organization is satisfied that the risk has been sufficiently reduced.

In addition to the risk treatment life cycle, subsequent risk assessments and other activities will identify risks that represent residual risk from earlier risk treatment activities. Over time, the nature of residual risk may change, based on changing threats, vulnerabilities, or business practices, resulting in an initially acceptable residual risk that is no longer acceptable.

Controls

A common outcome of risk treatment, when mitigation is chosen, is the enactment of controls. Put another way, when an organization identifies a risk in a risk assessment, the organization may decide to develop (or improve) a control that will mitigate the identified risk.

Suppose, for example, that an organization determined that its procedures for terminating access for departing employees were resulting in many user accounts *not* being deactivated. The existing control was a simple, open-loop procedure, in which analysts were instructed to deactivate user accounts. Often, they were deactivating user accounts late or not at all. To reduce this risk, the organization modified the procedure (updated the control) by introducing a step in which a second person would verify all account terminations daily.

Controls are measures put in place to ensure desired outcomes. Controls can come in the form of procedures, or they can be implemented directly in a system. There are many categories and types of controls, as well as standard control frameworks. You can find a thorough discussion of controls in the book *CISM Certified Information Security Manager All-In-One Exam Guide*, in Chapter 4.

Costs and Benefits

As organizations ponder options for risk treatment (and in particular, risk mitigation), they generally will consider the costs of the mitigating steps and the expected benefits they may receive. When an organization understands the costs and benefits of risk mitigation, this helps them develop strategies that are more cost effective or that result in greater cost avoidance.

When weighing mitigation options, an organization needs to understand several cost- and benefit-related considerations, including these:

- **Change in threat probability**   Organizations need to understand how a mitigating control changes the probability of threat occurrence and what that means in terms of cost reduction and avoidance.

- **Change in threat impact**   Organizations need to understand the change in the impact of a mitigated threat in terms of an incident's reduced costs and avoided costs versus the cost of the mitigation.

- **Change in operational efficiency**   Aside from the direct cost of the mitigating control, organizations need to understand the impact on the mitigating control on other operations. For instance, adding code review steps to a software development process may mean that the development organization may complete fewer fixes and enhancements in a given time period.

- **Total cost of ownership (TCO)**   When an organization considers a mitigation plan, the best approach is to understand its TCO, including the following costs:
  - Acquisition
  - Deployment and implementation

- Recurring maintenance
- Testing and assessment
- Compliance monitoring and enforcement
- Reduced throughput of controlled processes
- Training
- End-of-life decommissioning

- **Compliance-related fines and penalties** The matter of compliance with privacy and security laws and regulations often involves fines and penalties when there are findings of noncompliance. Fines and penalties need to be considered as potential consequences for failing to mitigate some risks.

While weighing costs and benefits, organizations need to keep in mind several things:

- Estimating the probability of a specific threat or event is difficult—particularly infrequent, high-impact events such as large-scale data thefts.

- Estimating the impact of any particular threat is difficult, especially those rare, high-impact events.

Thus, the precision of cost–benefit analysis is no better than estimates of event probability and impact.

An old adage in information security states that an organization would not spend $20,000 to protect a $10,000 asset. Although that may be true in some cases, there is more to consider than just the asset's replacement (or depreciated) value. For example, loss of the asset could result in an embarrassing and costly public relations debacle, or the asset may play a key role in the organization's earning hundreds of thousands of dollars in revenue each month.

Still, the principle of proportionality is valid and is often a good starting point for making cost-conscious decisions on risk mitigation. The principle of proportionality is described in NIST's generally accepted security systems principles (GASSP) and section 2.5 of its generally accepted information security principles (GAISP).

About the Online Content

This book comes complete with TotalTester Online customizable practice exam software with 300 practice exam questions.

System Requirements

The current and previous major versions of the following desktop browsers are recommended and supported: Chrome, Microsoft Edge, Firefox, and Safari. These browsers update frequently, and sometimes an update may cause compatibility issues with the TotalTester Online or other content hosted on the Training Hub. If you run into a problem using one of these browsers, please try using another until the problem is resolved.

Your Total Seminars Training Hub Account

To get access to the online content you will need to create an account on the Total Seminars Training Hub. Registration is free, and you will be able to track all your online content using your account. You may also opt in if you wish to receive marketing information from McGraw Hill or Total Seminars, but this is not required for you to gain access to the online content.

Privacy Notice

McGraw Hill values your privacy. Please be sure to read the Privacy Notice available during registration to see how the information you have provided will be used. You may view our Corporate Customer Privacy Policy by visiting the McGraw Hill Privacy Center. Visit the **mheducation.com** site and click **Privacy** at the bottom of the page.

Single User License Terms and Conditions

Online access to the digital content included with this book is governed by the McGraw Hill License Agreement outlined next. By using this digital content you agree to the terms of that license.

Access   To register and activate your Total Seminars Training Hub account, simply follow these easy steps.

1. Go to this URL: **hub.totalsem.com/mheclaim**

2. To register and create a new Training Hub account, enter your e-mail address, name, and password on the **Register** tab. No further personal information (such as credit card number) is required to create an account.

   If you already have a Total Seminars Training Hub account, enter your e-mail address and password on the **Log in** tab.

3. Enter your Product Key: `gm9t-0wsw-wrr5`

4. Click to accept the user license terms.

5. For new users, click the **Register and Claim** button to create your account. For existing users, click the **Log in and Claim** button.

   You will be taken to the Training Hub and have access to the content for this book.

Duration of License   Access to your online content through the Total Seminars Training Hub will expire one year from the date the publisher declares the book out of print.

Your purchase of this McGraw Hill product, including its access code, through a retail store is subject to the refund policy of that store.

The Content is a copyrighted work of McGraw Hill, and McGraw Hill reserves all rights in and to the Content. The Work is © 2021 by McGraw Hill.

Restrictions on Transfer   The user is receiving only a limited right to use the Content for the user's own internal and personal use, dependent on purchase and continued ownership of this book. The user may not reproduce, forward, modify, create derivative works based upon, transmit, distribute, disseminate, sell, publish, or sublicense the Content or in any way commingle the Content with other third-party content without McGraw Hill's consent.

Limited Warranty   The McGraw Hill Content is provided on an "as is" basis. Neither McGraw Hill nor its licensors make any guarantees or warranties of any kind, either express or implied, including, but not limited to, implied warranties of merchantability or fitness for a particular purpose or use as to any McGraw Hill Content or the information therein or any warranties as to the accuracy, completeness, correctness, or results to be obtained from, accessing or using the McGraw Hill Content, or any material referenced in such Content or any information entered into licensee's product by users or other persons and/or any material available on or that can be accessed through the licensee's product (including via any hyperlink or otherwise) or as to non-infringement of third-party rights. Any warranties of any kind, whether express or implied, are disclaimed. Any material or data obtained through use of the McGraw Hill Content is at your own discretion and risk and user understands that it will be solely responsible for any resulting damage to its computer system or loss of data.

Neither McGraw Hill nor its licensors shall be liable to any subscriber or to any user or anyone else for any inaccuracy, delay, interruption in service, error or omission, regardless of cause, or for any damage resulting therefrom.

In no event will McGraw Hill or its licensors be liable for any indirect, special or consequential damages, including but not limited to, lost time, lost money, lost profits or good will, whether in contract, tort, strict liability or otherwise, and whether or not such damages are foreseen or unforeseen with respect to any use of the McGraw Hill Content.

TotalTester Online

TotalTester Online provides you with a simulation of the CIPM exam. Exams can be taken in Practice Mode or Exam Mode. Practice Mode provides an assistance window with hints, references to the book, explanations of the correct and incorrect answers, and the option to check your answer as you take the test. Exam Mode provides a simulation of the actual exam. The number of questions, the types of questions, and the time allowed are intended to be an accurate representation of the exam environment. The option to customize your quiz allows you to create custom exams from selected domains or chapters, and you can further customize the number of questions and time allowed.

To take a test, follow the instructions provided in the previous section to register and activate your Total Seminars Training Hub account. When you register you will be taken to the Total Seminars Training Hub. From the Training Hub Home page, select **CIPM All-in-One TotalTester** from the Study drop-down menu at the top of the page, or from the list of Your Topics on the Home page. You can then select the option to customize your quiz and begin testing yourself in Practice Mode or Exam Mode. All exams provide an overall grade and a grade broken down by domain.

Technical Support

For questions regarding the TotalTester or operation of the Training Hub, visit **www.totalsem.com** or e-mail **support@totalsem.com**.

For questions regarding book content, visit **www.mheducation.com/customerservice**.

acceptable use   A security policy that defines the types of activities that are acceptable and those that are not acceptable.

access control   Any means that detects or prevents unauthorized access and that permits authorized access.

access control list (ACL)   An access control method whereby a list of permitted or denied users (or systems or services, as the case may be) is used to control access.

access control policy   A statement that defines the policy for the granting, review, and revocation of access to systems and work areas.

access management   A formal business process used to control access to networks and information systems.

access review   A review of the users, systems, or other subjects that are permitted to access protected objects to ensure that all subjects are authorized to have access.

acquisition   A business transaction in which an organization purchases and merges with another, usually smaller, organization.

administrative audit   An audit of operational efficiency.

advertising cookie   *See* persistent cookie.

aggregation   *See* data aggregation.

annualized loss expectancy (ALE)   The expected loss of asset value resulting from threat realization. ALE is defined as single loss expectancy (SLE) × annualized rate of occurrence (ARO).

annualized rate of occurrence (ARO)   An estimate of the number of times that a threat will occur every year.

anonymization   An irreversible de-identification procedure in which specific identifiers that relate personal information to a specific individual are removed. *See also* de-identification, pseudonymization.

antimalware   Software that uses various means to detect and block malware. *See also* antivirus software.

antivirus software   Software designed to detect and remove viruses and other forms of malware.

architecture standard   A standard that defines technology architecture at the database, system, or network level.

ARCI   *See* RACI (Responsible-Accountable-Consulted-Informed).

asset inventory   The process of confirming the existence, location, and condition of assets; also, the results of such a process.

asset management   The processes used to manage the inventory, classification, use, and disposal of assets.

asset value (AV)   The value of an IT asset, which is usually (but not necessarily) the asset's replacement value.

assets   The collection of property that is owned by an organization, including digitally stored information.

attorney–client privilege   A common legal practice that states that the communications between employees and an organization's general counsel are exempt from legal discovery.

attribute sampling   A sampling technique used to study the characteristics of a population to determine how many samples possess a specific characteristic. *See also* sampling.

audit logging   A feature in an application, an operating system, or a database management system that enables events to be recorded in a separate log.

audit objective   The purpose or goals of an audit. Generally, the objective of an audit is to determine whether controls exist and are effective in some specific aspect of business or technology operations in an organization.

audit procedures   The step-by-step instructions and checklists required to perform specific audit activities. Procedures may include a list of people to interview and questions to ask them, evidence to request, audit tools to use, sampling rates, where and how evidence will be archived, and how evidence will be evaluated.

audit report   The final, written product of an audit that includes a description of the purpose, scope, and type of audit performed; persons interviewed; evidence collected; rates and methods of sampling; and findings on the existence and effectiveness of each control.

audit scope   The process, procedures, systems, and applications that are the subject of an audit.

authentication   The process of asserting one's identity and providing proof of that identity. Typically, authentication requires a user ID (the assertion) and a password (the proof). However, authentication can also require stronger means of proof, such as a digital certificate, token, smart card, or biometric. *See also* multifactor authentication.

authorization   The process by which a system determines what rights and privileges a user has been granted.

availability management   Processes that ensure the sustainment of IT service availability.

back door   A section of code that permits someone to bypass access controls and access data or functions. Back doors are commonly placed in programs during development but are removed before programming is complete.

back up   The process of copying important data from one media device to another in the event of a hardware failure, an error, security incident, or a software bug that causes damage to data.

background check   The process of verifying an employment candidate's employment history, education records, professional licenses and certifications, criminal background, and financial background.

background verification   *See* background check.

beacon   *See* web beacon.

biometrics   Any use of a machine-readable characteristic of a user's body that uniquely identifies the user. Biometrics can be used for strong authentication. Types of biometrics include voice recognition, fingerprint, hand scan, palm vein scan, iris scan, retina scan, facial scan, and handwriting. *See also* authentication, multifactor authentication.

binding corporate rules   *See* standard contractual clauses.

Bluetooth   A short-range air-link standard for data communications between peripherals and low-power-consumption devices.

bring your own device (BYOD)   A practice in which workers use personally owned devices to connect to organization networks and conduct organization business.

budget   A plan for allocating resources over a certain time period.

business associate agreement (BAA)   As defined by HIPAA, a legal agreement between two parties in which the parties agree to enact general and specific measures to protect personal information, usually protected health information (PHI). *See also* Health Insurance Portability and Accountability Act (HIPAA).

business development   A corporate function tasked with identifying and developing new business opportunities to ensure continued growth.

business impact analysis (BIA)   A study used to identify the impacts of different disaster scenarios on ongoing business operations.

California Consumer Privacy Act (CCPA)   Privacy regulation enacted in 2018 in the US state of California.

California Privacy Rights Act (CPRA)   Privacy regulation enacted through a ballot initiative in 2020 in the US state of California.

capability maturity model   A model used to measure the relative maturity of an organization or of its processes.

Capability Maturity Model Integration (CMMI)   A process appraisal and improvement framework administered by the CMMI Institute.

capacity management   Activities that confirm sufficient capacity in IT systems and IT processes to meet service needs.

CAPTCHA   A challenge–response test requiring human interaction to distinguish human from machine input.

Center for Internet Security Critical Security Controls (CIS CSC)   A security controls framework developed by the Center for Internet Security (CIS).

chain of custody   Documentation that shows the acquisition, storage, control, and analysis of evidence. The chain of custody may be required for evidence that is to be used in a legal proceeding.

change advisory board   The group of stakeholders from IT and business who propose, discuss, and approve changes to IT systems.

change control   *See* change management.

change control board   *See* change advisory board.

change management   An IT function used to control changes made to an IT environment. *See also* IT service management (ITSM).

change request   A formal request for a change to be made in an environment. *See also* change management.

change review   A formal review of a requested change. *See also* change management, change request.

charter   A document that describes a program (such as a privacy program), including its scope, mission, objectives, roles and responsibilities, authorities, and key business processes.

citizen IT   *See* shadow IT.

cloud   A generalization referring to remote computers, storage, software, or networks, typically accessed through a commercial service.

cloud computing   A technique of providing a dynamically scalable and usually virtualized computing resource as a service.

cloud responsibility model   *See* shared responsibility model.

code of conduct   *See* code of ethics.

code of ethics   A statement that defines acceptable and unacceptable professional conduct within an organization.

collection   In the context of data privacy, the acquisition of personal information.

Common Vulnerability Scoring System (CVSS)   A standard methodology for rating system vulnerabilities based on the ease, method, and impact of exploitation.

compensating control   A control that is implemented because another control cannot be implemented or is ineffective.

compliance audit   An audit to determine the level and degree of compliance to a law, regulation, standard, contract provision, or an internal control.

compliance risk   Risk associated with failures to comply with laws, regulations, and other legal obligations.

configuration management   The process of recording and maintaining the configuration of IT systems.

configuration standard   A standard that defines the detailed configurations that are used in servers, workstations, operating systems, database management systems, applications, network devices, and other systems.

consent   Permission granted by a data subject for the collection and/or processing of his or her personal data.

contact tracing   The process of identifying persons who have been in close proximity to a person carrying an infectious disease.

contract   A binding legal agreement between two parties that may be enforceable in a court of law.

control   A policy, process, or procedure that is created to achieve a desired event or to avoid an unwanted event.

control objective   A foundational statement that describes desired states or outcomes from business operations.

control self-assessment (CSA)   A methodology used by an organization to review key business objectives, risks, and controls. Control self-assessment is a self-regulation activity.

controller   *See* data controller.

cookie   A block of data stored by a browser on a user's computer, as directed by a web site.

corroboration   An audit technique whereby an information systems (IS) auditor interviews personnel to confirm the validity of evidence obtained from others who were interviewed previously.

countermeasure   Any activity or mechanism that is designed to reduce risk.

covered entity   An organization that is obligated to comply with the Health Insurance Portability and Accountability Act (HIPAA).

cross-border data transfer   The transfer of data, typically personal information, across a state, provincial, or national border.

cryptography   The practice of hiding information so that it can be accessed only by the sender and intended recipient, with the intention of preventing access by other persons. *See also* encryption.

culture   The behavioral norms in an organization.

custodian   A person or group delegated to operate or maintain an asset.

Cybersecurity Framework (CSF)   *See* NIST CSF (National Institute for Standards and Technology Cybersecurity Framework).

data aggregation   The process of combining data sets to enrich available data.

data classification   The process of assigning a sensitivity classification to a data set or information asset.

data classification policy   A policy that defines sensitivity levels and handling procedures for information.

data controller   An entity that determines the purposes of and means for processing of personal data, which can include directing third parties to process personal data on the entity's behalf.

data destruction   The purposeful act of destroying data so that it cannot be recovered.

data discovery   A process, usually automated, whereby data stores are scanned to determine the presence of specific information, typically personal and other sensitive information.

data flow diagram (DFD)   A diagram that illustrates the flow of data within and between systems.

data governance   Policies and processes that result in management's visibility and control over all data management and data processing activities in an organization.

data loss prevention (DLP)   Any of several tools and methods used for gaining visibility and control into the presence and movement of sensitive data.

data marking   Any means for applying machine- or human-readable marks on a document to identify it as containing personal or other sensitive information. *See also* data tagging.

data minimization   The practice of collecting and retaining only those data elements required to perform agreed-upon processing. *See also* data retention.

data processor   An entity that processes data at the direction of a data controller. *See also* data controller.

data protection impact assessment (DPIA) An analysis of how planned changes to a business process or information system will impact an organization's ability to protect specific types of data, such as personally identifiable information (PII). *See also* privacy impact assessment (PIA).

data protection officer (DPO) A position tasked with ensuring that the organization's privacy policies and practices are compliant with applicable laws, regulations, and other legal obligations.

data retention As a portion of data governance, a formal approach for determining how long data should reside in an organization, and the process of developing procedures for removing data that has exceeded its retention limit. *See also* data retention schedule.

data retention schedule A formal statement that specifies how long various types of business records should be retained in an organization.

data sovereignty The idea that data is subject to laws and regulations within the jurisdiction in which it is collected.

data sprawl The uncontrolled accumulation and proliferation of data in an organization. When this data contains personal information, data sprawl is of particular concern to privacy leaders.

data subject An identifiable natural person.

data subject request (DSR) A request or inquiry sent to an organization by a data subject for the purpose of verification, correction, or removal of personal information.

data subject rights Legal rights granted to natural persons, generally concerning the collection and use of their personal information.

data tagging A typically automated process of applying an identifying mark on a data file if its contents meet specific criteria. *See also* data marking.

database A collection of organized and structured information.

decryption The process of transforming ciphertext into plaintext so that a recipient can read it.

default password A password associated with a user account or system account that retains its factory default setting.

degaussing The application of a strong magnetic field to erase the contents of magnetic storage media.

de-identification Any procedure through which specific identifiers about a data subject are removed or replaced. *See also* anonymization, masking, pseudonymization.

detective control A control that is used to detect events.

direct marketing Communication from an organization to selected individuals to inform them of products and services.

directory   A structure in a system that is used to store files and, optionally, other directories.

divestiture   A business transaction in which an organization sells or disposes of a portion of itself or its assets (often a business unit or department) to another organization.

Do Not Track   A web browser feature used to request that web site operators refrain voluntarily from tracking individual visitors.

documentation   The inclusive term that describes charters, processes, procedures, standards, requirements, and other written documents.

dynamic data loss prevention (dynamic DLP)   The use of tools to detect the movement of PII and other sensitive information. *See also* data loss prevention (DLP), static DLP.

eavesdropping   The act of secretly intercepting and, optionally, recording a voice or data transmission.

electronic protected health information (ePHI)   Patient-related health information in electronic form, as defined by the US Health Insurance Portability and Accountability Act (HIPAA).

e-mail   A network-based service used to transmit messages between individuals and groups.

encryption   The act of hiding sensitive information in plain sight. Encryption works by scrambling the characters in a message, using a method known only to the sender and receiver, making the message useless to anyone else who intercepts the message.

encryption key   A block of characters, used in combination with an encryption algorithm, to encrypt or decrypt a stream or block of data.

end user behavior analytics (EUBA)   *See* user behavior analytics (UBA).

endpoint   Any of several types of end-user devices, including desktop computers, laptop computers, tablet computers, and smartphones.

enterprise architecture   Activities that ensure that important business needs are met by IT systems; the model that is used to map business functions into the IT environment and IT systems in increasing levels of detail.

evidence   Information gathered by the auditor that provides proof that a control exists and is being operated.

exposure factor (EF)   The financial loss that results from the realization of a threat, expressed as a percentage of the asset's total value.

extraterritorial regulation   A government regulation that exercises jurisdiction beyond its land borders.

facial recognition   A capability, often coupled with video surveillance, to recognize specific individuals based upon their facial characteristics.

Factor Analysis of Information Risk (FAIR)   An analysis method that helps a risk manager understand the factors that contribute to risk, as well as the probability of threat occurrence and an estimation of potential losses.

fail closed   A situation in which all access requests will be denied if an access control system fails.

fail open   A situation in which all access requests will be permitted if an access control system fails.

feasibility study   An activity that seeks to determine the expected benefits of a program or project.

fiduciary duty   The accountability by board members to shareholders or constituents to act in the best interests of the organization with no appearance of impropriety, conflict of interest, or ill-gotten profit.

file   A sequence of zero or more characters that is stored as a whole in a system. A file may be a document, spreadsheet, sound file, computer program, data, or an image that is used by a program.

file server   A server used to store files in a central location, usually to make them available to many users.

file store   *See* file server.

financial audit   An audit of an accounting system, accounting department processes, and accounting procedures to determine whether business controls are sufficient to ensure the integrity of financial statements.

first-party cookie   A cookie whose origin matches the domain of the web server. *See also* cookie, third-party cookie.

functional requirements   Statements describing the required behavioral characteristics that a system must have to support business needs. *See also* nonfunctional requirements.

gate process   Any business process that consists of one or more review/approval gates, which must be completed before the process may continue.

general computing controls (GCC)   *See* IT general controls (ITGC).

General Data Protection Regulation (GDPR)   A European Union regulation enacted in 2018 that defines data privacy rights and remedies for residents of EU member states.

governance   Management's control over policy and processes.

guideline   A document that provides suggestions for compliance to a policy or standard.

hacker   A person who interferes with or accesses another's computer without authorization. Formerly, a benign hobbyist who strives to understand how complex mechanisms function.

hardening   A technique intended to reduce the "attack surface" of a system to its essential components by configuring the system and/or its security settings so that only its essential services and features are active, and all others are deactivated.

hardware   The physical machinery used for computing, storage, and networking.

Health Insurance Portability and Accountability Act (HIPAA)   A US regulation regarding the protection of electronic protected health information (ePHI) that applies to healthcare delivery organizations, health insurance companies, and other healthcare industry organizations.

human capital management (HCM) system   *See* human resources information system (HRIS).

human resources   A corporate function responsible for business records concerned with the hire, internal transfer, and termination of workers, and for activities including performance review, salary administration, benefits administration, and career development.

human resources information system (HRIS)   An information system used to facilitate tasks and store records of the employees in an organization.

identification   The process of asserting one's identity without providing proof of that identity. *See also* authentication.

identity management   The activity of managing the identity of each employee, contractor, temporary worker, and, optionally, customer for use in a single environment or multiple environments.

implementation   An activity whereby new or updated software is placed into the production environment and started.

incident   *See* privacy incident, security incident.

incident response   The organized response to a privacy or security incident. *See also* privacy incident response, security incident response.

independence   A characteristic of the relationship between an auditor and the party being audited. An auditor should be independent of the auditee; this permits the auditor to be objective.

information classification   *See* data classification.

information security management   The aggregation of policies, processes, procedures, and activities to ensure that an organization's security policy is effective.

information security management system (ISMS)   The collection of activities used for managing information security, as defined by ISO/IEC 27001.

information security policy   A statement that defines how an organization will classify and protect its important data assets.

infrastructure   The collection of networks, network services, devices, facilities, and system software that facilitates access to, communication with, and protection of business applications.

infrastructure as a service (IaaS)   A cloud computing model in which a service provider makes computers and other infrastructure components available to subscribers. *See also* cloud computing.

inherent risk   A risk expectation that asserts that material weaknesses are present in existing business processes and no compensating controls can detect or prevent them.

input authorization   Controls that ensure that all data input into an information system is authorized by management.

input controls   Administrative and technical controls that determine what data is permitted to be input into an information system. These controls exist to ensure the integrity of information in a system.

integrated audit   An audit that combines an operational audit and a financial audit. *See also* financial audit, operational audit.

intellectual property   A class of assets owned by an organization, which includes an organization's designs, architectures, software source code, processes, and procedures.

Internet   The interconnection of the world's TCP/IP networks.

Internet of Things (IoT)   The connection of physical objects other than human-interactive computers to networks and the Internet.

Internet Protocol Security (IPsec)   A suite of protocols used to secure IP-based communications by using authentication and encryption.

intrusion detection system (IDS)   A hardware or software system that detects anomalies that may be signs of an intrusion.

intrusion prevention system (IPS)   A hardware or software system that detects and blocks anomalies that may be indications of an intrusion.

IP address   An address assigned to a station on a TCP/IP network.

ISACA   An international professional association focused on IT governance, security, and privacy.

ISACA audit guidelines   Published documents that help the IS auditor apply ISACA audit standards.

ISACA audit procedures   Published documents that provide sample procedures for performing various audit activities and for auditing various types of technologies and systems.

ISACA audit standards   The minimum standards of performance related to security, audits, and the actions that result from audits. The standards are published by ISACA and updated periodically. ISACA audit standards are considered mandatory by IS auditors worldwide.

ISAE 3402 (International Standard on Assurance Engagement)   An international standard for the external audit of a service provider. An ISAE 3402 audit is performed according to rules established by the International Auditing and Assurance Standards Board (IAASB).

ISO/IEC 20000   An ISO/IEC standard for IT service management (ITSM).

ISO/IEC 27001   An ISO/IEC standard for IT security management.

ISO/IEC 27002   An ISO/IEC standard for IT security controls.

ISO/IEC 27005   An ISO/IEC standard for cybersecurity risk assessments and risk management.

ISO/IEC 27035   An ISO/IEC standard for cybersecurity incident response.

ISO/IEC 27701   An ISO/IEC standard for privacy information management.

IT Assurance Framework (ITAF)   An end-to-end framework that provides guidance to organizations in developing and managing IT assurance and IT audits.

IT general controls (ITGC)   A framework of controls established in an organization that applies across core business systems. Generally used in the context of Sarbanes–Oxley compliance. *See also* Sarbanes–Oxley.

IT governance   Management's control over IT policy and processes.

IT Infrastructure Library (ITIL)   *See* IT service management (ITSM).

IT service desk   *See* service desk.

IT service management (ITSM)   A set of business processes used to manage an IT organization.

job description   A written description of an employee's responsibilities within an organization that usually contains a job title, responsibilities, experience requirements, and knowledge requirements.

judgmental sampling   A sampling technique by which items are chosen based upon the auditor's judgment, usually with regard to risk or materiality. *See also* sampling.

jurisdiction   The authority granted to enforce laws; generally applies to a geographic area.

key goal indicator (KGI)   A measure of business activities related to the achievement of strategic goals and objectives.

key performance indicator (KPI)   A measure of business processes' performance and quality, used to reveal trends related to the efficiency and effectiveness of key processes in the organization.

key risk indicator (KRI)   A measure of business risk, used to reveal trends related to the risk levels of various activities, processes, and systems in an organization.

keylogger   A hardware device or a type of malware that records a user's keystrokes (and, optionally, mouse movements and clicks) and sends them to the keylogger's owner.

laptop computer   A portable computer used by an individual user.

least privilege   The concept whereby an individual user should have the lowest privilege level possible that will still enable him or her to perform required tasks.

legitimate interest   A rationale expressed for the justification for processing personal information that presupposes benefits for the data subject and the processor.

local area network (LAN)   An interconnection of computers within a limited area such as a single building. *See also* network.

logic bomb   A set of computer instructions designed to perform some damaging action when a specific event occurs; a popular example is a time bomb that alters or destroys data on a specified date in the future.

malware   The broad class of programs that are designed to inflict harm on computers, networks, or information. Types of malware include viruses, worms, Trojan horses, spyware, and rootkits.

marketing   An activity in an organization whereby targeted groups and individuals are informed of the organization's goods and services, generally in the form of offers for sale.

marking   The act of affixing a classification label to a document. *See also* data marking.

masking   A technique of concealing the contents of a data field.

maturity   The degree of formality and integrity of a business process.

merger   A business transaction in which two organizations of similar size join together to become a single organization.

mitigating control   *See* compensating control.

mobile device   A portable computer in the form of a smartphone, tablet computer, or wearable device.

mobile device management (MDM)   A class of enterprise tools used to manage mobile devices such as smartphones and tablet computers.

monitoring   The continuous or regular evaluation of a system or control to determine its operation or effectiveness.

multifactor authentication   Any means used to authenticate a user that requires more than a user ID and password. Examples of multifactor authentication include a user ID and password, plus any one or more of the following: digital certificate, token, smart card, or biometric.

NetFlow   A network diagnostic tool that collects network metadata, which can be used for network diagnostic or security purposes.

network   An interconnection of computers for the purpose of exchanging information.

network architecture   The overall design of an organization's network.

NIST CSF (National Institute for Standards and Technology Cybersecurity Framework)   A controls and controls management framework developed by the US National Institute for Standards and Technology.

NIST RMF (National Institute for Standards and Technology Risk Management Framework)   A process framework for risk management development by the US National Institute for Standards and Technology.

NIST SP 800-30   A NIST special publication regarding a standard methodology for risk management and conducting a risk assessment.

nonfunctional requirements   Statements describing the required inherent characteristics that a system must have to support business needs. *See also* functional requirements.

notebook computer   *See* laptop computer.

object   A resource, such as a computer, an application, a database, a file, or a record. *See also* subject.

objectivity   The characteristic of a person that relates to his or her ability to develop an opinion that is not influenced by external pressures.

open-source intelligence (OSINT)   Sources for, and methodology concerning, available cybersecurity vulnerability, threat, and breach information.

operational audit   An audit of IS controls, security controls, or business controls to determine control existence and effectiveness.

Operationally Critical Threat, Asset, and Vulnerability Evaluation (OCTAVE)   A risk analysis approach developed by Carnegie Mellon University and used to assess privacy and security risks.

orchestration   A scripted, automated response that is triggered when specific events occur.

organization chart   A diagram that depicts the manager–subordinate relationships in an organization or in a part of an organization.

owner   A person or group responsible for the operation of an asset.

passphrase   A longer password that is constructed from a string of words.

password   An identifier that is created by a system manager or a user to facilitate access to a system; this secret combination of letters, numbers, and other symbols is known (or should be known) only to the user who uses it.

patch management   The process of identifying, analyzing, and applying patches (including security patches) to systems.

Payment Card Industry Data Security Standard (PCI DSS)   A global security standard whose objective is the protection of credit card numbers while in storage, while processed, and while transmitted. The standard was developed by the Payment Card Industry, a consortium of credit card companies, including VISA, MasterCard, American Express, Discover, and JCB.

penetration test   A simulation of an attack on a system or network to identify the presence of exploitable vulnerabilities.

persistent cookie   A cookie used to identify a user and store user preferences. *See also* cookie.

Personal Information Protection and Electronic Documents Act (PIPEDA)   A Canadian data privacy law that went into effect in 2000 and seeks to ensure consumer data privacy in the context of e-commerce.

personally identifiable information (PII)   Any information relating to an identifiable natural person.

phishing   A social engineering attack whereby e-mail messages that resemble official communications entice victims to visit imposter web sites that contain malware or request credentials to sensitive or valuable assets.

platform as a service (PaaS)   A cloud computing delivery model in which the service provider supplies the platform on which an organization can build and run software. *See also* cloud computing.

playbook   A detailed procedure, typically the instructions to be followed in response to an event or incident.

policy   A statement that specifies what must be done (or not done) in an organization. A policy usually defines who is responsible for monitoring and enforcing it.

population   A complete set of subjects, entities, transactions, or events that are the focus of an audit.

preventive action   An action that is initiated to prevent an undesired event or condition.

preventive control   A control that is used to prevent unwanted events from occurring.

privacy   The protection of personal information from unauthorized disclosure, use, and distribution.

privacy awareness   A formal program used to educate employees, users, customers, or constituents on required, acceptable, and unacceptable privacy-related behaviors. *See also* security awareness.

privacy governance   Management's control over an organization's information privacy program.

privacy impact assessment (PIA)   An analysis of how personally identifiable information is collected, used, shared, and maintained as part of planned changes to a business process or information system to identify any changes in privacy risk. *See also* data protection impact assessment (DPIA).

privacy incident   An event in which personal information has been misused, accessed by unauthorized persons, or affected by a security incident. *See also* security incident.

privacy incident response   The organized response to a privacy incident. *See also* security incident response.

Privacy Information Management System (PIMS)   The collection of activities for managing information privacy, as defined by ISO/IEC 27701.

privacy office   A corporate oversight function that ensures that the organization complies with applicable privacy laws and other related requirements.

privacy policy   A policy statement that defines how an organization will protect, manage, and handle private information.

privacy requirements   Formal statements that describe required privacy safeguards that a system or service must support.

privacy steering committee   A body of senior managers or executives that establishes priorities and provides oversight for activities and issues related to information privacy in the organization.

privacy threshold analysis (PTA)   A brief analysis on a proposed addition or change to a business process or information system to determine whether personal information is involved, necessitating the performance of a full privacy impact assessment. *See also* privacy impact assessment.

problem   In the context of IT service management, a situation characterized by several similar incidents. *See also* incident, IT service management.

procedure   A written sequence of instructions required to complete a task.

process   A collection of one or more procedures required to perform a business function. *See also* procedure.

processor   *See* data processor.

program   An organization of many large, complex activities; a program can be thought of as a set of projects that work together to fulfill one or more key business objectives or goals.

program charter   A formal definition of the objectives of a program, its main timelines, its sources of funding, the names of its principal leaders and managers, and the business executive(s) who are sponsoring the program.

project   A coordinated and managed sequence of tasks that result in the realization of an objective or a goal.

protected health information (PHI)   Patient-related healthcare information, as defined by the US Health Insurance Portability and Accountability Act (HIPAA). *See also* electronic protected health information (ePHI).

provided by client (PBC) list   A list of evidence requested of an auditee at the onset of an audit.

provisioning   The creation of a user account and the issuance of credentials to the user.

pseudonymization   An irreversible de-identification procedure whereby a specific identifier is replaced by other values to make it less identifiable to the original data subject. *See also* anonymization, de-identification.

qualitative risk analysis   A risk analysis methodology whereby risks are classified on a nonquantified scale, such as High, Medium, and Low, or on a simple numeric scale, such as 1 through 5.

quantitative risk analysis   A risk analysis methodology whereby risks are estimated in the form of actual cost amounts.

RACI (Responsible-Accountable-Consulted-Informed)   The responsibility model used to track individual responsibilities in a business process or a project.

ransomware   Malware that performs some malicious action and requires payment from the victim to reverse the action. Malicious actions include data erasure, data encryption, extortion, and system damage.

records   Documents describing business events such as meeting minutes, contracts, financial transactions, decisions, purchase orders, logs, and reports.

redress   The correction of an error.

reduced sign-on   The use of a centralized directory service, such as LDAP (Lightweight Directory Access Protocol) or Microsoft Active Directory, for authentication into systems and applications. Users need to log in to each system and application using one set of login credentials. *See also* single sign-on (SSO).

regulatory requirements   Formal statements derived from laws and regulations that describe the required characteristics a system must support.

release management   The process of managing the release of changes to information systems.

remediation   The correction of a defect.

remote access   A capability that permits a user to establish a network connection from a remote location to access an internal host network at another location.

request for information (RFI)   A formal solicitation to a vendor for detailed information about specific types of products or services.

request for proposal (RFP)   Part of an organization's procurement process, this formal document is provided to vendors to solicit proposals and bids regarding the delivery of specific projects, products, or services.

requirements   Formal statements that describe required (and desired) characteristics of a system that is to be changed, developed, or acquired.

residual risk   The risk that remains after being reduced through other risk treatment options.

responsibility   A stated expectation of activities and performance.

right to audit   A clause in a contract that indicates that one party has the right to conduct an audit of the other party's operations.

risk   Generally, the fact that undesired events can happen that may damage property or disrupt operations; specifically, an event scenario that can result in property damage or disruption.

risk acceptance   The risk treatment option by which management chooses to accept the risk as-is.

risk analysis   The process of identifying and studying risks in an organization.

risk appetite   The level of risk that an organization is willing to accept while in pursuit of its mission, strategy, and objectives, and before action is needed to treat or manage a risk. *See also* risk capacity.

risk assessment   A process by which risks, in the form of threats and vulnerabilities, are identified for each asset.

risk avoidance   The risk treatment option involving a cessation of the activity that introduces identified risk.

risk capacity   The objective amount of loss that an organization can tolerate without its continued existence being called into question. *See also* risk appetite.

risk management   The management activities used to identify, analyze, and treat risks.

risk mitigation   The risk treatment option involving the implementation of a solution that will reduce the impact or probability of an identified risk.

risk tolerance   *See* risk appetite.

risk transfer   The risk treatment option involving the act of transferring risk to another party, such as an insurance company.

risk treatment   The decision to manage an identified risk. The available choices are mitigate the risk, avoid the risk, transfer the risk, or accept the risk.

role   A set of privileges in an application. Also, a formally defined set of work tasks assigned to an individual.

sample   A portion of a population of records selected for auditing.

sampling   A technique used to select a portion of a population when it is not feasible to test an entire population.

Sarbanes–Oxley Act   A US law requiring public corporations to enact business and technical controls, perform internal audits of those controls, and undergo external audits.

scanning   *See* static DLP, vulnerability scanning.

security awareness   A formal program used to educate employees, users, customers, or constituents on required, acceptable, and unacceptable security-related behaviors.

security governance   Management's control over an organization's security program.

security incident   An event in which the confidentiality, integrity, or availability of information (or an information system) has been compromised.

security incident response   The formal, planned response that is enacted when a security incident has occurred. *See also* security incident.

security information and event management system (SIEM)   An information system that collects event logs and generates alerts to inform personnel of events occurring that warrant attention and potential action.

security policy   *See* information security policy.

security requirements   Formal statements that describe the required security characteristics that a system, service, or product must support.

segregation of duties   The concept that ensures that single individuals do not possess excessive privileges that could result in unauthorized activities such as fraud or the manipulation or exposure of sensitive data.

separation of duties   *See* segregation of duties.

server   A centralized computer used to perform a specific task.

service continuity management   Processes to ensure the ability of the organization to continue providing services, primarily in the event of a natural or manmade disaster. *See also* business continuity planning.

service desk   The IT function that handles incidents and service requests on behalf of customers by acting as a single point of contact. *See also* IT service management (ITSM).

service level agreement (SLA)   A formal commitment by an individual or group to provide services at stated levels of quantity and quality.

service provider audit   An audit of a third-party organization that provides services to other organizations.

session cookie   A cookie used by a web server that uniquely identifies one logged-in user from other logged-in users. *See also* cookie.

shadow IT   The phenomenon whereby organization departments procure IT services directly, bypassing corporate IT.

shared responsibility model   A logical model that depicts and describes operational responsibilities in a cloud services environment. The model indicates the responsibilities belonging to the cloud service provider and those belonging to the customer.

shredding   Document destruction by means of cutting printed materials into narrow strips or small pieces that are not easily reconstituted.

single loss expectancy (SLE)   The financial loss when a threat is realized one time. SLE is defined as AV × EF. *See also* asset value (AV), exposure factor (EF).

single sign-on (SSO)   An interconnected environment in which applications are logically connected to a centralized authentication server that is aware of the logged-in and/or logged-out status of each user. A user can log in once to the environment; each application and system is aware of a user's login status and will not require the user to log in to each one separately. *See also* reduced sign-on.

smart card   A small, credit card–sized device that contains electronic memory and is used with a smart card reader in multifactor authentication.

smartphone   A mobile phone equipped with an operating system and software applications.

SOC   *See* system and organization controls (SOC) audit.

SOC 1   A system and organization controls audit of a financial services service provider using a bespoke set of controls. *See also* system and organization controls (SOC) audit.

SOC 2   A system and organization controls audit of a service provider using a standard set of controls. *See also* system and organization controls (SOC) audit.

social engineering   The act of using deception to trick an individual into revealing secrets.

software as a service (SaaS)   A software delivery model in which an organization obtains a software application for use by its employees, and the software application is hosted by the software provider rather than the customer organization. *See also* cloud computing.

SOX   *See* Sarbanes–Oxley Act.

spam   Unsolicited and unwanted e-mail.

split custody   The concept of splitting knowledge of a specific object or task between two persons.

spyware   A type of malware in which software performs one or more surveillance-type actions on a computer, reporting back to the spyware owner.

SSAE 18 (Statements on Standards for Attestation Engagements No. 18)   An external audit of a service provider. An SSAE 18 audit is performed according to rules established by the American Institute of Certified Public Accountants (AICPA). Also known as a SOC 1.

standard   A statement that defines the technologies, protocols, suppliers, and methods used by an IT organization.

standard contractual clauses   Privacy controls and practices defined in standard contract terms as defined by the European Commission to enable the transfer of personal data from the European Union.

static DLP   The use of scanning tools to identify files containing personally identifiable information (PII) or other sensitive information on file servers and other file stores. *See also* data loss prevention, dynamic DLP.

statistical sampling   A sampling technique whereby items are chosen at random; each item has a statistically equal probability of being chosen. *See also* sampling.

steward   *See* custodian.

stop-or-go sampling   A sampling technique used to permit sampling to stop at the earliest possible time. This technique is used when the auditor believes that there is low risk or a low rate of exceptions in the population. *See also* sampling.

strategic planning   Activities used to develop and refine an organization's long-term plans and objectives.

strategy   The plan to achieve an objective.

stratified sampling   A sampling technique whereby a population is divided into classes or strata, based upon the value of one of the attributes. Samples are then selected from each class. *See also* sampling.

strong authentication   *See* multifactor authentication.

structured data   Data that resides in database management systems and in other forms as part of information systems and business applications. *See also* unstructured data.

subject   In access controls, a person or a system. In information privacy, a natural person. *See also* data subject, object.

subject data request   *See* data subject request (DSR).

supervisory authority An organization that has been delegated to enforce laws, perform investigations, and/or resolve disputes.

system and organization controls (SOC) audit An audit of a service provider's controls, performed by a public accounting firm. *See also* SOC, SOC 1, SOC 2.

system hardening *See* hardening.

tablet A mobile device with a touchscreen interface. *See also* mobile device.

tabletop An exercise, usually of privacy incident response, security incident response, and business continuity plans, that consists of a scripted simulation of an actual incident or event.

technical control A control that is implemented in IT systems and applications.

technical requirements Formal statements that describe the required technical characteristics that a system or service must support.

termination The process of discontinuing the employment of an employee or contractor.

third-party cookie A cookie whose domain is different from the web server that creates the cookie. Often used for advertising tracking. *See also* cookie, first-party cookie.

third-party risk management (TPRM) A business process used to assess and treat risks related to third-party service providers.

threat An event that, if realized, would bring harm to an asset.

threat hunting The proactive search for intrusions, intruders, and indicators of compromise.

threat intelligence A human- or machine-readable feed of threat-related information that can help organizations better protect themselves from emerging threats.

threat realization An occurrence of a threat.

token A small electronic device used in two-factor authentication. A token may display a number that the user types into a login field, or it may be plugged into a workstation to complete authentication. *See also* multifactor authentication.

training The process of educating personnel; to impart information or provide an environment where personnel can practice a new skill.

transfer The process of changing an employee's job title, department, and/or responsibilities within an organization.

two-factor authentication *See* multifactor authentication.

unstructured data   Data that resides on end-user workstations and network file shares, usually as a result of the creation of reports and extracts. *See also* structured data.

user   A worker or customer who uses an information system.

user behavior analytics (UBA)   Tools and techniques that learn end-user behavior and generate alerts when end-user behavior exceeds norms.

user ID   An identifier created by a system manager and issued to a user for the purpose of identification or authentication.

variable sampling   A sampling technique used to study the characteristics of a population to determine the numeric total of a specific attribute from the entire population. *See also* sampling.

vendor standard   A standard that specifies which suppliers and vendors are used for various types of products and services.

virtual private network (VPN)   Any network encapsulation protocol that utilizes authentication and encryption; used primarily for protecting remote access traffic and for protecting traffic between two networks.

virus   A type of malware in which fragments of code attach themselves to executable programs and are activated when the program they are attached to is run. *See also* malware.

vulnerability   A weakness that may be present in a system that increases the probability of one or more threats occurring.

vulnerability management   A formal business process used to identify and mitigate vulnerabilities in an IT environment.

vulnerability scanning   The use of a tool that automatically identifies exploitable vulnerabilities on systems connected to a network.

web beacon   A tiny or invisible image on a web page or e-mail message that's used to track individual views of the image along with other properties, such as the IP address of the device viewing the web page or image.

web content filter   A central program or device that monitors and, optionally, filters web communications. A web content filter is often used to control the sites (or categories of sites) that users are permitted to access from the workplace. Some can also protect an organization from malware.

web server   A server that runs specialized software that makes static and dynamic HTML pages available to users.

web tracking   The use of any of several technologies and techniques for tracking the use of web page views and web site viewing.

Wi-Fi   The common name for a wireless LAN protocol.

works council   A body similar to a labor union that represents the rights of workers in an organization, and with whom an organization is required to negotiate on matters of the collection and use of workers' personal information.

XaaS   A term that is inclusive of IaaS, PaaS, SaaS, and other "as a service" (aaS) offerings. *See also* infrastructure as a service (IAAS), platform as a service (PaaS), and software as a service (SaaS).

INDEX

Health Insurance Portability and
Accountability Act (HIPAA)
requirements, 80
rules, 69–70
third parties, 143
HITECH (Health Information Technology for
Economic and Clinical Health Act), 70, 72
HRISs (human resources information
systems), 199
human capital management (HCM)
systems, 199
human resources, integrating into
organization processes, 199–201
human resources information systems
(HRISs), 199
hygiene in risk likelihood, 293

I

identification in remote access, 171
identifying
assets, 190–191, 278–280
devices, 118
privacy requirements, 104–105
risk, 266–267, 292
threats, 283–289
vulnerabilities, 156, 179, 289–291
identity and access management, 166
access controls, 166–169
remote access, 169–177
Identity Theft and Assumption Deterrence
Act, 72
IDS/IPS (intrusion detection/prevention
system), 91, 253
impact
BIAs, 19, 294
PIAs. *See* privacy impact assessments (PIAs)
risk analysis, 267
risk assessment, 294–295
risk identification, 292
incident commanders in incident response
plans, 255–256
incident management
auditing, 237–238
ITIL, 182, 185
incident response, 250
baselines, 139
description, 180

evidence, 254
legal and contract issues, 204
phases, 250–254
plan development, 254–257
playbooks, 257
regulations, 250
reporting, 254
third parties, 144
incidents
communicating, 28
logs, 19
reviews, 38
risk identification, 267
inertia, organizational, 31
information assets, 279–280
information gathering, 295–296
information security
human resources, 200
integrating into organization processes, 198
practices, 165
information security management system
(ISMS), 165–177
information systems audits, 229
Information Technology Assurance
Framework, 238
information workers, training, 51
informed people in RACI charts, 34
initiation phase in incident response, 252
input controls, 223
inquiries
business process owner responsibilities, 38
data usage, 108
insider threats, 283–286
insurance
legal and contracts, 204
privacy programs, 18
third parties, 144
integrated audits, 229
integrating privacy into organization processes
audits, 201
BCDR planning, 199
business development, 202
compliance and ethics, 201
finance, 204–205
human resources, 199–201
information security, 198
IT development and operations, 198–199

Risk Management Framework (RMF), 273–274
risk management life cycle
 analysis, 295–305
 asset classification, 280–281
 asset identification, 278–280
 asset valuation, 281–283
 data classification, 281
 FAIR, 277–278
 ISO/IEC standards, 274–277
 methodologies, 269–278
 NIST standards, 269–274
 overview, 265–266
 process, 266–268
 risk identification, 292
 risk impact, 294–295
 risk likelihood, 293
 threat identification, 283–289
 vulnerability identification, 289–291
risk mitigation, 147, 267–268, 302
risk registers, 268
risk tolerance, 3
risk treatment
 overview, 300–303
 privacy programs, 18
 risk analysis, 268
RMF (Risk Management Framework), 273–274
roadmap development, 24–27
roles
 data governance models, 6
 incident response plans, 255–256
 internal policies, 63–64
 roadmap development, 26
 team structure, 31–33

S

sampling audit evidence, 233–234
SAQ (Self-Assessment Questionnaire), 226
Sarbanes–Oxley Act audit requirements, 35, 225
scanners, 150
scanning
 data discovery, 106–107
 data loss prevention, 221
 vulnerabilities, 177–179

schedules, training, 52–53
scope
 auditing, 228
 gap analysis, 21
 risk management process, 266
scribes in incident response plans, 256
Secure Sockets Layer (SSL), 125
security advisories
 privacy programs, 28
 security-related events, 223–224
security and privacy, 10
security information and event management (SIEM), 220–222
security-related events
 data loss prevention, 221
 input controls, 223
 log reviews, 220
 monitoring, 219–224
 orchestration, 220–221
 responsibilities, 224
 security advisories, 223–224
 SIEM, 220
 threat hunting, 222–223
 threat intelligence, 222
 UBA, 223
security rule in HIPAA, 69
security steering committees, 37–38
segregation of duties (SOD)
 access controls, 167
 matrix reviews, 176
 RACI charts, 34
Self-Assessment Questionnaire (SAQ), 226
semiqualitative risk analysis, 296
sensitive employment data, 200
sensitive information classification, 281
service access controls, 166–167
service account reviews, 176
service continuity management, 189
service desks
 IT, 181
 team positions, 47
service-level ITSM management, 187–188
service provider audits, 230
session integrity, tracking, 118